PERGAMON GENERAL PSYCHOLOGY SERIES
EDITORS
Arnold P. Goldstein, *Syracuse University*
Leonard Krasner, *SUNY at Stony Brook*

Child Behavioral Assessment
Principles and Procedures

Edited by

Thomas H. Ollendick
Virginia Polytechnic Institute & State University

Michel Hersen
University of Pittsburgh School of Medicine

PERGAMON PRESS
New York   Oxford   Toronto   Sydney   Frankfurt

Pergamon Press Offices:

U.S.A.   Pergamon Press Inc., Maxwell House, Fairview Park,
                Elmsford, New York 10523, U.S.A.

U.K.   Pergamon Press Ltd., Headington Hill Hall,
                Oxford OX3 0BW, England

CANADA   Pergamon Press Canada Ltd., Suite 104, 150 Consumers Road,
                Willowdale, Ontario M2J 1P9, Canada

AUSTRALIA   Pergamon Press (Aust.) Pty. Ltd., P.O. Box 544,
                Potts Point, NSW 2011, Australia

FEDERAL REPUBLIC   Pergamon Press GmbH, Hammerweg 6,
OF GERMANY   D-6242 Kronberg-Taunus, Federal Republic of Germany

Library of Congress Cataloging in Publication Data
Main entry under title:

Child behavioral assessment.

   (Pergamon general psychology series ; 129)
   Bibliography: p.
   Includes index.
   1. Behavioral assessment of children.   I. Ollendick,
Thomas H.   II. Hersen, Michel.   III. Series.   [DNLM:
1. Child behavior.   2. Child behavior disorders—
Diagnosis. WS 350.6 C5367]
RJ503.5.C47 1984   155.4′028′7   83-13156
ISBN 0-08-029370-0
ISBN 0-08-029369-7 (pbk.)

Second printing, 1985.

Printed in Great Britain by A. Wheaton & Co. Ltd., Exeter

To Our Children
Laurie and Katie
and
Jonathan and Nathaniel

Contents

Preface   ix

PART I. GENERAL ISSUES

Chapter

1   An Overview of Child Behavioral Assessment   3
Thomas H. Ollendick and *Michel Hersen*

2   Developmental Considerations   20
Craig Edelbrock

3   Diagnostic Issues   38
Sandra L. Harris and *Michael D. Powers*

PART II. SPECIFIC ASSESSMENT STRATEGIES

4   Behavioral Interviewing   61
Alan M. Gross

5   Behavioral Checklists and Rating Scales   80
Robert J. McMahon

6   Self-Report Instruments   106
Al J. Finch, Jr. and *Tim R. Rogers*

7   Peer Sociometric Forms   124
Hyman Hops and *Lewis Lewin*

8   Self-Monitoring Procedures   148
Edward S. Shapiro

9   Direct Observation   166
Edward J. Barton and *Frank R. Ascione*

10   Intellectual and Academic Achievement Tests   195
      Alan S. Kaufman and *Cecil R. Reynolds*

PART III. COMPREHENSIVE ASSESSMENT

11   Integrated Assessment and Treatment   223
      Philip H. Bornstein, Marcy Tepper Bornstein,
      and *Brenda Dawson*

12   Ethical Issues in Child Behavioral Assessment   244
      George A. Rekers

Author Index   263

Subject Index   271

About the Contributors   273

Preface

While treatment strategies based on behavioral principles have a long and rich tradition in clinical psychology, assessment procedures based on these principles have lagged behind significantly. In recent years, this gap has been addressed and filled, at least with adults, as evidenced by a proliferation of books, journals, and research articles. Unfortunately, behavioral assessment of children has not developed concurrently. While the principles of behavioral assessment may be similar for adults and children, the procedures are not. Children are a special population. The automatic extension of adult behavioral assessment procedures is unwarranted and of dubious merit.

In this volume, we define child behavioral assessment as *an exploratory, hypothesis testing process in which a range of specific procedures is used in order to understand a given child, group, or social ecology and to formulate and evaluate specific intervention strategies.* As such, child behavioral assessment entails more than the specification and subsequent observation of highly discrete target behaviors and their controlling variables. Recent advances in child behavioral assessment have incorporated a wide variety of procedures, including behavioral interviews, self- and other-reports, self-monitoring, *and* behavioral observations. This approach can best be described as a multimethod one in which a complete "picture" of the child is obtained.

Two other features characterize behavioral assessment with children. First, and foremost, the procedures must be developmentally sensitive. The most distinguishing characteristic of children is developmental change. Developmental changes are of importance for selection of specific assessment procedures, for determination of response covariation at different age levels, and for stability and continuity of specific behavior problems. Second, procedures must be empirically validated. All too frequently, professionals working with children have used assessment procedures of convenience without due regard for psychometric issues related to reliability, validity, and clinical utility. Comparison across studies is difficult, if not impossible, and the advancement of an assessment technology, let alone an understanding of child behavior disorders, is not achieved with such practices.

Attention to such principles and procedures has guided us in soliciting contributors and topics for this volume. All contributors are practicing clinicians in the field of child behavioral assessment and therapy and are aware of the special considerations of developmental psychology as it relates to the assessment and treatment of children. Further, all contributors are empirically minded; consequently, the chapters are data-based, up-to-date, and clinically useful.

The volume is organized in three parts: general issues, specific assessment procedures, and integrative issues. In the first part, historical, developmental, and diagnostic issues are addressed in detail. The purpose of this section is to provide a framework for the various assessment procedures which follow. In the second part, specific assessment procedures that comprise the multimethod approach are described and illustrated. For each procedure, issues related to reliability, validity, and clinical utility are examined, and a case study depicting the use of the specific procedure is presented. In the final section, the integration of assessment procedures and treatment strategies is described, and sensitive ethical issues related to child behavioral assessment are highlighted. All in all, the volume is intended to be a source book for advanced undergraduate students, graduate students, and mental health professionals working with children.

In a project such as this, many persons are to be acknowledged. Among the foremost are the contributors, whose expertise and dedication to the project have been outstanding. Without them, up-to-date scholarly coverage of the various topics would not have been so easily achieved. We would also like to acknowledge Jerome B. Frank and the various professionals at Pergamon Press whose support, assistance, and patience have been welcomed. In addition, we would like to thank two special persons who have assisted us in secretarial and technical matters and provided day-to-day support for our continued efforts on this project: Trevia Moses and Mary Newell. Finally, our thanks and appreciation are extended to our children and spouses, who have supported us in less direct but nonetheless valuable ways. Their implicit support and encouragement, as well as their understanding, are deeply appreciated.

PART I
General Issues

1

An Overview of
Child Behavioral Assessment

Thomas H. Ollendick
and
Michel Hersen

The assessment and treatment of child behavior disorders are of relatively recent origin. Child behavior disorders, though occasionally acknowledged prior to the twentieth century, received little concerted attention. Up to that time, child behavior disorders were viewed no differently than adult behavior disorders. In all likelihood, this state of affairs resulted from the then prevailing viewpoint of children as little miniature adults. In general, children were viewed as small versions of adults, evincing problems similar to adults and benefiting from reasoned advice much like their adult counterparts (Aries, 1962; Brown, 1939; Rie, 1971).

By contrast, the twentieth century has witnessed extensive study of "childhood" and its associated child behavior disorders. Predating the first White House Conference on Children in 1909 and extending beyond the International Year of the Child in 1979, extensive efforts have been directed toward the *understanding, assessment,* and *treatment* of behavior disorders of *children as children* and not as miniature adults. Just how useful these new developments have been, or will be, is not completely known at this time. However, advances have been made, and our understanding of childhood and child behavior disorders has been enriched (Ollendick & Hersen, 1983).

Within this stream of historical events, the assessment and treatment of child behavior disorders from a behavioral perspective evolved. Although application of behavioral principles to the problems of children has a rich tradition (e.g., Holmes, 1936; Jones, 1924; Watson & Rayner, 1920), behavioral

3

assessment of child behavior disorders has lagged significantly behind and has received less attention in the intervening years. Two primary themes have characterized early developments in child behavioral assessment: (1) adherence to an operant perspective which placed emphasis on observable events, current behavior, the situational determinants of behavior, and intraindividual comparisons (Bijou & Peterson, 1971; Mash & Terdal, 1981); and (2) relative inattention to normal developmental processes and normative comparisons which permit specific child behaviors to be compared to appropriate reference groups (Ciminero & Drabman, 1977; Evans & Nelson, 1977; Ollendick & Cerny, 1981). Although it can be said that these early developments possessed definite shortcomings, they clearly provided the foundation for an *empirical* approach to the assessment of child behavior disorders.

In this introductory chapter, we shall briefly examine the foundations of child behavioral assessment and explore its theoretical underpinnings as well as procedural nuances. In doing so, we hope to provide a broader context in which child behavioral assessment can be viewed as an empirically based, developmentally sensitive, multimethod approach. In the remaining chapters, these themes will be developed in greater detail. In addition, a variety of approaches to assessment will be described, integrated assessment and treatment will be detailed, and sensitive issues related to ethical concerns in child behavioral assessment will be explored.

CHILD BEHAVIORAL ASSESSMENT

Psychological assessment has been defined as the "systematic use of a variety of special techniques in order to better *understand* a given individual, group, or social ecology" (McReynolds, 1968, p. 2, italics added). From a traditional perspective, this notion of assessment has led to the search for those underlying personality characteristics or traits that are "responsible" for current functioning. In contrast, psychological assessment from a behavioral perspective has been directed toward a description of current behavior and a specification of organismic and environmental conditions that occasion and maintain it. In short, behavioral assessment has led to the search for antecedent and consequent events of behavior rather than underlying causes.

Excellent reviews of the major conceptual differences between psychological assessment from traditional and behavioral perspectives have been presented elsewhere (e.g., Goldfried & Kent, 1972; Kanfer & Saslow, 1969). Suffice it to indicate that three major distinctions have been offered. *First,* differences have been noted in the underlying assumptions about what constitutes "personality." In the traditional approach, psychological traits or personality characteristics are assumed to produce consistency in behavior that is stable and which exists independent of situational variation. However, from a behavioral perspective, greater emphasis is placed upon the behavior itself, as determined by specific learning histories and organismic and situational events. From the behavioral perspective, temporal and cross-situational consistency in behavior are not necessarily expected. *Second,* differences have been noted in the specification and selection of test items. In the traditional approach, test items are selected on the basis of a priori theoretical assumptions regarding the role of personality variables in behavior. In the behavioral approach, on the other hand, items are selected on the basis of how well they adequately represent specific stimulus situations associated with behavior. Hence, behavioral assessment of a child's "noncompliance" might involve observation of him or her in varying stimulus conditions (e.g., home, school, clinic) rather than measuring a hypothetical construct like "hostility toward mother," which in turn is thought to be causative of noncompliant behavior. *Third,* basic differences exist in the level of inference and subsequent interpretation of test responses. In traditional assessment, a child's response is viewed as a "sign" or indirect manifestation of underlying personality traits such as "hostility" as described in the preceding example. In contrast, interpretation of test responses in behavioral assessment is based on a low level of inference and involves a "sampling" approach.

As described by Goldfried and Kent (1972), the behavioral approach requires that the specific behaviors sampled in the test comprise a subset of the actual behaviors to be targeted for change. Such similarity between test responses and criterion measures of behavior is one of the most important and distinguishing characteristics of child behavioral assessment.

Early distinctions between traditional and behavioral assessment have proven heuristic in highlighting basic differences in both the purposes and methods of assessment. Further, they have been instrumental in focusing child behavioral assessment more directly upon "target behaviors" and the events that immediately precede and follow these behaviors. Accurate observation and recording of target behaviors remains the hallmark of child behavior assessment and the benchmark upon which other methods are evaluated (Gelfand & Hartmann, 1975; Mash & Terdal, 1981; Sulzer-Azaroff & Mayer, 1977).

As behavioral approaches with children evolved from sole reliance on basic operant procedures to those incorporating cognitive and self-control procedures, the methods of assessment, though not the purposes, also have changed. In this process, specification of target behaviors has been widened to include evaluation of cognitions and affect as well as large-scale social systems that impact upon the child and his or her family. Further, the important role of affect and cognition in mediating behavior change, at least for some children, finally has been recognized (e.g., Kendall & Hollon, 1980; Meichenbaum, 1977). Similarly, the notion that the child is an active arranger and determiner of his or her environment, rather than simply a passive responder, has been observed (e.g., Bandura, 1969, 1977; Mischel, 1973, 1979). These recent developments expand the scope of child behavioral assessment to include broader and richer contexts in which ecological, social, cultural, and developmental influences on behavior can be examined more productively. At this point in time, child behavioral assessment can best be viewed as "a range of deliberate problem-solving strategies for understanding children and childhood disorders" (Mash & Terdal, 1981, p. 8). The outcome of these problem-solving strategies is to provide a "picture of the child" that is informative, accurate, and useful in both the understanding and modification of child behavioral disorders.

Explicit in this view of child behavioral assessment is the notion that multiple assessment strategies are useful in advancing our understanding of childhood disorders and in formulating and evaluating viable treatment regimens. Assessment strategies including the clinical interview, self-monitoring, behavioral observation, standardized testing, rating forms from significant others (e.g., peers, parents, and teachers), and self-report measures may all be worthwhile and even desirable. Given our current state of knowledge in this area, or perhaps more accurately, our lack thereof, this position appears defensible so long as the individual strategies have been empirically validated (Hersen & Bellack, 1976; Ollendick & Cerny, 1981). Inasmuch as individual assessment strategies are inadequate, the combination of them serves to compound rather than neutralize their inherent inadequacies. Thus, acceptability of the multiple assessment approach rests firmly on the availability of a range of psychometrically sound measures and the empirical demonstration of their additive utility. While a clear demonstration of the multiple assessment approach is only suggested at this time (Ollendick & Cerny, 1981; see chap. 11), firm conclusions are yet to be reached. Although advocating a multiple assessment approach, we are mindful of Evans's eloquent admonition: "taking careful aim is still more important than the bore of the barrel or the gauge of the shot" (Evans, 1982, p. 124).

In summary, child behavioral assessment can be described as an exploratory, hypothesis-testing process in which a range of specific procedures are used in order to understand a given child, group, or social ecology and to formulate and evaluate specific intervention strategies. Three primary characteristics guide the selection of specific procedures in child behavioral assessment: (1) a multimethod approach which yields the best "picture of the child," (2) the selection of procedures which have been empirically validated, and (3) the sensitivity of the procedures to developmental processes. These characteristics will be examined in greater detail in the subsequent sections.

CHARACTERISTICS OF CHILD BEHAVIORAL ASSESSMENT

Multimethod Approach

As we have noted, early child behavioral assessment procedures were directed primarily toward identification of discrete and highly specific target behaviors and their controlling variables. Observable behaviors like hitting, tantrums, sitting in a chair, and eye contact were isolated for study and modification. While the importance of systematic assessment of discrete target behaviors should not be underestimated, more recent advances have incorporated a broader view of child behavior and its assessment (Mash & Terdal, 1981). This new view more clearly encompasses activities of the organism which mediate antecedent and consequent events, including physiological reactions, affective responses, and covert cognitions. Further, it more clearly examines distal as well as proximal events which serve to affect child behavior.

Since Kanfer and Saslow's (1969) S-O-R-K-C model of assessment espouses a thorough analysis of both overt and covert behaviors and acknowledges that behavior is determined by a variety of events (including ecological, social, and cultural ones), we have found this approach useful in guiding the selection of child behavioral assessment strategies (Ollendick & Cerny, 1981). The S component includes antedecent events and refers to those internal or external stimulus events which are thought to be functionally related to the behavior in question. The O refers to the biological condition of the organism and includes those variables that place constraints on specific behaviors. The inclusion of the organism is particularly significant in child behavioral assessment since rapid developmental changes affect both the form and function of specific behaviors. R refers to observed (or reliably reported) behaviors and encompasses motor behavior, cognitive-verbal behavior, and physiological-emotional behavior (Lang, 1968). Most importantly, from a developmental standpoint, R allows for inclusion of cognitive events such as self-statements, expectancies, and plans. K describes the schedules or contingency-related conditions and includes such parameters as the frequency and timing of response outcomes. Examination of a child's learning history, including the duration of specific behaviors, provides valuable information in this regard. Finally, C refers to events following R, be they environmental or organismic.

In the S-O-R-K-C model, a wide range of assessment strategies may be used, including behavioral interviews, checklists, rating forms, standardized instruments, self-reports, self-monitoring forms, and behavioral observations. Collectively, these sources of information generate a wealth of data regarding the child, his or her behavior, and the context in which behavior occurs.

Prior to examining the psychometric properties of these various sources, we would like to briefly describe the procedural steps in the S-O-R-K-C model of child behavioral assessment. The first step involves an analysis of the presenting concerns and entails specification of behavioral excesses, deficits, or assets. As noted above, these behaviors might include motor behaviors, cognitive-verbal behaviors, and physiological-affective behaviors. In the second step, a standard functional analysis of the identified behaviors is undertaken. Antecedent and consequent events, both proximal and distal, are determined. In this step, the probable consequences of behavior change for the child and for those involved with him or her are also determined; that is, "an attempt is made to determine how the behavior is functional within the social milieu and what consequences might ensue if treatment is, or is not, successful" (Ollendick & Cerny, 1981, p. 29). A motivational analysis is undertaken in the third step to determine various incentives and aversive conditions that operate for the child both at the present time and from his or her learning history. In the fourth step, a developmental analysis of biological, cognitive, and social variables that affect the child's current behavior as well as probable response to treatment is conducted. Organic conditions (e.g., defective vision, glandular imbalances), cognitive limitations (e.g., inability to generate or use self-statements), and socioeconomic variables (e.g., lower class environment, paucity of environmental stimulation) that affect or interact with the problematic behaviors (and their resolution) are examined. In the fifth step, an analysis of the child's "self-control" capacity is undertaken. Information in this regard is obtained most directly from an analysis of those situations in which the child is able to control the problematic behavior and indirectly from specific self-report and other-report instruments. In the sixth step, the child's interpersonal relationships are reviewed, with special emphasis upon peer and family relationships. This analysis provides the basis for identifying those relationships that have affected the development of the child's problematic behavior and those social resources that might play a potentially significant role in treatment programming. In the final step, an analysis is made of the child's socio-cultural-physical environment to determine whether treatment goals are congruent with the norms or expectations of the child's particular background and current milieu.

Although assessment following the S-O-R-K-C model is time consuming, the thoroughness of the approach and its incorporation of diverse multiple assessment methods make it especially appealing to us. However, we must remind the reader once again of Evans's admonition that errors in clinical judgment are not necessarily minimized by inclusion of many different methods. As also noted by Mash and Terdal (1981), an implicit danger in the multimethod approach is that it is reminiscent of the old traditional "test battery" approach. In this approach, it is frequently assumed that the more information we have, the better we are able to understand and treat children. Although there is considerable empirical support for the notion that different methods yield varied information, there is little available support for the hypothesis that such additional information leads to a "truer" or more useful understanding of the child or that more efficacious treatment will follow necessarily. In this regard, it is important that child behavioral assessors "give some attention to the incremental validity associated with using multiple methods, in order to avoid the perpetration of potentially unnecessary and costly procedures" (Mash & Terdal, 1981, pp. 41–42). Incremental validity can be assessed by determining the relationship between the assessment information obtained and treatment outcomes (Mash, 1979).

Empirically Validated Measures

Undoubtedly, a variety of factors enter into determining exactly which methods of assessment should be used (Mash & Terdal, 1981). Among these are the nature of the target behaviors (e.g., self-statements, social skills, affective expression), characteristics of the child (e.g., age, sex, cognitive skills, particular learning history), the referral source (e.g, parents, teachers, social workers, law enforcement officers), the assessment setting (e.g., home, school, clinic, institution), the sociocultural milieu (e.g., socioeconomic status, religious affiliation), and the specific purpose of assessment (e.g., diagnosis, placement, intervention, understanding). Regardless of the exact methods selected, however, it is essential that the chosen ones possess sound psychometric qualities. All too frequently, child behavioral assessors have chosen or designed methods of convenience without due regard for adequate standardization, reliability, validity, or clinical utility. A comparison across studies is extremely difficult, if not impossible; and advancement of an assessment technology, let alone an understanding of child behavior disorders, is not realized with such an idiosyncratic approach.

The role of conventional psychometric standards in evaluating the adequacy of child behavioral assessment methods is highly controversial (e.g., Cone & Hawkins, 1977; Mash & Terdal, 1981). On the one hand, basic assumptions concerning the situational specificity and temporal instability of behavior appear to defy or preclude the use of psychometric standards. After all, how can a self-report or role-play test of assertiveness designed to "sample" heterogeneous social situations be expected to possess high internal consistency or good split-half reliability (McFall, 1982; Ollendick, in press-a)? Further, how can such instruments be expected to possess concurrent validity when cross-situational variability is the norm rather than a reflection of invalid instruments? Such notions of reliability and validity are most appropriate to traitlike, nomothetic conceptions in which behavior is viewed as reasonably stable over time and relatively consistent across situations. On the other hand, if no two situations are exactly alike, and there is no consistency in behavior over time, the prediction and generalizability of behavior becomes meaningless and impossible. Such an extreme idiographic stance precludes meaningful assessment except for a particular behavior in a particular setting and at a particular point in time.

It appears to us that child behavioral assessors have misinterpreted Mischel's (1973) intent when he first stated that the focus of assessment from a behavioral perspective "shifts from describing situation-free people with broad trait adjectives to analyzing the specific interactions between conditions and the cognitions and behaviors of interest" (p. 265). Mischel, as clarified in a later statement, did not intend to do away with personality or its measurement:

> My intentions . . . were not to undo personality but to defend individuality and the uniqueness of each person against what I saw as the then prevalent form of clinical hostility: the tendency to use a few behavioral signs to categorize people enduringly into fixed slots on the assessor's favorite nomothetic trait dimensions and to assume that these slot positions were sufficiently informative to predict specific behavior and to make extensive decisions about a person's whole life. (Mischel, 1979, p. 740)

It is evident from these statements, as well as recent research findings (e.g., Gresham, 1982; Ollendick, 1981), that we need not totally dismiss the notions of cross-situational and cross-temporal consistency of behavior. Though we cannot expect a high degree of congruence in behavior across diverse situations or over extended periods of time, we can expect a modicum of behavioral consistency across those situations that involve increasingly similar stimulus and response characteristics and which are temporarily related (Bem & Allen, 1974). Inasmuch as diverse methodologies (e.g., interviews, self-reports, other-reports, etc.) are used to assess various facets of behavior under these conditions, a modest relationship among the various measures can be expected. In such circumstances, application of conventional psychometric standards to the evaluation of child behavioral assessment strategies becomes less problematic and increasingly useful.

In the least, it seems to us that we must begin to develop standardized measures of child behaviors that possess adequate test-retest reliability and criterion validity. Within the tenets of the behavioral perspective, attention to such considerations is both desirable and possible (e.g., Cone, 1977). Regardless of the assessment methods used, we must expect our measures to be consistent over time and to be related to one another (as long as they are obtained under similar stimulus situations, and change due to an intervention program or a normal developmental process has not occurred). Further, under the same assumptions, we must expect our measures to be reasonably good predictors of subsequent behavior and adjustment (predictive validity). Such validity has already been demonstrated for certain classes of behavior with diverse measures such as behavioral observation (e.g., Olweus, 1979), self-report (e.g., Ollendick, 1981), teacher ratings (e.g., Cowen, Pederson, Barbigian, Izzo, & Trost, 1973), and sociometric ratings (e.g., Hartup, Glazer, & Charlesworth, 1967). Further, when these multiple measures have been used in the same studies, a moderate degree of both concurrent and predictive validity has been obtained, at least for socially dysfunctional behavior (e.g., Gresham, 1982; Ollendick, 1981).

It is not possible in this chapter to delineate the many factors related to standardization, reliability, validity, and clinical utility for each of the methods. However, some of the more important considerations and issues are addressed in each of the chapters that follow. Attention to these psychometric qualities directly guided the selection of specific methods for this volume. In subsequent chapters, each of these methods is described and its psychometric properties are reviewed. Prior to leaving this section, we must return briefly to the notion of multimethod assessment and the selection of specific methods to use. While a multimethod approach that is based on empirically validated instruments is recommended, it should be clear that it is not always possible or necessary to use all of the suggested methods. A "test battery" approach is not being recommended. The specific assessment devices to be used depend upon a variety of factors including the nature of the referral question and the personnel, time, and resources available to the child behavior assessor (Ollendick & Cerny, 1981). Nonetheless, given the limitations of the various procedures, as well as the desirability of having as complete a "picture of the child" as possible, we recommend that as many procedures as possible be used. Any one procedure, including direct behavioral observation, is not sufficient to meet the various assessment functions that are required for a thorough functional analysis of the child's behavior problems. The multimethod approach is not only helpful in assessing specific behaviors and in determining response to behavior change, but it may also be useful in understanding child behavior disorders and in advancing our knowledge in this area of study.

Developmental and Normative Comparisons

Just as assessment procedures must be psychometrically sound and empirically validated, they must also be sensitive to developmental changes when used with children. Perhaps the most noteworthy characteristic of children in general is developmental change (Ciminero & Drabman, 1977; Evans & Nelson, 1977; Mash & Terdal, 1981; see chap. 2). Such change, whether it is based on hypothetical stages of cognitive or social development or empirically derived developmental norms, has clear implications for the selection of specific assessment methods and the evaluation of behavior change.

Age-related verbal and cognitive abilities directly affect the appropriateness of certain methods of assessment. Self-monitoring, for instance, requires the ability to compare one's own behavior against a standard and to accurately judge occurrence or nonoccurrence of targeted events and behaviors. Most children below 6 years of age lack the requisite ability to self-monitor and may not profit from such procedures. In fact, the limited research available suggests that self-monitoring may be counterproductive when used with such children, resulting in confusion and impaired performance (e.g., Higa, Tharp, & Calkins, 1978; Ollendick & Cerny, 1981). These findings suggest that self-monitoring procedures are better suited for children who possess sufficient cognitive abilities to benefit from their use (see chap. 8). In a similar vein, age-related variables place constraints on the use of certain self-report and sociometric measures with young children. It often has been noted that sociometric devices must be simplified and presented in pictorial form to children under 6 years of age (McCandless & Marshall, 1957; see chap. 7). The picture sociometric provides the young child a set of concrete, visual cues regarding the children to be rated and, of course, does not require him or her to read the names of the children being rated. The roster-and-rating method, used so frequently with older children, is simply not appropriate for younger children.

Similarly, self-report measures need to be carefully designed with the verbal and cognitive abilities of the young child in mind. Recently, one of us (Ollendick, 1979, in press-b) undertook the revision and restandardization of the Fear Survey Schedule for Children (Scherer & Nakamura, 1968). This scale, while useful with older children, was found to be less applicable to children under 8 years of age. Although younger children appeared to understand the fear stimulus items, they were unable to grasp the notion of rating fear on a 5-point scale. When a 3-point scale was used, however, the children were able to reliably and validly rate their fear, as evidenced by good test-retest reliability and congruence with a behavioral measure of fear (Ollendick, in press-b).

Other methods of child behavioral assessment are not without their age-related constraints. Although untested at this time, it seems plausible that reactivity to behavioral observation may also be age related. For example, the social comparison literature suggests that as children become older, they compare and evaluate their own behavior against relevant social norms (e.g., Ollendick, Shapiro, & Barrett, 1982; Ruple, Parsons, & Ross, 1976). While an adult's presence might not serve as a cue for such an evaluative process with young children, or for that matter with adolescents, it might be predicted to do so for the older child. However, confirmation of this hypothesis awaits empirical verification.

In sum, age-related constraints are numerous and await clearer articulation and categorization. Until such time, it is imperative that child behavioral assessors be aware of developmental considerations and constraints when selecting specific methods of assessment. Certain procedures are more appropriate for specific age groups and ability levels than others. The continued and indiscriminate use of developmentally insensitive instruments will fail to advance our understanding and subsequent modification of child behavior disorders.

Rapid and uneven changes associated with normal developmental processes and experiences also have implications for selection of target behaviors and for evaluation of their change over time. In this regard, the development of normative information is invaluable. As noted by Mash and Terdal (1981), child behavioral assessors have emphasized intraindividual comparisons and have given little attention to normative comparisons. Normative comparisons provide information about the child's behavior relative to the behavior of other children in an appropriate reference group (e.g., age, sex, culture). While intraindividual comparisons examine an individual child's behavior relative to his or her own baseline rate of behavior, they provide little information about the child's behavior with respect to that of a suitable reference group. Clearly, intraindividual comparisons are necessary; however, so too are normative comparisons if we wish to establish the social validity of our assessment and treatment efforts (Kazdin, 1977; Wolf, 1978).

Several studies have described "normal" age trends in specific child behavior disorders. For example, specific fears and phobias have been shown to occur with regularity during the course of normal development. Most infants show a startlelike response (called the freeze reaction) to loss of support or to sudden and loud noises. Later, during the first year of life, babies evidence a fear of strangers in which they react with fearlike panic to unfamiliar people and unfamiliar situations. Fear of animals tends to appear between the ages of 2 and 3, while fear of the dark emerges between 3 and 4 years of age. School phobia characteristically occurs upon entry into school (and subsequent changes in schools or grade levels), while evaluative fear and social fear develop during middle childhood and adolescence. Presence of such regularity in fears and phobias, of course, does not "explain" their occurrence. Undoubtedly, emerging cognitive abilities (e.g., Bauer, 1980) as well as common situational events (Miller, Barrett, & Hampe, 1974; Ollendick, 1979; Ollendick & Mayer, 1983) interact to occasion their presence. Further, regularity in occurrence does not necessarily imply that such fears are transitory or not problematic to the child (Graziano, 1975). We now know that persistent and excessive fears are present in 3–8% of children (Ollendick, 1979). Further, we know that such fears are not transitory, as many fears persist into adulthood (e.g., Marks & Gelder, 1966), while other fears such as school phobia frequently serve as early precursors to agoraphobia in adults (Berg, 1976; Berg, Marks, McGuire, & Lipsedge, 1974; Ollendick & Mayer, 1983).

While caution must be exercised in the blind use of developmental norms, as stated above, they do provide good "markers" for target selection and behavior change. For example, a child whose fear of the dark is evident at 10 years of age is clearly exhibiting deviant behavior from a normative standpoint; on the other hand, the child who evinces fear of the dark at 4 years of age is not. Just as a 1-year-old child displays poor bowel control and a 5-year-old child frequently reverses "*b*'s" and "*d*'s" and "*p*'s" and "*q*'s," so too might a child at 4 years of age display fear of the dark. Fear of the dark itself may not be unusual for this age; however, its intensity, duration, and persistence may be of concern. Similar conclusions have been offered about aggressive behavior (Olweus, 1979), withdrawn behavior (Furman, 1980), and cross-dressing behavior (Rekers, 1978) in young children.

Thus, normative comparisons are most useful in the identification of behavioral excesses and deficits and in the evaluation of behavior change over time. To the extent that behaviors are not stable and that rapid and uneven developmental changes characterize child behavior, behavioral assessors must be aware of the extent to which behavior change is a function of intervention and developmental change. The combined use of intraindividual and normative comparisons will assist in both of these endeavors.

Based on these characteristics, several generalizations regarding child behavioral assessment are offered:

1. Children are a special population. The automatic extension of adult behavioral assessment methods to children is not warranted and often is inappropriate. Age-related variables affect the choice of methods as well as the procedures employed.

2. Given rapid developmental change in children, normative comparisons are required to ensure that appropriate target behaviors are selected and that change in behavior is related to treatment, not to normal developmental change. Such comparisons require identification of suitable reference groups and information about the "natural course" of child behavior problems.

3. Thorough child behavioral assessment involves multiple targets of change, including overt behavior, affective states, and cognitions. Further, such assessment entails determining the context (e.g., familial, social, cultural) in which the child's behavior occurs and the "function" that the targeted behaviors serve.

4. Given the wide range of targets for change, multimethod assessment is desirable and necessary. Multimethod assessment should not be viewed simply as a "test battery" approach; rather, methods should be selected on the basis of their appropriateness to the referral question. Regardless of the measures used, they should be empirically validated and developmentally sensitive.

In the chapters that follow, this empirically based, developmentally anchored, multimethod approach will be explicated in greater detail. A variety of methods will be explored, and their relevance to child behavioral assessment will be described. Before moving to a more detailed discussion of these principles and procedures, we shall briefly turn our attention to the role of the child in child behavioral assessment.

THE ROLE OF THE CHILD IN
CHILD BEHAVIORAL ASSESSMENT

All too frequently, child behavioral assessors have conceptualized children and child behavior disorders in a rather passive, static fashion. Tests are administered *to* children, ratings are obtained *on* children, and behaviors are observed *in* children. This process relegates the child to a role of passive responder, as someone who is incapable of actively shaping and determining his or her environment. Rarely are the thoughts, feelings, perceptions, attributions, or expectations of the child taken into consideration.

Although a thorough investigation of these organismic processes in children and their effects on child behavior has been explored only recently, they hold considerable promise in advancing our understanding of child behavior and our prediction of child behavior change. Illustratively, children's conceptions of behavior disorders are a potentially relevant, if not critical, area of further study. To what causes do children attribute aggressive or withdrawn behavior in themselves or in their peers? Do these attributions differ for psychotic or retarded behavior? Are there age-related trends in these attributions? Do causal attributions (as well as self-efficacy and outcome expectancies) interact with treatment efficacy? The answer to these questions are of both theoretical interest and applied clinical significance.

A partial answer to these questions can be found in recent research efforts. For example, studies by Coie and Pennington (1976) and Dollinger, Thelen, and Walsh (1980) have shown that an interesting developmental trend exists in children's conceptions of child deviance and their attributions of its causes. Younger children conceive of deviant behavior as that which is "different" from their own behavior or interests. Further, younger children attribute the cause of such deviant behavior to external factors like "mean parents," "a bad teacher," or "other kids." In contrast, older children and adolescents conceive of deviant behavior as that which deviates from some social norm. Moreover, they attribute the cause of deviant behavior to internal factors like "not having the ability" or "not trying hard enough." Interestingly, as a child matures into later adolescence, both conceptions and attributions approximate those held by adults (e.g., Compas, Friedland-Bandes, Bastien, & Adelman, 1981). What are the practical implications of these rapidly changing conceptions and attributions? The elucidation of these phenomena with children and parents in a clinical context seems especially critical since observations made by parents (or teachers) invariably precipitate clinical intervention. Consider the 8-year-old child who is brought to the clinic by his parents because he is inattentive in school, displays disruptive behavior, and is receiving low grades. The child, as well as his peers, perceives the problem as an external one — one demanding clear environmental change. However, the parents and teachers perceive the child's problems as a lack of "self-control" and that he "just has to try harder" and everything will work out. While adults and children are perceiving the situation differently, they both may be perceiving correctly (much like the proverbial elephant). Regardless, both sets of perceptions and attributions must be clarified and considered in the assessment, treatment, and evaluation aspects of child behavior therapy.

Recent research has also shown that treatment procedures may have differential effects depending on children's causal attributions. For instance, Bugental, Whalen, and Henker (1977) compared a self-instructional package to a contingent social reinforcement program with medicated and unmedicated hyperactive boys. The self-instruction program was most effective for unmedicated boys who were internal in their locus of control attributions. On the other hand, the social reinforcement program worked best for unmedicated boys who reported an external locus of control. From a similar perspective, Ollendick, Elliott, and Matson (1980) showed that self-reported locus of control was related to success of behavioral contracting and token economy programs with adjudicated male delinquents. The extension of Bandura's (1977) notion of self-efficacy to children would also likely prove productive in this regard. Recently, we have developed measures of self-efficacy and outcome expectancy for children's social skills. In our initial efforts, we have found these measures to be related to the presence of specific behavioral and cognitive skills and to be predictive of differential change following cognitive restructuring or behavioral interventions (Ollendick, 1982). Although considerably more research must be performed, such attributional and expectancy constructs appear to be of heuristic value in planning and implementing specific intervention strategies.

Thus, while this area of research is just now evolving, we view it as one of the most important developments in child behavioral assessment. Much remains to be learned; much is likely to be gained.

SUMMARY

In this introductory chapter, we have attempted to elucidate some of the more important principles and procedures of child behavioral assessment. We have described child behavioral assessment as an empirically based, developmentally sensitive, multimethod approach in which a range of specific procedures are used in order to *understand* a given child, group, or social ecology. We also argue that child behavioral assessment is an exploratory, hypothesis-testing process in which a wide range of information is reviewed in order to obtain a complete "picture of the child" and the meaningful context(s) in which his or her behavior occurs. From this standpoint, a wide range of methods is not only necessary but desirable; these methods include behavioral interviews, self-reports, self-monitoring, other-reports, standardized instruments, and behavioral observations.

We also have noted that the incremental validity of this approach is in need of verification, and important issues related to rapid changes in development in children need to be considered when using this approach. Nonetheless, at this stage of our knowledge of child behavioral assessment, such an approach is not only heuristic but also appears warranted. Advancement in this area of research and clinical practice demands concerted effort and systematic attention. In particular, the role of the child in the behavioral assessment paradigm is likely to be a most important area of investigation.

REFERENCES

Aries, P. *Centuries of childhood.* New York: Vintage Books, 1962.

Bandura, A. *Principles of behavior modification.* New York: Holt, Rinehart, & Winston, 1969.

Bandura, A. Self-efficacy: Toward a unifying theory of behavioral change. *Psychological Review,* 1977, *84, 191*-215.

Bauer, D. Childhood fears in developmental perspective. In L. Hersov & I. Berg (Eds.), *Out of school.* New York: Wiley, 1980.

Bem, D. J., & Allen, A. On predicting some of the people some of the time: The search for cross-situational consistencies in behavior. *Psychological Review,* 1974, *81,* 506-520.

Berg, I. School phobia in the children of agoraphobic women. *British Journal of Psychiatry,* 1976, *128,* 86-89.

Berg, I., Marks, I., McGuire, R., & Lipsedge, M. School phobias and agoraphobia. *Psychological Medicine,* 1974, *4,* 428-434.

Bijou, S. W., & Peterson, R. F. The psychological assessment of children: A functional analysis. In P. McReynolds (Ed.), *Advances in psychological assessment* (Vol. 2). Palo Alto, CA: Science and Behavior Books, 1971.

Brown, F. J. *The sociology of childhood.* Englewood Cliffs, NJ: Prentice-Hall, 1939.

Bugental, B. D., Whalen, C. K., & Henker, B. Causal attributions of hyperactive children and motivational assumptions of two behavior-change approaches: Evidence for an interactionist position. *Child Development,* 1977, *48,* 874-884.

Ciminero, A. R., & Drabman, R. S. Current developments in the behavioral assessment of children. In B. B. Lahey and A. E. Kazdin (Eds.), *Advances in clinical child psychology* (Vol. 1). New York: Plenum Press, 1977.

Coie, J. D., & Pennington, B. F. Children's perceptions of deviance and disorder. *Child Development,* 1976, *47,* 407-413.

Compas, B. E., Friedland-Bandes, R., Bastien, R., & Adelman, H. S. Parent and child causal attributions related to the child's clinical problem. *Journal of Abnormal Child Psychology,* 1981, *9,* 389-397.

Cone, J. D. The relevance of reliability and validity for behavioral assessment. *Behavior Therapy*, 1977, *8*, 411–426.

Cone, J. D., & Hawkins, R. P. (Eds.). *Behavioral assessment: New directions in clinical psychology*. New York: Brunner/Mazel, 1977.

Cowen, E. L., Pederson, A., Barbigian, H., Izzo, L. D., & Trost, M. A. Long-term follow-up of early detected vulnerable children. *Journal of Consulting and Clinical Psychology*, 1973, *41*, 438–445.

Dollinger, S. J., Thelen, M. H., & Walsh, M. L. Children's conceptions of psychological problems. *Journal of Clinical Child Psychology*, 1980, *9*, 191–194.

Evans, I. M. Review of *Multimethod clinical assessment* by W. R. Nay. *Behavioral Assessment*, 1982, *4*, 121–124.

Evans, I. M., & Nelson, R. O. Assessment of child behavior problems. In A. R. Ciminero, K. S. Calhoun, & H. E. Adams (Eds.), *Handbook of behavioral assessment*. New York: Wiley-Interscience, 1977.

Furman, W. Promoting social development: Developmental implications for treatment. In B. B. Lahey & A. E. Kazdin, *Advances in clinical child psychology* (Vol. 3). New York: Plenum Press, 1980.

Gelfand, D., & Hartmann, D. P. *Child behavior analysis and therapy*. New York: Pergamon Press, 1975.

Goldfried, M. R., & Kent, R. N. Traditional versus behavioral personality assessment: A comparison of methodological and theoretical assumptions. *Psychological Bulletin*, 1972, *77*, 409–420.

Graziano, A. M. *Behavior therapy with children* (Vol. 2). Chicago: Aldine, 1975.

Gresham, F. M. Social interactions as predictors of children's likeability and friendship patterns: A multiple regression analysis. *Journal of Behavioral Assessment*, 1982, *4*, 39–54.

Hartup, W. W., Glazer, J. A., & Charlesworth, R. Peer reinforcement and sociometric status. *Child Development*, 1967, *38*, 1017–1024.

Hersen, M., & Bellack, A. S. *Behavioral assessment: A practical handbook*. New York: Pergamon Press, 1976.

Higa, W. R., Tharp, R. G., & Calkins, R. P. Developmental verbal control of behavior: Implications for self-instructional training. *Journal of Experimental Child Psychology*, 1978, *26*, 489–497.

Holmes, F. B. An experimental investigation of a method of overcoming children's fears. *Child Development*, 1936, *7*, 6–30.

Jones, M. C. The elimination of children's fears. *Journal of Experimental Psychology*, 1924, *7*, 382–390.

Kanfer, F. H., & Saslow, G. Behavioral diagnosis. In C. M. Franks (Ed.), *Behavior therapy: Appraisal and status*. New York: McGraw-Hill, 1969.

Kazdin, A. E. Assessing the clinical or applied importance of behavior change through social validation. *Behavior Modification*, 1977, *1*, 427–452.

Kendall, P. C., & Hollon, S. D. (Eds.). *Cognitive-behavioral intervention: Assessment methods*. New York: Academic Press, 1980.

Lang, P. J. Fear reduction and fear behavior: Problems in treating a construct. In J. M. Shlien (Ed.), *Research in psychotherapy* (Vol. 3). Washington, DC: American Psychological Association, 1968.

Marks, I. M., & Gelder, M. G. Different ages of onset in varieties of phobia. *American Journal of Psychiatry*, 1966, *123*, 218–221.

Mash, E. J. What is behavioral assessment? *Behavioral Assessment*, 1979, *1*, 23–29.

Mash, E. J., & Terdal, L. G. Behavioral assessment of childhood disturbances. In E. J. Mash & L. G. Terdal (Eds.), *Behavioral assessment of childhood disorders*. New York: Guilford Press, 1981.

McCandless, B. R., & Marshall, H. R. A picture sociometric technique for preschool children and its relation to teacher judgment of friendship. *Child Development,* 1957, *28,* 139–148.

McFall, R. M. A review and reformulation of the concept of social skills. *Behavioral Assessment,* 1982, *4,* 1–33.

McReynolds, P. *Advances in psychological assessment* (Vol. 1). Palo Alto, CA: Science and Behavior Books, 1968.

Meichenbaum, D. H. *Cognitive-behavior modification.* New York: Plenum Press, 1977.

Miller, L. C., Barrett, C. L., & Hampe, E. Phobias of childhood in a prescientific era. In A. Davids (Ed.), *Child personality and psychopathology: Current topics.* New York: Wiley, 1974.

Mischel, W. Toward a cognitive social learning reconceptualization of personality. *Psychological Review,* 1973, *80,* 252–283.

Mischel, W. On the interface of cognition and personality: Beyond the person-situation debate. *American Psychologist,* 1979, *34,* 740–754.

Ollendick, T. H. Fear reduction techniques with children. In M. Hersen, R. M. Eisler, & P. M. Miller (Eds.), *Progress in behavior modification* (Vol. 8). New York: Academic Press, 1979.

Ollendick, T. H. Assessment of social interaction skills in school children. *Behavioral Counseling Quarterly,* 1981, *1,* 227–243.

Ollendick, T. H. *The Self-Efficacy Questionnaire for Children's Social Skills.* Unpublished manuscript, Virginia Polytechnic Institute and State University, 1982.

Ollendick, T. H. Development and validation of the Children's Assertiveness Inventory. *Child Behavior Therapy,* in press. (a)

Ollendick, T. H. Reliability and validity of the Revised Fear Survey Schedule for Children (FSSC-R). *Behaviour Research and Therapy,* in press. (b)

Ollendick, T. H., & Cerny, J. A. *Clinical behavior therapy with children.* New York: Plenum Press, 1981.

Ollendick, T. H., Elliott, W. R., & Matson, J. L. Locus of control as related to effectiveness in a behavior modification program for juvenile delinquents. *Journal of Behavior Therapy and Experimental Psychiatry,* 1980, *11,* 259–262.

Ollendick, T. H., & Hersen, M. (Eds.). *Handbook of child psychopathology.* New York: Plenum Press, 1983.

Ollendick, T. H., & Mayer, J. School phobia. In S. M. Turner (Ed.), *Behavioral treatment of anxiety disorders.* New York: Plenum Press, 1983.

Ollendick, T. H., Shapiro, E. S., & Barrett, R. P. Effects of vicarious reinforcement in normal and severely disturbed children. *Journal of Consulting and Clinical Psychology,* 1982, *50,* 63–70.

Olweus, D. Stability of aggressive reaction patterns in males: A review. *Psychological Bulletin,* 1979, *86,* 852–875.

Rekers, G. A. Sexual problems: Behavior modification. In B. B. Wolman (Ed.), *Handbook of treatment of mental disorders in childhood and adolescence.* Englewood Cliffs, NJ: Prentice-Hall, 1978.

Rie, H. E. (Ed.). *Perspectives in child psychopathology.* Chicago: Aldine-Atherton, 1971.

Ruple, D. N., Parsons, J. E., & Ross, J. Self-evaluative responses of children in an achievement setting. *Child Development,* 1976, *47,* 990–997.

Scherer, M. W., & Nakamura, C. Y. A Fear Survey Schedule for Children (FSS-FC): An analytic comparison with manifest anxiety (CMAS). *Behaviour Research and Therapy,* 1968, *6,* 173–182.

Sulzer-Azaroff, B., & Mayer, G. R. *Applying behavior analysis procedures with children and youth.* New York: Holt, Rinehart, & Winston, 1977.

Watson, J. B., & Rayner, R. Conditioned emotional reactions. *Journal of Experimental Psychology,* 1920, *3,* 1–14.

Wolf, M. M. Social validity: The case for subjective measurement or how behavior analysis is finding its heart. *Journal of Applied Behavior Analysis,* 1978, *11,* 203–214.

2

Developmental Considerations

Craig Edelbrock

This chapter discusses the importance of accounting for age and developmental level when assessing children's behavior disorders. The necessity of accounting for age differences when assessing behavior is obvious in many ways but requires reiteration here, if only as a reminder. Sooner or later everyone involved in child behavioral assessment confronts the fact that adult assessment devices and procedures cannot be applied to children. Even careful attempts to extrapolate adult measures down to children by simplifying wording, modifying administration and scoring procedures, and revising norms typically fail. Children's behavior is qualitatively so different from that of adults that a completely different approach is required.

Assessment of clinically relevant child behaviors involves a number of special problems and issues (Mash & Terdal, 1981, pp. 25-29; Ollendick & Cerny, 1981). Unlike adults, children rarely refer themselves for mental health services, report on their own problems, or play a significant role in the negotiation and evaluation of treatment interventions. Behavioral assessment of the child depends heavily on information derived from adults, such as parents, teachers, and trained observers. Childhood disorders are not characterized by a few pathognomonic signs and symptoms but entail a wide range of emotional, behavioral, and social difficulties that arise in diverse situations, such as home, school, and with peers. Thus, multiproblem and multisituation analyses are the rule. It is also necessary to consider a broad range of demographic and background variables, such as home environment, family psychopathology, and socioeconomic status, which influence children's behavior and development as well as the types of professional services atypical children are likely to receive. In addition, children are characterized by constant change in behavior and abilities, which creates special problems in selecting target behaviors and appropriate methods of assessment.

Despite general consensus that behavioral assessment of children involves unique considerations, there has been remarkably little attention paid to differences *among* children of various ages. A surprising number of behavioral measures are designated as being for "children" of broad or unspecified age. This is a major deficiency. The behavior of children depends to a large degree on age, experience, and developmental level. Moreover, behavioral norms and expectations differ markedly for children of different ages. Assessment materials and procedures must therefore be closely attuned to developmental status if they are to provide useful information. There is also an unfortunate gap between the study of normal child behavior and development and the study of psychopathological disorders of childhood. Although much developmental research is designed to be clinically relevant, few links to clinical research or practice have been forged.

The next part of this chapter presents the delineation of the normative-developmental perspective on child behavior and its implications regarding assessment. Differences between behavioral and developmental approaches to the study of child behavior disorders will be discussed, and ways of integrating developmental concepts and principles into child behavioral assessment will be illustrated by recent research findings. Many of these illustrations will be drawn from research using the Child Behavior Checklist and Child Behavior Profile (Achenbach, 1978; Achenbach & Edelbrock, 1979, 1981; Edelbrock & Achenbach, 1980) because our goal in developing these instruments has been to bridge the gap between studies of normal development and the clinical assessment of children's behavior.

THE NORMATIVE-DEVELOPMENTAL PERSPECTIVE

Psychopathological disorders of childhood are so diverse and variously determined that no single "sovereign" theory can solve all prevailing clinical and research problems. Although there are several theories of child development (Baldwin, 1967), they provide only partial explanations of limited aspects of behavioral and psychological development (Rutter, 1980, p. 6). The developmental approach to children's behavioral disorders is not a comprehensive theory. It is rather a perspective or point of view which takes into account the overwhelming changes that occur as the child grows from birth to maturity. This perspective does not provide definitive answers regarding appropriate methods of assessment, diagnosis, or treatment. However, it does provide an essential framework for the construction of assessment materials and for the interpretation of behavioral differences among children.

The developmental point of view is perhaps best termed the "normative-developmental" perspective, since it involves two fundamental principles. The "developmental" principle stresses the importance of accounting for the quantitative and qualitative changes that occur as the child grows older. These changes encompass not only quantum leaps in biological structure and functioning, but also complex and closely intertwined changes in emotional, behavioral, cognitive, and social functioning. These changes are generally systematic, orderly, and progressive but during certain periods can be rapid and uneven. To some extent, stages or phases can be identified in which a stable level of structure and functioning is maintained for a period of time. Moreover, behaviors and abilities acquired during one stage may be essential to further development. Thus, appraisal of a child's current level of behavioral functioning requires consideration of developmental antecedents as well as future consequences.

According to the second or "normative" principle, children's behavior must be evaluated with respect to some reference group. There is no absolute yardstick for measuring children's behavioral problems and adaptive competencies. Each attempt to evaluate a child's level of behavioral functioning must be met with the question: Compared to whom? Given the overwhelming age contingencies in behavior, the appropriate reference group typically involves children of the same age. Age is obviously a crude index of developmental level; however, it serves as a convenient summary of a child's developmental standing in several areas. In general, it would be an advantage to obtain more precise and detailed information regarding a child's functioning in specific areas. Nevertheless, age is simply and reliably assessed and serves as an acceptable index of global developmental status.

Although developmentalists acknowledge variability in the behavior of children of the same age, there is considerably more variability across ages. Sequences, rates, and patterns of developmental changes can be determined for children in general. Given baselines for normal age-related changes, "developmental deviations" can be identified wherein a child's behavioral functioning is clearly outside the normal range. It is also possible to identify children with a "developmental lag," a term which describes a child who is behind his or her agemates in terms of developmental achievements but may still be progressing through the normal sequence of steps and stages.

In summary, the normative-developmental perspective encompasses two general principles. One emphasizes the central importance of change in the study of children's behavior, the other underscores the need for age-graded norms against which individual children can be compared.

DEVELOPMENTAL VS. BEHAVIORAL APPROACHES

Behavioral and developmental approaches to child psychopathology are in no way incompatible, but there are some major differences between the two perspectives. The first, and perhaps most important difference, involves the distinction between the *idiographic* and *nomothetic* approach. Behavioral assessment is predominantly idiographic. As Mash and Terdal (1981, p. 28) have pointed out, this orientation is largely due to the role of behavioral assessment in treatment evaluation, where intraindividual changes in behavior are of primary concern. In contrast, the developmental approach is nomothetic; the goal is to establish general laws that pertain to groups of individuals. Thus, developmental research has concentrated more on the establishment of group norms than on the study of individual differences in development.

Second, as Voeltz and Evans (1982) have recently pointed out, behavioral assessment emphasizes the quantification of specific behaviors which may be isolated from more complex behavioral patterns. The judicious selection of specific target behaviors is a hallmark of behavioral assessment. However, behaviors are interrelated in complex ways, and relationships among behavioral responses may be overlooked or ignored. In contrast, much of the developmentally attuned research has focused on the identification of patterns of covariation among behaviors. Numerous factor analytic studies, for example, have identified groups of behavior problems that co-occur and form distinct syndromes of child psychopathology (see Achenbach & Edelbrock, 1978, for a review).

The concept of a syndrome has been rejected within the field of behavioral assessment because it connotes traditional notions of unseen etiological factors or implies a medical model. However, the concept of a syndrome can be employed in a more limited statistical sense to refer to groups of behaviors that co-occur. There is a growing realization that the association among behaviors is a crucial consideration in child behavioral assessment and therapy (Voeltz & Evans, 1982).

Third, behavioral and developmental approaches differ in terms of the emphasis placed on the role of the current environment in determining behavior. The behavioral approach emphasizes the salience of the current environment in shaping and controlling behavior, whereas the developmental perspective includes consideration of the historical antecedents or developmental precursors of current functioning. It is important to note, however, that the developmental perspective does not discount the importance of the current environment or deny the situational specificity of current behavior. Instead, both historical antecedents and current environmental contingencies are integrated into one explanation of behavior.

The developmental perspective also entails consideration of the future consequences of current behavior. Stability and change in behavior is viewed not simply as a function of stability and change in the environment. To some degree, prior experiences shape future behavior. Difficulty getting along with peers in a kindergarten class, for example, cannot be properly evaluated and explained as an isolated set of current behaviors. Nor can this problem be fully attributed to contemporaneous aspects of the environment. In addition to appraisal of current situational contingencies, possible developmental precursors must be considered. Moreover, these behaviors must be evaluated with respect to potential long-term consequences for the child.

INTEGRATING DEVELOPMENTAL AND BEHAVIORAL APPROACHES

Whereas the importance of accounting for developmental level when assessing behavior is obvious, ways of integrating developmental concepts and principles into behavioral assessment are less clear. How can the developmental perspective improve child behavioral assessment? Surprisingly, answers to this question arise from the differences between behavioral and developmental approaches just discussed. Rather than representing insurmountable problems, these differences represent fertile areas for the synthesis of developmental and behavioral principles. The remainder of this chapter examines three areas of research which blend the developmental perspective with behavioral assessment. These areas, which are directly related to the aforementioned differences, include (a) the establishment of normative baselines for behaviors, (b) the determination of age differences in the patterning of behaviors, and (c) the study of stability and change in behavior over time.

Establishing Normative Baselines

As discussed previously, a major difference between behavioral and developmental perspectives involves the distinction between idiographic and nomothetic analyses. These two analytical approaches are not mutually exclusive, and their synthesis, involving the evaluation of an individual's behavior within a normative context, has several advantages. One way to integrate normative-developmental principles into child behavioral assessment, for example, is to establish normative baselines for the behavior of children of different ages.

Establishing such norms is a formidable task. It would require the construction of comprehensive data bases describing the behavior of large representative samples of both referred and nonreferred children of different ages. Such data would be most useful if they tapped a wide range of clinically relevant behaviors and if the assessment methods were widely adoptable in both clinical and research contexts. It would also be an advantage to account for variables such as gender, race, and socioeconomic status, so that the contribution of these variables to behavioral differences could be evaluated.

To date, few surveys have provided data that meet these requirements. The most widely cited epidemiological surveys of children's behavioral problems are based on parents' reports of nonreferred children (Lapouse & Monk, 1958; Mitchell & Shepherd, 1966; Rutter, Tizard, & Whitmore, 1970). Cost and time requirements have thus far precluded use of direct observations in large scale epidemiological surveys. Previous studies are also limited in that information was obtained on relatively few behaviors or on children of very narrow age range. Among the published comparisons of clinical and nonclinical samples (Ferguson, Partyka, & Lester, 1974; Shectman, 1970, 1971; Wolff, 1967), data were combined for boys and girls and children of broad age ranges, and the samples were not representative of larger populations.

In an attempt to overcome these limitations, we recently completed a study designed to determine the prevalance of behavioral problems and adaptive competencies among normal and disturbed boys and girls aged 4 through 16 (Achenbach & Edelbrock, 1981). Data on 1,300 children referred for mental health services and a matched sample of 1,300 randomly selected nonreferred children were obtained using the Child Behavior Checklist. These samples were comprised of 50 boys and 50 girls at each age from 4 through 16. Within each group of 50, there was approximately equal representation of lower, middle, and upper socioeconomic status and an 80 : 20 ratio of white : black children.

The checklist is comprised of 20 social competence items and 188 behavioral problems (e.g., argues a lot, gets in fights, feels worthless) and serves as a standard format for obtaining parents' descriptions of their children's behavior. Parents respond to behavioral problem items according to a 0–1–2 scale in which 0 indicates that the problem is *not true* of the child, 1 indicates that the problem is *somewhat* or *sometimes true,* and 2 indicates that it is *very* or *often true.* In the analyses presented in the following section, responses of 1 and 2 were combined to reflect the presence or absence of specific behaviors. Data derived from the checklist are also directly applicable to clinical assessment in that the checklist is scorable in terms of the Child Behavior Profile, a standardized instrument for assessing and classifying children's behavioral disorders (Achenbach, 1978; Achenbach & Edelbrock, 1979; Edelbrock & Achenbach, 1980).

The study provides some unique examples of the contributions that normative baselines can make to behavioral assessment. It also raises a host of problems and issues related to the use of behavioral norms. For these reasons, I will briefly summarize our major findings, with emphasis on age differences. Detailed results and more complete discussions of our findings are available elsewhere (Achenbach & Edelbrock, 1981).

Age Differences. Our findings related to age differences are most pertinent to the discussion of developmental considerations in behavioral assessment. Of the 118 behavior problems on the checklist, 84 showed significant ($p < .01$) age effects. Most of these items showed a linear decrease in prevalence from age 4 through 16, with higher prevalence among younger children than older children. Figure 2.1 portrays age differences for checklist item number 109 (*Whining*), for clinically referred and nonreferred boys and girls. As shown in this figure, whining was reported to be a problem for 44–55% of the nonreferred 4- and 5-year-olds. This prevalence rate declined steadily with age and was only 5–7% among nonreferred children aged 12–16. The checklist item pertaining to *fears* also showed a linear decline in prevalence for all groups of children (see fig. 2.1). Other behaviors that manifested similar age trends included acting too young, encopresis, enuresis, hyperactivity, dependency, crying, demanding attention, destructiveness, disobedience, poor peer relations, jealousy, nightmares, showing off, speech problems, and thumb sucking.

In addition to these age trends, 19 checklist items showed a linear increase in prevalence over the age range from 4 through 16. The most dramatic age increases were found for items reflecting *alcohol and drug abuse* and *truancy* (fig. 2.1). These behaviors were rarely reported for children aged 4–10 but became increasingly common after age 11, particularly among clinically referred children. Other behaviors manifesting linear age increases included: fears school, hangs around children who get into trouble, preferring to be alone, obesity, headaches, poor schoolwork, refusing to talk, running away from home, secrecy, swearing, suicidal talk, sexual preoccupation, and underactivity.

Finally, a few behavior problems manifested nonlinear age trends. Item 48 (*Is teased*), for example, was reported more commonly for children aged 8–13 than for either younger or older children (fig. 2.1). Other items manifesting nonlinear age differences included confused, daydreams, harms self, feels worthless, self-conscious, and worrying.

Disturbed vs. Normal Children. In our analyses, significant differences related to clinical status were obtained for 108 of the 118 behavioral problem items; each difference reflected higher prevalence among clinically referred children than nonreferred children. Moreover, these differences were consistently larger than those due to age, race, and socioeconomic status. Item 103 (*Unhappy, sad, or depressed*) showed the largest difference between referred and nonreferred samples. As shown in figure 2.1, this behavior was reported for 40–90% of the clinically referred children (depending on age and gender) but only about 10% of the nonreferred children. Other behaviors that showed large effects of clinical status included: cannot concentrate, demands attention, disobedient at home, disobedient at school, poor peer relations, feels worthless, lying or cheating, and poor schoolwork. Surprisingly, several behavioral problems that have received considerable attention in the clinical literature (e.g., allergies, asthma, behaves like opposite sex) manifested negligible differences between our clinical and normal samples.

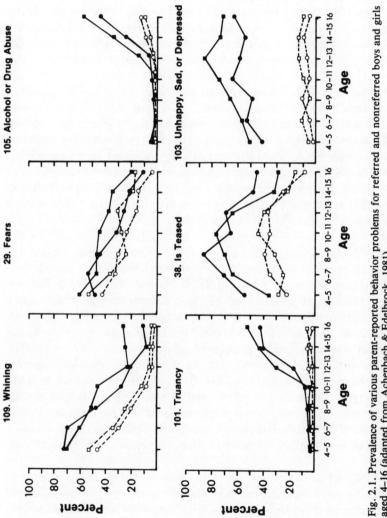

Fig. 2.1. Prevalence of various parent-reported behavior problems for referred and nonreferred boys and girls aged 4–16 (adapted from Achenbach & Edelbrock, 1981).

● Referred boys
■ Referred girls
○ Nonreferred boys
□ Nonreferred girls

Gender, Race, and Socioeconomic Status (SES) Differences. Compared to the differences related to age and clinical status, the effects of age, race, and SES were negligible. Significant differences between boys and girls were obtained for 51 behavioral problems but most entailed small effects accounting for less than 1% of the variance in scores. Of these items, 26 reflected higher prevalence among girls, whereas 25 reflected higher prevalence among boys. Problems characteristic of boys tended to be associated with "externalizing" behaviors such as aggression, hyperactivity, and delinquency; whereas problems more characteristic of girls tended to be associated with "internalizing" behaviors such as depression, withdrawal, and somatic complaints.

Only 14 of the 118 behavior problem items manifested significant differences between black and white children. All of these differences were small and accounted for less than 1% of the variance in scores. Furthermore, there was no discernible pattern in these race differences, with six items reflecting higher scores for blacks and eight items reflecting higher scores for whites.

Significant SES differences were detected for 53 behavior problems, with 49 reflecting higher prevalence among lower class children. Despite the statistical significance of these differences, most are trivial in that they account for less than 1% of the variance in scores.

Uses of Norms. Analysis of behavioral differences between normal and disturbed children of various ages can serve diverse clinical and research functions (Hartmann, Roper, & Bradford, 1979; Mash & Terdal, 1981). For one, such epidemiological comparisons can help determine what constitutes a disorder. Systematic data on the incidence and prevalence of behavioral problems would help establish standards for what constitutes a clinically significant behavioral deviation. Because of the number and size of age differences in reported behaviors, the judgment of whether a behavior is deviant depends heavily on the age of the child. Behavioral problems such as fears, whining, crying, demanding attention, and wetting the bed, for example, are relatively common among normal preschoolers and are not necessarily pathognomonic. If such behaviors persist into middle childhood or early adolescence, however, they may be more likely to represent clinically significant problems.

A second and closely related function of norms is that they can serve as guidelines for selecting appropriate target behaviors. Few clinically referred children manifest only one or two presenting symptoms, and child behavioral disorders are typically characterized by a wide range of maladaptive behaviors. Thus, selection of appropriate target behaviors can be difficult and prone to errors. Furman (1980) has recently pointed out that behavioral norms can help prevent the error of targeting behaviors that are occurring at normal rates as well as the error of failing to target behaviors that are genuinely deviant.

In our epidemiological analyses, high normative baselines were obtained for many behavioral problems. Arguing, for example, was reported to be a problem for more than half of the nonreferred boys and girls of all ages. Arguing may be particularly irritating to parents, but the fact that it is such a common complaint about normal children suggests that it should not receive high priority as a target behavior for clinical treatment.

Behavioral norms can also be used to address the validity of informants' descriptions of children's behavior. Assessment of many clinically relevant behaviors depends upon reports by unsophisticated and potentially biased observers such as parents and teachers. One question that often arises is whether informants' ratings represent veridical descriptions of the child's behavior or whether they reflect the informant's peculiar perceptions and biases. Behavioral norms can help determine whether the problem lies "in the child" or in the informant's perception. For example, a couple may instigate clinical behavior, but *their own descriptions* of the child's aggressiveness may fall well within the normal range. In this situation, it may be more appropriate to deal with the parents' inability to cope with normal childhood behavior than to attempt to modify the child's behavior.

Behavioral norms can also play a crucial role in the evaluation of treatment interventions. A given treatment may reduce problem behavior significantly, but the rate or severity of target behaviors may still exceed normal limits. Behavioral norms could thus be used to establish benchmarks for determining the applied or social significance of treatment effects (Kazdin, 1977; Walker & Hops, 1979).

Finally, normative data can also facilitate the direct comparison of behavioral assessments derived from different informants and/or different instruments. For example, parents and teachers may complete behavior rating scales describing the same target phenomena (e.g., child hyperactivity). Their ratings may differ due to differences in the children's behavior at home and at school or due to inherent differences in the ratings scales themselves (e.g., number of items, response scaling, etc.). Data derived from parents and teachers could be more easily compared and integrated if separate norms were available for each instrument. It would be possible, for example, to identify children who were two standard deviations above the mean on both parent and teacher ratings.

Statistical vs. Clinical Significance. Comparisons of demographically similar referred and nonreferred samples can also reveal which behaviors signify more serious psychopathology. In our analyses, for example, unhappiness, poor schoolwork, and poor peer relations were more strongly related to clinical status than problems such as allergies and asthma, which have been presumed to reflect underlying psychopathology. These findings suggest at least that highly discriminating behaviors are viewed as more serious problems by adults such as parents.

It is tempting to simply equate the "clinical significance" of behavioral problems with the size of differences between referred and nonreferred samples, but this can be very misleading. Referral for services is recognized as a fallible criterion for child psychopathology. Problems such as fire setting, hallucinations, encopresis, pica, suicidal and self-destructive acts, and sexual disturbances are rare among all children. Such behaviors can hardly be considered insignificant, but they do not discriminate well between referred and nonreferred criterion groups. Judgments regarding the clinical significance of childhood behaviors require consideration of additional factors such as the degree to which they impede development, hamper social relations, are dangerous to the child or others, or predict future and perhaps more serious maladaptation. Nevertheless, differences between normal and disturbed children can provide guidelines for selecting target behaviors for purposes of screening. Using such guidelines, statistically efficient screening inventories can be constructed to identify children whose behavior resembles those judged to need mental health services (Edelbrock, 1981).

Stratification of Norms. Normative data of the type collected using the Child Behavior Checklist can also be used to standardize behavioral rating scales. Standardization permits the location of an individual's scores on a continuum, relative to some reference group. But what is the appropriate reference group for evaluating a given child's behavior? Should children's behavior be compared to that of other children in general or children of the same age or gender? Should behavioral norms be stratified according to additional variables such as race, socioeconomic status, community environment, and region of the country?

One way to answer these questions is to consider how much variance in scores can be attributed to such variables. In our analyses, for example, clinical status, gender, and age accounted for considerable amounts of variance in parents' ratings. Failure to account for such variables when constructing norms can thus create misleading inferences. Haphazard and heterogeneous samples of normal and referred children are clearly inadequate for standardization purposes. The number, size, and direction of gender differences in our analyses dictate separate standardization samples for boys and girls. Even in the nonreferred sample, girls manifested more behavior associated with *"internalizing"* problems, whereas boys manifested more behaviors associated with *"externalizing"* problems. Thus, scoring girls according to boys' norms (or vice versa) or combining boys and girls in one standardization sample can yield very erroneous conclusions regarding the degree and patterning of behavioral deviations. Age must also be considered when constructing normative samples. Many behavioral problems (such as bedwetting, whining, and dependency, for example) are more common among younger children and are not necessarily pathognomonic at those ages. Thus, scoring behavioral descriptions of preschoolers according to norms based on older or heterogeneous age groups can exaggerate their behavioral deviance.

Accounting for race and SES differences when constructing norms appears to be less crucial, at least for parents' reports. Although these variables were significantly related to many parent-reported child behaviors, the effects were small and the direction of race differences was inconsistent. Developing separate norms for lower, middle, and upper SES groups or for black and white children results in standard scores having very similar distributions. The benefits of slightly increasing the precision of such scores are far outweighed by the cost and complexity of producing separate scoring procedures for each subgroup.

Age Differences in the Patterning of Behaviors

A second way to integrate developmental principles into child behavioral assessment is to identify age differences in the relations among behaviors. As mentioned previously, much of the developmentally attuned research on child psychopathology has focused on the identification of behavioral problem syndromes (Achenbach & Edelbrock, 1978). Several investigators, employing multivariate statistical procedures such as factor analysis, have identified groups of behavioral problems that co-occur and form distinct syndromes. Unfortunately, almost all of these analyses have been based on heterogeneous samples of children representing broad age ranges or have been limited to very narrow age ranges. Few investigators have sought to identify age contingencies in the patterning of behavioral symptoms.

One exception is the development of the Child Behavior Checklist and Child Behavior Profile. In order to account for age and gender differences in the patterning of behaviors, behavior problem syndromes were derived separately for boys and girls aged 4–5, 6–11, and 12–16. These age groups are somewhat arbitrary but correspond to major developmental milestones in children's lives, including transitions in school and social, cognitive, and biological changes. As Achenbach (1980) has pointed out, combining groups for these analyses could produce three types of misleading results. For one, syndromes specific to one age group or gender could be obscured. Second, age and gender differences in the specific content of similar syndromes could be obscured. Third, the generality of syndromes across groups could be exaggerated.

Our factor analyses were based on checklists completed on clinically referred children because many behavioral symptoms are too infrequent among normal children to permit meaningful correlational analysis. Sample sizes for these analyses were 450 for boys and girls aged 6–11 and 12–16, and 250 for boys and girls aged 4–5. Principal components analysis followed by both orthogonal and oblique rotations was used to identify robust factors that had a substantial number of items with loadings of .30 and above. These "narrow-band" behavioral problem syndromes, which represent specific groupings of behaviors, were also used as a basis for second-order factor analysis aimed at identifying more global broad-band factors. Two broad-band groupings of factors were obtained in each analysis and were labeled *Internalizing* and *Externalizing*. Descriptive labels given to the narrow-band factors and their relations to the broad-band *Internalizing* and *Externalizing* factors are shown in table 2.1. Factors listed under the *mixed* heading were not clearly aligned with either of the two second-order factors.

Several narrow-band syndromes, including *Somatic Complaints, Delinquent, Aggressive, Depressed, Obsessive-Compulsive,* and *Hyperactive,* occurred in all or almost all analyses. Syndromes related to *withdrawal* and *schizoid* behavior also occurred in most analyses but were sometimes mixed with other syndromes. More importantly, these analyses revealed both gender and age differences in the patterning of behavior problems. For example, the *Uncommunicative* syndrome, which was comprised of behaviors such as refusing to talk, secrecy, and self-consciousness, was obtained only for boys. Alternatively, the *Cruel* syndrome, reflecting behaviors such as cruelty to others and destructiveness, was obtained only for girls.

The importance of accounting for age differences can be illustrated by comparison of findings for children aged 6–11 versus 12–16. For both boys and girls aged 6–11, clear-cut *Depressed* syndromes were obtained that were not evident in the analyses of the older groups. Moreover, when age groups were combined for analysis, the *Depressed* syndromes completely disappeared.

What do these age and gender differences mean, and what are their implications for behavioral assessment? First of all, the absence of a factor for any one gender or age group does not mean that the items related to the factor are infrequent or unimportant for that group. Items related to the *Cruel* syndrome found for girls, for example, are more commonly reported for boys than girls. Likewise, many of the items related to the *Depressed* syndrome found for boys and girls aged 6–11 are more common among children aged 12–16. The absence of a factor, however, does indicate that the items that comprise it do not covary and form a distinct syndrome. Among girls, for example, items that comprised the *Depressed* factor for 6–11 year olds were scattered across the *Anxious-Obsessive, Depressed-Withdrawal,* and *Immature-Hyperactive* factors derived for girls aged 12–16. For boys aged 12–16, items that comprised the *Depressed* factor for boys 6–11 were scattered across several factors, particularly those labeled *Uncommunicative* and *Hostile-Withdrawal*.

These findings illustrate how indicators of specific disturbances for one age group or gender can be diffuse indicators of generalized disturbances for another group. Behavioral problem scales constructed for one group may

Table 2.1. Behavioral Problem Syndromes Derived for Boys and Girls aged 4–5, 6–11, and 12–16.

INTERNALIZING	MIXED	EXTERNALIZING
Boys 4-5		
1. Social Withdrawal	5. Sex Problems	6. Schizoid
2. Depressed		7. Aggressive
3. Immature		8. Delinquent
4. Somatic Complaints		
Girls 4–5		
1. Somatic Complaints	5. Obese	6. Aggressive
2. Depressed		7. Sex Problems
3. Schizoid		8. Hyperactive
4. Social Withdrawal		
Boys 6–11		
1. Schizoid	6. Social Withdrawal	7. Hyperactive
2. Depressed		8. Aggressive
3. Uncommunicative		9. Delinquent
4. Obsessive-Compulsive		
5. Somatic Complaints		
Girls 6–11		
1. Depressed		6. Sex Problems
2. Social Withdrawal		7. Delinquent
3. Somatic Complaints		8. Aggressive
4. Schizoid-Obsessive		9. Cruel
5. Hyperactive		
Boys 12–16		
1. Somatic Complaints	6. Hostile-Withdrawal	7. Delinquent
2. Schizoid		8. Aggressive
3. Uncommunicative		9. Hyperactive
4. Immature		
5. Obsessive-Compulsive		
Girls 12–16		
1. Anxious-Obsessive	5. Immature-Hyperactive	6. Delinquent
2. Somatic Complaints		7. Aggressive
3. Schizoid		8. Cruel
4. Depressed-Withdrawal		

Note: For each group, factors are numbered according to their loadings on the second-order Internalizing and Externalizing factors. Factor number 1 had the highest loading on the Internalizing factor, factor number 2 had the next highest, and so on.

therefore yield misleading inferences when applied to other groups. These findings also reveal how fatuous arguments regarding the existence and characteristics of certain childhood disorders can be fueled by the lack of understanding of developmental differences in the expression of psychopathology. Current debates regarding the validity of childhood depression as a diagnostic construct, for example, seem meaningless when pursued outside of a developmental context (Schulterbrandt & Raskin, 1977).

Age and gender differences in the patterning of behavioral problems have additional implications regarding both assessment and treatment of child psychopathology. There is a growing realization that an understanding of response-response relationships is crucial in child behavioral assessment and therapy. Voeltz and Evans (1982) have argued quite convincingly that knowledge of behavioral interrelationships is crucial in the identification of meaningful response units and controlling variables and the evaluation of treatment outcomes. For purposes of assessment, knowledge of interrelations among behaviors may yield valuable guidelines for choosing among target variables. In the context of intervention, such knowledge may also provide a basis for predicting concomitant treatment effects.

Longitudinal Studies

The attention to the past is another distinguishing feature of the developmental perspective. Although the salience of the current environment in shaping and maintaining behavior is not discounted, greater emphasis is placed upon the role of prior experiences and previous levels of functioning to determine current behavior. This also implies that current behavior and abilities will influence future functioning. The integration of this perspective into the assessment process yields many benefits. Longitudinal studies of normal and disturbed children can address many questions that are crucial to the field of child mental health (Robins, 1979). For example, such studies can provide discontinuities in children's behavior and can yield insight into the origins and consequences of behavioral differences and deviations. Such findings have far-reaching implications regarding child behavioral assessment.

A complete review of longitudinal studies of child behavior and a discussion of the conceptual and methodological problems they involve is outside the scope of this chapter (see Robins, 1979; Mednick & Baert, 1981; Rutter, 1977; Schulsinger, Mednick, & Knop, 1981, for more complete discussions). My goal here is to illustrate a few findings from longitudinal studies that have assessment implications.

Stability and Change in Behavior. Several longitudinal studies have documented that the prevalence of specific behaviors varies according to age and that some behavioral problems tend to persist, while others are transient (Macfarlane, Allen, & Honzik, 1954; Rutter, Tizard, Yule, Graham, & Whitmore, 1976; Thomas & Chess, 1976). Whereas young children with many behavioral problems tend to have continuing difficulties in later childhood and early adolescence, the bulk of findings suggest that behavioral problems occurring before the age of 6 are not good predictors of later maladjustment (see Robins, 1979, for a review).

Some findings suggest that the behavior of preschoolers is simply too unstable over time and across situations to yield accurate predictions. Both direct observations and interview data derived from the Fels Longitudinal Study (Kagan & Moss, 1962) revealed that aggressive behavior prior to about age 3 did not predict later aggressiveness. Only after age 5 or 6 was aggressive behavior found to predict later aggressive acts. This rather simple developmental picture is complicated by the possibility that different types of behaviors stabilize at different ages. There is longitudinal data, for example, that suggest that disturbances in cognitive functioning and in parent-child relations stabilize as early as age 6, but antisocial behaviors show little stability until age 10 or so (Gersten, Langner, Eisenberg, Simcha-Fagan, & McCarthy, 1976). In addition, there is evidence which indicates that the persistence of behavioral problems depends upon the nature of the disorder. In their longitudinal followup of children on the Isle of Wight, Graham and Rutter (1973) found that the majority of emotional disorders evident at ages 10–11 cleared up by ages 14–15, whereas the majority of conduct disorders did not.

Age of Onset. Longitudinal studies have also revealed that the age of onset of behavioral disorders, which is often overlooked in child behavioral assessment and therapy, is an important consideration. Rutter et al. (1976), for example, studied a large sample of children at ages 10–11 and again at ages 14–15. Two groups of psychiatrically disturbed adolescents were identified: those whose disorders were evident at ages 10–11 and those whose disorders arose during the follow-up period. Surprisingly, disorders with an early age of onset were more common in boys than girls, whereas those with later onset were almost equally common among boys and girls. In addition, age of onset was significantly related to a number of background variables. Disorders arising early, for example, were strongly associated with marital discord, divorce, parental psychiatric disturbances, and reading difficulties on the part of the child. Thus, there appear to be different patterns and associations related to psychiatric disturbances that arise during adolescence versus those that arise in early or middle childhood.

SUMMARY

The normative-developmental perspective emphasizes: (a) the importance of accounting for the overwhelming changes in behavior and abilities that occur as the child grows older, and (b) the necessity of establishing normative baselines against which the individual child can be compared. Behavioral and developmental approaches to the study of child psychopathology differ in important respects but have been integrated in recent studies. The results of these studies have underscored the need to account for age and developmental variables when assessing children's behavior. The prevalence and patterning of children's behavioral problems have been shown to vary markedly according to age. Longitudinal studies have documented differences in duration and prognostic significance of problem behaviors occurring at different ages. Moreover, age of onset of disorders has been shown to be an important clinical consideration. These findings have numerous implications regarding the development and standardization of child behavioral rating scales, selection of target behaviors for assessment, and nature and timing of behavioral interventions.

REFERENCES

Achenbach, T. M. The Child Behavior Profile: I. Boys aged 6–11. *Journal of Consulting and Clinical Psychology,* 1978, *46,* 478–488.

Achenbach, T. M. The role of taxonomy in developmental psychopathology. In M. E. Lamb & A. E. Brown (Eds.), *Advances in developmental psychology.* Hillsdale, NJ: Erlbaum, 1980.

Achenbach, T. M., & Edelbrock, C. S. The classification of child psychopathology: A review and analysis of empirical efforts. *Psychological Bulletin,* 1978, *85,* 1275–1301.

Achenbach, T. M., & Edelbrock, C. S. The Child Behavior Profile: II. Boys aged 12–16 and girls aged 6–11 and 12–15. *Journal of Consulting and Clinical Psychology,* 1979, *47,* 223–233.

Achenbach, T. M., & Edelbrock, C. S. Behavioral problems and competencies reported by parents of normal and disturbed children aged 4 through 16. *Monographs of the Society for Research in Child Development,* 1981 (46, Serial No. 188).

Baldwin, A. L. *Theories of child development.* New York: Wiley, 1967.

Edelbrock, C. A comparison of strategies for identifying children in need of mental health services. In N. J. Anastasiow, W. K. Frankenburg, & A. W. Fandal (Eds.), *Identifying the developmentally delayed child.* Baltimore: University Park Press, 1981.

Edelbrock, C., & Achenbach, T. M. A typology of Child Behavior Profile patterns: Distribution and correlates for disturbed children aged 6–16. *Journal of Abnormal Child Psychology,* 1980, *8,* 441–470.

Ferguson, L. R., Partyka, L. B., & Lester, B. M. Patterns of parent perception differentiating clinic from nonclinic children. *Journal of Abnormal Child Psychology,* 1974, *2,* 169–181.

Furman, W. Promoting social development: Developmental implications for treatment. In B. B. Lahey & A. E. Kazdin (Eds.), *Advances in Clinical Child Psychology* (Vol. 3). New York: Plenum Press, 1980.

Gersten, J. C., Langner, T. S., Eisenberg, J. B., Simcha-Fagan, O., & McCarthy, E. D. Stability and change in types of behavioral disturbance of children and adolescents. *Journal of Abnormal Child Psychology,* 1976, *4,* 111–127.

Graham, P., & Rutter, M. Psychiatric disorder in the young adolescent: A followup study. *Proceedings of the Royal Society of Medicine,* 1973, *66,* 1226–1229.

Hartmann, D. P., Roper, B. L., & Bradford, D. C. Some relationships between behavioral and traditional assessment. *Journal of Behavioral Assessment,* 1979, *1,* 3–21.

Kagan, J., & Moss, H. A. *Birth to maturity.* New York: Wiley, 1962.

Kazdin, A. E. Assessing the clinical or applied importance of behavior change through social validation. *Behavior Modification,* 1977, *1,* 427–452.

Lapouse, R., & Monk, M. A. An epidemiologic study of behavior characteristics in children. *American Journal of Public Health,* 1958, *48,* 1134–1144.

Macfarlane, J. W., Allen, L., & Honzik, M. P. *A developmental study of behavior problems of normal children between 21 months and 14 years.* Berkeley: University of California Press, 1954.

Mash, E. J., & Terdal, L. G. (Eds.). *Behavioral assessment of childhood disorders.* New York: Guilford Press, 1981.

Mednick, S. A., & Baert, A. E. *Prospective longitudinal research.* Oxford: Oxford University Press, 1981.

Mitchell, S., & Shepherd, M. A comparative study of children's behavior at home and at school. *British Journal of Educational Psychology,* 1966, *36,* 248–254.

Ollendick, T. H., & Cerny, J. A. *Clinical behavior therapy with children.* New York: Plenum Press, 1981.

Robins, L. N. Followup studies. In H. C. Quay & J. S. Werry (Eds.), *Psychopathological disorders of childhood.* New York: Wiley, 1979.

Rutter, M. Prospective studies to investigate behavioral change. In J. S. Strauss, H. M. Babigian, & M. Roff (Eds.), *The origins and course of psychopathology.* New York: Plenum Press, 1977.

Rutter, M. Introduction. In M. Rutter (Ed.). *Developmental psychiatry.* London: Hienemann, 1980.

Rutter, M., Tizard, J., & Whitmore, K. (Eds.). *Education, health, and behavior.* London: Longman, 1970.

Rutter, M., Tizard, J., Yule, W., Graham, P., & Whitmore, K. Research report: Isle of Wight studies, 1964–1974. *Psychological Medicine,* 1976, *6,* 313–332.

Schulsinger, F., Mednick, S. A., & Knop, J. (Eds.). *Longitudinal research: Methods and uses in behavioral science.* Boston: Nijhoff, 1981.

Schulterbrandt, J. G., & Raskin, A. (Eds.). *Depression in childhood: Diagnosis, treatment, and conceptual models.* New York: Raven, 1977.

Shechtman, A. Psychiatric symptoms in normal and disturbed children. *Child Development,* 1970, *41,* 683–693.

Shectman, A. Psychiatric symptoms observed in normal and disturbed black children. *Journal of Clinical Psychology,* 1971, *27,* 445–447.

Thomas, A., & Chess, S. Evolution of behavior disorders into adolescence. *American Journal of Psychiatry,* 1976, *133,* 539–542.

Voeltz, L. M., & Evans, I. M. The assessment of behavioral interrelationships in child behavior therapy. *Behavioral Assessment,* 1982, *4,* 131–165.

Walker, H. M., & Hops, H. Use of normative peer data as a standard for evaluating classroom treatment effects. *Journal of Applied Behavior Analysis,* 1979, *9,* 159–168.

Wolff, S. Behavioral characteristics of primary school children referred to a psychiatric department. *British Journal of Psychiatry,* 1967, *113,* 885–893.

3

Diagnostic Issues*

Sandra L. Harris
and
Michael D. Powers

The American Psychiatric Association's third *Diagnostic and Statistical Manual of Mental Disorders* (DSM-III, 1980) must be acknowledged as the most extensive, detailed, and careful attempt in psychiatric history to develop a comprehensive diagnostic system. As a consequence, the child behavioral therapist has an intellectual responsibility to examine this system with great care rather than simply to dismiss the notion of traditional diagnosis in favor of behavioral assessment. To facilitate that goal, the present chapter examines the historical development of DSM-III, its current status, and the strengths and weaknesses of the system in relation to children. We will also consider how DSM-III might be integrated into a behavioral assessment.

AN HISTORICAL VIEW

In 1952, the American Psychiatric Association published its first *Diagnostic and Statistical Manual of Mental Disorders* (DSM-I). It contained 132 pages, of which approximately one-third were devoted to a description of specific psychiatric disorders. Very little attention was paid to children. This neglect of children and consequent lack of utility for the child clinician was noted by Rosen, Bahn, and Kramer (1964), who found that 30% of the children seen

---

*Our thanks to JoLynn Powers who read the manuscript and provided useful feedback and to Linda Hoffman who typed the chapter for us.

at 1,200 clinics were given no diagnosis, and an additional 40% were labeled as *Adjustment Reaction*. Essentially the same observations were made by Dreger, Lewis, Rich, Miller, Reid, Overlake, Taffer, and Fleming (1964) that same year in their survey of child clients at 40 different clinics in the state of Florida. They found that diagnosticians were reluctant to use any but the most nondescript diagnoses with children. Discussing this situation, Dreger et al. (1964) wrote: "Looked at realistically, what this means is that after the elaborate procedures used in most clinics are completed, the child is placed in a category, which says exactly what we knew about him in the first place, that he has a problem" (p. 1). Thus, DSM-I had little redeeming value for the child client beyond setting the scene for the introduction of DSM-II and a somewhat more complex diagnostic scheme.

The publication of DSM-II in 1968 brought with it a moderately expanded consideration of psychopathology in childhood. Nevertheless, clinicians showed little more inclination to use these new categories than they had with the more limited variety in DSM-I. Thus, Cerreto and Tuma (1977) reported that 38% of the children being diagnosed according to DSM-II were called *Adjustment Reaction* and 30% were classified as some form of *Behavior Disorder*.

This reluctance of child clinicians to use any but the most nondescript labels may be attributed to at least two different sources. One is our appropriate hesitation to apply labels to children which will haunt them through their lives. We doubtless want to feel very sure of ourselves and the function of the diagnostic label before we use it. The other may be our reluctance to use diagnostic labels when they are remote from the problems of our young clients. If a diagnostic system does not make provision for the behaviors we confront, we are likely to find ourselves forced to use only the blandest of labels for lack of more precise alternatives. *Adjustment Reaction* is one of those diagnostic terms which has been widely used in talking about children but tells us essentially nothing about what is bothering the child or how the youngster would appear if we met him or her. Although it suggests that the problem, whatever it might be, is related to environmental events, we know neither what the stressor might be nor how the child has attempted to cope.

The relative neglect of children in DSM-I and DSM-II, with a consequent lack of utility by either of the first two editions of the *Diagnostic and Statistical Manual of Mental Disorders*, posed a major problem to the framers of DSM-III. They were required to develop a system which would be broad enough to describe the many varieties of childhood problems and which would invite the clinician to become more open to the use of formal and precise diagnoses with child clients.

If more is better, then DSM-III is way ahead of earlier attempts at diagnosis. This is strikingly clear for the child categories since, as Spitzer, Williams, and Skodol (1980) note in their introduction to this new system, there are more than four times as many child categories in DSM-III as there were in DSM-II. They attribute this vast increase to a substantial growth in our knowledge of child psychopathology.

Will DSM-III be a more useful, reliable system of psychiatric diagnosis than its predecessors? All of the facts are not yet in. Nevertheless, we can examine the system with some care and consider those studies that have been published to date in an effort to make at least a logical, rational, if not fully data-based, judgement.

WHAT DOES DSM-III LOOK LIKE?

Because DSM-II has been the diagnostic system in widest use in the United States since the late 1960s, we will focus our description of DSM-III on a comparison between these two systems.

The differences between DSM-II and DSM-III are evident at first glance. DSM-II totals 134 pages in a spiral-bound book. DSM-III with all of its appendices comes to nearly 500 pages, and the pocket-sized paperback *Quick Reference to Diagnostic Criteria from DSM-III* (American Psychiatric Association, 1980) is 264 pages long. This length reflects the many new categories that have been added to both adult and child diagnostic possibilities. It also indicates the much expanded discussion of each diagnosis. Thus, each diagnosis is described in terms of:

1. Essential features
2. Associated features
3. Age at onset, sex ratio, and prevalence
4. Course
5. Familial pattern
6. Impairment
7. Complications
8. Predisposing factors
9. Differential diagnosis

Such greatly enhanced detail should make it possible for the clinician to form more reliable decisions than were possible with DSM-II. Indeed, Spitzer, Forman, and Nee (1979), in a preliminary look at the reliability of clinical decisions using DSM-III, found the overall reliability to be better than had been possible with DSM-II. The more explicit nature of DSM-III, as compared to DSM-II, may improve the research as well as the clinical potential of this instrument (Treece, 1982).

Of course, simply providing greater detail does not necessarily mean that decision making will always be greatly enhanced. As Schacht and Nathan

(1977) note, clinicians often lack sufficient information to make all of the necessary discriminations and end up making some decisions on a probability rather than data basis. Nevertheless, DSM-III does have a sounder set of decision rules than DSM-II, and clinicians are likely to benefit from this more detailed structure.

Another major departure from DSM-II was the use of five different axes for diagnosis in DSM-III. These are:

- Axis I. Clinical Syndromes
- Axis II. Personality Disorders (adult) and Specific Developmental Disorders (child)
- Axis III. Physical Disorders and Conditions
- Axis IV. Severity of Psychosocial Stressor (range 1–7)
- Axis V. Highest level of adaptive behavior past year (range 1–7)

Axis II is of interest to the child clinician since it is here that one may note such problems as *Developmental Reading Disorder* or *Developmental Language Disorder,* which occur in an otherwise normal child. This inclusion of Axis II was intended to ensure that secondary but important problems are not overlooked in the process of assessment.

The use of multiple dimensions for diagnosis is appealing in that it permits the clinician to convey additional information beyond the clinical label of Axis I. It should also serve to ensure that the diagnostician has examined the client's functioning along a number of dimensions and thus developed a fuller picture than necessary to determine a diagnostic label. The initial reliability data for the axes are somewhat better than might have been predicted (Russell, Cantwell, Mattison, & Will, 1979; Spitzer & Forman, 1979). However, as Schacht and Nathan (1977) note, while these axes are a substantial improvement over previous diagnostic systems, they are nevertheless somewhat simplistic in contrast to the complexity of the decisions clinicians must make. As Nathan and Harris (in press) suggest, one must also ask whether the particular dimensions chosen are in fact the ones of greatest potential value. For example, response to treatment might have been valuable to include. Looking specifically at children, Axis IV, *Severity of Psychosocial Stressor,* may be problematic because of a lack of use of empirical data for ranking the impact of stress (Rutter & Shaffer, 1980) while Axis V's use of the previous year as a measure of adaptive behavior might better be replaced by premorbid level (Rutter & Shaffer, 1980). Earls (1982) has pointed to the limited value of Axis V for preschool children.

DSM-III is superior to its predecessors in terms of its careful avoidance of psychodynamic assumptions in formulating diagnoses. The emphasis is much more upon observable behavior than was true in previous editions of the manual and this is one factor that should make the system more attractive to the behavior therapist than previous efforts.

Disorders of Infancy, Childhood, or Adolescence

An entire section of DSM-III is devoted to those disorders which typically arise in childhood. As Spitzer, Williams, and Skodol (1980) note, although an adult occasionally will be given a diagnosis from this section and children and adolescents will sometimes receive other diagnoses, this section contains the majority of disorders appropriate to children.

The disorders of childhood can be subdivided into five broad categories: *Intellectual, Behavioral* (overt), *Emotional, Physical,* and *Developmental.* We will examine each of these subgroups and consider many of the specific categories under each heading.

Intellectual Disorders. Under the heading of *Intellectual Disorders* there falls the single category of *Mental Retardation.* By definition, *Mental Retardation* occurs before the age of 18 years. If the behavior were to begin after the age of 18, one would use one of the categories of *Organic Mental Disorder.* Within the heading of *Mental Retardation* are four subheadings: *Mild* (IQ 50–70); *Moderate* (IQ 35–49); *Severe* (IQ 20–34) and *Profound* (IQ below 20). Although DSM-II included the concept of *Borderline Retardation* (IQ 68–83), this has been dropped in DSM-III, thus removing the label of *Mental Retardation* from a substantial number of people. The DSM-III definition of *Mental Retardation* was written to be consistent with the definition of the American Association on Mental Deficiency. Rutter and Shaffer (1980) argue persuasively that mental retardation would better have been included on a separate axis rather than on Axis I since this condition reflects an abnormal level rather than type of mental functioning.

If a person has a specific biological cause for mental retardation such as Down's Syndrome or PKU, this is described in Axis III (Physical Disorders and Conditions).

Behavioral Disorders. Two different categories are included under the heading of *Behavioral Disorders: Attention Deficit Disorder* and *Conduct Disorder.*

1. *Attention Deficit Disorder* is the term used to describe children who in the past were labeled as *Minimal Brain Dysfunction, Hyperkinetic Reaction of Childhood, Minimal Brain Damage,* etc. The authors of DSM-III elected to use the term *Attention Deficit Disorder* because they viewed the problems in attention as primary for these youngsters. They identified two different categories of *Attention Deficit Disorder: With Hyperactivity* and *Without Hyperactivity.* No assumption was made that the two conditions are related to one another. The term *Attention Deficit Disorder* also eliminates the presumption of a biological dysfunction that was implicit in many of the earlier labels such as *Minimal Brain Dysfunction.*

Although the focus upon attention rather than activity level is a plausible one, research is needed to examine the question of the extent to which attending problems of hyperactive children are due to their hyperactivity per se or simply co-occur with hyperactivity.

In one illustration of the potential usefulness of DSM-III for treatment purposes, Wender, Reimherr, and Wood (1981) found that adults who continued to exhibit the symptoms of *Attention Deficit Disorder* and who had met the DSM-III criteria when they were children showed a positive reaction to the use of medication to treat their symptoms in adulthood.

2. *Conduct Disorder* was scattered among several different categories in DSM-II including *Unsocialized Aggressive Reaction of Childhood, Group Delinquent Reaction,* and *Runaway Reaction.* DSM-III has integrated the various forms of *Conduct Disorder* in a four part classification system: *Undersocialized, Aggressive; Undersocialized, Nonaggressive; Socialized, Aggressive;* and *Socialized, Nonaggressive.* These four categories offer a neat system, but the data are not yet in concerning the empirical validity of the grouping. For example, we do not know how skillfully clinicians can distinguish among the four categories nor to what extent these distinctions dictate differences in intervention strategy. In addition, DSM-III fails to address varying cultural norms and life-styles that may give rise to certain patterns of behavior.

Emotional Disorders. Under the heading of *Emotional Disorders* we find two categories: *Anxiety Disorders of Childhood* and *Other Disorders.* Each of these is further divided into several specific diagnostic categories.

1. *Anxiety Disorders* include *Separation Anxiety Disorder, Avoidant Disorder,* and *Overanxious Disorder.* In addition, one may apply to children any of the categories of adult *Anxiety Disorders* or *Affective Disorders* which appear appropriate. Thus, a child's behavior may be labeled as *Simple Phobia, Panic Disorder, Obsessive-Compulsive Disorder,* etc.

Separation Anxiety Disorder refers to the child's fear of leaving family or home while *Avoidant Disorder* is used to describe those youngsters who are fearful of social contacts in general. It is probably unfortunate that the categories of *Anxiety Disorders of Childhood* are not further refined since we know little about the extent to which anxious, obsessive, compulsive or other behaviors in children relate to these same behaviors in adults. Achenbach (1980, 1982) has argued that most major adult disorders do not have clear child counterparts; therefore, it may be an error to dub these children with an adult diagnosis. In addition, in light of all that we know about phobic behavior in terms of cognitive, behavioral, and physiological components, it is surprising that this triple response framework was not used to organize thinking about anxiety disorders.

Given the extensive debate which has raged over the question of whether children experience clinical depression (e.g., Lefkowitz & Burton, 1978), one has to wonder about the wisdom of including children within the general adult category of *Affective Disorders.* Without more widespread agreement that children experience depression in the same sense that adults do, it might have been wiser to designate their depressive experiences as different from those of adults.

2. *Other Disorders* include *Reactive Attachment Disorder* (failure to thrive), *Schizoid Disorder* (deficient social relationships), *Oppositional Disorder* (negativism), *Identity Disorder* (difficulty forming a unified sense of self) and *Elective Mutism* (refusal to speak in social situations). *Schizoid Disorder* is seen as a precursor to adult *Schizoid Personality Disorder* or *Schizophrenia* in some children, and *Oppositional Disorder* may develop into adult *Passive-Aggressive Personality Disorder.*

Physical Disorders. Three separate categories are included under the heading of *Physical Disorders: Eating Disorders, Stereotyped Movement Disorders, and Other Disorders with Physical Manifestations.*

1. *Eating Disorders* include the diagnoses of *Anorexia Nervosa, Bulimia, Pica,* and *Rumination Disorder of Childhood.* In an article on the validity of the *Anorexia Nervosa* criteria for children, Irwin (1981) notes that of 13 girls under 13 years of age hospitalized for *Anorexia Nervosa,* 7 did not meet the DSM-III criteria. He argues that the DSM-III definition may not be suitable for preadolescents because the 25% weight loss required for the DSM-III diagnosis may not occur with young girls since their adipose distribution is different from that of adolescents. In spite of this flaw in the system, it is encouraging to see that DSM-III offers far more detailed guidelines for diagnosis of *Eating Disorders* than did DSM-II under the old heading of *Special Symptom of Feeding Disturbance.*

2. *Stereotyped Movement Disorders* include *Transient Tic Disorder, Chronic Motor Tic Disorder, Tourette's Disorder,* and *Atypical Stereotyped Movement Disorder* (sometimes called self-stimulation).

One item missing from the diagnosis of *Atypical Stereotyped Movement Disorder is specification of the movement.* For example, body rocking, finger play, and light gazing might all be diagnosed as *Atypical Stereotyped Movement Disorder* (although we do not at present know whether they are all equivalent in terms of etiology, response to treatment, etc.). Carr (1977) has noted that self-injurious behavior can arise from a variety of causes and that it is an error in assessment to lump these behaviors into a single unit. Thus, it might have been helpful to provide more refined descriptions of these behaviors. In addition, since Rincover and his colleagues (Rincover, Cook, Peoples, & Packard, 1979; Rincover, Newsom, & Carr, 1979) have identified sensory reinforcement as important in some (but perhaps not all) self-stimulation, identification of relevant sensory channels for stereotyped behaviors might have considerable diagnostic significance. *Atypical Stereotyped Movement Disorder* is frequently seen in conjunction with *Mental Retardation* or *Pervasive Developmental Delay* but may occur independently of these disorders.

3. *Other Disorders with Physical Manifestations* include *Stuttering, Functional Enuresis, Functional Encopresis, Sleepwalking Disorder,* and *Sleep Terror Disorder.* The authors of DSM-III acknowledge that these problems may not be a reflection of mental disorder but have been included within the diagnostic system because of the once widespread assumption that they were a manifestation of psychological conflict. They recognize that recent research has raised questions about this assumption. Many behavior therapists may have grave reservations about inclusion of bed wetting and stuttering as part of a manual of mental disorders, even with the qualification that the children do not exhibit an associated mental disorder.

Developmental Disorders. There are two broad categories of *Developmental Disorders: Pervasive Developmental Disorders* and *Specific Developmental Disorders.*

1. *Pervasive Developmental Disorders,* severely debilitating disorders of early onset, include *Infantile Autism* and *Childhood Onset Pervasive Developmental Disorder.* This reflects an important change from DSM-II, which had failed to acknowledge the category of *Infantile Autism* but had included *Schizophrenia, Childhood Type. Childhood Schizophrenia* has been deleted from DSM-III with the note than when children exhibit the symptoms of schizophrenia, they should be diagnosed according to the adult categories for that disorder. However, Cantor, Evans, Pearce, and Pezzot-Pearce (1982) argue that some children may meet all the DSM-III criteria for schizophrenia except that onset was so early that they fail to show the required deterioration from a previous level of functioning. Since they exhibit thought disorder, they may not be labeled autistic and, therefore, cannot be accommodated in DSM-III.

The inclusion of *Infantile Autism* in DSM-III is an excellent reflection of the current state of the art in terms of classifying psychotic conditions in childhood. It indicates recognition that *Infantile Autism* is not a downward extension of an adult condition of schizophrenia, but a distinct disorder (or set of disorders) with different prognostic and treatment implications than adult schizophrenia. The diagnostic criteria for *Infantile Autism* closely resemble those of Rutter (1978) and, therefore, can draw upon a substantial body of research.

Childhood Onset Pervasive Developmental Disorder is differentiated from *Infantile Autism* in that the former starts at a later age and does not carry the full syndrome of *Infantile Autism.* One study examining the ability of diagnosticians to apply the label of *Childhood Onset Pervasive Developmental Disorder* following a 2½-day training seminar found a 77.1% agreement for this label with that of an expert judge (Webb, Gold, Johnstone, & DiClemente, 1981).

Differences in the utility of DSM-III for adults and children may be noted in examining psychotic behavior. Nathan (1981), in a discussion of the merits of DSM-III, notes that symptomatic diagnosis for adults has greatest utility in the treatment of psychotic disorders where drug treatment is the treatment of choice. This observation has considerable validity for adult psychotic disorders such as schizophrenia or manic-depression. However, it has less significance in the case of the pervasive developmental disorders such as *Infantile Autism* or *Childhood Onset Pervasive Developmental Disorder* where drug treatments have yet to provide substantial relief.

2. *Specific Developmental Disorders,* unlike all of the diagnostic categories we have discussed to this point, are coded on Axis II since they frequently co-occur with other diagnostic categories and are too important to be overlooked. The diagnostic categories of *Specific Developmental Disorders* include *Developmental Reading Disorder, Developmental Arithmetic Disorder, Developmental Language Disorder* (expressive and receptive types), and *Developmental Articulation Disorder.* Some of these behaviors may appear to clinicians not to warrant the application of a psychiatric diagnosis. As in the case of *Other Disorders with Physical Manifestations,* the authors of DSM-III recognized the somewhat marginal status of these problems as psychiatric conditions, but nonetheless believed they merited inclusion in the manual.

V-Code Conditions. DSM-III describes briefly a series of conditions called "*V* Codes" in ICD-9-CM that are not attributable to a mental disorder but may be a focus of professional treatment. The categories relevant to children under this heading include *Borderline Intellectual Functioning* (IQ 71–84), *Childhood or Adolescent Antisocial Behavior* (isolated antisocial acts, not a pattern of such behavior), *Academic Problem* (poor academic work in absence of any mental disorder or *Specific Developmental Disorder*), *Phase of Life Problem* (problem related to developmental phase such as starting school or separating from parents), *Parent-Child Problem* (parent-child problem not due to a mental disorder of the person being evaluated), and *Other Specified Family Circumstances* (interpersonal difficulty such as sibling rivalry not due to mental disorder). Essentially, these categories reflect life problems within the normal realm of adaptation which may derive benefit from professional help but 1) which do not reflect a mental disorder; or 2) where the presence of a mental disorder has not been identified; or 3) where the person may suffer from a mental disorder, but the problem being treated is not a reflection of that disorder.

EMPIRICAL EVALUATION
OF DSM-III FOR CHILDREN

In a series of four papers, Cantwell, Russell, Mattison, and Will (Cantwell, Mattison, Russell, & Will, 1979; Cantwell, Russell, Mattison, & Will, 1979; Mattison, Cantwell, Russell, & Will, 1979; Russell, Cantwell, Mattison, & Will, 1979) compared DSM-II and DSM-III in the diagnosis of childhood psychiatric disorders. This evaluation went beyond those categories specifically designated for children to include *Depressive Disorders, Anxiety Disorders,* and *Organic Brain Disorders.* The four studies were from the same set of data based upon the diagnosis of 24 actual case histories by 20 psychiatrists who had no previous experience with DSM-III. These physicians were given a draft version of DSM-III, current as of 1976, and asked to familiarize themselves with it.

The first of the papers (Cantwell, Russell, Mattison, & Will, 1979) asked to what extent the raters would agree in their diagnosis with the "expected diagnosis" conferred by the authors as most appropriate to the case. Agreement with the experts varied according to the category. The mean percentage agreement for psychotic disorders was 55%; depressive disorders, 39%; anxiety disorders, 37%; attention deficit disorders and conduct disorders, 58%; mental retardation and organic brain disorders, 72%; miscellaneous disorders (e.g., motor tic, elective mutism), 42%. These results led to some changes in the final draft of DSM-III with the expectation that communication about diagnostic intent could be improved in the manual's descriptive material. Cantwell, Russell, Mattison, and Will (1979) point out that the relatively low overall agreement (49%) may be due to correctable problems in DSM-III plus the lack of experience of the raters.

The second study in the series (Mattison et al., 1979) compared interrater agreement using DSM-II and DSM-III. The average interrater agreement for DSM-II was 57% and for DSM-III's Axis I (clinical psychiatric syndrome), 54%. For DSM-II the agreements by category were: psychotic disorders, 71%; depressive disorders, 41%; anxiety disorders, 48%; attention deficit disorders and conduct disorders, 72%; mental retardation and organic brain disorders, 77% miscellaneous disorders, 49%. Comparable figures for DSM-III were psychotic disorders, 76%; depressive disorders, 42%; anxiety disorders, 50%; attention deficit disorders and conduct disorders, 63%; mental retardation and organic brain disorders, 85%; miscellaneous, 49%. Thus, the two systems yielded roughly comparable results. The expanded number of categories for DSM-III did not appear to have diminished reliability of ratings between observers. Both DSM-II and DSM-III were notably weak in describing depressive and anxiety disorders in children, conditions frequently seen in outpatient settings.

One bit of evidence suggesting that clinicians will use alternatives to *Adjustment Reaction* was that Mattison et al. (1979) found that while *Adjustment Reaction of Childhood* was the most frequent of the DSM-II ratings, *Depressive Disorder, Single Episode* led the DSM-III list.

A third study (Russell et al., 1979) examined the use of the multiaxial system of DSM-III. The average agreement on Axis II (Specific Developmental Disorders) was 80%; Axis III (Physical Disorders and Conditions), 90%; Axis IV (Psychosocial Stressors) 63%; and Axis V (degree of impairment of adaptive functioning), 64%. Russell et al. (1979) conclude that the multiaxial system may be a valuable new addition to the diagnostic process.

Finally, Cantwell, Mattison, Russell, and Will (1979) asked their 20 psychiatric raters their preference for DSM-II versus DSM-III and found the new system consistently preferred to the old.

The Developmental Factor in Diagnosis

The diagnosis of psychopathology in childhood requires a special sensitivity to the developmental component of behavior. Children, by definition, are rapidly changing and variable individuals from whom we expect considerable plasticity of behavior. It is, therefore, essential that the clinician consider a child's age and general level of development in arriving at a diagnostic decision. The framers of DSM-III, while not ignoring the developmental aspect of child psychopathology, paid it relatively brief notice and did not address themselves adequately to the need for the diagnostician to be sensitive to developmental factors. An orienting statement about the importance of considering the child's developmental status in decision making would have been appropriate.

To their credit, there are scattered references in DSM-III to developmental factors in diagnostic decision making with children. One of the most explicit of these is in conjunction with *Oppositional Disorder,* where the reader is advised that oppositional behavior is a normal phase in the development of the 18- to 36-month-old child. Similarly, in discussing *Reactive Attachment Disorder of Infancy,* specific infant behaviors, such as visual tracking of eyes and face at 2 months of age or reaching to be picked up at 4–5 months of age, are discussed. Unfortunately, the diagnostic criteria for this disorder may run counter to empirical data (Rutter & Shaffer, 1980). Likewise, in the diagnosis of *Attention Deficit Disorder,* the inappropriate attending behavior is described simply as "developmentally inappropriate inattention" with little further guidance to help the clinician determine what is appropriate attending behavior for a 3-year-old, 7-year-old, or 11-year-old. A similar lack of guidance is offered for *Conduct Disorder* where the child is described as deficient in "age-appropriate societal norms."

This lack of normative guidelines for the diagnosis of children's behavioral disorders is not to be laid squarely on the shoulders of the authors of DSM-III. Clinicians in general have done a poor job of integrating normative data from developmental psychology into our diagnostic decision making. Behavior therapists, with some notable exceptions (e.g., Kazdin, 1977; Patterson, 1974), have not looked closely at the extent to which their clients' target behaviors deviate from the behaviors of other people. This failure to use developmental data may well be due in part to a lack of adequate research on the development of those behaviors which are of most central interest to the child clinician. This is an area where a closer integration of clinical and developmental research might be fruitful.

Closely related to the importance of developmental factors in diagnostic decision making is the importance of considering situational factors in the child's behavior. Not only is a child's behavior variable over time, it is also variable in different settings. Perhaps one of the most striking illustrations of this is seen in the diagnosis of hyperactive behavior. For example, Klein and Gittleman-Klein (1975) noted that in evaluating 155 children labeled as hyperactive, only 25% were unanimously given that label by mother, teacher, social worker, and clinician, and that almost 60% were not viewed as hyperactive in the clinic. Similarly, Lambert, Sandoval, and Sassone (1978) found that only 1% of 5000 elementary school children were identified as hyperactive by parent, teacher, and physician. Barkley (1981) notes the importance of using more than one informant in assessing hyperactive behavior in children. As a consequence, it becomes very important for the diagnostician to consider carefully the context in which he or she examines a child and the sample of behavior upon which the diagnosis is based. If a child fails to exhibit any hyperactive behavior during a clinic interview but is reported by the teacher to be hyperactive in school, is it appropriate for the child to be labeled as *Attention Deficit Disorder?* DSM-III acknowledges that it is rare for a child to exhibit the signs of *Attention Deficit Disorder* across all settings. It also is stated that some inadequate or chaotic environments may lead to disorganized behavior on the part of the child. Nonetheless, the clinician is not given explicit guidance about how much hyperactive behavior, in how many settings, is essential for the label to be applied.

The Social Factor in Diagnosis

Applying a diagnostic label to a client carries with it important social consequences, some of which are desirable and some of which may have aversive implications. It is, therefore, important to consider the social/interpersonal consequences of giving a child a DSM-III diagnosis.

One of the important, pragmatic reasons for providing a diagnostic label is to make an individual eligible for services which require such a designation. In this respect, DSM-III is an improvement over previous versions of the diagnostic manual since its expanded coverage and respectable reliability make it more acceptable for clinical use than previous versions. Since most clinicians are confronted by utilitarian reasons to use diagnoses, we should be pleased to use an instrument that is more accurate and reliable than those we have had available in the past. Most mental health centers, insurance companies, courts of law, public schools, and other official agencies expect the clinician to be able to confer a diagnosis as part of his or her assessment of an individual's psychological status. DSM-III allows behavior therapists to feel somewhat more comfortable than we did before about such labels because we have been freed from the psychodynamic assumptions that pervaded DSM-I and DSM-II. DSM-III provides a more explicitly behavior-based diagnostic system than DSM-II and, thus, is more amenable to study and verification than were previous versions of the manual.

Although in general the expanded coverage of DSM-III is a desirable event, there are some drawbacks to this feature. Specifically, one has to be concerned about the social/interpersonal implications of including the *Specific Developmental Disorders* and some of the *Other Disorders with Physical Manifestations* as part of a psychiatric diagnostic system. These problems are more likely to be evaluated in a school setting or a speech clinic than a psychiatric setting, and, to some, it may seem like stretching the bounds of psychiatry to encompass these problems. Rutter and Shaffer (1980) note that the diagnostic criteria for these disorders are vague in comparison to other disorders and may be misleading. We do not doubt that stuttering, bed wetting, or a reading disability can create problems for child and parents. But, ought we include these children under the psychiatric umbrella because of these difficulties? Might they not more accurately have been listed as conditions not attributable to mental disorder ("*V* code")?

The goal of expanding DSM-III to encompass a broader range of disorders than was possible in DSM-II was an admirable one to the extent that it allows the clinician to be more precise in describing a child's problems. Nonetheless, the authors of DSM-III may have gone a bit too far in their efforts to be broad and incorporated some behaviors which really do not merit a psychiatric diagnosis. This question of whether DSM-III is overinclusive is not to be treated lightly. Almost every undergraduate textbook in child psychopathology addresses the question of the consequences of labeling, and this concern is well founded. Although diagnostic labels have utilitarian functions, their overuse can prove counterproductive for any client — perhaps especially for children.

Once a child has received a diagnostic label and been designated as special, his or her parents, teachers, and others in the community are likely to

treat that youngster as different from others in the peer group. Perhaps equally as important, the child may perceive himself or herself as different. For
example, Whalen and Henker (1976) note that children who call themselves
hyperactive may be less likely to control their behavior than those children
who do not give themselves this label. The label may lead to a reduced sense
of self-control in a person who views himself or herself as a helpless victim
of a disorder.

Applying a diagnostic label to a person may also tend to focus intervention upon the individual rather than encouraging the clinician to look at the
child within the social/interpersonal context in which he or she operates. A
child "owns" a problem when a label is applied, and other people may be perceived as peripheral to the difficulties. Of course, a skilled clinician would
go beyond the label, using it as only one bit of information in the total assessment. Nonetheless, records are often read in a cursory fashion and the
outsider may come away with one primary piece of information in his or her
head: the label for the child. Therefore, the practice of encompassing many
disorders of only borderline relevance in DSM-III may be counter to the child
client's best interests.

Consistent with this observation of ownership of problems by the child
is the statement by Spitzer and Cantwell (1980) that DSM-III assumes that
"mental disorders are conditions that occur in persons" (p. 362). Such an assumption is an explicit rejection of the view that psychopathological disorders of infancy, childhood, or adolescence can be the result of dysfunctional
family, school, or community systems. Not only does such an extreme view
place an inordinate responsibility for "cure" within the disordered child, but
it also renders DSM-III useless as a diagnostic tool for clinicians with a sys-
temic/ecological understanding of psychotherapeutic change. Spitzer and
Cantwell (1980) note that the Task Force on Nomenclature and Statistics was
initially receptive to a classification of disturbed family units but abandoned
the idea for a variety of reasons.

Behavioral Assessment and DSM-III:
The Integration in Practice

While DSM-III is not without its marked limitations, it does offer the clinician access to data and to a common ground of communication with other
clinicians for describing psychopathological disorders of childhood. Given
this view, DSM-III might best be regarded as a "work-in-progress" or a suc-
cessive approximation of the comprehensive assessment process we all wish
existed. As part of a continuing process of evolution of that diagnostic pro-

cess, we wish to propose a model of assessment that compensates for some of the weaknesses of DSM-III by drawing upon the strengths of behavioral assessment.

Broadly speaking, the goals of behavioral assessment are to identify antecedent and consequent events that serve as controlling variables for a target behavior and to design and evaluate a treatment program for such behavior. In our view, these controlling variables include overt behavior as well as subjectively felt cognitions and physiological behavior. Through the use of one of several assessment processes such as S-O-R-K-C analysis (Goldfried & Sprafkin, 1976; Kanfer & Saslow, 1969) or Multimodal Assessment (Lazarus, 1981), the clinician gathers data providing a functional analysis of the target behavior, which in turn guides treatment and defines the parameters of ongoing assessment (Mash & Terdal, 1981). How shall we relate these activities to the process of traditional diagnosis?

Several authors have compared traditional and behavioral assessment procedures (e.g., Cone & Hawkins, 1977; Goldfried & Kent, 1972). One important difference concerns nomothetic and idiographic descriptions of behavior. It should be noted that both these levels of description are important and useful, albeit for different reasons (Nelson & Barlow, 1981; Nelson & Hayes, 1979). Thus, traditional assessment can be described as nomothetic in that it focuses upon developing generalizations that apply to many people while behavioral assessment takes an idiographic approach that emphasizes the uniqueness of a given individual. By describing a client symptomatically, DSM-III generates a series of nomothetic statements that have a given probability of applying to any one client. Such generalizations guide the clinician's behavior, summarize clinical and research information, and facilitate communication among professions. They do not lead directly to the development of treatment goals for an individual client (Nelson & Hayes, 1979). In contrast, the idiographic approach of behavioral assessment leads to an emphasis on the specification of person, setting, event, and organismic controlling variables so that treatment planning takes on an individualized focus.

Nomothetic data are potentially valuable in treatment planning in that they suggest response covariations and controlling variables that the clinician might examine with care (Nelson & Barlow, 1981). To the extent that it is possible to specify these variables, nomothetic data can be conceptualized as a starting point of the idiographic assessment of particular responses and specific controlling variables that influence a child's behavior. Identification of these idiographic data then leads directly to treatment planning.

Behavioral therapists frequently reject traditional diagnosis because of issues such as reliability, psychodynamic assumptions about etiology, and the irrelevance of symptomatic diagnosis to treatment (Mash & Terdal, 1981). These criticisms are less valid for DSM-III than for earlier versions of this diagnostic system. To the extent that the foundation for diagnosis in DSM-

III can be shown to have a data base, it is important for us to recognize and attempt to use these findings in our behavioral practice.

These considerations lead us to the development of our model for integrating traditional and behavioral assessment. The integrative model we are offering resembles the funnel strategy proposed by Hawkins (1979) with symptomatic diagnosis providing an initial, broad-band assessment function. Individual DSM-III criteria serve to prompt extensive inquiry about controlling variables and range of response and lead the therapist to do a functional analysis of the behavior nomothetically described by the diagnostic criteria. This in turn leads to an examination of the relevant literature, followed by treatment hypotheses, intervention, and evaluation of the treatment protocol (table 3.1).

Although it is beyond the scope of the present chapter to describe in detail each phase of this model, a brief explanation may be helpful. Let us consider the use of the proposed model for a child diagnosed as *Childhood Onset Pervasive Developmental Disorder Full Syndrome Present*. In order to qualify for this label, a child must meet several criteria. For example, the clinician must note: 1) a gross and sustained impairment in social functioning; 2) at least three of seven severe behavioral excesses or deficits (e.g., self-mutilation, inappropriate affect, and resistance to change in the environment); 3) onset of the syndrome after 30 months of age but before 12 years; and 4) the absence of hallucinations and delusions (American Psychiatric Association, 1980, p. 91).

The first criterion of social impairment is a general term and can be satisfied in different ways. Should our hypothetical child cling inappropriately to a significant adult, we would propose a very different treatment program than if he or she ignored other people. In either case the therapist would do

Table 3.1. A Model for the Synthesis of DSM-III and Child Behavioral Assessment.

DSM-III Diagnosis
Screening and general disposition of client
Operational definition(s) of target behavior(s)
Examination of the relevant literature
Determination of controlling variables via S-O-R-K-C analysis
Design and implementation of intervention
Ongoing evaluation of treatment progress
Follow-up

well to go to the literature to identify relevant instruments for the assessment of social behavior. One such instrument would be the Adaptive Behavior Scale (American Association on Mental Deficiency, 1975).

In order to meet the second criterion of severe behavioral excesses or deficits, the child could exhibit a variety of different behaviors. The identification of each specific behavior should prompt the therapist to return to the literature seeking methods of assessment particular to that behavior. For example, presence of self-mutilation might well lead one to Carr's (1977) screening sequence for determining the motivation of self-injury. Similarly, presence of language abnormalities warrants use of Schuler and Goetz's (1981) assessment strategies. This same process of going from the diagnostic criteria to the assessment of each behavior would continue until all diagnostic criteria are satisfied. In this fashion, DSM-III offers guidelines for where to probe in doing one's evaluation of the client.

Being realistic, it is not likely that all DSM-III criteria for diagnosis will have a previously developed assessment protocol in the professional literature. In such cases, the child therapist is hampered only by his or her imagination in the use of innovative behavioral assessment techniques.

SUMMARY

The purpose of the present chapter has been to summarize the current status of DSM-III and to evaluate this diagnostic system from the perspective of the child behavioral therapist. The strengths and weaknesses of DSM-III in relation to children have been detailed, with special emphasis on what behavioral assessment offers the process of symptomatic diagnosis of childhood disorders. We have briefly presented an integrative model, which suggests that traditional diagnosis can provide signposts for the behavioral assessment process by suggesting important areas to be examined in doing a comprehensive evaluation. The behavioral therapist who uses this model gains access to nomothetic considerations inherent in the use of symptomatic diagnosis.

REFERENCES

Achenbach, T. M. DSM-III in light of empirical research on the classification of child psychopathology. *Journal of the American Academy of Child Psychiatry,* 1980, *19,* 395–412.
Achenbach, T. M. *Developmental psychopathology* (2nd ed.). New York: Wiley, 1982.
American Association on Mental Deficiency. *Adaptive Behavior Scales* (Rev. ed.). Washington, DC: Author, 1975.
American Psychiatric Association. *Diagnostic and Statistical Manual of Mental Disorders.* Washington, DC: Author, 1952.

American Psychiatric Association. *Diagnostic and Statistical Manual of Mental Disorders* (2nd ed.). Washington, DC: Author, 1968.

American Psychiatric Association. *Diagnostic and Statistical Manual of Mental Disorders* (3rd ed.). Washington, DC: Author, 1980.

American Psychiatric Association. *Quick reference to diagnostic criteria from DSM-III.* Washington, DC: Author, 1980.

Barkley, R. A. Hyperactivity. In E. J. Mash & L. G. Terdal (Eds.), *Behavioral assessment of childhood disorders.* New York: Guilford Press, 1981.

Cantor, S., Evans, J., Pearce, J., & Pezzot-Pearce, T. Childhood schizophrenia: Present but not accounted for. *American Journal of Psychiatry,* 1982, *139,* 758–762.

Cantwell, D. P., Mattison, R., Russell, A. T., & Will, L. A comparison of DSM-II and DSM-III in the diagnosis of childhood psychiatric disorders. IV. Difficulties in use, global comparison, and conclusions. *Archives of General Psychiatry,* 1979, *36,* 1227–1228.

Cantwell, D. P., Russell, A. T., Mattison, R., & Will, L. A comparison of DSM-II and DSM-III in the diagnosis of childhood psychiatric disorders I. Agreement with expected diagnosis. *Archives of General Psychiatry,* 1979, *36,* 1208–1213.

Carr, E. G. The motivation of self-injurious behavior: A review of some hypotheses. *Psychological Bulletin,* 1977, *84,* 800–816.

Cerreto, M. C., & Tuma, J. M. Distribution of DSM-II diagnoses in a child psychiatric setting. *Journal of Abnormal Child Psychology,* 1977, *5,* 147–153.

Cone, J. D., & Hawkins, R. P. (Eds.). *Behavioral assessment: New directions in clinical psychology.* New York: Brunner/Mazel, 1977.

Dreger, R. M., Lewis, P. M., Rich, T. A., Miller, K. S., Reid, M. P., Overlake, D. C., Taffer, C., & Fleming, E. L. Behavioral classification project. *Journal of Consulting Psychology,* 1964, *28,* 1–13.

Earls, F. Application of DSM-III in an epidemiological study of preschool children. *American Journal of Psychiatry,* 1982, *139,* 242–243.

Goldfried, M. R., & Kent, R. N. Traditional versus behavioral personality assessment: A comparison of methodological and theoretical assumptions. *Psychological Bulletin,* 1972, *77,* 409–420.

Goldfried, M. R., & Sprafkin, J. N. Behavioral personality assessment. In J. T. Spence, R. C. Carson, & J. W. Thibaut (Eds.), *Behavioral approaches to therapy.* Morristown, NJ: General Learning Press, 1976.

Hawkins, R. P. The functions of assessment: Implications for selection and development of devices for assessing repertoires in clinical, educational, and other settings. *Journal of Applied Behavior Analysis,* 1979, *12,* 501–516.

Irwin, M. Diagnosis of anorexia nervosa in children and the validity of DSM-III. *American Journal of Psychiatry,* 1981, *138,* 1382–1383.

Kanfer, F. H., & Saslow, G. Behavioral diagnosis. In C. M. Franks (Ed.), *Behavior therapy: Appraisal and status.* New York: McGraw-Hill, 1969.

Kazdin, A. E. Assessing the clinical or applied importance of behavior change through social validation. *Behavior Modification,* 1977, *1,* 427–452.

Klein, D. F., & Gittelman-Klein, R. Problems in the diagnosis of minimal brain dysfunction and the hyperkinetic syndrome. In R. Gittelman-Klein (Ed.), *Recent advances in child psychopharmacology.* New York: Human Sciences Press, 1975.

Lambert, N., Sandoval, J., & Sassone, D. Prevalence of hyperactivity in elementary school children as a function of social system definers. *American Journal of Orthopsychiatry,* 1978, *48,* 446–463.

Lazarus, A. A. *The practice of multi-modal therapy.* New York: McGraw-Hill, 1981.

Lefkowitz, M. M., & Burton, N. Childhood depression: A critique of the concept. *Psychological Bulletin,* 1978, *85,* 716–726.

Mash, E. J., & Terdal, L. G. (Eds.). *Behavioral assessment of childhood disorders.* New York: Guilford Press, 1981.

Mattison, R., Cantwell, D. P., Russell, A. T., & Will, L. A comparison of DSM-II and DSM-III in the diagnosis on childhood psychiatric disorders. II. Interrater agreement. *Archives of General Psychiatry,* 1979, *36,* 1217–1222.

Nathan, P. E. Symptomatic diagnosis and behavioral assessment: A synthesis? In D. H. Barlow (Ed.), *Behavioral assessment of adult disorders.* New York: Guilford Press, 1981.

Nathan, P. E., & Harris, S. L. *The diagnostic and statistical manual of mental disorders:* History, comparative analysis, current status, and appraisal. In C. E. Walker (Ed.), *Handbook of clinical psychology: Theory, research, and practice.* Homewood, IL: Dow Jones-Irwin, in press.

Nelson, R. O., & Barlow, D. H. Behavioral assessment: Basic strategies and initial procedures. In D. H. Barlow (Ed.), *Behavioral assessment of adult disorders.* New York: Guilford Press, 1981.

Nelson, R. O., & Hayes, S. C. Some current dimensions of behavioral assessment. *Behavioral Assessment,* 1979, *1,* 1–16.

Patterson, G. R. Interventions for boys with conduct problems: Multiple settings, treatments, and criteria. *Journal of Consulting and Clinical Psychology,* 1974, *42,* 471–481.

Rincover, A., Cook, R., Peoples, A., & Packard, D. Sensory extinction and sensory reinforcement principles for programming multiple adaptive behavior change. *Journal of Applied Behavior Analysis,* 1979, *12,* 221–233.

Rincover, A., Newsom, C. D., & Carr, E. G. Using sensory extinction procedures in the treatment of compulsive-like behavior of developmentally disabled children. *Journal of Consulting and Clinical Psychology,* 1979, *47,* 695–701.

Rosen, B. M., Bahn, A. K., & Kramer, M. Demographic and diagnostic characteristics of psychiatric clinic outpatients in the U.S.A., 1961. *American Journal of Orthopsychiatry,* 1964, *34,* 455–468.

Russell, A. T., Cantwell, D. P., Mattison, R., & Will, L. A comparison of DSM-II and DSM-III in the diagnosis of childhood psychiatric disorders. III. Multiaxial features. *Archives of General Psychiatry,* 1979, *36,* 1223–1226.

Rutter, M. Diagnosis and definition of childhood autism. *Journal of Autism and Childhood Schizophrenia,* 1978, *8,* 139–161.

Rutter, M., & Shaffer, D. DSM-III: A step forward or back in terms of the classification of child psychiatric disorders? *Journal of the American Academy of Child Psychiatry,* 1980, *19,* 371–394.

Schacht, T., & Nathan, P. E. But is it good for psychologists? Appraisal and status of DSM-III. *American Psychologist,* 1977, *32,* 1017–1025.

Schuler, A. L., & Goetz, L. The assessment of severe language disabilities: Communicative and cognitive considerations. *Analysis and Intervention in Developmental Disabilities,* 1981, *1,* 333–346.

Spitzer, R. L., & Cantwell, D. P. The DSM-III classification of the psychiatric disorders of infancy, childhood, and adolescence. *Journal of the American Academy of Child Psychiatry,* 1980, *19,* 356–370.

Spitzer, R. L., & Forman, J. B. W. DSM-III field trials: II. Initial experience with the multiaxial system. *American Journal of Psychiatry,* 1979, *136,* 818–820.

Spitzer, R. L., Forman, J. B. W., & Nee, J. DSM-III field trials: I. Initial interrater diagnostic reliability. *American Journal of Psychiatry,* 1979, *136,* 815–817.

Spitzer, R. L., Williams, J. B. W., & Skodol, A. E. DSM-III: The major achievements and an overview. *American Journal of Psychiatry,* 1980, *137,* 151–164.

Treece, C. DSM-III as a research tool. *American Journal of Psychiatry,* 1982, *139,* 577–583.

Webb, L. J., Gold, R. S., Johnstone, E. E., & DiClemente, C. C. Accuracy of DSM-III diagnoses following a training program. *American Journal of Psychiatry,* 1981, *138,* 376–378.

Wender, P., Reimherr, F. W., & Wood, D. R. Attention deficit disorder ("minimal brain dysfunction") in adults. *Archives of General Psychiatry,* 1981, *38,* 449–456.

Whalen, C. K., & Henker, B. Psychostimulants and children: A review and analysis. *Psychological Bulletin,* 1976, *83,* 1113–1130.

PART II
Specific Assessment Strategies

4

*Behavioral Interviewing**
Alan M. Gross

Behavioral assessment involves the identification and measurement of response units and their controlling variables for the purpose of understanding and modifying human behavior (Nelson & Hayes, 1981). Of the many techniques employed by clinicians when conducting a behavioral assessment, the interview is the most widely used (Swan & MacDonald, 1978). Although it may often be supplemented by other procedures, it is generally considered an indispensible part of clinical assessment strategy (Linehan, 1977).

Haynes and Wilson (1979) define the behavioral interview as a structured interaction between target subjects or mediators and the behavior analyst for (1) purposes of gathering information about patient concerns and goals, (2) identifying factors that maintain or elicit problem responses, (3) eliciting historical information, (4) identifying reinforcers, (5) assessing mediation potential, (6) educating the patient, (7) obtaining informed consent, and (8) communicating explicitly about the procedures and goals of assessment and intervention. An experienced behavioral clinician knows, however, that assessment does not stop with identification of the target response. Treatment is then implemented, and the interview provides a vehicle to monitor the progress of therapy as well as obtain feedback for making clinically sound adjustments in treatment (Gross, in press). Additionally, the interview can be used as a measure of treatment effectiveness.

The popularity of the interview as a data collection technique in behavioral assessment may be due in part to a number of practical considerations as well

*The author thanks Jean Anderson for her helpful comments on an earlier version of this manuscript.

as to the advantages it offers over other assessment strategies. The emphasis in assessment in behavior therapy clearly has been on the use of direct observation. However, this procedure is not always possible, and at times, the patient's verbal report or the verbal report of significant others is the only data base on which to perform a behavioral analysis. This is particularly the case in outpatient therapy. More importantly, before therapists can make any direct observations of the target behavior, they must know what they are looking for and where to look. The interview offers the most economical method of obtaining such crucial information (Wahler & Cormier, 1970).

When the behavioral interview is compared to other methods of gathering self-report data, such as paper-and-pencil measures, additional benefits become apparent. The flexibility of the interview allows the clinician to obtain both general information regarding overall functioning and detailed information about specific areas. This flexibility may help the clinician broaden the assessment band and obtain information the patient might have otherwise omitted because of general reluctance or the belief that the clinician may find this information unimportant (Mischel, 1968; Peterson, 1968). The interview situation also provides a setting in which the potential for the perception of greater confidentiality between patient and therapist exists. The patient may be more likely to divulge information verbally than to write it and provide a permanent record (Linehan, 1977). Information can also be obtained from people who, because of poor communication skills, are unable to provide it in other ways.

Finally, the interview allows the therapist an opportunity to directly observe the patient's social behavior. The patient's behavior in the interview may not be completely representative of his or her interpersonal responding in all situations, but it can be used to generate hypotheses about behavioral deficits and assets (Linehan, 1977).

The purpose of the present chapter is to discuss the behavioral interview in child behavioral assessment. In particular, the focus will be on the practical issues involved in interviewing. Included in this chapter will be a brief discussion of various behavioral approaches to assessment, followed by a presentation of the applied aspects of interviewing children and their families. The issues of reliability and validity of interview data will also be addressed, and a case description will be included to help illustrate the methodology.

GENERAL GUIDELINES IN
BEHAVIORAL ASSESSMENT

As previously noted, the primary objective of behavioral assessment is to obtain descriptive information about problem behavior and the conditions maintaining it. In recent years, a variety of general guidelines for conducting a thorough behavioral assessment have been proposed (Morganstern & Tevlin, 1981). Kanfer and Saslow (1969) have described one of the most comprehensive assessment schemes. Their approach incorporates variables from the patient's current situation and past history, although the historical data are relevant only if they contribute to the description of present problem responses or future interventions. Kanfer and Saslow suggest that to perform a thorough analysis of behavior, the following areas should be examined: (1) an analysis of the problem situation; (2) an elucidation of the factors maintaining the problem response; (3) a motivational analysis; (4) a developmental analysis; (5) an analysis of self-control; (6) an analysis of social relationships; and (7) an analysis of the socio-cultural-physical environment. In addition to being extremely encompassing, Kanfer and Saslow's assessment approach was one of the first to emphasize the importance of assessing the patient's behavioral strengths along with response deficits (Morganstern & Tevlin, 1981).

Unlike Kanfer and Saslow (1969), Goldfried and Pomeranz (1968) and Goldfried and Sprafkin (1974) place more emphasis on specification of organismic variables in behavioral assessment. Suggesting that many behaviorists oversimplify the target for assessment, they speculate that cognitive sets and perceptions also are important variables for consideration. They suggest that a comprehensive assessment consists of an investigation of the following four classes of variables: (1) the antecedent situational variables, (2) organismic variables (cognitive and physiological), (3) the problem response, and (4) the consequent changes in the environment.

Another theorist who emphasizes the importance of cognitive variables in behavioral assessment is Mischel (1973). Like most behaviorists, Mischel agrees with the belief that major emphasis in assessment should be placed on determining the specific environmental events maintaining maladaptive behavior. However, he also suggests that "person variables" or cognitive social learning factors must be examined. He speculates that "person variables" develop as a function of an individual's social learning history. These factors influence the way in which environmental conditions affect human responding. Because "person variables" are unique to each individual, it is imperative to study them if effective behavioral control is to be established. The person variables Mischel suggests for investigation include: (1) cognitive and behavioral construction competencies, (2) encoding strategies, (3) behavior-outcome and stimulus-outcome expectancies, (4) subjective stimulus values, and (5) self-regulatory systems and plans.

Rather than focusing on cognitive variables, the assessment system of Stuart (1970) emphasizes the precise specification of target behaviors, antecedents, and consequences. Furthermore, Stuart breaks both the antecedent and consequence variables into four classes. The four types of antecedent variables for assessment are instructional, discriminative, potentiating, and facilitating variables. The four types of consequence stimuli that need to be investigated are positive reinforcement, extinction, punishment, and negative reinforcement. Additionally, like Kanfer and Saslow (1969), Stuart encourages assessment of the patient's response strengths because therapists have a larger repertoire for increasing desired behaviors than for decreasing maladaptive responses.

Lastly, Peterson (1968) suggests that assessment concentrate on two broad sets of variables. The first set includes defining the target and examining the severity and generality of the problem. The second category focuses on the determinants of the target response. These include antecedents and consequences associated with the response. More importantly, Peterson (1968) was an early proponent of assessment going beyond the identification of behavior and its determinants. He suggested that the behavioral assessment interview be used for extended inquiry, including periodic reappraisal of intervention effectiveness throughout treatment and a final follow-up of the maintenance of behavior change.

While there are other theorists who have proposed guidelines for conducting comprehensive behavioral assessments (e.g., Lazarus, 1973), it is safe to say that their approaches, along with those described here, share a common emphasis on the clarification of the problem behavior and the controlling antecedent and consequent stimuli. The approaches differ primarily in their relative emphasis on cognitive variables and the extent of historical data to be obtained. For example, Mischel (1973) places more weight on cognitive variables than does Peterson (1968).

Although it might be argued that the clinician should attempt to gain as much information as possible about patients and their problems in order to increase the likelihood of developing an effective intervention, no data exist to support this idea. Also, this kind of assessment may not always be practical or useful. When conducting an assessment, the clinician's strategy should be guided by an attempt to obtain data directly relevant to treatment planning. Data collection should focus on the factors likely to influence the maintenance and generalization of treatment gains following the withdrawal of the treatment program.

CHILD VERSUS ADULT ASSESSMENT

While the goals of the behavioral interview are the same regardless of the target population, there are two aspects of child behavioral assessment that differentiate it from adult assessment. Unlike most adult outpatients who attend therapy after identifying themselves as having behavioral difficulties, a child usually appears at the therapist's office because an adult (parent or teacher) has determined that a behavioral problem exists. As such, it is not uncommon for the child and adult to disagree over the existence of the problem as well as over the exact specifics of the problem area. When these differences in opinion exist, the therapist must exhibit great sensitivity to both the child and his or her family if efficient and effective data collection is to occur. Moreover, failure to address the disparity in perceptions may inhibit the development of cooperation between parent, child, and therapist during the treatment intervention.

Behavioral interviewing with children also differs from adult interviewing by the number of individuals from whom information is obtained. Behavior is a function of its consequences, and adults are able to control many of the rewarding and aversive events children experience. Additionally, because of the limited verbal repertoire of many children, the significant adults in a youngster's life are often better able to describe his or her behavior. For these reasons, the behavior therapist working with children continues beyond the target child during assessment and conducts interviews with parents, teachers, siblings, and, at times, peers (Ciminero & Drabman, 1977).

THE INTERVIEW

As just noted, in the process of treating a child behavioral problem, a variety of individuals may be interviewed. To determine which adults are relevant and significant to the child's situation and should be included in the assessment and treatment process, the behavioral problem first must be defined. As such, the assessment process is generally initiated with both the child and his or her parents during the first interview (Ollendick & Cerny, 1981). Therapists differ in their approach to structuring this initial contact, but it is generally agreed that the child and his or her parents should be seen alone and together. With children under 6 years of age, the parents are usually seen first, followed by the child alone, and finally all three together. With older children, the order of interview may be altered.

Whether interviewing the parents or the child (or teacher), the interviewer is attempting to identify the target behavior, to identify alternative appropriate behaviors, to discover the controlling antecedent and consequent stimuli, to assess the parents' mediational potential, and to identify potential rewarding and aversive stimuli that may be useful in treatment planning. Furthermore, some investigators advocate the collection of developmental history data. Haynes (1978) suggests that, although this information may not be directly relevant to treatment development, it may identify situations in which the problem is likely to reemerge.

Meeting with Parents

The therapist generally begins the first interview by gathering demographic information about the child (e.g., age, grade in school, number of siblings, etc). This procedure is followed by an attempt to gather data concerning typical parent-child interactions that are considered to be problems. General questions from the therapist initiate this process. For example, parents may be asked what prompted them to come to the clinic or to describe the types of problems they are having with their child. Because the emphasis of the behavioral assessment interview is to obtain precise accounts of the situation, the therapist prompts parents to describe these interactions in great detail. After the problem situation has been identified, the therapist may begin to probe in more depth. Questions asking for a description of the child's behavior ("Tell me what your child does exactly."), the parents' behavior ("What do you do when your child behaves in this manner?"), the youngster's response to parental actions ("What does your child do after you do that?"), and descriptions of the situation in which this interaction takes place ("Tell me where you are and what is happening when the problem usually occurs.") are appropriate. Additionally, information concerning frequency and duration of problem responses is also collected. These questions are designed to obtain information that will allow the therapist to select the target responses and identify the antecedent and consequent stimuli that may be controlling the behavior.

Following this stage of data collection, the interviewer then begins to assess the youngster's behavioral assets in order to determine appropriate alternative responses to teach the child. Asking parents to specify the preferred behavior for a particular setting often provides this information (e.g., "What behavior do you want him to exhibit when that occurs?"). Discussion of appropriate alternative responses helps to determine therapy goals as well as to assess parental expectations for child behavior. Moreover, questions about a child's good behaviors may help the parents begin to notice that, contrary to their perception, there are a number of settings in which their youngster displays very positive responses.

The interview should also focus on potential rewarding and aversive stimuli for use in the treatment program. The majority of behavioral therapy programs involve the reinforcement of appropriate responding and the extinction or punishment of inappropriate responding. As such, discovering which events in the youngster's life may be effective reinforcers and punishers is important. Asking parents about their child's likes and dislikes ("What does he or she do after school? Does he or she like T.V.?") is often an efficient technique for gathering this information.

A nonspecific variable which therapists also attempt to assess during the interview is parents' mediation potential. In other words, the therapist assesses the probability that the parents will successfully complete the treatment intervention. This potential is inferred from a number of variables: degree of behavioral insight, degree of distress, value of contingencies for successful behavioral change, reliability of patient, and degree of interference from competing problems in parents' lives (Haynes, 1978). The interviewer must use the behavioral sample provided by observing the parents in the interview to evaluate some of the variables mentioned. However, the ability of parents to comply with instructions over time will also provide objective data regarding mediation potential.

Meeting with the Child

The purposes of interviewing the youngster are similar to those of interviewing parents. An attempt is made to hear the child's definition of the problem situations, to assess behavioral strengths, and to identify potential consequent stimuli. With children under 6 years of age, however, the therapist can expect that this tactic will lead to little useful content information, although such is not necessarily the case with older children. This interview generally begins with the therapist asking the child why he or she thinks he or she has been brought to the clinic. Following the youth's response, the therapist usually shares his or her opinion about this issue with the youngster. The clinician's reply conveys to the child that the entire family would like to work to make things more pleasant for everyone at home. The therapist may also ask about family and peer interactions as well as about preferred activities (e.g., "What do you like to do with your friends?"). These questions help the therapist to determine events that may serve as rewards in the treatment program. It is important to note that although some practical information can be obtained in the interview with the child, the major goal of this phase of the interview process is to convey to the youth that the family and not the child is going to be the focus of treatment and that the child's thoughts and feelings will be important factors in the formulation of the intervention strategy.

In addition to descriptive data, interviewing the child and his or her parents provides other very useful information. This procedure affords the clinician the opportunity to directly observe how the parents and child behave during the interview. These observations may lead to hypotheses about social skill development. For example, noting how the child responds to parental questions and commands provides an important sample of the youngster's behavior. Additionally, it also is possible that the therapist will be able to see how the parents respond to inappropriate and appropriate child behavior. Despite the novelty of the interview situation and the possibility that the family is attempting to present itself at best, or worst, the interview with the child and his or her family is the first direct observation (and in some cases the only direct observation) provided to the therapist. The information gathered as a result should be used to develop hypotheses and lead to further exploration (e.g., additional specific questioning).

After the interview with the child, the initial interview is generally closed with a brief summary discussion with the youngster's parents. During this time the therapist presents his or her conceptualization of the problem(s) to the parents. Suggestions as to which problem area should immediately be targeted are also discussed. This summary provides parents with a behavioral framework with which to redefine and view the problem. When additional information is desired, this is also a good time for the therapist to give parents homework assignments (e.g., "Please write down each time you have a problem getting Jerome to finish eating. Also, briefly describe the situation."). During the final part of the interview, parents are given an overview regarding the therapist's approach to treating this type of disorder.

Meeting with the Teacher

Very often the primary setting outside the home in which children are treated is the school. Furthermore, children are frequently brought to the therapist's office because of behavioral problems reported by the teacher. As such, the teacher is an important person to consider during the assessment process. Additionally, interviewing the teacher may provide corroboration of parental reports of child behavior.

As in the interview with parents, teachers are asked to provide a description of the problem responses, the setting in which they occur, and the controlling variables. Questions such as those recommended for use with parents are also appropriate with teachers.

Interviewing the teacher may lead to identification of areas of behavioral assets and deficits that are not easily obtained from parents. Social skills may be assessed by inquiring about the child's social interactions with peers (e.g., "Does he have many friends?", "Does she interact with boys and girls?", "Do the other children include him when they are selecting team players?"). Teachers are frequently very accurate at identifying children with a high likelihood of developing school problems (Ciminero & Drabman, 1977; Keefe, Kopel, & Gordon, 1978; Ollendick, 1981). As such, questions regarding academic performance may delineate important areas for intervention. A good set of questions to ask in this area includes: Does he or she do his or her work?; Are assignments completed on time?; Relative to classmates, how would you evaluate his or her performance in math, science, etc?; Does he or she require more time to complete assignments than the other children?; and Does he or she have difficulties staying on a task?

Lastly, the interview with the teacher should result in an assessment of the willingness of the teacher to assist in the intervention program. Generally, teachers are very interested in the performance of their students. An interviewer who consults with a child's teacher and exhibits a sincere appreciation of his or her observations and comments is likely to readily elicit a cooperative response.

Interview Structure

The preceding section describes the informational content that is crucial to a thorough behavioral assessment interview. There is little disagreement among researchers as to the importance of the topics listed. It has been debated, however, whether the interview format used to gather this information should be structured or unstructured (Maloney & Ward, 1976).

The flexible, or unstructured interview, imposes minimum constraints on the topics discussed by parents. The interviewer simply follows the cues of parents and is not restricted to a specific sequence of topics. This may be a good approach when there are multiple behavioral problems (Haynes, 1978). It is important to note, however, that even in the unstructured behavioral interview, there is a degree of structure. The therapist asks questions in order to meet the goals and functions of the interview (e.g., problem specification, antecedent and consequent stimuli identification). The major characteristic of unstructured interviews is that the sequence of topics discussed is less standardized and may vary across interviewers.

In structured interviews, the topics discussed follow a prearranged format. The therapist directs the conversation of the parents and is not likely to follow up tangential topics. Holland (1970) has suggested a standard interview method for parent-child interactions. He suggests that the therapist ask questions covering 21 topic areas. In summary, the following areas should be explored: parent goals, problem definition, alternative behaviors, potential positive and negative reinforcers, behavioral strengths, use of positive reinforcement and negative reinforcement, use of time out, use of intermittent reinforcement, and how to apply two treatment procedures simultaneously.

An interview format that appears to be a modified version of the structured interview is suggested by Patterson, Reid, Jones, and Conger (1975). Rather than simply asking open-ended questions, they begin the interview by having parents fill out a symptom checklist. Each symptom is clearly defined so that parents are sure to understand the meanings of terms. If parents consider a behavior from the checklist to be a problem, the therapist asks detailed questions regarding that particular problem situation in order to identify the controlling variables.

The structured interview increases the probability that interviewers will cover the same material in the same manner with all families. A potential benefit of this style is that it may facilitate the therapist's development of a frame of reference from which to view child behavioral problems.

There is no one correct way to conduct a behavioral interview. Rather than strictly adhering to either a structured or unstructured format, it might be best to view the interview procedure along a continuum (Maloney & Ward, 1976). The therapist might begin the process with minimal structure, using open-ended questions designed to determine what problem prompted the family to seek treatment. After establishing the nature of the difficulty, the therapist might begin to increase the structure of the interview. At this point he or she could employ a set of questions that would result in the specification of controlling variables. The highest degree of structure would be appropriate for the final phase of the interview, during which the clinician would present his or her clinical impressions to the child's parents. Conducting the interview according to a combination of both formats would provide benefits associated with both.

Interviewer Behavior

Interviewer behavior has been shown to have a significant impact on the verbal responding of patients during the interview (e.g., Matarrazo & Wiens, 1967). While the paucity of research on interviewing children and their families prevents presentation of a standard set of rules regarding valid interviewer behavior, a number of investigators have suggested that incorporating certain responses into the interview process can enhance the validity of the data obtained (Haynes & Wilson, 1979).

Scheiderer (1977) has suggested that efficiency and effectiveness of interviews could be improved if, rather than simply beginning the interview process with open-ended questions designed to identify the problem, therapists prepare patients for assessment by telling them how to respond. Additionally, he suggests that therapists model the type of verbal behaviors they desire. To evaluate this hypothesis, Scheiderer (1977) videotaped counseling patients experiencing their first interview session after exposure to one of four experimental conditions. One group of patients received detailed verbal instructions to be very open and specific regarding the nature of their difficulties. A second group observed a 9-minute videotape in which the model displayed the above-mentioned desirable behaviors. A third group of subjects received a combination of the videotape and verbal instructions, while the fourth group was given no treatment. He found that, in comparison to the no-treatment control, subjects in the three treatment groups exhibited significantly more self-disclosure and less impersonal discussion. He also reported that instructions alone were more effective than modeling or the combination treatment, which were equally effective. Scheiderer (1977) concluded that providing patients with instructions at the onset of the interview can enhance the quality of information gathered. Doster (1972) has reported similar findings.

The therapist's use of reinforcement can also contribute to the effectiveness of the interview (Morganstern & Tevlin, 1981). The function of reinforcement in the interview is to establish the interviewer as a dispenser of social rewards (e.g., praise), to increase the likelihood that the patient returns for additional sessions, and to raise the frequency of desirable types of speech (e.g., problem specifics) (Haynes, 1978). Reinforcing behaviors may include eye contact, body posture, verbal praise, and affective comments (i.e., remarks which communicate to the patient that the therapist has been listening) (Morganstern & Tevlin, 1981). These behaviors can be used with adults and children. Primary reinforcers such as food can also be employed to reward children for their good interview performance. As with all stimuli used as rewards, each may not be an effective stimulus for all patients. As such, the interviewer needs to be aware of the parameters involved in the effective use of reinforcers.

Maloney and Ward (1976) suggest that therapists use open-ended questions when interviewing (e.g,. "Describe what happens when you ask Jerome to pick up his toys."). They state that this type of question prevents patients from assuming a passive responder role. While a closed question (e.g., "Is it difficult to get Jerome to pick up his toys?") can be responded to with a *yes* or *no* response, open-ended questions require the patient to decide what is pertinent, where to start, and what to include in his or her response. Not only does this type of question provide the therapist with an opportunity to listen to the subject's perspective on the problem, but it also affords the opportunity to see how parents and children handle themselves in a relatively unstructured situation. Moreover, phrasing of open-ended questions may be less biased and, therefore, result in more valid information (Haynes, 1978).

Lastly, the interview process can be greatly facilitated by the education of parents, and to a lesser extent their children, in behavioral theory. This education process can be accomplished via the therapist's combined use of modeling and selective reinforcement. As the interview progresses, the therapist should model speech content (e.g., "You said that Jerome is allowed to stay up an extra half hour every night he does the dishes. When the performance of a specific behavior is followed by a reward, we refer to this as reinforcement. Do you systematically reinforce any of his other behaviors?") and selectively reinforce patient verbal behavior (e.g., "That account of Jerome's response to your instructions to go to bed was really nicely detailed and very helpful."). Following a continued exposure to this procedure, patients will begin to talk in more precise terms and use phrases that are behavioral in content. Information becomes easier to obtain and fewer questions must be asked in order to gather the details necessary for conducting a behavioral analysis. Additionally, detailed responding of parents during the treatment phases of intervention will facilitate the therapist's making adjustment in the treatment program.

Reliability and Validity

There has been a paucity of research on the reliability and validity of behavioral interview data in child behavioral assessment. This lack of investigation is problematic given the important functions of interview data in assessment and treatment. While it is asserted that therapists should view patient reports as the individual's verbal construction of events, rather than as an accurate reflection of events, in practice it appears that clinicians often assume patients' reports to be accurate.

Performing a behavioral analysis from information gathered during an interview rests on two assumptions: that parents are capable of accurately observing and reporting their own behavior, environment, and behavior-consequence relationships, and that they are reporting these events accurately (Linehan, 1977). Until recently, reports concerning the accuracy of recall of children's behavior suggested that parents are highly inaccurate data souces. Yarrow, Campbell, and Burton (1970) and Chess, Thomas, and Birch (1966) found that parents' retrospective reports of their children's behavior did not reflect actual behavioral development. They noted that parent recall was greatly influenced by social desirability and theories of child rearing. However, those results were based on responses to open-ended questions about child behavior occurring 3–30 years earlier. Behavioral interviews generally do not require reliance on long-term memory, since the focus is on current behavioral difficulties (Wells, 1981).

Schnelle (1974) also demonstrated that parents are not accurate reporters of their children's behavior. Youngsters and their families were treated for school truancy using behavioral contracting. Four weeks following termination of the intervention, parents were mailed a questionnaire regarding parental perception of improvement. But, 92% of the parents failed to return the questionnaire. Case workers were then sent to each of these homes in order to collect the follow-up data. Comparisons between parent reports of school attendance and school records revealed a complete lack of relationship. However, these results may, in part, be a function of the low educational level of parents and the demand characteristics resulting from the case worker collecting follow-up data.

Despite the data presented in the above studies, a number of researchers have found that parents and children can be valid data sources. Herjanic and Campbell (1977) interviewed parents and children using a standard interview format. One group of those interviewed was selected from a clinic sample and the other was a matched control group. The psychiatric sample was clearly distinguishable from the control group on the basis of interview responses. Similar findings have been reported by Graham and Rutter (1968). Although these studies were diagnostic in nature, they provide indirect evidence for the criterion-related validity of interview data in child behavioral assessment.

A second index of the validity of interview data is the reliability of the parent report (Haynes, 1978). Herjanic, Herjanic, Brown, and Wheatt (1975) interviewed parents and their children using the same set of interview questions. The questions were designed to obtain: factual information, a description of the problem areas, psychiatric symptoms, and mental status. A comparison of parent and child responses showed an overall agreement level of 80%. Furthermore, higher agreement was found (84%) when only factual questions were considered. The authors concluded that child behavior can be reliably observed by parents and their children.

While the results are contradictory, there does seem to be some evidence that children and their parents can provide reliable and valid information in the behavioral interview. Clearly, further research is needed to determine the variables that enhance these factors. While parental and child reports should be viewed with caution, there appear to be ways to increase the clinician's confidence in this type of data. Obtaining accounts of the behavior from other involved individuals may provide evidence for the accuracy of parental reports. For example, teacher observations may validate parental accounts of a child's behavioral difficulties. Interviewing mother and father separately may also point out areas of agreement and disagreement that need to be addressed. Additionally, comparing both parents' descriptions will provide opportunities for the therapist to reinforce parents for accurate reporting, thus enhancing accurate data provision. Asking questions about recent events and focusing on specific behaviors and events may also increase the accuracy of the data. Training parents and children to be behavior monitors and reinforcing performance also can be used to increase the accuracy of verbally reported data. Finally, supplementing verbal reports with direct observations will provide the strongest test of the validity of this information.

CASE STUDY

Having described a general interviewing strategy for use in child behavioral assessment, it seems appropriate to provide a brief case report to illustrate the application of these procedures in the clinical setting.

Jake is a 5-year-old Caucasian male brought to the outpatient clinic by his parents because of his noncompliant behavior. At the initial interview, the therapist first met with Mr. and Mrs. B. while Jake remained in the waiting room. The therapist began the session and explained the purpose of the first meeting. He emphasized to Mr. and Mrs. B. the importance of describing the problem in detail. Mr. and Mrs. B. were then asked to outline the difficulties that prompted them to seek help.

T: Please tell me what has prompted you to make an appointment.

Mrs. B: We are having trouble getting Jake to behave. He just never seems to listen when he is asked to do something.

T: Please give me an example.

Mrs. B: Well, just before we came today, he was outside playing. I called him and asked him to come in and he said yes but continued to play.

T: What happened then?

Mrs. B: I called him again and he still didn't listen.

T: What did you do next?

Mrs. B: I was getting really mad. My husband was on his way to pick us up and I wanted to be ready when he arrived. I guess I began to yell and then went in and got Jake's and my things together.

T: Did Jake ever come in before you left?

Mrs. B: No. I just told him that if he didn't care how he looked then neither did I. When his father arrived we just left.

T: Did Jake readily stop playing when you arrived to pick them up?

Mr. B: He was playing in the yard when I pulled up. She called him and he didn't listen. So I told him to get in the car, and he said he didn't want to go.

T: What did you do next?

Mr. B: I just went over and picked him up and put him in the car.

T: How did he respond to that?

Mr. B: He did a bit of screaming and crying, but he calmed down after a while.

T: Does he usually have a tantrum when he doesn't get his way?

Mr. B: Yeah, he does. It's gotten to the point where unless I really have to I'll just leave him alone so I don't have to listen to all that screaming.

Continuing with this questioning strategy, the therapist asked Mr. and Mrs. B. about a number of other examples of their son's noncompliant behavior. After obtaining a fairly clear description of parent-child behavior in these situations, the therapist began to ask questions designed to identify controlling variables.

T: You stated that often when you tell Jake to do something that he doesn't want to do, he ignores you. You also said that then you often scold him. Does that have any effect?

Mrs. B: Not usually. It really just makes me mad at myself.

T: If he doesn't do what you ask, do you do it for him?

Mrs. B: Yes, I guess so.

T: Give me an example.

Mrs. B: Well, yesterday I asked him to put his toys away. After his usual failure to comply, I just didn't want to argue about it so I did it myself.

T: Do you respond to him the same way?

Mr. B: I don't think it's quite so bad for me since I'm not home all day. But, yeah, I guess I leave him alone or do things myself to avoid fighting.

The therapist's line of questioning identified some likely variables that may have been contributing to the maintenance of the behavior problem. That is, Jake's noncompliant behavior was followed by not having to perform the requested response. Noncompliance often resulted in avoidance or escape from some undesirable task. Once the target behavior and its controlling factors had been described, questioning then proceeded to identify the youngster's desirable behaviors as well as potential rewards.

T: Describe some situations when Jake behaves very appropriately.
Mrs. B: Well, if we take him places with us, he is generally pretty good.
T: Give me an example.
Mr. B: I have to admit that the other night I took him to a Braves' game, and for a five year old, he did pretty well.
T: How do you mean?
Mr. B: Well, I told him that he could have a soda and some popcorn and nothing else. That seemed great to him. He didn't nag me, and he paid attention to me when I asked him to sit down and remain in his seat.
T: Does he like baseball?
Mr. B: He is always asking me to play catch when I get home from work.
T: Are there other times when he behaves the way you want?
Mrs. B: He's really pretty good when there are other kids around. If he has friends over and I ask him to share a toy or play outside, he is pretty good about listening.
T: Is that what you want in terms of behavior change, that he listen and comply to requests?
Mrs. B: Yeah, that would be great.
T: It appears that he does that some of the time but not consistently enough.
Mrs. B: Hadn't really thought of it that way, but I guess you're right.
T: You mentioned that he likes baseball. What else does he really like?
Mrs. B: Like all kids he seems addicted to some television programs, and he seems to really get excited if his father takes him on an errand or plays some sport with him.

After obtaining information regarding target behavior, controlling variables, alternative responses, and potential rewarding stimuli, the therapist met alone with Jake. The therapist attempted to assess the youngster's knowledge of why he was in the clinic as well as to identify potential rewarding stimuli.

T: Do you know why you are here, Jake?
Jake: No. Maybe 'cause I get in trouble at home.
T: Well, your mom and dad want to learn how you and they can get along without yelling. Would you like that?
Jake: Yeah.

T: I think we can make that happen if you, your mom and dad, and I work together.

Jake: O.K.

T: Your dad tells me you like to play baseball.

Jake: Uh-huh. I like to pitch. Sometimes I play with dad. Next year I'm going to play Little League.

T: He told me that you and he went to see the Braves.

Jake: Yeah and the Braves won.

T: Do you ever watch the Braves on T.V.?

Jake: Sometimes.

T: Do you like T.V.

Jake: I love to watch T.V. My favorite program is the Hulk.

At the conclusion of his interview with Jake, the therapist met with Jake's parents and presented a brief summary of his assessment observations.

T: Your descriptions of the problem situation were very detailed and clearly presented. It appears that there are a few things that are occurring that I believe can be used to alleviate your problems with Jake.

Mr. B: That would be great.

T: It is very stressful and frustrating to ask your child to do something and get no response. Frequently, after experiencing this a number of times parents become impatient, scold their child, and then complete the task themselves just to end the difficulty. You essentially described this pattern of interaction regarding the incident with putting away his toys. Unfortunately, in alleviating their own stress by completing the task, parents teach their child that if he ignores mom or dad's request then they will do the chore after they finish yelling. Hence, noncompliance is rewarded by not having to perform an unpleasant behavior. When a behavior is strengthened by being followed by a reward, we call this reinforcement.

Mrs. B: That is characteristic of what often occurs at home. Sometimes it is just easier to do it myself and not argue.

T: Another result of child noncompliance is that it results in a great deal of one-to-one parent attention. Some of this attention may appear aversive to you and me, such as scolding, but it is attention. For example, when Jake is being a good boy, it is easy not to say anything to him. If he stops being good, however, and becomes disruptive, he is immediately spoken to. As such, bad behavior receives all of the attention, and appropriate behavior is largely ignored. Adult attention can be a very strong reinforcer for children.

Mrs. B: I understand what you are saying, but it is really hard to ignore him when he is being disruptive.

T: I understand that. However, there are a number of strategies we will discuss in order to strengthen Jake's good behavior and eliminate his inappropriate responding. Between now and next week I would like you to keep a record of the frequency of Jake's deviant behavior as well as the situation in which it occurs and your responses to this behavior. Again, let me emphasize the importance of being precise and detailed in your observations. You did an excellent job today of clearly presenting a picture of what has been going on at home. Keep up the good work.

The results of the assessment interview indicated that Jake's behavior was most likely being supported by parental attention and avoidance of performing unenjoyable tasks. Additionally, potential stimuli (e.g., T.V., sports, time with dad) were specified for use as rewards in the treatment program. As such, following the interview, the parents were given a homework assignment of monitoring the identified target behavior. At the subsequent treatment session this information would be used to begin teaching parenting skills. In particular, Jake's parents were taught to use direct commands, to state clearly response-reinforcer relationships, to use time out, and to deliver rewards for appropriate behavior. These procedures were described in detail in the therapist's office and then practiced in the playroom while being observed by the therapist. Mr. and Mrs. B. were also required to continue to collect data on Jake's deviant behavior throughout the treatment intervention. By questioning Mr. and Mrs. B. about these data, the therapist was able to evaluate treatment effectiveness. Additionally, this information helped delineate practical problems associated with application of the procedures and identify new problem situations. A total of 10 weekly therapy sessions was required to alter Jake's and his parents' behavior.

The case described is a relatively straightforward and simple assessment and treatment program. A youngster was brought to the clinic by his parents because of his noncompliant behavior. They reported no academic or school-related problems. An interview assessment identified the target behaviors and the controlling variables. A parent training program was implemented. Data collection by parents and their verbal reports indicated that the treatment resulted in a large improvement in the youngster's behavior.

It is clear that not all interview assessments in child behavior therapy will be as uncomplicated as the one presented. At times, the interview with parents will reveal the importance of speaking with the child's teachers. The interview may also result in data that indicate the need for additional types of assessment (e.g., direct observation, intelligence testing). However, it is hoped that the example presented provides a general strategy for behavioral interviewing. Following these guidelines, the therapist should be able to gather enough adequate information to serve as a solid foundation on which to build further assessment and treatment plans.

SUMMARY

The present chapter describes a systematic approach to the use of behavioral interviews in child behavioral assessment. Practical issues involved in interview assessment have been noted in addition to a discussion of the validity and reliability of data obtained via interviews. A case study illustrating the use of these procedures also has been presented. Presented with both the strengths and weaknesses of behavioral interviewing in child behavioral assessment, clinicians will be able to utilize these techniques in the most successful manner possible.

REFERENCES

Chess, S., Thomas, A., & Birch, H. G. Distortions in developmental reporting made by parents of behaviorally disturbed children. *Journal of the American Academy of Child Psychiatry,* 1966, *5,* 226–231.

Ciminero, A. R., & Drabman, R. S. Current developments in the behavioral assessment of children. In B. B. Lahey & A. E. Kazdin (Eds.), *Advances in clinical child psychology* (Vol. 1). New York: Plenum Press, 1977.

Doster, J. A. Effects of instructions, modeling, and role rehearsal on interview verbal behavior. *Journal of Consulting and Clinical Psychology,* 1972, *39,* 202–209.

Goldfried, M. R., & Pomeranz, D. Role of assessment in behavior modification. *Psychological Reports,* 1968, *23,* 75–87.

Goldfried, M. R., & Sprafkin, J. N. *Behavioral personality assessment.* Morristown, NJ: General Learning Press, 1974.

Graham, P., & Rutter, M. The reliability and validity of the psychiatric assessment of the child. II. Interview with the parent. *British Journal of Psychiatry,* 1968, *114,* 581–592.

Gross, A. M. Conduct disorders. In M. Hersen (Ed.), *Practice of outpatient behavior therapy: A clinician's handbook.* New York: Grune & Stratton, in press.

Haynes, S. N. *Principles of behavioral assessment.* New York: Gardner Press, 1978.

Haynes, S. N., & Wilson, C. C. *Behavioral assessment.* San Francisco: Jossey-Bass, 1979.

Herjanic, B., & Campbell, W. Differentiating psychiatrically disturbed children on the basis of a structured interview. *Journal of Abnormal Child Psychology,* 1977, *5,* 127–133.

Herjanic, B., Herjanic, M., Brown, F., & Wheatt, T. Are children reliable reporters? *Journal of Abnormal Child Psychology,* 1975, *3,* 41–48.

Holland, C. J. An interview guide for behavioral counseling with parents. *Behavior Therapy,* 1970, *1,* 70–79.

Kanfer, F. H., & Saslow, G. Behavioral Diagnosis. In C. M. Franks (Ed.), *Behavior therapy: Appraisal and status.* New York: McGraw-Hill, 1969.

Keefe, F. J., Kopel, S. A., & Gordon, S. B. *A practical guide to behavioral assessment.* New York: Springer, 1978.

Lazarus, A. A. Multimodal behavior therapy: Treating the BASIC ID. *Journal of Nervous and Mental Disease,* 1973, *156,* 404–411.

Linehan, M. M. Issues in behavioral interviewing. In J. D. Cone & R. P. Hawkins (Eds.), *Behavioral assessment: New directions in clinical psychology.* New York: Brunner/Mazel, 1977.

Maloney, M. P., & Ward, M. P. *Psychological assessment: A conceptual approach.* New York: Oxford University Press, 1976.

Matarazzo, J., & Wiens, A. Interviewer influence on duration of interviewee silence. *Journal of Experimental Research in Personality,* 1967, *2,* 56–59.

Mischel, W. *Personality and assessment.* New York: Wiley, 1968.

Mischel, W. Toward a cognitive social learning reconceptualization of personality. *Psychological Review,* 1973, *80,* 252–283.

Morganstern, K. P., & Tevlin, H. E. Behavioral interviewing. In M. Hersen & A. S. Bellack

(Eds.), *Behavioral assessment: A practical handbook*. New York: Pergamon Press, 1981.

Nelson, R. O., & Hayes, S. C. Nature of Behavioral Assessment. In M. Hersen & A. S. Bellack (Eds.), *Behavioral assessment: A practical handbook*. New York: Pergamon Press, 1981.

Ollendick, T. H. (1981) Assessment of social interactive skills in schoolchildren. *Behavioral Counseling Quarterly,* Vol. 1, pp. 227-243.

Ollendick, T. H., & Cerny, S. A. *Clinical behavior therapy with children.* New York: Plenum Press, 1981.

Patterson, G. R., Reid, J. B., Jones, R. R., & Conger, R. E. *A social learning approach to family intervention: Families with aggressive children.* Eugene, OR: Castalia Press, 1975.

Peterson, D. R. *The clinical study of social behavior.* New York: Appleton-Century-Crofts, 1968.

Rutter, M., & Graham, P. The reliability and validity of the psychiatric assessment of the child. *British Journal of Psychiatry,* 1968, *114,* 563-579.

Scheiderer, E. G. Effects of instructions and modeling in producing self-disclosure in the initial clinical interview. *Journal of Consulting and Clinical Psychology,* 1977, *45,* 378-384.

Schnelle, J. F. A brief report on invalidity of parent evaluation of behavior change. *Journal of Applied Behavior Analysis,* 1974, *7,* 341-343.

Stuart, R. B. *Trick or treatment: How and when psychotherapy fails.* Champaign, IL: Research Press, 1970.

Swan, G. E., & MacDonald, M. C. Behavior therapy in practice: A national survey of behavior therapists. *Behavior Therapy,* 1978, *9,* 799-807.

Wahler, R. G., & Cormier, W. H. The ecological interview: A first step in out-patient child behavior therapy. *Journal of Behavior Therapy and Experimental Psychiatry,* 1970, *1,* 279-289.

Wells, K. C. Assessment of children in outpatient settings. In M. Hersen & A. S. Bellack (Eds.), *Behavioral assessment: A practical handbook.* New York: Pergamon Press, 1981.

Yarrow, M. R., Campbell, J. D., & Burton, R. V. Recollections of childhood: A study of the retrospective method. *Monograph of the Society for Research in Child Development,* 1970, *35* (5, Serial No. 138).

5

Behavioral Checklists
and Rating Scales*
Robert J. McMahon

Behavioral therapists have typically eschewed the use of "indirect" methods of assessment such as self-report, self-monitoring, and ratings by others (Cone & Hawkins, 1977). At best, these measures were employed as a last resort when direct observation was not possible. As the area of behavioral assessment has matured, however, such indirect assessment methods have been used more frequently (e.g., Cairns & Green, 1979). A recent survey of assessment methods employed in studies published in the major behavioral journals during the 1970s found that these indirect methods were employed in approximately 30% of the studies (Bornstein, Bridgewater, Hickey, & Sweeney, 1980).

The purpose of this chapter is to describe the role of one of these indirect methods (ratings by others) in child behavioral assessment. This method has played an important role in the assessment of psychopathology in general and child psychopathology in particular (Conners, 1979). Yet, in the survey cited above, ratings by others was the least frequently employed indirect method, being used by behavioral assessors in only 6% of the studies. Despite this infrequent use, I will attempt to document the potentially important role that ratings by others may serve in child behavioral assessment.

The types of instruments that usually fall under the heading "ratings by others" are behavioral checklists and rating scales. There is a certain amount of confusion in the literature as to whether the terms "behavioral checklists"

*The author would like to express his appreciation to Glen Davies, Rex Forehand, and Eric Mash for their comments on an earlier draft of this chapter.

and "rating scales" are synonymous or if they describe different types of ratings by others. Cone and Hawkins (1977) define a behavioral checklist as a "list of fairly specific, objectively described behaviors whose presence or absence in a learner's repertoire is rated" (p. 27). Other writers distinguish between behavioral checklists and rating scales in that the former require the informant to make a binary decision as to the presence or absence of a certain behavior or characteristic while the latter utilizes at least 3-point scales (Humphreys & Ciminero, 1979; Wilson & Prentice-Dunn, 1981). Conners and Werry (1979) offer a more traditional definition of a rating scale, which is defined as an " . . . algebraic summation, over variable periods of time and numbers of social situations, of many discrete observations by parents, teachers, or other caretakers in which an unconscious data reduction process operates to produce a global score or frequency estimate" (p. 341). According to this definition, ratings are a product of both characteristics of the child over a period of time and the rater, such as perception of the child, personality, and so on (Cairns & Green, 1979; Mash, in press).

The diversity of definitions concerning ratings by others is partly a function of historical antecedents concerning perceived theoretical differences between behavioral and traditional assessment and partly a function of the diversity of available instruments that are referred to as checklists, rating scales, or both. For purposes of this chapter, I will use the term "behavioral rating scales" in a broad sense to describe assessment instruments that are completed by adults in reference to a child's behavior or characteristics. Instruments designed specifically to assess personality factors, even when completed by adults about the child (e.g., Personality Inventory for Children), will not be discussed in this chapter. Self-report measures (in which the child is the informant about his or her own behavior), ratings provided by the child's peers, and structured interviews will be discussed in other chapters of this volume.

There are literally hundreds of behavioral rating scales for assessing children. I will first provide an overview of some of the dimensions along which these scales vary, such as the informants and the scope and structure of the scales themselves. A discussion of the most common uses of behavioral rating scales in child behavioral assessment is followed by a consideration of relevant psychometric issues such as reliability, validity, and clinical utility. Several of the better designed rating scales are then briefly described and discussed. Finally, a case study will be presented as an example of how rating scales can be employed in child behavioral assessment. Throughout the chapter, I will emphasize practical issues in the development, selection, and use of behavior rating scales.

DIMENSIONS OF BEHAVIORAL RATING SCALES

Informants

A primary dimension concerns who is to complete the rating scale. Possible informants include parents, teachers, mental health workers, and more recently, "naive" observers. Some of the behavioral rating scales were developed for use with specific informants while others may be completed by any of these respondents. A few rating scales include parallel forms for different types of informants (e.g., Conners Parent and Teacher Rating Scales: Conners, 1969, 1970).

Parents and teachers have been the most frequently utilized informants since they are usually the ones who initiate the referral process and who typically have the greatest exposure to the child's behavior (Evans & Nelson, 1977). Achenbach and Edelbrock (1978) have argued that parents are the most important single data source since they will have seen the child in a wider variety of settings and over a longer period of time than teachers or other respondents. However, teachers have the advantage of being able to compare the child's behavior with that of a much larger sample of children. It may also be that the parents' importance as a primary data source declines as the child grows older and enters school. Once the child is in school, teacher and peer ratings will assume increasing importance, and with older children, self-report and self-monitoring measures become more feasible. While there are a variety of teacher rating scales for elementary school-age children, there is a relative dearth of well-designed instruments to assess high school students (Spivack & Swift, 1973). This is particularly unfortunate since this is the population for whom teacher ratings might prove to be of most value. Given the variability of behavior across situations, parent and teacher ratings should provide useful and complementary sets of information about the child.

Many of the rating scales employed by parents and teachers have been used by mental health workers as well. Other behavioral rating scales have been developed specifically for assessing children in residential treatment centers (e.g., the Devereux Child Behavior Rating Scale: Spivack & Spotts, 1965). A recent innovation in child behavioral assessment has been to have observers trained in a behavioral coding system also provide ratings of the child and/or family members at the conclusion of the observation (Weinrott, Reid, Bauske, & Brummett, 1981). In this investigation, observers completed a 25-item behavioral rating scale (Observer Impressions Inventory) immediately after a 40–60 minute in-home observation of a family referred for treatment of child management problems. The combination of the observational data with the more subjective rating provided better prognostic information about child behavior at treatment termination than either measure alone. While this study suggests the potential utility of gathering observer impressions, the parameters of this use of behavioral rating scales await further investigation (Wein-rott et al., 1981).

Scope

The majority of behavioral rating scales used in the assessment of deviant children have focused on describing maladaptive child behaviors and characteristics. These scales typically apply to children from preschool age through adolescence. A few scales are designed for more restricted age groups such as preschool-age children (Preschool Behavior Questionnaire: Behar & Stringfield, 1974) or high school students (Hahnemann High School Behavior Rating Scale: Spivack & Swift, 1977). While most of the scales assess a wide variety of such behavioral problems, others have focused upon a single type of behavioral problem. Examples of the more general behavioral rating scales are the Behavior Problem Checklist (Quay & Peterson, 1979) and the Child Behavior Checklist (Achenbach, 1978; Achenbach & Edelbrock, 1979). There are also rating scales that are designed to assess a single type of child behavioral problem such as hyperactivity (e.g., Conners Parent and Teacher Rating Scales: Conners, 1969, 1970), conduct disorders (Eyberg Child Behavior Inventory: Eyberg, 1980), and fears (Louisville Fear Survey for Children: Miller, Barrett, Hampe, & Noble, 1972). Two rating scales for assessing children's self-control have recently been developed (Humphrey, 1982; Kendall & Wilcox, 1979).

Several behavioral rating scales have been developed that include an assessment of adaptive behaviors or competencies in the child either as part of a broad rating scale or, in a few cases, as the sole content (see Hops, 1983, for a discussion of the status of children's social competence in behavioral assessment and therapy). It has been suggested that inclusion of such items provides a more complete picture of the child and may improve the clinical utility of the instrument (Sandoval, 1981; Wilson & Prentice-Dunn, 1981). Examples of rating scales that include an assessment of positive child behaviors or characteristics are the Pittsburgh Adjustment Survey Schedules (Ross, Lacey, & Parton, 1965) and the Child Behavior Checklist. The latter is noteworthy in that it provides a more extensive assessment of social competency than do the other general rating scales.

There are two other types of assessment instruments that focus primarily on positive child behaviors or competencies. So-called "adaptive behavioral scales" have been developed as assessment instruments for use with the mentally retarded. The best known of these scales are the Vineland Social Maturity Scale (Doll, 1964) and the American Association of Mental Deficiency's Adaptive Behavior Scales (Nihira, Foster, Shellhaas, & Leland, 1969). In recent years, there has been a proliferation of this type of rating scale (see

Meyers, Nihira, & Zetlin, 1979, for a review). Many of the adaptive behavioral scales have been developed by institutions in an ad hoc fashion for their own use. Walls, Werner, Bacon, and Zane (1977) catalogued more than 100 behavioral checklists of various types, many of which were developed in this manner. Although the use of adaptive behavioral scales has been restricted almost entirely to the mentally retarded, some authors have suggested that these or similar measures be standardized with other populations such as children on inpatient psychiatric units (Matson & Beck, 1981).

The second type of assessment instrument that focuses on positive child characteristics is the reinforcement survey schedule. While some of these are self-report measures, there are instruments for children that are completed by *significant others* such as the parents (e.g., Children's Reinforcement Survey: Clement & Richard, 1976). Unfortunately, there is not a great deal of psychometric data to support the use of these instruments. In addition, there is little evidence to support a link between stated preferences as reported by a second party and the actual reinforcing properties of an event (Mash & Terdal, 1976, p. 200). However, Mash and Terdal suggest that these ratings by others can be interpreted as indicative of the informants' perceptions of what the child finds reinforcing.

Structure of the Rating Scales

Behavioral rating scales also vary with regard to certain structural aspects. First, these scales range in length from a single item (e.g, the NIMH Early Clinical Drug Evaluation Unit's (ECDEU) Clinical Global Impressions: Guy, 1976) to over 150 items (e.g., Louisville Child Behavior Checklist: Miller, 1967). Ideally, a rating scale will have a sufficient number of items to reliably assess the behaviors or factors of interest, while at the same time not including so many items as to be overly demanding for the informant. There is some evidence to suggest that behavioral rating scales with more than 50 items are necessary to increase the likelihood of the appearance of replicable "narrow-band" syndromes when the scale is factor analyzed (Achenbach & Edelbrock, 1978).

Second, prior research has indicated that rating scales with more global items are susceptible to biasing information (e.g., Shuller & McNamara, 1976), while rating scales with specific items are not, at least when the raters have also been trained in observational procedures (Siegel, Dragovich, & Marholin, 1976). It may be that training in observational procedures is the relevant factor, since Weinrott (1977) found that teachers with prior training in tracking child behavior in the classroom were able to provide more accurate global ratings than teachers who did not receive the training in observing and tracking behavior. Conners (1973) has suggested that descriptive global ratings that require a moderate level of inference are more likely to be reliable than either very specific, molecular items or very global items. This is an interesting hypothesis that warrants further investigation.

Third, most authors suggest that the provision of more than two response alternatives is likely to improve the reliability and validity of the instrument and provides the clinician with more information than does a dichotomous response (Barkley, 1981; O'Leary & Johnson, 1979). This would seem particularly relevant with respect to treatment outcome data. However, the number of response alternatives appears robust when the rating scale is used for classification purposes (Achenbach & Edelbrock, 1978). The Eyberg Child Behavior Inventory (Eyberg, 1980) uses two different formats. On the "Intensity Scale," the parent rates the frequency of the behavior on a 7-point scale, while on the "Problem Scale," the parent states whether or not the behavior is a problem (a 2-point scale). This permits a much more fine-grained analysis of the problem and may provide useful information concerning the role of parental perception of the child in the rating process (Robinson, Eyberg, & Ross, 1980).

A fourth structural dimension is the specificity of the anchors on the rating scale. There are some data to suggest that the use of behavioral descriptors as anchors, as opposed to more global indicators, reduces some of the methodological artifacts (e.g., lack of precision) that can be associated with the use of rating scales (Sandoval, 1981).

Finally, temporal factors may also vary. The time period which the informant is supposed to use as a frame of reference in making the rating ranges from a 25-minute observation (Siegel et al., 1976) to a period of 6 months or more (Achenbach, 1979). The time elapsed between the "observation" and the rating also varies. It may be that restricting the time frame to a relatively brief period that has just occurred would result in more objective ratings than those which cover a longer period of time farther in the past.

USES OF BEHAVIORAL RATING SCALES

Behavioral rating scales have been utilized primarily in large-scale population research studies (usually for epidemiological and/or classification purposes) and in clinical settings (to provide idiographic information about a child or group of children). Each of these two major categories of use will be described below.

Epidemiology and Classification

Epidemiology is the populationwide study of problems as they occur in groups of people and is intimately linked to classifying childhood behavioral disorders (Graham, 1979). Classification systems for child behavioral disorders have either been clinically derived (e.g., DSM-III: American Psychiatric Association, 1980) or developed via multivariate statistical approaches (see Achenbach & Edelbrock, 1978; Quay, 1979, for reviews). The multivariate studies have made extensive use of behavioral rating scales and have been consistent in identifying two "broad-band" syndromes of child behavioral disorders: *Undercontrolled,* which includes behaviors such as aggression, noncompliance, and hyperactivity; and *Overcontrolled,* in which the child is overly shy, anxious, and withdrawn (Achenbach & Edelbrock, 1978). These studies have also identified various replicable "narrow-band" syndromes such as schizoid, aggressive, delinquent, socially withdrawn, etc. Employing teachers as informants has been less useful in developing the narrow-band syndromes, perhaps, because the teacher rating scales tend to have fewer items than those completed by other informants and because teachers may have less opportunity to observe certain types of problems (Achenbach & Edelbrock, 1978). A potential advance has been the development of methods for identifying patterns of reported problems that characterize groups of children (i.e., profile types: Edelbrock & Achenbach, 1980).

One of the major methodological problems with the multivariate classification studies, thus far, has been a failure to systematically evaluate important subject parameters such as sex, age, race, and clinical status of the child; socioeconomic status of the family; or characteristics of the raters (Achenbach & Edelbrock, 1978). When such studies have been carried out (e.g., Achenbach & Edelbrock, 1981; Campbell & Steinert, 1978; Touliatos & Lindholm, 1975), important differences among these subgroups emerge. Skinner (1981) has recently proposed a model for classification research that increases the likelihood that a more systematic evaluation of relevant parameters will occur.

Clinical Uses

While classification research certainly has direct clinical implications, in this section more idiographic uses of behavioral rating scales in child behavioral assessment will be discussed. Wilson and Prentice-Dunn (1981) described an "hourglass" model of assessment in which the assessment proceeds from a broad focus (e.g., screening) to more narrow ones (e.g., pinpointing target behaviors) and then widens again (e.g., follow-up assessment). The appropriateness of using behavioral rating scales varies according to the type of rating scale and the stage of the assessment process (Cone & Hawkins, 1977; Wilson & Prentice-Dunn, 1981). For purposes of this chapter, I will discuss the use of behavioral rating scales for screening, diagnosis, treatment selection, and treatment evaluation. Behavioral rating scales have not been especially useful for pinpointing target behaviors or in monitoring progress from session to session. Instead, more "narrow-band, high-fidelity" measures (Cone & Hawkins, 1977) such as behavioral observation have proven to be more useful. It may be that behavioral rating scales that utilize a very brief time sample (e.g., 1 hour) might be of some use in these situations. As noted earlier, preliminary evidence suggests that ratings of short time periods can be quite accurate and can enhance predictive validity (Siegel et al., 1976; Weinrott et al., 1981).

There seems to be consensus that behavioral rating scales are a valuable assessment tool for such "broad-band, low-fidelity" purposes as screening (e.g., Cone & Hawkins, 1977). Since screening involves the assessment of a large number of children, an assessment instrument should be easily administered and should cover a wide variety of potential problem behaviors. Most behavioral rating scales have no difficulty meeting these criteria. When employed as screening instruments, rating scales alert the clinician to areas where more narrow-band, high-fidelity assessment is warranted. Thus, the more broadly based general behavioral rating scales are most likely to be used for screening. By employing a general behavioral rating scale that has also been well validated with respect to more narrow-band syndromes (e.g., the Child Behavior Checklist), it may also be possible to draw some tentative diagnostic conclusions. For example, the Teacher's Report Form of the Child Behavior Checklist has been shown to be able to reliably discriminate boys diagnosed as *Attention Deficit Disorder with Hyperactivity* from boys diagnosed as *Attention Deficit Disorder without Hyperactivity* (Edelbrock, Costello, & Kessler, 1983).

One area where behavioral rating scales have the potential to be of considerable utility is with respect to treatment selection (i.e., assigning particular treatments to children on the basis of information gathered in the assessment). Although the empirical basis of using rating scales for this purpose is generally lacking (Evans & Nelson, 1977; Wilson & Prentice-Dunn, 1981), one example of how behavioral rating scales might be used for treatment selection is the suggestion that a high anxiety factor score on the Conners Parent or Teacher Rating Scales may contraindicate the treatment of hyperactivity by stimulant medication (Barkley, 1981).

There are other ways in which information from behavioral rating scales could be utilized for treatment selection. By rating the child in different settings, data regarding the situational specificity of the child's behavior may be obtained. When behavioral rating scales are completed by *different* informants in the *same* setting (e.g., mother and father) and compared to more direct measures of the child's behavior in that setting (e.g., home observations), then several treatment implications may be revealed. If the parents rate the child differently on one or more dimensions, this may suggest that the child adjusts his behavior depending upon which parent he or she is with, and/or that one of the parents perceives the child inaccurately. By comparing these ratings to home observation data of the child with each parent, the clinician may be able to determine whether the problem lies with the child's behavior or with the parent's faulty perception of that behavior.

Behavioral rating scales are frequently utilized as outcome measures. They are a "mainstay" of drug evaluation studies (Conners & Werry, 1979, p. 342), and a number of them have been incorporated into the ECDEU standard package of outcome measures. Behavioral rating scales have also been employed as outcome measures in child behavioral therapy. In a review of studies that employed multiple outcome measures to assess the effectiveness of behavioral parent training for problem children, Atkeson and Forehand (1978) reported that 19 of 24 studies employed a parent-completed behavioral rating scale as one of the outcome measures. In a subsequent investigation that utilized a fine-grained analysis of data gathered via observation and parent-completed rating scales, Forehand, Griest, and Wells (1979) found that while there were significant correlations *within* each of the measurement categories of observation and rating scales, there were no significant relationships *across* the categories. This suggests that parent-completed behavioral rating scales may be assessing independent aspects of family functioning from those assessed by various observational methods.

Even if behavioral rating scales fail to reflect the child's actual behavior (and behavioral changes), the parent's or teacher's perception of the child is an important source of social validational data (Kazdin, 1977), and may be an important treatment goal in its own right. If the significant adult still perceives the child as deviant, despite objective evidence to the contrary, then referrals may reoccur. Behavioral rating scales are a primary source of such perceptual data (Mash, in press; Mash & Terdal, 1981). A recent investigation of a parent training program by Forehand, Wells, and Griest (1980) illustrates how behavioral rating scales can be utilized to assess social validity. Prior to treatment, mothers of clinic-referred children perceived their children as less well adjusted than did mothers of a comparison group of "normal" children. At the end of treatment, mothers of the clinic-referred children had a more positive perception of their children than prior to treatment and by a 2-month follow-up, maternal ratings of child adjustment were the same for the two groups.

Some behavioral clinicians working with children have begun to examine parental perceptual processes more directly. As noted earlier, Robinson et al. (1980) have suggested that comparisons of the Problem and Intensity scores on the Eyberg Child Behavior Inventory may represent a useful index of different types of parental perceptions of the child. Forehand and his colleagues have examined the role of maternal distress in parental perceptions of the child and have found that for clinic-referred conduct disorder children, maternal personal distress (anxiety, depression) is a more powerful predictor of the mother's rating of the child than is the child's behavior per se (see Forehand,

Furey, & McMahon, in press, for a review). Other investigators have employed a signal-detection paradigm in the laboratory to assess parental perception of the child (Holleran, Littman, Freund, & Schmaling, 1982).

PSYCHOMETRIC CONSIDERATIONS

Adequate reliability, validity, and clinical utility are the hallmarks of a good assessment instrument (O'Leary & Johnson, 1979). The role and perceived value of these psychometric considerations in behavioral assessment has been a matter of some debate. While early behavioral assessors eschewed psychometrics, in the past few years several authors have argued for the adaptation of psychometric concepts to behavioral assessment (e.g., Cone, 1977; Furman & Drabman, 1981; but, see Cone, 1981, for an alternate view). In this section, I will not review psychometric theory or debate the relative advantages and disadvantages of psychometrics to behavioral assessment. Instead, I will attempt to delineate some of the relevant issues as they relate to the use of rating scales in child behavioral assessment. Given the tremendous diversity of rating scales that is available and the variety of purposes for which they are intended, it should be made clear from the outset that questions of reliability, validity, and clinical utility must be asked for each instrument and for each purpose to which it is applied. For example, while the reliability and validity of various behavioral rating scales have been well documented for purposes of classification (Achenbach & Edelbrock, 1978), fewer data are available pertaining to more idiographic uses of these instruments. The adaptation of various psychometric concepts to situations without individual clients awaits the development of adequate analytical methods (Nelson, 1981).

The types of reliability that are most relevant to behavioral rating scales are internal consistency, test-retest, and interrater. The relevance of internal consistency to behavioral rating scales varies as a function of whether the rating scale is supposed to measure some unitary factor or set of factors or whether the scale is comprised of a wide variety of behaviors or characteristics that may be mutually exclusive (Nay, 1979). In the former case, high internal consistency is required, while in the latter case, high internal consistency would be neither necessary nor expected.

Given the variability of behavior across situations, test-retest reliability may be confounded for behavioral rating scales that focus on very specific behaviors versus those scales that assess more global characteristics. In general, the shorter the interval between assessments, the higher the reliability (Achenbach & Edelbrock, 1978). One way to improve test-retest reliability is by using descriptors that delimit and specify the time frame for which the rating is to occur (the preceding 30-minute observation, the past month, etc.) (Wilson & Prentice-Dunn, 1981). While the test-retest reliability of many behavioral rating scales is adequate, it is necessary to also assess whether or not the absolute value of the rating changes over time (Glow, Glow, & Rump, 1982). Several investigators have noted a tendency for raters to report fewer behavioral problems on subsequent administration of many of the rating scales (e.g., Achenbach & Edelbrock, 1978). This has usually been described as a practice effect, although recent investigations suggest that statistical regression (Milich, Roberts, Loney, & Caputo, 1980) or reactivity (Glow et al., 1982) is a more accurate explanation. When rating scales are employed in treatment outcome research, it is important to also obtain the ratings on an untreated control group to assess whether decrements in behavioral problem scores from pretreatment to posttreatment reflect the effects of the intervention or are a result of one or more of these biases.

Interrater reliability may also be confounded by the situational specificity of behavior when raters have contact with the child in different contexts (parent versus teacher, mother versus father). However, the clinical significance of such differences has been pointed out earlier. A recent study by Jacob, Grounds, and Haley (1982) illustrates the influence of various factors on interrater reliability between parents. In this case, the Behavior Problem Checklist was employed. Overall parent agreement was found to be at moderate levels. However, it was substantially higher between parents of non-clinic-referred children than between parents of clinic-referred children. Agreement was also higher on the *Conduct Problem* factor than on the *Personality Problem* factor. Jacob et al. hypothesized that this was likely due to the more global nature of the items on the *Personality Problem* factor compared to the more specific behaviorally based items on the *Conduct Problem* factor. Finally, interrater agreement for both samples was substantially lower when reliability was calculated with respect to individual items, as opposed to the total score.

There are several types of validity relevant to behavioral assessment. Content validity has been cited as essential in the construction of a behavioral assessment instrument, whether on a nomothetic or an idiographic level (Linehan, 1980). Criterion-related validity encompasses concurrent validity (in which the instrument and criterion are administered at the same time) and predictive validity (in which the criterion measure is administered at a later point in time). A practical aspect of predictive validity is whether data obtained from a behavioral rating scale can predict treatment outcome (Ciminero & Drabman, 1977). As noted earlier, there are few data concerning this issue. It is important to note that when criterion-related validity studies are carried out, investigators must be careful to control for method of assessment confounds (i.e., failure to find a relationship between the assessment device and the criterion may be a function of differences in content, method, or interactions between content and method) (Cone, 1979). Cone has proposed a multicontent-multimethod-multibehavior matrix to sort out these factors.

In addition to adequate reliability and validity, a behavioral rating scale should possess clinical utility. The clinical utility of behavioral rating scales is enhanced when they are easy to administer, require relatively little time on the part of the informant or the clinician, can be completed outside the treatment session, and are sensitive to treatment effects. These considerations are especially important to clinicians in private practice or in settings with very heavy clinical case loads. These aspects of behavioral rating scales are also likely to facilitate the involvement of practitioners in clinical outcome research (Emmelkamp, 1981; Nelson, 1981).

What else can be done to enhance the clinical utility of behavioral rating scales? Clinicians must be careful to investigate the pertinent literature on an instrument prior to its adoption in a clinical setting, to determine whether it is appropriate for use with the population of interest. Relevant population variables include age, sex, and race of the child; nature of informants; and clinical versus nonclinical status of children in the standardization samples. Mash and Terdal (1981) have suggested that clinical utility may be enhanced by an increased focus on the situational specificity of behavioral rating scales. Other suggestions include the provision of more than two response choices, a rating scale of moderate length, and the inclusion of positive child behaviors and competencies.

One potential method of enhancing clinical utility is the development of "individualized behavior rating scales" (Finch, Deardorff, & Montgomery, 1974; O'Leary & Johnson, 1979). Detailed descriptions of the child's behavior are gathered from a variety of sources (significant others, the child, case notes, direct observation), grouped into specific categories, and then items within each category are ranked according to some dimension (intensity, severity, etc.) and assigned numerical ratings. Potential advantages of these individualized scales are that they employ the exact language of the raters, they are relatively easy to develop, and the descriptors on the scale are specifically designed to apply to that individual (Finch et al., 1974). To date, this approach has not been extensively utilized in behavioral assessment but warrants more systematic investigation.

While behavioral rating scales appear to have some clinical utility, there are also several potential disadvantages to their use. First, there are a number of factors that may affect the reliability and validity, and therefore the clinical utility, of these instruments. Wiggins (1973, p. 313) presents several sources of error characteristic of rating scales in general (e.g., halo effects, leniency error, proximity error). Second, a further complication occurs when the informant is asked to make these ratings on the basis of retrospective events. Third, social desirability may also be a factor in how informants respond to these behavioral rating scales. The socially desirable response is obvious in most of the rating scales and may increase reactivity on the part of the raters (Humphreys & Ciminero, 1979). Furthermore, the degree of social desirability most likely varies among particular items on a behavioral rating scale and/or among different informants (Haynes, 1978; Robinson & Anderson, 1981). Fourth, situational factors may also play a role. For example, parents may rate their child as more deviant at the initial assessment to access treatment resources and rate their child as less deviant at treatment termination to please the therapist. Alternatively, after completing a behavioral rating scale during baseline assessment, the informant may realize that the child is not nearly as deviant as he or she imagined and decide that treatment is not necessary. While this type of reactivity may be somewhat less likely to occur than with more direct assessment methods such as self-monitoring, it is worthy of consideration.

REVIEW OF SELECTED BEHAVIORAL RATING SCALES

Several behavioral rating scales that appear to offer the greatest utility to child behavioral assessment will be briefly described and reviewed in this section. These include two of the more comprehensive behavioral rating scales: the Behavior Problem Checklist (Quay & Peterson, 1979) and the Child Behavior Checklist (Achenbach, 1978; Achenbach & Edelbrock, 1979). Some of the rating scales that are utilized for more circumscribed problems will also be described: the Conners Teacher and Parent Rating Scales (Conners, 1969; 1970) for hyperactivity, and the Eyberg Child Behavior Inventory (Eyberg, 1980) for conduct disorders. There are several reviews that can be consulted for information concerning other behavioral rating scales for children (Humphreys & Ciminero, 1979; Spivack & Swift, 1973; Walls et al., 1977).

The Behavior Problem Checklist consists of 55 items describing various problem behavioral "traits" that are rated on a 3-point scale. The instrument is usually completed by parents or teachers. The items range from very specific behaviors (e.g., steals, disobedient) to more global personality characteristics (e.g., lack of self-confidence) (Spivack & Swift, 1973). The rating scale was originally developed for school-age children, but the original scale or adaptations have been employed with various populations (e.g., preschool children: O'Donnell & Van Tuinan, 1979; institutionalized delinquents: Kelley, 1981; and visually impaired children: Schnittjer & Hirshoren, 1981). Various factor analyses with these different populations have yielded two very robust dimensions (*Conduct Problem, Personality Problem*) as well as two other dimensions (*Inadequacy-Immaturity, Socialized Delinquency*). Quay (1977) has recently summarized the large body of research concerning the reliability and validity of the Behavior Problem Checklist. Adequate reliability and validity coefficients have been obtained with either parents or teachers as informants. As noted earlier, interparent agreement has been shown to be higher in nondistressed than distressed samples and for the *Conduct Problem* items than the *Personality Problem* items (Jacob et al., 1982).

In a clinical setting, the Behavior Problem Checklist can be used as a general screening device, to identify dimensions of deviant behavior, and as a measure of treatment outcome (e.g., Oltmanns, Broderick, & O'Leary, 1977). Normative data in the school setting (e.g., Touliatos & Lindholm, 1975) permit comparisons between an individual child and deviant and normal groups. However, as noted by these authors, it is preferable to use local norms (e.g., from a particular classroom, school, or teacher) when assessing a child in this manner. One major limitation of the Behavior Problem Checklist is that it fails to assess positive behaviors or competencies.

The Child Behavior Checklist (CBCL) is designed for use with children between the ages of 4 and 16. There eventually will be parallel forms of the CBCL for parents, teachers, and observers. To date, only the parent form has been completely standardized, although the Teacher's Report Form of the CBCL and the teacher version of the Child Behavior Profile have now been standardized for boys aged 6–11 (Edelbrock & Achenbach, 1983). In addition, preliminary investigations have been completed with the observer version (Reed & Edelbrock, 1983).

The parent form of the CBCL includes both social competency and behavioral problem scales, and takes approximately 15 minutes to complete. The CBCL scores are summarized on the Child Behavior Profile, which indicates the child's standing on various narrow- and broad-band syndromes. The Child Behavior Profile has separate norms for boys and girls at three age levels (4–5, 6–11, 12–16). Scales from the behavioral problem items representing narrow-band syndromes were derived from separate factor analyses for each age group and sex, so the scales vary somewhat. However, the broad-band syndromes have been found in each of the six groups. The social competency scales were derived in an a priori manner, and include items related to various activities, social relationships, and success in school. A preliminary typology of Child Behavior Profile patterns has been developed via cluster analysis (Edelbrock & Achenbach, 1980) and potentially represents an important advance in the use of behavioral rating scales. Achenbach has presented data that indicate the CBCL has adequate reliability and effectively discriminates clinic-referred from non-clinic-referred children (e.g., Achenbach & Edelbrock, 1981). The Child Behavior Profile is currently being revised to extend the *T* scores to 100, and there are minor content changes on the behavioral problem scales for girls aged 4–5 (Achenbach, personal communication).

The behavioral problem items on the Teacher's Report Form of the CBCL were adapted from the parent version of the CBCL, with several items being replaced by ones that were more appropriate to classroom situations. The social competency items from the parent version have been replaced by items that assess the child's school performance and adaptive functioning. The teacher version of the Child Behavior Profile consists of eight behavioral problem scales derived from factor analysis (two of which form an *Internalizing* grouping and three of which form an *Externalizing* grouping similar to those reported for the parent version) as well as six scale scores related to school performance and adaptive functioning. While there is significant overlap of the behavioral problem scales on the parent and teacher versions, there is not a one-to-one correspondence between the scales derived from the parent and teacher forms. Scores on both the narrow- and broad-band behavioral problem scale have correlated with classroom observational measures (Edelbrock & Reed, 1983).

The CBCL offers a number of compelling advantages. First, it represents the culmination of extensive empirical analyses of data gathered from a variety of informants concerning both child behavioral problems and competencies. Second, normative data are provided for children of different ages and sexes, and its psychometric qualities appear to be more than adequate (Achenbach & Edelbrock, 1981). Third the development of equivalent forms for different informants will hopefully maximize the amount of information that can be gathered about the child and permit comparisons across informants and situations. Fourth, the provision of both broad-band and narrow-band syndromes in the Child Behavior Profile means that the CBCL can be used for both general and more specific purposes, including classification, screening, diagnosis, and treatment evaluation.

A major disadvantage of the CBCL is that, because it is a new instrument, the development and refinement of the various forms is ongoing. Although the CBCL has been available for only a short while, it has come into widespread use. As its empirical base becomes even more substantial, the CBCL will perhaps become a standard assessment instrument in child clinical settings.

A third set of behavioral rating scales in wide use are those developed by Conners (1969, 1970, 1973) to identify hyperactive children and evaluate the effects of pharmacological interventions with this population. There are separate rating scales for teachers and parents, both of which have been revised recently (Goyette, Conners, & Ulrich, 1978).

The original form of the Conners Teacher Rating Scale (CTRS) consists of 39 items which are rated on a 4-point scale. Earlier factor analyses with hyperactive (Conners, 1969) and normal (Werry, Sprague, & Cohen, 1975) children revealed five factors, although a recent factor analysis of the CTRS that employed an extremely large stratified random sample (9,583 school-age children) has resulted in a revised six-factor structure (Trites, Blouin, & Laprade, 1982). Internal consistency coefficients for each factor are moderate to high, and adequate test-retest and interrater reliability have also been reported (Trites, Dugas, Lynch, & Ferguson, 1979). Norms for the various factor scores for boys and girls aged 4–12 have been developed. Several recent investigators have demonstrated that the CTRS may be sensitive to both the attentional and activity components of hyperactivity (Brown & Wynne, 1982; King & Young, 1982; Roberts, Milich, Loney, & Caputo, 1981).

The original form of the Conners Parent Rating Scale (CPRS) consisted of 93 items rated on a 4-point scale. A recent reanalysis of normative data on this rating scale indicated eight factors (Conners & Blouin, 1980). The Conners Abbreviated Parent-Teacher Questionnaire (CAPTQ) or Hyperkinesis Index (Conners, 1973) consists of 10 items common to both the CTRS and CPRS and is designed to provide a very brief measure of hyperactivity per se. Also, ratings by parents and teachers can be compared directly since they respond to the same items. Because of its sensitivity to drug changes and brevity, the CAPTQ is reported to be useful for dosage titration in the early stages of pharmacotherapy and for frequent follow-up assessments (Conners, 1973, 1979).

The revised versions of these behavioral rating scales have been shortened and slightly reworded (Goyette et al., 1978). The CTRS now consists of 28 items that comprise three of the five factors from the original version: *Conduct Problems, Hyperactivity,* and *Inattentive-Passive.* The revised CPRS consists of 48 items that comprise five of the eight original factors: *Conduct Problem, Learning Problem, Psychosomatic, Impulsive-Hyperactive,* and *Anxiety.* The 10-item CAPTQ has been retained in the revised versions of these scales, with slight rewording of some of the items. Adequate interrater reliability between mothers and fathers has been demonstrated for each of the factors on the CPRS and for the CAPTQ. As might be expected, correlations between parents and teachers on common factors of the two rating scales were lower. Parents tended to rate their children as more deviant than did the teachers. Norms for children of both sexes aged 3–17 on the various factors of each rating scale have been reported (Goyette et al., 1978).

The various Conners rating scales have been shown to reliably discriminate hyperative from nonhyperactive children (e.g., Werry et al., 1975) and to be sensitive to various drug (Conners & Werry, 1979) or behavioral treatment effects (O'Leary & Pelham, 1978) on such children. In addition, these scales have recently been shown to be able to discriminate children labeled as depressed from nondepressed children (Leon, Kendall, & Garber, 1980).

The Eyberg Child Behavior Inventory (ECBI) is another example of a behavioral rating scale that has been designed to assess a limited type of child behavioral problem; in this case, conduct disorders. The ECBI is composed of 36 items that describe specific behaviors and is completed by parents. As noted earlier, each item is rated on both the frequency of occurrence (*Intensity* score) and identification as a problem (*Problem* score). The ECBI is intended for use with children from ages 2 to 16. Adequate test-retest reliability and internal consistency have been reported (Robinson et al., 1980). Scores on both dimensions of the ECBI (Eyberg & Ross, 1978) and on individual items (Robinson et al., 1980) have been shown to discriminate conduct-disorder children from other clinic-referred children and from normal children. The ECBI has been found to correlate significantly with various clinic-based observational coding systems, but only modestly with a maternal-report measure of child temperament (Robinson & Eyberg, 1981; Webster-Stratton & Eyberg, 1982). Responses on the ECBI have been shown to be independent of social desirability factors (Robinson & Anderson, 1981). The ECBI is also sensitive to behavioral treatment effects (Eyberg & Robinson, 1982; Eyberg & Ross, 1978). Normative data for children aged 2–12 have been presented (Robinson et al., 1980), and tentative cutting points for treatment selection have been suggested (Eyberg & Ross, 1978). The ECBI shows a great deal of promise as a useful rating scale in clinical settings, a screening instrument, and a treatment outcome measure.

CASE STUDY

Gene is a 6-year, 8-month-old boy referred to a psychology clinic by his pediatrician. He was referred because of parental concern about various behavioral problems that had been occurring at home and at school. His mother, Mrs. F., stated that Gene's excessive noncompliance, temper tantrums, destructiveness, and demands for attention were problematic. Mrs. F. was also concerned about reports from Gene's teacher describing his disruptive behavior and his excessive demands for attention in the classroom. The teacher had recommended to Mrs. F. that Gene be evaluated for hyperactivity. An intellectual assessment conducted by the school psychologist indicated that Gene is functioning in the high-average range of intellectual ability, with particular strengths in the verbal area. The behavioral assessment consisted of several types of measures including behavioral rating scales, interviews, and direct observation. However, the use of behavioral rating scales will be the focus of this discussion. See table 5.1 for a summary of the behavioral rating scales employed in this case example.

In order to get a general idea as to whether intervention was appropriate, and to pinpoint more specific areas to be assessed, Mr. and Mrs. F. each were asked to complete the parent version of the Child Behavior Checklist (CBCL) prior to the first session at the clinic. The importance of completing the CBCL independently was emphasized. When the parents' CBCL responses were scored on the Child Behavior Profile for Boys Aged 6–11, the following was revealed. On the behavioral problem scales, both parents endorsed a large number of items that load on the broad-band *Externalizing* syndrome, and especially items that loaded on the narrow-band *Aggressive* syndrome. The parents' ratings were more than two standard deviations above the mean for 6- to 11-year-old boys. Ratings of the broad-band *Internalizing* syndrome and the narrow-band syndromes that comprise it were within normal limits, as

Table 5.1. Case Study — Behavioral Rating Scales.

	Time of Assessment			
RATING SCALE	BASELINE	POST-HOME INTER-VENTION	POST-SCHOOL INTER-VENTION	6-MONTH FOLLOW-UP
Parent-Completed Child Behavior Checklist	D[a]	N[b]	N	N
Eyberg Child Behavior Inventory	D	N	N	N
Conners Abbreviated Parent-Teacher Questionnaire	N	Not administered		
Teacher-Completed Child Behavior Checklist	D	D	N	N
Conners Abbreviated Parent-Teacher Questionnaire	N	Not administered		

[a]Deviant — scores obtained on the behavioral rating scale are above the cut-off points for appropriate behavior determined by normative data.
[b]Normal — scores obtained on the behavioral rating scale are within the appropriate range according to normative data.

were ratings on the *Social Withdrawal* syndrome. Both parents rated Gene in a reasonably similar manner, although Mrs. F. tended to endorse more of the items on the behavioral problem scales than did Mr. F. The scores on the social competency scales indicated that both parents saw Gene as comparable to other 6- to 11-year-old boys with regard to his participation in activities, social interactions, and school performance.

On the basis of the parental ratings on the CBCL, it was decided to have the parents also complete the Eyberg Child Behavior Inventory (ECBI), which focuses on conduct disorders. On the ECBI, the parents rated Gene well above the recommended cut-off points (Eyberg & Ross, 1978) on both the *Problem* and *Intensity* scores. Since the teacher had raised the issue of hyperactivity, the revised version of the Conners Abbreviated Parent-Teacher Questionnaire (CAPTQ) was also given as an additional screening measure for this behavioral disorder (both parents had rated Gene within normal limits on this syndrome on the CBCL). Parental ratings on the CAPTQ were below the cut-off point for hyperactivity on this scale.

With the parents' permission, Gene's teacher was contacted, and she agreed to complete the Teacher Report Form of the CBCL and the CAPTQ. A time was also scheduled for the clinician to meet with the teacher at the school and to observe Gene in the classroom. On the CBCL, the items loading on the

Externalizing syndrome of the teacher version of the Child Behavior Profile and the narrow-band syndromes of *Inattentive* and *Aggressive* were endorsed most frequently. Compared to other 6- to 11-year-old boys, Gene was clearly perceived as deviant on these dimensions, although there was no evidence of an attention deficit disorder, with or without hyperactivity. The teacher rated Gene below the normal range on the various *Adaptive Functioning* scales. The ratings on the CAPTQ were similar to the parents' ratings on this measure.

In this particular case, the ratings of the child's behavior were consistent across informants (mother, father, and teacher) and settings (home, school). Based on data from both the general and more specific rating scales, the clinician conducted behavioral interviews with the parents and teacher to delineate the antecedent and consequent events occurring in conjunction with Gene's inappropriate behavior at home and at school. Behavioral observations in the clinic and in the classroom, parent monitoring of child behaviors at home, and parental report measures of personal and marital adjustment (e.g., Beck Depression Inventory, Dyadic Adjustment Scale) extended the data base on which the clinician based his treatment recommendations. Because the data from the observations and rating scales were similar, and the measures of personal adjustment and marital satisfaction were generally in the normal range, the likelihood that the parental concerns were simply the result of parental perceptual biases or distortions was deemed unlikely.

Because of the relatively greater severity of behavioral problems at home, it was decided to implement treatment in that setting first. The parents participated in a 6-week behavioral management program specifically designed to assist them in dealing with their child's noncompliance and other conduct disorder behaviors (Forehand & McMahon, 1981). At the conclusion of this phase of treatment, the CBCL and the ECBI were readministered to the parents to assess possible treatment gains. (Since the CAPTQ had been utilized only as a screening measure of hyperactivity, it was not readministered.) Results for both scales indicated that Gene's behavior was now viewed within the normal range compared to other children his age. By examining the other behavioral problem scales of the CBCL, the clinician assessed whether other aspects of Gene's behavior had worsened over the course of treatment. In this case, there was no evidence of such contrast effects.

The Teacher Report Form of the CBCL was also readministered at this time. Previous research has indicated that, while there is no systematic effect of behavioral treatment of home-based problems on behavioral problems in the classroom, for any individual child there may be either positive or negative transfer (McMahon & Davies, 1980). The CBCL indicated that Gene's teacher had not noted any improvement or deterioration in his behavior. At this point, consultation in behavioral management strategies for dealing with Gene's classroom behavior was conducted with the teacher over the next several weeks. Following the completion of the classroom intervention, both the teacher and parents again completed the rating scales. At this point, Gene's behavior was perceived by both his teacher and parents as within the normal range. Observations in the clinic and home corroborated this conclusion, and the case was closed. Completion of the CBCL and ECBI by the parents and the CBCL by the teacher 6 months following the conclusion of treatment, as well as intermittent contact with the family during this period, indicated that Gene's improved behavior has generally maintained in both the home and classroom.

SUMMARY

In this chapter, I have provided an overview of various characteristics of behavioral rating scales and addressed several issues associated with their use in child behavioral assessment. There are literally hundreds of such behavioral rating scales, and they vary tremendously on a large number of dimensions. These scales are most often completed by parents and teachers because of the critical role these individuals play in the referral process and their familiarity with the child. The scales can also be completed by mental health workers or naive observers. One-to-one correspondence of ratings across informants rarely occurs, nor is it expected, because of the unique perceptual framework each informant incorporates into the rating as well as the situationally specific nature of child behavior. Data from each source are likely to be of use in a comprehensive behavioral assessment.

Most behavioral rating scales focus on maladaptive child behaviors or characteristics, although the importance of also assessing adaptive behaviors and competencies has been recognized. Some of the rating scales are very general and cover a number of types of child behavioral disorders, while others focus on a single disorder (e.g., fears). The rating scales also differ with respect to structural dimensions, such as the number of items and degree of specificity of the items in the rating scale, the number of response alternatives, the specificity of the anchors on the rating scale, and the time period to be used as a frame of reference in rating the child.

Unfortunately, empirically based guidelines to assist child behavioral therapists in making decisions regarding the type of rating scale that is most appropriate are lacking. Two guidelines that can be of some assistance in this regard concern the intended use of the rating scale and its clinical utility. Behavioral rating scales have been used extensively in the classification of child behavioral disorders. On a more idiographic clinical level they have been used for screening and diagnosis, for the evaluation of treatment outcome, and to a lesser extent, for treatment selection. Different behavioral rating scales may be appropriate for some, but not all, of these functions. The clinical utility of behavioral rating scales is partly dependent on the reliability and validity of the instrument. Some of the relative advantages and disadvantages of behavioral rating scales have been discussed, and suggestions for enhancing clinical utility provided. Finally, a selective review of a few of the more useful behavioral rating scales and an illustration of their use indicated the necessity of assessing the relative merits of a particular rating scale for a particular purpose with a particular population.

A tremendous diversity of behavioral rating scales exists. If they are to be developed and utilized to their fullest potential in child behavioral assessment, clinicians and researchers must employ one or a few of the well-validated measures so that an adequate data base for these instruments can be built. The proliferation of behavioral rating scales with nothing more than face validity only perpetuates the use of poorly constructed instruments with minimal validity or clinical utility. Research is needed to empirically validate particular rating scales with different populations and for various purposes as well as to compare different types of rating scales used for the same purpose (e.g., Roberts et al., 1981).

In concluding this chapter, I would like to make several observations concerning the use of behavioral rating scales in a clinical setting. A recommended strategy is to have the person who has referred the child for treatment (e.g., parent, teacher) complete one of the more general behavioral rating scales early in the assessment process. This allows the clinician to screen inappropriate referrals and to structure a more detailed behavioral interview. Rating scales that can be completed by different informants may facilitate comparisons across informants (and prevent informant-rating scale confounds). Given the situational specificity of child behavior and the potential biases inherent in rating scales, multiple informants should be utilized whenever feasible.

Depending upon the referral problem (data derived from the general rating scale and/or data gathered through interview and observation) the clinician might decide to employ a more specific rating scale as well (e.g., a scale for hyperactivity, conduct disorder, fears, etc.). These same measures could then be readministered at treatment termination and at follow-up intervals as one facet of treatment-outcome evaluation. In some cases, these behavioral rating scales might be helpful in the selection of appropriate treatment procedures. The further development of profile types (e.g., from Achenbach's CBCL and Child Behavior Profile) will perhaps increase the utility of behavioral rating scales for treatment selection. Finally, it is important to note the role of rater characteristics such as perception of the child in the rating process (Cairns & Green, 1979). For example, while the CBCL may be employed as a relatively objective measure of child behavioral problems, it can also be interpreted as a measure of the rater's perceptions of the child's adjustment. In the latter case, the instrument has become an adult self-report measure. Adult perception of the child's behavior is a legitimate assessment and intervention target, and behavioral rating scales seem to be the best approach for obtaining such information.

Ratings of the child by significant others is a very important source of data in the assessment process. The clinical utility of this method can be enhanced greatly through more careful development of the behavioral rating scales, extensive evaluation of a few of these instruments for a variety of uses and with different populations, and a recognition of the strengths and weaknesses of using significant adults to rate various child behaviors or characteristics.

REFERENCES

Achenbach, T. M. The Child Behavior Profile: I. Boys aged 6–11. *Journal of Consulting and Clinical Psychology,* 1978, *46,* 478–488.

Achenbach, T. M. The Child Behavior Profile: An empirically based system for assessing children's behavioral problems and competencies. *International Journal of Mental Health,* 1979, *7,* 24–42.

Achenbach, T. M., & Edelbrock, C. S. The classification of child psychopathology: A review and analysis of empirical efforts. *Psychological Bulletin,* 1978, *85,* 1275–1301.

Achenbach, T. M., & Edelbrock, C. S. The Child Behavior Profile: II. Boys aged 12–16 and girls aged 6–11 and 12–16. *Journal of Consulting and Clinical Psychology,* 1979, *47,* 223–233.

Achenbach, T. M., & Edelbrock, C. S. Behavioral problems and competencies reported by parents of normal and disturbed children aged four through sixteen. *Monographs of the Society for Research in Child Development,* 1981, *46* (1, Serial No. 188).

American Psychiatric Association. *Diagnostic and statistical manual* (3rd ed.). Washington, DC: American Psychiatric Association, 1980.

Atkeson, B. M., & Forehand, R. Parent behavioral training for problem children: An examination of studies using multiple outcome measures. *Journal of Abnormal Child Psychology,* 1978, *6,* 449–460.

Barkley, R. A. *Hyperactive children: A handbook for diagnosis and treatment.* New York: Guilford Press, 1981.

Behar, L. B., & Stringfield, S. A behavior rating scale for the preschool child. *Developmental Psychology,* 1974, *10,* 601–610.

Bornstein, P. H., Bridgewater, C. A., Hickey, J. S., & Sweeney, T. M. Characteristics and trends in behavioral assessment: An archival analysis. *Behavioral Assessment,* 1980, *2,* 125–133.

Brown, R. T., & Wynne, M. E. Correlates of teacher ratings, sustained attention, and impulsivity in hyperactive and normal boys. *Journal of Clinical Child Psychology,* 1982, *11,* 262–267.

Cairns, R. B., & Green, J. A. How to assess personality and social patterns: Observations or ratings? In R. B. Cairns (Ed.), *The analysis of social interactions: Methods, issues, and illustrations.* Hillsdale, NJ: Lawrence Erlbaum Associates, 1979.

Campbell, S. B., & Steinert, Y. Comparisons of rating scales of child psychopathology in clinic and nonclinic samples. *Journal of Consulting and Clinical Psychology,* 1978, *46,* 358–359.

Ciminero, A. R., & Drabman, R. S. Current developments in the behavioral assessment of children. In B. B. Lahey & A. E. Kazdin (Eds.), *Advances in clinical child psychology* (Vol. 1). New York: Plenum Press, 1977.

Clement, P. W., & Richard, R. C. Identifying reinforcers for children: A children's reinforcement survey. In E. J. Mash & L. G. Terdal (Eds.), *Behavior therapy assessment: Diagnosis, design, and evaluation.* New York: Springer, 1976.

Cone, J. D. The relevance of reliability and validity for behavioral assessment. *Behavior Therapy,* 1977, *8,* 411–426.

Cone, J. D. Confounded comparisons in triple response mode assessment research. *Behavioral Assessment,* 1979, *1,* 85–95.

Cone, J. D. Psychometric considerations. In M. Hersen & A. S. Bellack (Eds.), *Behavioral assessment: A practical handbook* (2nd ed.). New York: Pergamon Press, 1981.

Cone, J. E., & Hawkins, R. P. *Behavioral assessment: New directions in clinical psychology.* New York: Brunner/Mazel, 1977.

Conners, C. K. A teacher rating scale for use in drug studies with children. *American Journal of Psychiatry,* 1969, *126,* 884–888.

Conners, C. K. Symptom patterns in hyperkinetic, neurotic, and normal children. *Child Development,* 1970, *41,* 667–682.

Conners, C. K. Rating scales for use in drug studies with children. *Psychopharmacology Bulletin* (Special Issue, Pharmacotherapy with Children), 1973, 24–84.

Conners, C. K. Rating scales. In J. D. Noshpitz (Ed.), *Basic handbook of child psychiatry* (Vol. 1). New York: Basic Books, 1979.

Conners, C. K., & Blouin, A. Hyperkinetic syndrome and psychopathology in children. Paper presented at the meeting of the American Psychological Association, Toronto, 1980.

Conners, C. K., & Werry, J. S. Pharmacotherapy. In H. C. Quay & J. S. Werry (Eds.), *Psychopathological disorders of childhood* (2nd ed.). New York: Wiley, 1979.

Doll, E. A. *Vineland Scale of Social Maturity.* Minneapolis: American Guidance Service, 1964.

Edelbrock, C., & Achenbach, T. M. A typology of child behavior profile patterns: Distribution and correlates for disturbed children aged 6–16. *Journal of Abnormal Child Psychology,* 1980, *8,* 441–470.

Edelbrock, C., & Achenbach, T. M. The teacher version of the Child Behavior Profile: I. Boys Aged 6–11. Manuscript submitted for publication, 1983.

Edelbrock, C., Costello, A. J., & Kessler, M. D. Empirical corroboration of the Attention Deficit Disorder. Manuscript submitted for publication, 1983.

Edelbrock, C., & Reed, M. L. Relations between the teacher version of the Child Behavior Profile and behavioral observations in the classroom. Manuscript in preparation, 1983.

Emmelkamp, P. M. G. The current and future status of clinical research. *Behavioral Assessment,* 1981, *3,* 249–253.

Evans, I. M., & Nelson, R. O. Assessment of child behavior problems. In A. R. Ciminero, K. S. Calhoun, & H. E. Adams (Eds.), *Handbook of behavioral assessment.* New York: Wiley, 1977.

Eyberg, S. M. Eyberg Child Behavior Inventory. *Journal of Clinical Child Psychology,* 1980, *9,* 29.

Eyberg, S. M., & Robinson, E. A. Parent-child interaction training: Effects on family functioning. *Journal of Clinical Child Psychology,* 1982, *11,* 130–137.

Eyberg, S. M., & Ross, A. W. Assessment of child behavior problems: The validation of a new inventory. *Journal of Clinical Child Psychology,* 1978, *7,* 113–116.

Finch, A. J., Deardorff, P. A., & Montgomery, L. E. Individually tailored behavioral rating scales: A possible alternative. *Journal of Abnormal Child Psychology,* 1974, *2,* 209–217.

Forehand, R., Furey, W. M., & McMahon, R. J. A review of the role of maternal distress in a parent training program to modify one aspect of aggression: Noncompliance. *Analysis and Intervention in Developmental Disabilities,* in press.

Forehand, R., Griest, D. L., & Wells, K. C. Parent behavioral training: An analysis of the relationship among multiple outcome measures. *Journal of Abnormal Child Psychology,* 1979, *7,* 229–242.

Forehand, R., & McMahon, R. J. *Helping the noncompliant child: A clinician's guide to parent training.* New York: Guilford Press, 1981.

Forehand, R., Wells, K. C., & Griest, D. L. An examination of the social validity of a parent training program. *Behavior Therapy,* 1980, *11,* 488–502.

Furman, W., & Drabman, R. S. Methodological issues in child behavior therapy. In M. Hersen, R. M. Eisler, & P. M. Miller (Eds.), *Progress in behavior modification* (Vol. 11). New York: Academic Press, 1981.

Glow, R. A., Glow, P. H., & Rump, E. E. The stability of child behavior disorders: A one year test-retest study of Adelaide versions of the Conners Teacher and Parent Rating Scales. *Journal of Abnormal Child Psychology,* 1982, *10,* 33–60.

Goyette, C. H., Conners, C. K., & Ulrich, R. F. Normative data on revised Conners Parent and Teacher Rating Scales. *Journal of Abnormal Child Psychology,* 1978, *6,* 221–236.

Graham, P. Epidemiological studies. In H. C. Quay & J. S. Werry (Eds.), *Psychopathological disorders of childhood* (2nd ed.). New York: Wiley, 1979.

Guy, W. *ECDEU assessment manual for psychopharmacology* (DHEW Publication #76-338). Washington, DC: U.S. Government Printing Office, 1976.

Haynes, S. N. *Principles of behavioral assessment.* New York: Gardner Press, 1978.

Holleran, P. A., Littman, D. C., Freund, R. D., & Schmaling, K. B. A signal detection approach to social perception: Identification of negative and positive behaviors by parents of normal and problem children. *Journal of Abnormal Child Psychology,* 1982, *10,* 547–558.

Hops, H. Children's social competence and skill: Current research practices and future directions. *Behavior Therapy,* 1983, *14,* 3–18.

Humphrey, L. L. Children's and teacher's perspectives on children's self-control: The development of two rating scales. *Journal of Consulting and Clinical Psychology,* 1982, *50,* 624–633.

Humphreys, L. L., & Ciminero, A. R. Parent report measures of child behavior: A review. *Journal of Clinical Child Psychology,* 1979, *8,* 56–63.

Jacob, T., Grounds, L., & Haley, R. Correspondence between parents' reports on the behavior problem checklist. *Journal of Abnormal Child Psychology,* 1982, 10, 593–608.

Kazdin, A. E. Assessing the clinical or applied importance of behavior change through social validation. *Behavior Modification,* 1977, *1,* 427–452.

Kelley, C. Reliability of the Behavior Problem Checklist with institutionalized male delinquents. *Journal of Abnormal Child Psychology,* 1981, *9,* 243–250.

Kendall, P. C., & Wilcox, L. E. Self-control in children: Development of a rating scale. *Journal of Consulting and Clinical Psychology,* 1979, *47,* 1020–1029.

King, C., & Young, R. D. Attentional deficits with and without hyperactivity: Teacher and peer perceptions. *Journal of Abnormal Child Psychology,* 1982, *10,* 483–496.

Leon, G. R., Kendall, P. C., & Garber, J. Depression in children: Parent, teacher, and child perspectives. *Journal of Abnormal Child Psychology,* 1980, *8,* 221–235.

Linehan, M. M. Content validity: Its relevance to behavioral assessment. *Behavioral Assessment,* 1980, *2,* 147–159.

Mash, E. J. Families with problem children. In A. Doyle, D. Gold, & D. Moscowitz (Eds.), *Children in families under stress.* San Francisco: Jossey-Bass, in press.

Mash, E. J., & Terdal, L. G. Assessment for potential reinforcers. In E. J. Mash & L. G. Terdal (Eds.), *Behavior therapy assessment: Diagnosis, design, and evaluation.* New York: Springer, 1976.

Mash, E. J., & Terdal, L. G. Behavioral assessment of childhood disturbances. In E. J. Mash & L. G. Terdal (Eds.), *Behavioral assessment of childhood disorders.* New York: Guilford Press, 1981.

Matson, J. L., & Beck, S. Assessment of children in inpatient settings. In M. Hersen & A. S. Bellack (Eds.), *Behavioral assessment: A practical handbook* (2nd Ed.). New York: Pergamon Press, 1981.

McMahon, R. J., & Davies, G. R. A behavioral parent training program and its side effects on classroom behavior. *B. C. Journal of Special Education,* 1980, *4,* 165–174.

Meyers, C. E., Nihira, K., & Zetlin, A. The measurement of adaptive behavior. In N. Ellis (Ed.), *Handbook of mental deficiency, psychological theory, and research.* Hillsdale, NJ: Lawrence Erlbaum Associates, 1979.

Milich, R., Roberts, M. A., Loney, J., & Caputo, J. Differentiating practice effects and statistical regression on the Conners Hyperkinesis Index. *Journal of Abnormal Child Psychology,* 1980, *8,* 549–552.

Miller, L. C. Louisville Behavior Checklist for males, 6–12 years of age. *Psychological Reports,* 1967, *21,* 885–896.

Miller, L. C., Barrett, C. L., Hampe, E., & Noble, H. Factor structure of childhood fears. *Journal of Consulting and Clinical Psychology,* 1972, *39,* 264–268.

Nay, W. R. *Multimethod clinical assessment.* New York: Gardner Press, 1979.

Nelson, R. O. Realistic dependent measures for clinical use. *Journal of Consulting and Clinical Psychology,* 1981, *49,* 168–182.

Nihira, K., Foster, R., Shellhaas, M., & Leland, H. *Adaptive behavior scales: Manual.* Washington, DC: American Association on Mental Deficiency, 1969.

O'Donnell, J. P., & Van Tuinan, M. Behavior problems of preschool children: Dimensions and congenital correlates. *Journal of Abnormal Child Psychology,* 1979, *7,* 61–75.

O'Leary, K. D., & Johnson, S. B. Psychological assessment. In H. C. Quay & J. S. Werry (Eds.), *Psychopathological disorders of childhood* (2nd ed.). New York: Wiley, 1979.

O'Leary, S. G., & Pelham, W. E. Behavior therapy and withdrawal of stimulant medication with hyperactive children. *Pediatrics,* 1978, *61,* 211–217.

Oltmanns, T. F., Broderick, J. E., & O'Leary, D. K. Marital adjustment and the efficacy of behavior therapy with children. *Journal of Consulting and Clinical Psychology,* 1977, *45,* 724–729.

Quay, H. C. Measuring dimensions of deviant behavior: The Behavior Problem Checklist. *Journal of Abnormal Child Psychology,* 1977, *5,* 277–287.

Quay, H. C. Classification. In H. C. Quay & J. S. Werry (Eds.), *Psychopathological disorders of childhood* (2nd ed.). New York: Wiley, 1979.

Quay, H. C., & Peterson, D. R. *Manual for the Behavior Problem Checklist.* Published by the authors at 59 Fifth St., Highland Park, New Jersey, 08904, 1979.

Reed, M. L., & Edelbrock, C. Reliability and validity on the observational version of the Child Behavior Checklist. Manuscript in preparation, 1983.

Roberts, M. A., Milich, R., Loney, J., & Caputo, J. A multitrait-multimethod analysis of variance of teachers' ratings of aggression, hyperactivity, and inattention. *Journal of Abnormal Child Psychology,* 1981, *9,* 371–380.

Robinson, E. A., & Anderson, L. L. Family adjustment, parental attitudes, and social desirability. Paper presented at the meeting of the American Psychological Association, Los Angeles, 1981.

Robinson, E. A., & Eyberg, S. M. The dyadic parent-child interaction coding system: Standardization and validation. *Journal of Consulting and Clinical Psychology,* 1981, *49,* 245–250.

Robinson, E. A., Eyberg, S. M., & Ross, A. W. The standardization of an inventory of child conduct problem behaviors. *Journal of Clinical Child Psychology,* 1980, *9,* 22–29.

Ross, A. O., Lacey, H. M., & Parton, D. A. The development of a behavior checklist for boys. *Child Development,* 1965, *36,* 1013–1027.

Sandoval, J. Format effects in two teacher rating scales of hyperactivity. *Journal of Abnormal Child Psychology,* 1981, *9,* 203–218.

Schnittjer, C. J., & Hirshoren, A. Factors of problem behavior in visually impaired children. *Journal of Abnormal Child Psychology,* 1981, *9,* 517–522.

Shuller, D. Y., & McNamara, J. R. Expectancy factors in behavioral observation. *Behavior Therapy,* 1976, *7,* 516–527.

Siegel, L. J., Dragovich, S. L., & Marholin, D. The effects of biasing information on behavioral observations and rating scales. *Journal of Abnormal Child Psychology,* 1976, *4,* 221–233.

Skinner, H. A. Toward the integration of classification theory and methods. *Journal of Abnormal Psychology,* 1981, *90,* 68–87.

Spivack, G., & Spotts, J. The Devereux Child Behavior Rating Scale: Symptom behaviors in latency age children. *American Journal of Mental Deficiency,* 1965, *69,* 839–853.

Spivack, G., & Swift, M. The classroom behavior of children: A critical review of teacher-administered rating scales. *Journal of Special Education,* 1973, *7,* 55–89.

Spivack, G., & Swift, M. The Hahnemann High School Behavior (HHSB) Rating Scale. *Journal of Abnormal Child Psychology,* 1977, *5,* 299–307.

Touliatos, J., & Lindholm, B. W. Relationships of children's grade in school, sex, and social class to teachers' ratings on the Behavior Problem Checklist. *Journal of Abnormal Child Psychology,* 1975, *3,* 115–126.

Trites, R. L., Blouin, A. G. A., & Laprade, K. Factor analysis of the Conners Teacher Rating Scale based on a large normative sample. *Journal of Consulting and Clinical Psychology,* 1982, *50,* 615–623.

Trites, R. L., Dugas, F., Lynch, G., & Ferguson, H. B. Prevalence of hyperactivity. *Journal of Pediatric Psychology,* 1979, *2,* 179–188.

Walls, R. T., Werner, T. J., Bacon, A., & Zane, T. Behavior checklists. In J. D. Cone & R. P. Hawkins (Eds.), *Behavioral assessment: New directions in clinical psychology.* New York: Brunner/Mazel, 1977.

Webster-Stratton, C., & Eyberg, S. M. Child temperament: Relationship with child behavior problems and parent-child interactions. *Journal of Clinical Child Psychology,* 1982, *11,* 123–129.

Weinrott, M. R. Improving the validity of global ratings. *Journal of Abnormal Child Psychology,* 1977, *5,* 187–197.

Weinrott, M. R., Reid, J. B., Bauske, B. W., & Brummett, B. Supplementing naturalistic observations with observer impressions. *Behavioral Assessment,* 1981, *3,* 151–159.

Werry, J. S., Sprague, R. L., & Cohen, M. N. Conners Teacher Rating Scale for use in drug studies with children: An empirical study. *Journal of Abnormal Child Psychology,* 1975, *3,* 217–229.

Wiggins, J. S. *Personality and prediction: Principles of personality assessment.* Reading, MA: Addison-Wesley, 1973.

Wilson, D. R., & Prentice-Dunn, S. Rating scales in the assessment of child behavior. *Journal of Clinical Child Psychology,* 1981, *10,* 121–126.

6

Self-Report Instruments

Al J. Finch, Jr.
and
Tim R. Rogers

One of the major tenets of early behavioral therapy was that observable behavior was the only acceptable piece of data for the evaluation of research and therapy outcome. In addition, it was maintained that this data should be collected by unbiased observers who were trained rigorously to make accurate observations. Consequently, it is not surprising that self-report measures were rarely employed by researchers and therapists working within the behavioral framework. The main exception to this avoidance of self-report was self-monitoring wherein subjects counted their own targeted behaviors and reported them to the investigator/therapist. However, even these reports were treated skeptically due to well-known problems inherent in self-report measures.

To a large extent, the negative bias against self-report was an outgrowth of research indicating that reports of subjective states did not coincide with observable behavior. The question then became which was the more appropriate target for measuring change—what the subject reported or what was observed. Since the early behavioral emphasis was a movement away from subjective data, the overwhelming choice was for observable behavior. In no area was this more evident than in behavioral assessment of children for whom target behaviors were more easily quantifiable and with whom use of self-report was considered questionable due to limited verbal development. If adults were poor reporters, could children be anything but worse?

It is not surprising then that early texts of behavioral therapy and assessment typically excluded self-report instruments in their discussions. When authors included self-report measures, they were limited to self-monitoring of countable behaviors which could also be observed by others. More subjective measures were considered susceptible to demand characteristics or social desirability and of questionable validity and reliability. Recently, however, a trend toward incorporating a broader range of data into assessment and treatment evaluation has been evidenced. This expanded range of data includes not only observable behavior but, also, more subjective measures of the child's point of view, including self-report. With adults who frequently initiate their own referral, perception of the problems has come to be a standard facet of assessment. As Finch, Nelson, and Moss (in press) and others have stated, to ignore a person's own perception of reality is to lose a vital data base from which to draw treatment goals. Furthermore, Atkeson and Forehand (1978) have argued that although differing assessment approaches yield different information, data from these sources should be considered complementary rather than competitive. These authors call for a multimethod assessment approach with all data being utilized for comparison in order to derive meaningful treatment goals (see Ollendick & Cerny, 1981).

The present chapter follows in the spirit of the recent trend for multimethod assessment. The authors agree that serious errors are made when therapists and/or researchers ignore an individual's perception. At the same time, the authors recognize limitations of self-report measures when employed in isolation and advocate their use in combination with other measures. In the present chapter, select measures of anxiety, depression, locus of control, and anger will be reviewed. While other self-report measures exist and are useful in the measurement of behaviors such as fear (e.g., Scherer & Nakamura, 1968; Ollendick, in press, b) and assertion (e.g., Deluty, 1979), they will not be reviewed here. The instruments selected for inclusion are intended to be illustrative of the utility of self-report measures with children in the clinical setting.

MEASUREMENT OF ANXIETY

Despite the popular view of childhood as a happy-go-lucky period, it has become increasingly clear to researchers and clinicians alike that children often experience many of the same doubts and fears as do their more articulate adult counterparts. In an attempt to more precisely identify this subjective experience which children often are unable or unwilling to identify for themselves, several self-report inventories have been developed which assist the child in labeling his or her experience. The two most prominent anxiety inventories will be described here.

The first assessment instrument designed to measure anxiety in adults (Manifest Anxiety Scale) was constructed by Taylor (1951) and consisted of items drawn from the MMPI. Castaneda, McCandless and Palermo (1956) subsequently revised Taylor's scale into what was termed the Children's Manifest Anxiety Scale (CMAS). For more than twenty years, the CMAS was widely used as a self-report measure of anxiety in children. However, Reynolds and Richmond (1978) reported several criticisms of the CMAS while calling for a revision of the inventory. Specific problems identified by these authors were: (1) the narrow scope of areas of anxiety polled, (2) items which were too difficult for primary and mentally retarded children, (3) an inability to measure developmental changes in anxiety, and, most importantly, (4) that only 12 of the 42 items actually met criteria for a good test item recommended by Flanigan, Peters, and Conry (1969).

Thus, Reynolds and Richmond (1978) proposed the Revised Children's Manifest Anxiety Scale (RCMAS) that was developed by adding 20 items to the CMAS, which the authors felt assessed indicators of anxiety not covered by the original CMAS (a total of 73 items). Wording was then revised such that third graders would be able to complete the instrument alone while it could be understood by first and second graders if read to them. Data were initially collected on 329 children in grades 1–12. All items, with the exception of the *Lie* scale, that did not meet the criteria (i.e., difficulty index $.30 \leq p \leq .70$ and biserial correlation of that test item to test score, $r_{bis} \geq .40$) of Flanigan et al. (1969) were eliminated. *Lie* scale items which did not correlate significantly with other *Lie* items or correlated $\geq .30$ with the *Anxiety* items were also eliminated. The result was an inventory consisting of 28 *Anxiety* items and 9 *Lie* items. The child completing the inventory is instructed to respond either yes or no to statements depending on whether they are or are not like him or her.

To assess reliability of the new instrument, 167 students were selected from a separate district than the above children; the resulting Kuder-Richardson coefficient was .85. Reliability data are available from other sources as well. In use with Nigerian children, Pela and Reynolds (1981) reported internal consistency coefficients in the .80 range. Test-retest reliabilities with the same population were reported to be $\geq .90$ for both males and females. Drawing from a larger sample, Reynolds (1981) reported a 9-month test-retest correlation of .68 for 534 fourth, fifth, and sixth graders. In the most ambitious investigation of the RCMAS to date, Reynolds and Paget (1982) collected RCMAS data on 4,972 children between the ages of 6 and 19 years, representing 13 states and 80 school districts. The sample contained 2,208 white males; 2,176 white females; 289 black males; and 299 black females. Coefficient alpha reliability estimates by age, race, and sex are provided for all subjects with a range from .42 to .87 with the majority $\geq .80$. Thus the internal consistency and test-retest reliabilities are within acceptable ranges.

Less extensive data are available concerning the validity of the RCMAS. In a study of 42 children referred for psychological evaluation, Reynolds (1980) administered both the RCMAS and the State-Trait Anxiety Inventory for Children (STAIC: Spielberger, 1973). A significant correlation ($r = .85$,

$p \leq .001$) was found between the RCMAS and the A-trait scale of the STAIC, while no significant correlation was found between the RCMAS and the A-state scale of the STAIC. Reynolds (1980) concluded that evidence existed for the RCMAS as a measure of chronic manifest anxiety. In another study, Reynolds (1982) reports that RCMAS anxiety scores correlated positively with teacher observations of classroom behavioral problems.

Drawing on an earlier factor analysis of the CMAS by Finch, Kendall, and Montgomery (1974) (which identified the factors tapping: physiological indicators of anxiety, worry and hypersensitivity, and concentration difficulties), Reynolds and Richmond (1978) and Reynolds and Paget (1981) subjected the RCMAS to factor analysis. They found similar factors which they labeled *Physiological Anxiety, Worry and Oversensitivity,* and *Concentration Anxiety.* These factors held across sex and race (Reynolds & Paget, 1981). Presently, the only reliability data for these factors are those presented by Reynolds and Paget (1982). Reliability coefficients (coefficient alpha) for individual factors are generally in the .60–.80 range, although it appears that the factors may be less reliable with young black females as several coefficients fell within the .15–.25 range with this group.

Until recently, about the only source of normative data for the RCMAS was the original study reporting the revision of the instrument (Reynolds & Richmond, 1978). This investigation utilized a pool of 329 children in grades 1–12 and reported normative data by grade, race, and sex. Also, in a downward extension of the RCMAS, Reynolds, Bradley, and Steele (1980) reported normative data for a group of 97 kindergarten children. Fortunately, a recent investigation has provided large-scale normative data for children aged 6–19 years (Reynolds & Paget, 1982). Given the large sample size (4,972 children) and that the norms are separated by age rather than grade level (which can include a span of 3–4 years) and are broken into age, sex, and race combinations, this is considered the best source of normative information for the RCMAS.

As with the RCMAS, the State-Trait Anxiety Inventory for Children (STAIC: Spielberger, 1973) was developed as a downward extension of an anxiety inventory designed for adults. As is true of the parent scale, the STAIC consists of two separate self-report inventories which measure two distinct concepts of anxiety: trait anxiety (A-trait), a measure of anxiety proneness; and state anxiety (A-state), a measure of transitory anxiety. Designed originally for children aged 9–12, the STAIC may be used with younger children for whom reading ability is above average or with older children for whom reading ability is decreased. Both the A-state and A-trait scales consist of 20 items to which the child responds as to how he or she feels at a particular moment in time for the A-state or how she or he typically feels for the A-trait.

Reliability data for the two scales of the STAIC have been reported for both normal and emotionally disturbed children. Test-retest reliabilities (after 8 weeks) for the A-trait scale from a sample of 246 school children were .65 for males and .71 for females; modest correlations which are interpreted as an indication of instability of personality structure in young children (Spielberger, 1973). If the A-state scale actually measures a transitory anxiety state, the more appropriate measure of its reliability, as opposed to test-retest, would appear to be a measure of internal consistency. Spielberger (1973) reports alpha coefficients of .82 for males and .87 for females. Interestingly, in a reliability study of the STAIC with emotionally disturbed children, Finch, Montgomery and Deardorff (1974) found higher test-retest reliabilities for the A-state and lower reliabilities for the A-trait scale than did Spielberger. In their report Finch, Montgomery, and Deardorff (1974) administered the STAIC to 30 emotionally disturbed children in residential treatment. Test-retest reliabilities after 3 months were .63 and .44 for the A-state and A-trait scales respectively, the reverse of that reported by Spielberger (1973). The authors' hypotheses were: (a) emotionally disturbed children experience relatively constant high levels of anxiety at any given moment, thus inflating the test-retest reliability of the A-state scale, and (b) emotionally disturbed children report their level of trait anxiety more inconsistently than normals, which decreases reliability.

Data exist which support both the construct and concurrent validity of the STAIC. Spielberger (1973) reports correlations of .75 and .63 between the A-trait scale and the Children's Manifest Anxiety Scale (Castenada et al., 1956) and the General Anxiety Scale for Children (Sarason, Davidson, Lightfall, Waite & Ruebush, 1960). Montgomery and Finch (1974) administered the STAIC to 60 emotionally disturbed and 60 normal control children and found that by establishing cut-off scores they could correctly discriminate 65% of the disturbed group using the A-state, 63% using the A-trait, and 65% with a combined score. Despite some overlap and misclassification of normals, the authors concluded that the results had demonstrated acceptable validity for the STAIC.

Two investigations are the primary source of data demonstrating validity of the STAIC A-state form. Using a sample of 900 fourth, fifth, and sixth graders, Spielberger (1973) administered the A-state scale under two conditions: (1) Norm — standard instructions, and 2) Test — how they thought they would feel just before taking a major final exam. Scores on the A-state scale were able to discriminate significantly the two conditions for both males and females. Similarly, Newmark, Wheeler, Newmark, and Stabler (1975) found increases in A-state anxiety in response to psychological testing for normals but no changes in A-trait. Interestingly, Sitarz (1974) found exactly the opposite effect when the STAIC was administered to 30 emotionally disturbed children under the induced stress of psychological testing. The author reports that A-state scores remained constant while A-trait scores increased under increasing stress conditions.

Since some question as to the validity of the STAIC with emotionally disturbed children existed, Finch, Kendall, Montgomery, and Morris (1975) further investigated the sensitivity of the STAIC to changes in anxiety associated with failure experiences of emotionally disturbed children. Increases in anxiety ratings on both the A-state and A-trait scales were reported under failure conditions, leading the authors to propose that personality traits, such as A-trait anxiety, were not firmly established with emotionally disturbed children. Noting the discrepant results of earlier studies, Finch, Kendall, Dannenburg, and Morgan (1978) set out to unravel the confusion concerning the STAIC with emotionally disturbed children. Realizing that some discrepancy existed among the sets of instruction under which the STAIC had been used in previous reports, the authors determined to use instructions similar to those in the original Spielberger (1973) report with their group of emotionally disturbed children following the administration of easy and difficult tasks. Results of the authors' investigation were taken to support the validity of the STAIC in that, at least with older children, A-state scores increased with failure experiences, while A-trait scores were not significantly changed.

Normative data for both scales of the STAIC are available for both normal and child guidance children. Norms for elementary school children are available from Spielberger (1973) and are based on 1554 Florida elementary school children in grades 4, 5, and 6, approximately 35–40% of which were black. Both T-scores and percentile ranks are available by sex for this group. McAdoo (1981) has provided norms for 60 girls and 140 boys visiting child guidance clinics. Unfortunately, the norms are by sex only and are not available by age, grade, or race due to small sample sizes.

From the above information, it appears there are sufficient data to support both the RCMAS and STAIC as reliable, valid measures of anxiety in children. As for advantages of one scale over another, each has its strong points. Normative data for children of kindergarten age to age 19 are available for normal children with the RCMAS. Normative data for both scales of the STAIC are available for a more restricted age range, though the advantage of having norms for emotionally disturbed children exists. Thus, the RCMAS appears to be applicable to a wider age range of children, but, presently, normative data for emotionally disturbed children do not exist for this scale. The STAIC has the special advantage of containing both a state and a trait measure, which the RCMAS does not, though as discussed above, care must be taken when making the state-trait distinction with emotionally disturbed children.

Both the STAIC and RCMAS have been widely used in clinical and research settings and appear to have demonstrated utility as self-report measures of anxiety in children. In choosing between the two measures for use in a research/clinical setting, the authors recommend giving attention to the population for which the measures will be used and whether the state-trait distinction may be useful as a dimension. For many investigations, a combination of both scales appears justified.

MEASUREMENT OF DEPRESSION

Within the last few years, no other area in child psychiatry has received more attention than depression in children. Many issues regarding its existence, nature, assessment, and treatment have been investigated (see Finch & Saylor, in press), and considerable confusion exists within the area. As has been noted by Cantwell and Carlson (1979), one of the major obstacles to systematic research in the area of childhood depression has been the absence of a well-developed assessment methodology. At least a portion of this assessment methodology is self-report. Currently, there are several self-report measures of depression under investigation.

The most widely used measure of depression in children is the Children's Depression Inventory (CDI: Kovacs, 1978). The CDI is a 27-item severity measure of depression which is a downward extension and revision of the well-known Beck Depression Inventory (Beck & Beamesderfer, 1974). Each of the 27 items consists of three sentences designed to range from normalcy, to definite but not clinically significant symptoms, and finally to fairly severe and clinically significant symptoms. Each item then can be scored from 0–2 resulting in a range of scores from 0–54. Kovacs (1982) reports that the scale is suitable for youngsters aged 8–17 years of age.

Kovacs (1978) reports on the psychometric properties of the CDI. Employing a sample of 860 normal school children, she found an internal consistency of .87. With a sample of 75 psychiatrically referred children, an internal consistency of .86 was found, while .71 was the internal consistency Kovacs reports for pediatric-medical outpatients. In our own work, we have found the CDI to have an internal consistency of .94 with normals and .80 with emotionally disturbed children (Saylor, Finch, Spirito & Bennett, 1983).

Another measure of internal consistency is item-total score correlations. According to Kovacs (1982), these values are generally good with some variation being found between different populations. Test-retest reliability has been investigated over varying intervals and with various populations. Friedman and Butler (1979) found a test-retest reliability of .72 with normal children. Similarly, Miezitis, Friedman, Butler, and Blanchard (1978) found a value of .84 over a 9–13 week interval. However, Saylor et al. (1983) found the reliability value to be .38 over a 1-week period with normal fifth and sixth graders. With emotionally disturbed samples, Saylor et al. (1983) reported a .87 value for a 1-week interval and a .59 value for a 6-week period. The results of these studies generally support the reliability of the CDI but, given the poor values found with normal children over a 1-week period, additional work is needed.

Saylor et al. (1983) also report on the split half reliability of the CDI with both normal and emotionally disturbed children. Spearman-Brown correlations for even/odd items were .61 and .74 for the two populations, respectively; while the values were .73 and .57 for the first half/second half for the same groups.

With regard to the validity of the CDI, Kovacs (1978) reports that with a sample of 51 emotionally disturbed children, there was a high correlation of CDI scores with self-esteem scores ($r = .59$, $p < .0001$). Similar results have been reported by Fleming and Kelley (1982) with emotionally disturbed children, and by Green (1980) and Friedman and Butler (1979) with normal children.

Kovacs (1978) reports that the CDI scores can discriminate between emotionally disturbed children diagnosed as depressed and those who are not and between depressed and normal children. However, O'Brien (1982) failed to find a significant correlation between the CDI scores and therapists' ratings of depression in a group of emotionally disturbed children. Similarly, Saylor et al. (1983) failed to find a difference between the CDI scores of children rated as depressed versus those rated nondepressed by their individual therapists. In addition, there was no relationship between the child's self-report of depression on the CDI and the ratings given to him by his peers or the unit staff on the various symptoms of depression.

Other measures of depression in children are not as well investigated as the CDI. Lange and Tisher (1978) introduced the Children's Depression Scale (CDS). This scale contains 48 items which focus on depressive symptoms and reactions plus 18 items which focus on more positive types of experiences. The items are presented on separate cards which the child is asked to place into one of five boxes, ranging from "very right" to "very wrong." This scale has the advantage of being presented in a format which seems to be more enjoyable for the youngster. However, other than the research conducted by the developers of the scale, there seems to be little additional research available at this time. Its overall psychometric properties appear to be reasonably good, and, certainly, it should be investigated further. However, at this time cross validation and extensive work with clinical populations are not available.

Birleson (1980) introduced an 18-item rating scale for depression. On this scale, children are required to indicate whether or not each item applies to them most of the time, sometimes, or never. Again, the data which are available on this scale are very limited, and there is extensive need for further validation and reliability studies. The preliminary data look encouraging but few subjects were examined. Also, because the amount of cross validation was limited, caution is warranted in applying this scale in clinical and research settings.

The Short Children's Depression Inventory (SCDI) (Carlson and Cantwell, 1980) is a modification of the Beck Depression Inventory and is designed for use with children. The 13 items included in this scale are designed to encompass mood, anhedonia, guilt, helplessness, and other dimensions. There is limited data available on the psychometric properties of this scale, but preliminary results would suggest that it might have potential application to research and clinical work in the area. Again, before it can be applied extensively, considerably more research needs to be done to establish its reliability and validity.

After reviewing the available material on the four previously discussed self-report measures of depression, one must conclude that the published data supporting the wide-scale use of any of these scales are not available at this time. In each case, there is a need for additional work demonstrating the reliability of these scales with a variety of both normal and clinical populations. In addition, there is a need for cross-validational studies with each scale. Until these studies are available, one needs to employ extreme caution in interpretation of the results obtained on any of these measures.

LOCUS OF CONTROL MEASURES

The measurement of the construct of locus of control of reinforcement depends, as does measurement of any construct, on a reliable and valid instrument. Following the proliferation of research on adult locus of control following Rotter's (1966) monograph, child researchers/clinicians have attempted to measure the concept of locus of control in children.

Early measures included those developed by Bialer (1961); Battle and Rotter (1963); Mischel, Zeiss, and Zeiss (1974); Bachrach and Peterson (1975), and Nowicki and Strickland (1973). Many of the above scales, as well as others, have been criticized for various reasons by several authors (Bachrach & Peterson, 1975; Gorsuch, Henigan, and Barnard, 1972; MacDonald, 1973; Nowicki & Strickland, 1973). Of the available scales, the most widely accepted and utilized instrument is the Children's Nowicki-Strickland Internal-External control scale (CNS-IE). MacDonald, in a review of the literature, concluded that the CNS-IE is the best available measure of locus of control for children (MacDonald, 1973). Thus, for the purposes of this review, the focus will lie mainly on the CNS-IE as the primary measure of locus of control of reinforcement for children.

Based on Rotter's (1966) definition of internal-external control, the CNS-IE is a 40 item yes/no questionnaire with an approximate reading level of grade 5. The individual items assess attribution of control across multiple situations including achievement, dependency, and affiliation and were constructed following consultation with schoolteachers. Originally 59 items were included, however, 19 were discarded following original item analyses.

The original standardization study is reported by Nowicki and Strickland (1973) and includes data from approximately 1000 children in grades 3–12. Normative data are reported by grade for both males and females and indicate a general trend for scores to decrease (i.e., become more internal) with increasing age. This trend is consistent across sex.

Three reliability measures of the CNS-IE are reported from this sample. First, biserial item correlations with total score are presented for grades 3, 7, and 11 and generally fall in the .25–.45 range with a few more extreme scores present. Split-half Spearman-Brown correlations were $r = .63$ (for grades 3, 4, 5); $r = .81$ (grade 12). The authors argue the point that these split-half reliabilities tend to underestimate the true internal consistency of the scale as the individual items sample various situations and, therefore, are not comparable. Test-retest reliabilities were .63, .66, and .71 for grades 3, 7, and 10, respectively, when readministered 6-weeks later.

Evidence for the construct validity of the instrument includes significant correlations of CNS-IE scores with the 1 + but not 1 − scores on the Intellectual Achievement Responsibility Scale as well as with the Bialer-Cromwell score (Bialer, 1961). Furthermore, significant relationships between internal control and higher grade-point averages have been found with 12th graders, although no significant relationship was found with internal locus and IQ for the same students (Nowicki, 1971; Nowicki & Roundtree, 1971). This finding appears to hold with emotionally disturbed children (Finch, Pezzuti, & Nelson, 1975).

Thus, it appears that the CNS-IE is a valid and reliable instrument for the measurement of attribution of control of reinforcement in children. Multiple reports (too numerous to mention here) have utilized the CNS-IE to assess locus of control across cultures, ages, and social status; to investigate locus of control as a moderating variable; and as a prediction of treatment outcome in clinical situations, to name but a few.

As the CNS-IE is generally limited to use with children at or above third grade level, attempts have been made to extend it downward to preschool and primary children aged 4–8 (Nowicki & Duke, 1974). The original scale consisted of 78 yes/no items at a 4-year-old word level, many of which were directly taken from the CNS-IE. Following ratings by 10 raters, all items not consistently rated were eliminated, leaving 44 items. The resulting instrument was administered to 80 children (36 males, 44 females). Data from this administration were then analyzed to determine which items met the following criteria: (1) Mean ranging from .3–.7, (2) "moderate" item-total correlations, and (3) inclusion in an item analysis of the 10 highest and lowest scores. There were 36 resultant items cross validated in a population of preschool children; 26 of those items were deemed acceptable in both groups and were retained in the Preschool and Primary NS-IE (PPNS-IE). The next stage of construction consisted of having artists illustrate each item to make each item intrinsically interesting for children with both male and female form resulting.

The resulting scale was validated on 240 children (120 males, 120 females). Normative data are reported by sex and age groups (5- and 6-year-olds are together as are 7- and 8-year-olds). Reliability information reported is biserial correlations of item with total score (moderate to low) as well as a 6-week test-retest correlation for 7-year-olds of $n = .79$ ($p \le .001$). As evidence for validity, the authors cite the fact that the PPNS-IE correlates significantly with the CSN-IE for 8-year-olds, is related to the same factors as the CNS-IE (i.e., achievement scores), and internality was correlated with less interpersonal distancing (Nowicki & Duke, 1974). It should be noted that the PPNS-IE has drawn criticism from other authors. Herzhergen, Linney, Seidman, and Rappaport (1979) have subjected the PPNS-IE to renewed examination and concluded the psychometric properties are inadequate as internal consistency measures are quite low. Thus, caution in using the PPNS-IE is advised.

MEASUREMENT OF ANGER

Of all the problems which result in children being referred for psychiatric/psychological services, anger management is one of the most common. In fact, Montgomery, Nelson, and Finch (1979) have reported that 75% of children admitted to one inpatient hospital exhibited anger management problems. Given the prevalence of anger management problems, it is surprising that relatively little research has been done in this area.

One of the obvious problems in studying anger is that it is a subjective emotional state and not subject to direct observation by others. Consequently, it cannot be equated with aggressive behavior since aggression represents only one of several options in dealing with the subjective experience of anger. Since anger is an internal experience, it would appear logical to assume that self-report is the more direct method of measurement. The present section presents data on the development of the Children's Inventory of Anger (CIA: Nelson & Finch, 1978). The results presented here remain preliminary, and continued refinement and investigation are needed before the scale is acceptable for other than research purposes.

In order to obtain the initial pool of items, normal and emotionally disturbed children were interviewed about what made them angry. Following these interviews, four clinical child psychologists condensed the information into 71 items designed to assess the various parameters of anger. The language of the scale was limited to a relatively simple and straightforward one. Two elementary reading specialists were consulted on adjusting the language to a fourth-grade reading level.

Drawing on previous research which suggests that impulsive/aggressive children are more likely to think in pictures than words (Finch & Montgomery, 1973; Stein, Finch, Hooke, Montgomery, & Nelson, 1975), and to further simplify the nature of the test, the decision was made to employ stick figures as visual aids. Four stick figures with varying facial expressions were drawn on the front of the test booklet with a brief statement, corresponding to the adjacent ratings from 1 to 4, describing a range of reactions depicted by the item. Furthermore, at the top of each page containing the items, the faces of these figures appeared again with the corresponding numbers appearing below. The printed verbal reactions of the accompanying figure drawings ranged from "I don't care. That situation doesn't even bother me. I don't know why that would make anyone mad (angry)." to "I can't stand that! I'm furious! I feel like really hurting or killing that person or destroying that thing!" Table 6.1 presents sample items from the CIA with the faces at the top.

The first study was designed to determine the test-retest reliability of the CIA with emotionally disturbed children (Montgomery, et al., 1979). Thirty hospitalized children were administered the inventory at the beginning and end of a three-month period. The mean age of this group was 11.39 years with a range from 9 years, 0 months to 15 years and 1 month. Diagnoses of these children were primarily one of the behavioral disorders of childhood or one of the neurotic disorders. Each child was individually administered the questionnaire in a room alone with the examiner to facilitate cooperation. The test-retest reliability of the CIA was found to be .823.

In order to determine the split-half reliability, the CIA was administered

Table 6.1. Sample CIA items.

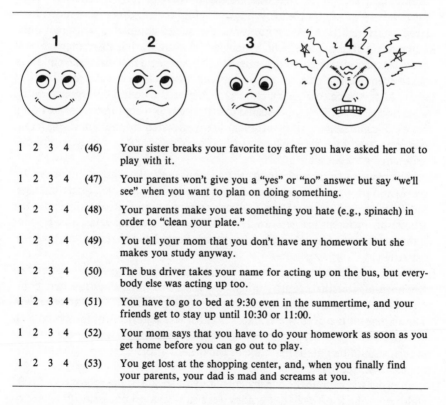

1	2	3	4	(46)	Your sister breaks your favorite toy after you have asked her not to play with it.
1	2	3	4	(47)	Your parents won't give you a "yes" or "no" answer but say "we'll see" when you want to plan on doing something.
1	2	3	4	(48)	Your parents make you eat something you hate (e.g., spinach) in order to "clean your plate."
1	2	3	4	(49)	You tell your mom that you don't have any homework but she makes you study anyway.
1	2	3	4	(50)	The bus driver takes your name for acting up on the bus, but everybody else was acting up too.
1	2	3	4	(51)	You have to go to bed at 9:30 even in the summertime, and your friends get to stay up until 10:30 or 11:00.
1	2	3	4	(52)	Your mom says that you have to do your homework as soon as you get home before you can go out to play.
1	2	3	4	(53)	You get lost at the shopping center, and, when you finally find your parents, your dad is mad and screams at you.

to 460 children enrolled in parochial schools and 61 emotionally disturbed children in residential treatment. The items were read to the "normal" children in the classroom in standard group administration format and administered individually to the emotionally disturbed children. The Spearman-Brown correlation for the first half-second half was .91 while the Spearman-Brown correlation for odd-even items was .95. The Rulon (1939) method of calculating split-half reliability resulted in a first half-second half reliability of .90 and an odd-even reliability of .99.

In order to determine the internal consistency of the CIA, the responses of 911 children were used to calculate the Kuder-Richardson reliability. This measure was felt to be important since we were attempting to measure a relatively homogeneous domain in anger. The alpha coefficient of the CIA was .96, indicating a very homogeneous domain.

Another important psychometric measure of consistency has to do with item-total score correlations. The responses of 376 normal children were employed to determine these correlations which ranged from .34 to .59 with 64 of the 71 items being correlated above .40 with the total score.

In order to investigate the concurrent validity of the CIA, two studies have been conducted. In the first one, 38 emotionally disturbed children, hospitalized in a state-supported psychiatric facility for children, were individually administered the CIA. In addition, each child completed a 40-item peer-nomination of anger scale which included items indicating anger management problems as well as items suggesting anger management skills. Each child was asked to name the child in his or her unit who was best described by each item. At the same time, each child's teacher was asked to complete a rating scale composed of 29 items selected to reflect anger from three separate rating scales. Finally, each child's problem list, generated by the admitting team, was evaluated by a rater who was blind as to whether or not anger control problems were present.

The results of this study indicated a significant relationship between CIA scores and peer-rated anger control problems ($r = .36$, $p < .05$), anger management skills ($r = .36$, $p < .05$), and the presence of anger control problems in the admission problem list ($x^2 = 16.29$, $p < .001$) but was not related to teacher ratings. Interestingly, teacher's ratings were not related to the child's problem list either.

In the second study of concurrent validity, the CIA was administered to 199 normal, fourth–seventh graders. At the same time, their teachers completed the Walker Problem Behavior Identification Checklist (Walker, 1976). The acting-out factor of the Walker checklist was significantly correlated with the CIA score ($r = .14$, $p < .05$) although the relationship was modest. However, it should be noted that none of the other factors were significantly correlated with the CIA.

In order to examine the construct validity of the CIA, the responses of 1000 children in the fourth–eighth grades were subjected to one principal component factor analysis with a varimax rotation. Six factors emerged which accounted for 75% of the total variance. Fifty-eight of the original pool of 71 items loaded on one of the factors. A group of six mental health professionals who work with children independently reviewed the factors and gave brief descriptions of what each one reflected. The six factors reflected the following areas: (1) At the mercy of authority figures, (2) at the mercy of uncontrollable events, (3) injustice, (4) embarrassment or threat to self-esteem, (5) frustration of desires, and (6) sibling conflict.

A final measure of the validity of a scale is its ability to reflect change as a result of a manipulation designed to change the variable the scale is reportedly measuring. Finch, Nelson, and Moss (in press) report a case study in which the CIA was found to change in the expected direction for a 15-year-old male in a stress-inoculation program for anger management. Similarly, Fleming (1982) found that the scores of a group of emotionally disturbed children with anger management problems decreased significantly following stress inoculation for anger management in contrast to a treatment control group.

While the CIA would appear to have potential as a measure of anger in children, there is continued need for psychometric work on the validity of this scale. Furthermore, its length presents a problem and there are efforts presently underway to shorten the scale to make it more practical.

CLINICAL APPLICATIONS

In this section we will discuss briefly cases illustrating how self-report measures can be used in actual clinical practice. First, Nelson (1981) employed the STAIC with an 11-year-old dental phobic girl undergoing stress inoculation for disproportionate dental anxiety and pain. In this case study, severe fear and disruptive behaviors such as crying, screaming, attempting to leave the dental chair, and so forth, were making it impossible for the dentist to complete badly needed dental work. Nelson employed deep-breathing relaxation, distraction, and cognitive self-statements in an attempt to reduce this youngster's fear and disruptive behaviors. The State-Trait Anxiety Inventory for Children (1973) was employed to obtain measures of subjective feelings of anxiety immediately prior to and after each dental visit, and, also, he employed ratings to obtain measures of "in-chair" disruptive behavior.

Results indicated that in-chair disruptive behavior was drastically reduced and that such improvements were maintained over follow-up. In addition, the amount of anticipatory anxiety as measured by the A-state scores declined moderately following the stress inoculation training and greatly prior to her next two dental visits. There was some increase in anxiety before later sessions (although it was still before baseline) but no increase in in-chair disruptive behaviors.

Nelson pointed out the varied relationship between self-report measures of anxiety and the behavioral manifestations defined by the child's in-chair behaviors. He emphasized that it is essential to include self-report measures as well as behavioral and physiological assessment of change in treatment approaches which are designed to alter maladaptive subjective states. He continues by stating that only through analyzing what specific changes (behavioral, self-report, or physiological) are brought about by what specific treatment procedures can understanding of the process of change come about. We agree completely.

In a second case reported by Finch et al. (in press), the Children's Inventory of Anger (CIA) was employed as one of the measures in evaluating stress inoculation for anger management in an adolescent boy. This youngster was an inpatient with a long history of anger management problems which had resulted in his being removed from several foster and group homes. Since he was a large youngster who was very strong, his aggressive outbursts, which involved hitting others, were of major concern. Initial assessment with the CIA indicated a youngster who reported many situations which would result in near-rage reactions. Of particular interest and importance was that nearly every item involving peer interactions received a maximum rating.

Treatment included relaxation, self-instructional training, the development of coping strategies and skills, role playing and rehearsal through imagery, and self-reinforcement for appropriate skill development. A detailed description including actual transcripts is provided by Finch et al. (in press).

The results indicated that there were marked reductions in anger management problems which corresponded to reduction in the CIA scores. Of particular interest was the finding that the CIA was extremely useful in identifying specific problem areas for treatment and evaluation.

SUMMARY

We believe that self-report measures serve a definite purpose in assessment with children. They provide unique subjective reports that facilitate our understanding of the nature of the problems presented and, consequently, improve effectiveness of our treatment approaches. However, it must be emphasized that we also recognize the need to include other sources of information such as behavioral ratings and/or observations. The need for systematic research into the interrelationship of the various measurement sources is great. In addition, treatment research which examines the correspondence of change in self-report and behavioral measures is needed. Fleming (1982) has suggested that internal statements (self-report) might be the first variables to reflect change in cognitive behavioral programs. Nelson (1981), on the other hand, has suggested that behavioral changes might be necessary before cognitive ones occur. Certainly, there is a need for additional research into this area.

REFERENCES

Atkeson, B. M., & Forehand, R. Parent behavioral training for problem children: An examination of studies using multiple outcome measures. *Journal of Abnormal Child Psychology*, 1978, *6*, 449–460.

Bachrach, R., & Peterson, R. A. Test-retest reliability and intercorrelation among three locus of control measures for children. *Perceptual and Motor Skills*, 1975, *43*, 260–262.

Battle, E. S., & Rotter, J. B. Children's feelings of personal control as related to social class and ethnic group. *Journal of Personality*, 1963, *31*, 482–490.

Beck, A., & Beamesderfer, A. Assessment of depression: The depression inventory. In P. Pichot (Ed.), *Psychological measurements in psychopharmacology, modern problems in pharmacopsychiatry* (Vol. 7). Switzerland: 1974.

Bialer, I. Conceptualization of success and failure in mentally retarded and normal children. *Journal of Personality*, 1961, *29*, 303–320.

Birleson, P. The validity of depressive disorder in childhood and development of a self-rating scale: A research report. *Journal of Child Psychology and Psychiatry*, 1980, *22*, 73–88.

Cantwell, D., & Carlson, G. Problems and prospects in the study of childhood depression. *The Journal of Nervous and Mental Disease*, 1979, 167, 522–529.

Carlson, G. A., & Cantwell, D. P. A survey of depressive syndromes and disorder in a child psychiatric population. *Journal of Child Psychology and Psychiatry*, 1980, *21*, 19–25.

Casteneda, A., McCandless, B. R., & Palermo, D. S. The Children's form of the Manifest Anxiety Scale. *Child Development*, 1956, *27*, 317–326.

Deluty, R. H. Children's Action Tendency Scale: A self-report measure of aggressiveness, assertiveness, and submissiveness in children. *Journal of Consulting and Clinical Psychology*, 1979, *47*, 1061–1071.

Finch, A. J., Jr., Kendall, P. C., Dannenburg, M. A., & Morgan, J. R. Effects of task difficulty on State-Trait Anxiety in emotionally disturbed children. *Journal of Genetic Psychology*, 1978, *133*, 255–259.

Finch, A. J., Jr., Kendall, P. C., & Montgomery, L. E. Multidimensionality of anxiety in children: Factor structure of the Children's Manifest Anxiety Scale. *Journal of Abnormal Child Psychology*, 1974, *2*, 331–336.

Finch, A. J., Jr., Kendall, P. C., Montgomery, L. E., & Morris, T. Effects of two types of failure on anxiety in emotionally disturbed children. *Journal of Abnormal Psychology*, 1975, *84*, 583–585.

Finch, A. J., Jr., & Montgomery, L. E. Reflection-impulsivity and information seeking in emotionally disturbed children. *Journal of Abnormal Child Psychology*, 1973, *1*, 358–362.

Finch, A. J., Jr., Montgomery, L. E., & Deardorff, P. Reliability of State-Trait Anxiety with emotionally disturbed children. *Journal of Abnormal Child Psychology*, 1974, *2*, 67–69.

Finch, A. J., Jr., Nelson, W. M., III, & Moss, J. H. A cognitive-behavioral approach to anger management with emotionally disturbed children. In A. J. Finch, Jr., W. M. Nelson, III, & E. S. Ott (Eds.), *Cognitive-behavioral approaches to treatment with children*. Jamaica, NY: Spectrum Publications, in press.

Finch, A. J., Jr., Pezzuti, K. A., & Nelson, W. M., III. Locus of control and academic achievement in emotionally disturbed children. *Journal of Consulting and Clinical Psychology*, 1975, *43*, 103.

Finch, A. J., Jr., & Saylor, C. F. An overview of child depression. In J. V. Lavigne & W. Burns (Eds.), *Review of pediatric psychology* (Vol. 1), New York: Grune and Stratton, Inc., in press.

Flanigan, P. J., Peters, C. J., & Conry, J. L. Item analysis of the Children's Manifest Anxiety Scale with the retarded. *Journal of Educational Research*, 1969, *62*, 472–477.

Fleming, C. C. *Evaluation of an anger management program with aggressive children in resi-*

dential treatment. Unpublished doctoral dissertation, Virginia Polytechnic Institute and State University, 1982.

Fleming, C. C., & Kelly, M. M. *Valid assessment of childhood depression.* Paper presented at the 29th Annual Meeting of the Southeastern Psychological Association, New Orleans, 1982.

Friedman, R. J., & Butler, L. F. *Development and evaluation of a test battery to assess childhood depression.* Final report to Health and Welfare, Canada, Project #606-1533-44, June 15, 1979.

Gorsuch, R. L., Henigan, R. P., & Barnard, C. Locus of control: An example of dangers in using children's scales with children. *Child Development,* 1972, *43,* 579–590.

Green, B. J. Depression in early adolescence. An exploratory investigation of its frequency, intensity, and correlates. *Dissertation Abstracts International,* 1980, *41,* 3890-B.

Herzbergen, S. D., Linney, J. A., Seidman, E., & Rappaport, J. Preschool and Primary Locus of Control Scale: Is it ready for use? *Developmental Psychology,* 1979, *15,* 320–324.

Kovacs, M. *Children's Depression Inventory* (CDI) . Unpublished manuscript, University of Pittsburgh, 1978.

Lange, M., & Tisher, M. *Children's Depression Scale.* The Australian Council for Educational Research Limited, Victoria, Australia, 1978.

MacDonald, A. P. Internal-external locus of control. In J. Robinson & P. Shaver (Eds.), *Measures of social psychological attitudes.* Ann Arbor: University of Michigan Institute for Social Research, 1973.

McAdoo, G. *T-scores and percentile ranks for children referred to a child guidance clinic.* Unpublished manuscript, Indiana University, 1981.

Miezitis, S., Friedman, R. J., Butler, L. F., & Blanchard, J. P. *Development and evaluation of school-based assessment and treatment approaches for depressed children.* The Ontario Institute for Studies in Education, Toronto, Canada, August 1978.

Mischel, W., Zeiss, R., & Zeiss, A. Internal-external control and persistence: Validation and implications of the Stanford Preschool Internal-External Scale. *Journal of Personality and Social Psychology,* 1974, *29,* 265–278.

Montgomery, L. E., & Finch, A. J., Jr. Validity of two measures of anxiety in children. *Journal of Abnormal Child Psychology,* 1974, *2,* 293–298.

Montgomery, L. E., Nelson, W. M., III, & Finch, A. J., Jr. *Anger in children: Preliminary investigations of anger-evoking stimuli in children.* Paper presented at the 25th Annual Meeting of the Southeastern Psychological Association, New Orleans, 1979.

Nelson, W. M., III. A cognitive-behavioral treatment for disproportionate dental anxiety and pain: A case study. *Journal of Clinical Child Psychology,* 1981, *10,* 79–82.

Nelson, W. M., III, & Finch, A. J., Jr. *The Children's Inventory of Anger.* Unpublished manuscript, Xavier University, 1978.

Newmark, C. S., Wheeler, D., Newmark, L., & Stabler, B. Test-induced anxiety with children. *Journal of Personality Assessment,* 1975, *39,* 409–413.

Nowicki, S., Jr. *Achievement and popularity as related to locus of control across different age groups.* Unpublished manuscript, Emory University, 1971.

Nowicki, S., Jr., & Duke, M. P. A preschool and primary internal-external control scale. *Developmental Psychology,* 1974, *6,* 874–880.

Nowicki, S., Jr., & Roundtree, J. Correlates of locus of control in a secondary school population. *Developmental Psychology,* 1971, *4,* 477–478.

Nowicki, S., Jr., & Strickland, B. R. A locus of control scale for children. *Journal of Consulting and Clinical Psychology,* 1973, *40,* 148–154.

O'Brien, P. A. *Construct validity of the Children's Depression Inventory: A multi-trait, multi-method approach.* Paper presented at the 28th Annual Meeting of the Southeastern Psychological Association, New Orleans, 1982.

Ollendick, T. H. Development and validation of the Children's Assertiveness Inventory. *Child & Family Behavior Therapy,* in press. (a)

Ollendick, T. H. Reliability and validity of the Revised Fear Survey Schedule for Children (FSSC-R). *Behaviour Research and Therapy,* in press. (b)

Ollendick, T. H., & Cerny, J. A. *Clinical behavior therapy with children.* New York: Plenum Press, 1981.

Pela, O. A., & Reynolds, C. R. *Cross-cultural application of the Revised Children's Manifest Anxiety Scale: Normative and reliability data for Nigerian primary school children.* Manuscript in review, 1981.

Reynolds, C. R. Concurrent validity of What I Think and Feel: The Revised Children's Manifest Anxiety Scale. *Journal of Consulting and Clinical Psychology,* 1980, *48,* 774–775.

Reynolds, C. R. Long-term stability of scores on the Revised Children's Manifest Anxiety Scale. *Perceptual and Motor Skills,* 1981, *53,* 702.

Reynolds, C. R. *Convergent and divergent validity of What I Think and Feel: The Revised Children's Manifest Anxiety Scale.* Manuscript in review, 1982.

Reynolds, C. R., Bradley, M., & Steele, C. Preliminary norms and technical data for use of the Revised Children's Manifest Anxiety Scale with kindergarten children. *Psychology in the Schools,* 1980, *17,* 163–167.

Reynolds, C. R., & Paget, K. D. Factor analysis of the Revised Children's Manifest Anxiety Scale for blacks, whites, males, and females. *Journal of Consulting and Clinical Psychology,* 1981, *49,* 352–359.

Reynolds, C. R., & Paget, K. D. *National normative and reliability data for the Revised Children's Manifest Anxiety Scale.* Paper presented at the annual meeting of the National Association of School Psychologists, Toronto, March 1982.

Reynolds, C. R., & Richmond, B. O. "What I Think and Feel": A revised measure of children's manifest anxiety. *Journal of Abnormal Child Psychology,* 1978, *6,* 271–280.

Rotter, J. B. Generalized expectancies for internal versus external control of reinforcement. *Psychological Monographs,* 1966, (Whole No. 80).

Rulon, P. J. A simplified procedure for determining the reliability of test of split-halves. *Harvard Educational Review,* 1939, *9,* 99–103.

Sarason, S. B., Davidson, K. S., Lightfall, F. F., Waite, R. R., & Ruebush, B. K. *Anxiety in elementary school children.* New York: Wiley, 1960.

Saylor, C. F., Finch, A. J., Jr., Spirito, A., & Bennett, B. *A systematic evaluation of the Children's Depression Inventory.* Manuscript under review, 1983.

Scherer, M. W., & Nakamura, C. Y. A fear survey schedule for children (FSS-FC): An analytic comparison with manifest anxiety. *Behaviour Research and Therapy,* 1968, *6,* 173–182.

Sitarz, A. M. *Effects of psychological testing on State-Trait Anxiety in emotionally disturbed children.* Unpublished master's thesis, Virginia Commonwealth University, Richmond, 1974.

Spielberger, C. D. *State-Trait Anxiety Inventory for Children.* Palo Alto, CA: Consulting Psychological Press, 1973.

Stein, A. B., Finch, A. J., Jr., Hooke, J. F., Montgomery, L. E., & Nelson, W. M., III. Cognitive tempo and the mode of representation in emotionally disturbed children and normal children. *Journal of Psychology,* 1975, *90,* 197–201.

Taylor, J. A. The relationship of anxiety to the conditioned eyelid response. *Journal of Experimental Psychology,* 1951, *42,* 183–188.

Walker, H. M. *Problem behavior identification checklist.* Western Psychological Services, Los Angeles, CA, 1976.

7

*Peer Sociometric Forms**†

Hyman Hops
and
Lewis Lewin

The study of children's peer relationships has long been the concern of educators, sociologists, and psychologists. The objectives of such research have ranged from interest in the basic normal development of childhood social relations to the identification of factors contributing to social maladjustment and childhood psychopathology. Current research into the developmental processes involved in children's peer relationships has extended the focus downward into infancy, showing that child-child interactions do indeed occur earlier than previously expected (Field, 1981). Furthermore, such social

*This manuscript was prepared with the assistance of NIMH Grant Number MH33205 and DOE Grant Number G008001339. The authors wish to acknowledge the valuable critique of Wendy Weissman on an earlier draft. The assistance of Agatha McLean in the typing and preparation of the manuscript and Linda Rangus for graphics is greatly appreciated.

†A variant of the nomination procedure requires children to nominate classmates who best fit a series of descriptions of behavior, characteristics, and attitudes. Examples include the frequently used Pupil Evaluation Inventory (Pekarik, Prinz, Liebert, Weintraub, & Neale, 1976) and the Class Play (Bower, 1960). We will not consider these measures as sociometric indices, however, even though they are often classified as such. They are more accurately defined as peer assessment procedures (Kane & Lawler, 1978), which are peers' judgments of whether specific behavioral characteristics apply to each child. Sociometric scores, in contrast, simply measure the valence of an individual's attraction toward other peer group members. Thus, attribution by peers of specific characteristics, whether obtained through interviews or systematic tests, may be used to validate sociometric measures by examining the relationship between the children's behavioral characteristics described by their peers and the peers' attraction toward them.

relations appear to account for unique aspects of children's social development (Hartup, in press; Mueller, 1972).

There are several reasons for the current interest in children's social development. First, increases in the number of working parents have produced a substantial increase in the number of children placed in day-care centers and preschools, thus providing an abundant population for researchers interested in the social behavior of children (Field, 1981). A second influence can be seen in studies demonstrating the short- and long-term deleterious effects of social maladjustment. Peer rejection, for example, has been shown to have long-term predictive validity for later behavioral adjustment (Cowen, Pederson, Babigian, Izzo, & Trost, 1973; Roff, Sells, & Golden, 1972). Problems in peer group social relations have also been found to be one of the most frequently mentioned factors in children's referrals for treatment at mental health centers (Achenbach & Edelbrock, 1981; Rinn & Markle, 1979). A third influence from the adult literature demonstrates highly significant relationships between the lack of social competence and various forms of psychopathology (Bellack & Hersen, 1979; Kazdin, 1979). Taken together, the combined influences of (a) an increasing preschool and day-care population and both social and scientific interest therein, and (b) the increasing number of studies demonstrating the relationship of both childhood and adult psychopathology to social behavior, have given rise to an increasing concern with the assessment (Hops & Greenwood, 1981) and treatment of children's maladaptive social relationships (Hops, 1982).

Strategies used to assess a child's social relationships or social status and to evaluate intervention programs aimed at improving those that are problematic have included interviewing, naturalistic observation, role play, and sociometrics (Cartledge & Milburn, 1980). The sociometric procedure, developed in the 1930s (Koch, 1933; Moreno, 1934), has been one of the most frequently used methods for measuring a child's social status or popularity with the peer group. Sociometrics provide information about the extent to which a child is liked or disliked by his or her peers by simply asking the peers to make written or verbal responses or nominations to questions about the child's playmates or best friends. Literally hundreds of studies have used this procedure to obtain estimates of peer popularity, friendship, social adjustment, and social competence among children (Glidewell, Kantor, Smith, & Stringer, 1966; Hallinan, 1981; Hartup, 1970, in press).

The sociometric method, however, is not a single well-defined set of procedures. Specifically, it has included nominations, Likert-type rating scales, and paired comparisons. The criteria for ranking or ratings have been both positive and negative. Nominations may have a fixed-choice or free-choice format. The referent situations, for which choices are made, have also varied considerably. Consequently, sociometric data must be examined in the light of the procedural context within which they were obtained.

In the following sections, we will discuss the major types of sociometric procedures, the variables which can be derived, and their advantages and disadvantages. Following that we will examine the supporting reliability and validity studies. Next, several studies will be reviewed in which the treatment of socially problematic children has been evaluated with sociometric instruments. A brief discussion will follow on some of the major prevailing issues that affect the usefulness of the procedure. Finally, a case study will be presented illustrating how peer status variables can be used to evaluate treatment effects of social skills training.

TYPES OF SOCIOMETRIC PROCEDURES

The three most commonly used types of sociometric procedures are: (a) the restricted nomination or partial-rank-order, (b) the rating scale, and (c) the paired-comparison procedure. We will present and discuss the prominent features of each of these types, their most commonly used formats, the measures each can provide, and their advantages and disadvantages.

Restricted Nominations

The restricted nomination or partial-ranking procedure is probably the most widely used sociometric procedure. Children of a given social group (e.g., the classroom) are asked to choose a predetermined number of classmates for a given referent situation. For example, to estimate a child's status as a playmate, children are asked generally to select three of their peers "whom you would most like to play (or work) with," "you like most," or as "best friends." Social status scores derived from such measures indicate levels of popularity or acceptance based on the percentage of positive nominations. Some investigators consider nomination of individuals as an index of friendship.

Negative nominations have also been used to provide a different measure of peer group relationships (Dunnington, 1957). Children are asked to identify classmates who they "would *not* like to (or *least* like to) play with." The percentage of negative nominations provides a measure of the level of rejection of each child by the peer group.

With children who read, the nominations can be obtained by each child writing down the names of his or her choices on a slip of paper or checking off nominees on a seating chart or class roster. For younger children with undeveloped reading and writing skills, McCandless and Marshall (1957) developed the picture-sociometric procedure. Head and shoulder photographs are taken of each child in the classroom with the pictures presented in a random fashion on a poster board to the children in individual interviews. Each child is first asked to identify his or her own picture and next to name all of the peers one at a time. The examiner provides the name of each child whose name is not known. Next, the child is asked to point to the nominees for the particular referent situation (e.g., "Point to the child you like [or would like to play with] the most"). In this way, the procedure is not dependent upon writing or reading skills or upon whether the child knows or remembers all of the names of his or her classmates.

Negative nominations have been used less frequently than positive nominations (Asher & Hymel, 1981) because of some parental and school administrative concern. This is generally based on the assumption that making negative nominations promotes negative concepts about, and negative interactions with, the rejectees, although there is no empirical data to support this belief. It is important to note that positive and negative nominations are only moderately correlated (Asher, Singleton, Tinsley, & Hymel, 1979) and have different behavioral correlates (Hartup, Glazer, & Charlesworth, 1967). Furthermore, interventions which increased acceptance scores of integrated EMR children had minimal effect on their rejection scores (Ballard, Corman, Gottlieb, & Kaufman, 1977). Taken together, these data suggest that the scores derived from positive and negative nominations may be conceptually and functionally independent.

Positive and negative nomination procedures can be combined to provide greater precision for diagnosing socially problematic children. True isolate or neglected children may be those who receive no positive or negative nominations. True rejected children may be defined as those receiving no positive but a large number of negative nominations. On a sample of 205 elementary grade children, Hymel and Asher (1977) found that 5% of the children were isolates and 3% were rejected. If different interventions are required for each diagnostic type then it is extremely important that both positive and negative nominations be used to precisely identify those in each category.

Derived Scores

Peery (1979) has suggested that combining positive and negative nominations can provide a measure of the total *social impact* a child has on the classroom. Similarly, subtracting the number of negative choices from the number of positive votes can provide an estimate of a child's *social preference* by the peer group. (The latter score has been used extensively in the literature as a measure of social status.) Using the two dimensions of social impact and social preference orthogonally, Peery defines four classification categories: *Popular* (high social impact, positive social preference), *Rejected* (high social impact, negative social preference), *Isolate* (low social impact, negative social preference), and *Amiable* (low social impact, positive social preference).

Coie, Dodge, and Coppotelli (1982) further differentiate social status. They suggest that there are "controversial" children who receive high proportions of both positive and negative nominations. Thus, they create a more homogeneous popular group while identifying another group of potentially problematic children.

The major advantage of the nomination procedure is that it is easy to administer, especially with children who read. A 3- or 6-choice nomination procedure can be administered to a classroom of 15–30 students in a 10-minute period. Its disadvantages occur primarily for preschoolers, for whom test-retest reliability is lower and who require longer administration time.

Peer Ratings

A second method for determining peer status involves the use of a Likert-type rating scale. Children are provided with a list or roster of their classmates and asked to rate each one according to the criterion specified in the referent situation. For example, elementary school children are asked to circle a number from 1 to 5 that best describes how much they like to play with (or work with) each class member (Hymel & Asher, 1977; Oden & Asher, 1977). Each child's score is the mean of all the ratings received. In some instances, faces ranging from a smile to a frown are paired with the rating scale to assist the children in assigning numeric values to their ratings (Singleton & Asher, 1977).

The major advantage of the sociometric rating procedure is that each child is rated by every other child in the group or classroom. Consequently, the distribution of scores tends to be significantly less skewed than that obtained with the partial-ranking procedure. It also reduces the probability that a child will not be chosen because a peer could not spell, write, or remember his or her name. In addition, there is some suggestion that the scores derived from the rating sociometric are more sensitive to changes in social status than the nomination procedure depending upon the referent situation (Asher & Hymel, 1981). Following coaching in social skills, low-status children changed on the "play with" ratings but not on the "work with" ratings (Oden & Asher, 1977). Similarly, white children rated black children higher for play, as opposed to work, situations (Singleton & Asher, 1977).

A variant of the rating-scale procedure combined with the picture sociometric has been developed by Asher et al. (1979) for preschool children. Children were first taught to assign values to boxes paired with a happy, neutral, and frowning face to represent "like something a lot," "kinda like something," and "don't like something," respectively. They were then asked to place the pictures of each of their classmates in one of the three boxes, indicating their ratings. The test-retest reliabilities of the ratings were found to be superior to the nominations.

Paired-Comparison Procedure

The first demonstration of the paired-comparison sociometric was conducted by Koch in 1933 with a sample of preschool children. Each child was asked to choose between every pair of children in the classroom, excluding themselves, for each referent situation. The number of pairs presented to each child equals $(n-1)(n-2)/2$. Koch (1933) took 4 months to administer the test to her 17 subjects by presenting all possible pairs of names orally. More recently, Cohen and Van Tassel (1978) used a variation of the picture sociometric to preclude the likelihood that children will not be selected because the peers cannot remember their names.

The major advantage of the paired-comparison procedure is its exceptional temporal stability (Cohen & Van Tassel, 1978; Vaughn & Waters, 1980) for preschoolers as well as older children (Wytrol & Thompson, 1953). Furthermore, the procedure can be used to establish reliable estimates of friendships or mutual relationships within the peer group. Studies have shown that mutually selected choices behave differently than unreciprocated choices on curiosity tasks and in social situations (e.g., Cohen & Melson, 1979).

The major drawback of the paired-comparison procedure is its lengthy administration requiring up to 300 choices to be made in a class of 25. With a maximum of 40–50 pairs shown at each administration, it requires six 10-minute sessions with each child in the classroom. However, Cohen and Van Tassel (1978) have shown recently that a partial but representative sample of choices will produce valid scores of popularity and dyadic relationships.

Multimethod Procedures

The use of both the nomination and the peer-rating procedures may provide a more distinct picture of the social relationships within the classroom to aid in identifying problematic children. Hymel and Asher (1977) found a moderately high correlation (.63) between positive nominations and peer ratings. However, 11 of the 23 children who received no positive nominations also received ratings of 3 or more on a 5-point rating scale! The effects of race on sociometric ratings may be less than that previously reported in studies using positive nominations alone (Singleton & Asher, 1977, 1979). In both these studies, the authors suggest that a rating scale provides a measure of a child's likability or acceptability, whereas positive nominations identify a child's popularity as a playmate or friend.

These interpretations, of course, must be viewed with caution partly because of the methodological differences that exist between the two procedures and because of the frequent confusion made between friendship and popularity (see *Issues*). The rating scale requires that each child evaluate every other child in the classroom. If the nomination procedure were unrestricted so that each child rank ordered the entire class, then the ratings and positive nominations would be likely to be more highly correlated. Thus, ratings and nominations may differ primarily in the restrictions placed on the number of choices allowed.

RELIABILITY

The test-retest reliability of a sociometric measure is affected by a number of factors including: (a) the type of sociometric strategy used (e.g., paired comparison vs. restricted nomination vs. ratings), (b) the age of the children (preschool vs. elementary), (c) the period of time elapsed between the test and retest, (d) the type of behavior studied (choices given vs. choices received vs. reciprocal choices), and (e) the referent situation or context (play vs. work) for which the child is rated or chosen. The impact of these factors on the temporal stability will be discussed using the major types of sociometric procedures as an organizing framework.

Restricted Nominations

Restricted nomination or partial-rank-order procedures have been used in the majority of sociometric studies reporting temporal reliability. A review of this research indicates that (a) stability increases with age – at least from preschool through sixth grade, (b) positive nominations are more stable than negative nominations, (c) reciprocal choices are more stable than positive choices received, and (d) stability decreases with increasing time between test and retest (Busk, Ford, & Schulman, 1973).

Most studies using preschoolers have reported test-retest coefficients ranging from .30 to .78 levels (Asher et al., 1979; Greenwood, Walker, Todd, & Hops, 1979; Hartup et al., 1967; Moore & Updegraff, 1964). While the introduction of the picture sociometric has reduced the error in test administration significantly, the stability of preschoolers' nominations remains highly variable. Generally, the test-retest reliabilities of acceptance scores are better than those for rejection scores or for the unilateral selection of peers ("individual friendships") (Cohen & Van Tassel, 1978; Hartup et al., 1967). Four- and 5-year-olds tend to be more stable than 3-year-olds (Cohen & Van Tassel, 1978; Moore & Updegraff, 1964). Research using nomination scores conducted with preschool children should automatically check the temporal stability in the group of interest.

The use of the nomination procedure with elementary-age children generally results in higher reliabilities than with preschool children. In a study of fourth and sixth graders, Busk et al. (1973) used an unlimited, positive-nomination-only procedure. In general, the stability of "choices received" (popularity) was higher than that of the "choices given" (friendships) for both grades, although the older students produced more stable scores overall. The authors concluded that a sixth grader's social status seems more firmly established; the stability of popularity in sixth graders remained at similar levels when the test-retest interval was increased from 8 weeks to 7 months. The reliability of other measures showed considerable decreases over larger intervals. However, overall, popularity and friendship measures were affected more by the length of the test-retest interval and the child's age than were reciprocal choices.

Peer Ratings

Relatively high stability coefficients have been found consistently for peer ratings of both preschool and elementary-age students. Asher et al. (1979) demonstrated correlations of .84 for peer ratings on a 3-point scale for 4-year-old preschoolers over a 4-week period. Similarly, studies with elementary school children have shown test-retest correlations in the seventies and eighties for periods ranging from 4 (Oden & Asher, 1977) and 9 weeks (Ladd, 1981) to 4 months (Hymel & Asher, 1977).

A single exception to these findings was in the work reported by Gresham (1981). The stability of "play with" and "work with" ratings ranged from .20 to .63 over a 6-week period for third- and fourth-grade students. The subjects, however, were all of low-sociometric status, and the lower correlations may have been an artifact of the reduced variability in a homogeneous group.

Paired-Comparison Sociometric

As indicated above, a major disadvantage of the paired-comparison sociometric is the lengthy administrative procedure. Consequently, Cohen and Van Tassel (1978) compared the test-retest reliability of the full paired comparison with a partial procedure on a sample of 3-year-olds ($n = 16$) and 4-year-olds ($n = 18$). The partial method consisted of various combinations of five shorter equally formed sublists, which were administered one or two at a time to each child on each day of testing.

The data support the substantial temporal stability of the paired-comparison procedure for both 3-year-olds and 4-year-olds. However, the younger children require a longer period of time initially to become acquainted and for choices to stabilize. Furthermore, it appears that scores based on the administration of only 60% of the possible pairs provide adequate reliability that is superior to that obtained on the partial-rank-order procedure, as described earlier. Similar comparisons have been found between paired-comparison methods and partial-ranking methods obtained on samples of sixth-grade children (Wytrol & Thompson, 1953). The stability of the unilateral "friendship" choices, however, remain much lower, especially for the 3-year-old children. The entire administration is required to achieve adequate test-retest reliability.

COMMENTS ON RELIABILITY

There has been a recent tendency to adapt some traditional psychometric concepts to behavioral assessment procedures. Not all have agreed with this approach, however. The concept of reliability has been borrowed from classical psychometric test theory which incorporates the assumptions underlying a trait-theory approach to human behavior (Cone, 1981). In its simplest form, behavior is assumed to remain relatively stable over time since it is simply the manifestation of inflexible traits. Thus, the instability of behavioral scores is indicative of "instrument or measurement error." This assumption of behavioral stability has been recently challenged by Mischel (1968) and Cone (1981), and at best is highly controversial. For example, instability in preschoolers' peer nominations or ratings may reflect: (a) "measurement error"—the instrument is simply not adequate for assessing the play preferences of 3- to 5-year-olds, or (b) the instability of a preschool child's individual choices. We have collected data which suggest that both of these possibilities should be considered. The stability of individual choices was examined in a classroom of 20 preschool children over a 1-month period using the paired-comparison procedure. We found consistently high stability for the majority of the students' individual choices. However, low stability was found for those children who were least popular, probably reflecting their particular difficulty in entering the peer group and establishing stable friendships (Hops, Finch, & Stevens, in preparation). Similar results have been reported by Dygdon, Conger, and Ward (1981) with older children. Thus, these findings highlight the difficulty in distinguishing between error due to poor test construction for a particular age group and actual variability in behavioral events. Only an individual analysis would demonstrate such differences.

The differences in reliability estimates between the nomination procedures and the rating or paired-comparison procedure must also be examined in psychometric terms as well as conceptual ones. Several investigators have argued that ratings and paired-comparison choices provide a measure of a child's likability as opposed to the friendship index measured by the nominations procedure (Asher & Hymel, 1981; Cohen & Van Tassel, 1978). Thus, they conclude that likability is more stable than individual friendships (we will examine the concept of friendship in more detail elsewhere). However, it is also true that the lower stability of the nomination method is due to its computation based on a smaller number of scores with a skewed distribution. Since reliability is influenced by changes in relative ranking within the distribution, rankings are more likely to change when they are based on fewer children's input, as in the nomination system, rather than data obtained from all of the children, as in the rating or paired-comparison procedures. Thus, data must be examined both conceptually and psychometrically to identify all of the possible sources of variability over time.

VALIDITY

Considerable research has been conducted on the relationship between various measures of peer status and a host of criterion measures. The latter have included the assessment of social, academic, and behavioral adjustments in both playground and classroom settings. Measurements have included direct observation methods and ratings obtained from peers, teachers, and parents. However, the research has been largely correlational and quasi-experimental. The experimental validation of these correlational findings has received proportionately little attention.

We will examine the validity of each of the major sociometric types. Studies will be grouped within each sociometric method according to the type of criterion, measurement, and setting studied.

Nomination Procedures

Direct Observation. Research on the relationship between preschoolers' social status based on nominations and social behavior observed *in vivo* has had at least a 30-year history. Overall, studies have consistently shown low to moderate relationships between positive social behavior and social acceptance and between negative social behavior and rejection (Greenwood et al., 1979; Hartup et al., 1967; Marshall & McCandless, 1957; Moore & Updegraff, 1964). Furthermore, acceptance and rejection scores are not significantly related, which indicates they are measuring independent dimensions of social status (Hartup et al., 1967; Moore & Updegraff, 1964).

Research with grade school children has been more elaborate. One of the better designed studies was conducted by Dodge, Coie, and Brakke (1982). Direct observation of third and fifth graders showed that rejected children spent less time in appropriate solitary activity, made more inappropriate initiations to the peer group in the classroom, and were likely to be twice as aggressive as popular and average children on the playground. The major deficit shown in the neglected child was a low initiation rate to peers on the playground. Like rejected children, however, neglected children's invitations were often rejected by their peers. With this study, Dodge and his colleagues have further differentiated the behavioral correlates of the accepted and two types of low-status children, the neglected and rejected.

The peer status-social behavior relationship has also been studied in contrived or analogue settings by Gottman and his associates. Compared to popular children, unpopular children do worse on a role-play test of how to make friends (Gottman, Gonso, & Rasmussen, 1975) and have difficulty entering small game-playing groups. Popular children demonstrate effective entry behaviors such as: (a) commenting on how well a player is doing, or (b) exchanging information without trying to control the group (Putallaz & Gottman, 1981). The major weaknesses in Gottman's creative research are: (a) the dependence on analogue situations for which generalization data are weak (Van Hasselt, Hersen, & Bellack, 1981), and (b) the absence of negative nominations to clearly differentiate the sociometric subgroupings.

Social Agents. Although the social behaviors of the subjects have most frequently served as the criterion in sociometric validity research, the ratings and ranking of other significant social agents, most noticeably teachers, have also been studied. Convergent validation has been consistently found for peer acceptance with teachers' rankings of peer popularity at the preschool level (Greenwood et al., 1979; Connolly & Doyle, 1981). However, in all studies, teacher judgment was more highly correlated with measures based on direct observation than were sociometrics. At the elementary school level, only low to moderate correlations were obtained between teachers' ratings of behavioral maladjustment and peer rejection and acceptance in the predicted directions (Green, Forehand, Beck, & Vosk, 1980).

Children's descriptions of their peers also have been used to validate sociometrics status (Coie, Dodge, & Coppotelli, 1982). The major behavioral correlates of positive and negative nominations for a sample of third, fifth, and eighth graders were prosocial behaviors and negative/aggressive behaviors, respectively. Descriptions were also obtained for each of the four sociometric types (i.e., popular, rejected, isolate, and amiable children). The unique finding isolated "controversial" children (high positives *and* negatives) who were seen having the features of both popular (leaders) and rejected children (starts fights). Neglected children were the opposite of controversial types. No differences were noted across age groups.

Of the few long-term predictive studies available, one of the most important is that of Roff, Sells, and Golden (1972). They found that children with low sociometric status (positive minus negative) in the third–sixth grades had the highest incidence of contact with juvenile police authorities some 3 years later, regardless of the level of SES. However, in lower SES areas, a higher incidence of juvenile delinquency was noted for students with high- as well as low-status scores.

Overall, the moderate discriminative validity of the positive and negative nomination system has been well established at the preschool and elementary-age levels. Generally, positive correlations were found between prosocial behavior and social acceptance and between negative-aggressive social behavior and rejection. Elementary students' classroom and academic work also appears to be related to their peer standing, but more research is required to explain this effect.

The recent work of Coie, Dodge, and their associates offers some new directions. In delineating the specific behavioral correlates of different problematic sociometric categories (i.e., the rejected, neglected, and controversial), they provide a more precise treatment focus for clinicians interested in working with such children.

Peer Ratings

Since scores derived from nomination procedures have received so much attention and partial validation, they have been used, in turn, to validate peer ratings. Generally, play ratings are moderately correlated with sociometric status based on both positive and negative nominations for preschool (Asher, Singleton, Tinsley, & Hymel, 1979) and elementary-age children (Green et al., 1980; Gresham, 1981, Van Hasselt et al., 1981). However, Gresham (1981) found ratings, nominations, and direct observation of social behavior loading on independent factors. Furthermore, the ratings alone do not discriminate between rejected and neglected children. Hymel and Asher (1977) found that 1 of 7 rejected children (no positives, 2 or more negatives) received a mean rating above 3.00. But 6 of 11 neglected children received ratings below 3.00 and 5 above 3.00.

The convergent validity of peer and teacher ratings has also been investigated. Peer ratings and teachers' estimates of the average peers' rating each child received were moderately correlated (Green et al., 1980). Moderate and positive correlations were also noted for teacher ratings of children's social skills (Van Hasselt et al., 1981). Lower correlations were found with teachers' ratings of childhood maladjustment (Green et al., 1980). A child's sex, however, may affect the relationship between peers and teachers' ratings (LaGreca, 1981). Both Hymel and Asher (1977) and Gresham (1981) conclude that ratings measure a child's acceptability in the peer group, whereas nominations assess friendship or high priority playmates. Gresham (1981) suggests that a differential diagnosis based on both nominations and ratings will aid in the selection of specific treatment procedures. However, more research is required to precisely identify the methodology and the expected advantages of such a procedure.

Paired Comparisons

Few studies have been conducted with the paired-comparison procedure and consequently there is less evidence of its validity. However, Cohen and Van Tassel (1978) have shown moderate correlations with sociometric status derived from nominations for both 3- and 4-year-olds. Further support was found in a study of over two hundred preschool children (Hops & Finch, 1983). Popularity was moderately correlated with the amount of social behavior displayed by children during free play and highly correlated with teachers' rankings of popularity. Further research is required to see whether such relationships hold for elementary school children.

COMMENTS ON VALIDITY

Although there have been many attempts to identify the correlates of sociometric status, few investigators have used a sociometric assessment procedure which permits subjects to be classified in a system that is both comprehensive and can discriminate between popular, rejected, withdrawn, and controversial children (Coie et al., 1982). Most studies at the preschool and elementary school level have shown positive correlations between social acceptance and positive social behavior and between social rejection and negative-aggressive social behavior. We need to further delineate the behaviors of each of the socially problematic groups, as Coie and his colleagues have done, to identify the social skills that underlie social competence and to target behaviors for treatment (Hops, 1982). In addition, experimental manipulation of these correlates is needed by treating rejected, neglected, and controversial children to determine whether the identified "skills" are causally related to sociometric status. It is quite possible that there are other moderating variables such as motor skills (Hops, 1982) or physical attractiveness (Hartup, in press) that account for a large proportion of the variance in children's popularity, thus mitigating any intervention efforts on our part. In the following section, we will describe a few of the experimental treatment studies that have been conducted using sociometric measures for both assessment and evaluation of treatment outcome.

THE USE OF SOCIOMETRICS
IN CLINICAL ASSESSMENTS

A number of studies have been directed at changing children's social status over the years (Ballard et al., 1977; Bonney, 1971; Gresham & Nagle, 1980; Lilly, 1971) with mixed success. However, very few of these were designed to experimentally test the causal relationship of specific correlates of social status.

Oden and Asher (1977) provided coaching in four categories of social skills that appeared to be related to social acceptance: participation, cooperation, communication, and validation/support. Ratings received by the coaching group increased significantly beyond those achieved by peer-pairing and no-treatment control groups. One-year follow-up data suggested that these gains were maintained over time. A replication of this study was unsuccessful (Hymel & Asher, 1977). However, Gottman, Gonso, and Schuler (1976) provided instruction for two isolated children in behaviors shown previously to discriminate between popular and unpopular children (Gottman, et al., 1975). Improvement in sociometric status was noted for only one of the two children treated.

Coaching and coaching plus modeling were compared in a sophisticated design (Gresham & Nagle, 1980). A single significant pre-posttreatment effect was noted for children defined as non-peer oriented on "play with" ratings. Pre-follow-up increases were found for all experimental groups. The relationship between changes in observational data and sociometric scores was not clear. A more precise delineation of social status groups may have reduced some of the pretreatment variability noted by Hops (1982) in his review. It is also possible that sociometric measures are not sensitive to short-term treatments (Gresham & Nagle, 1980).

Coaching and modeling were tested in another short-term intervention effort on a sample of third, fourth, and fifth graders (LaGreca & Santogrossi, 1980). The behavioral targets were a number of social skills extracted from a review of the literature. No effects of the treatment were noted on sociometric ratings; however, improvements were noted on a skill knowledge test, a role-play test, and in the initiation rate. Unfortunately, the observation code did not provide a full test of whether the specific skills taught actually generalized to the natural setting.

One of the best-designed studies was conducted by Ladd (1981), who selected his target children on the basis of sociometric ratings and direct observation measures of the behaviors targeted for treatment. The results showed that verbal skill training was effective in producing generalized increases in two of the three target behaviors in the classroom setting. Moreover, the children showed a concomitant increase in ratings at posttreatment and at the

1-month follow-up. Ladd's study is one of the few to offer experimental validity for the relationship between specific social skills and peer ratings. However, it should be noted that the selection procedure eliminated those low-status children who did *not* show deficits on these skills. Thus, low ratings do not necessarily indicate these specific skill deficits. Both sociometrics and direct observations are required to identify similar targets for intervention.

Recently, we conducted a study aimed at identifying specific sociometric types with the positive and negative nomination procedure. Children identified as isolated or rejected, using Peery's (1979) criteria, were subjected to the Procedures for Establishing Effective Relationship Skills (PEERS) program for socially withdrawn or isolate children (Hops et al., 1978). The program was shown to produce changes in sociometric status and positive social interaction rates. All of the children's social impact and preference scores placed them in the *Amiable* category (low impact, high preference) following intervention. Thus, the program not only increased the overall percentage of the children's social behavior but their social status as well.

The results of the few experimental validation studies clearly show that considerable work has yet to be done. In spite of the authors' delineation of previously identified behavioral correlates, it is difficult to determine whether the behaviors targeted for treatment were in fact the same ones that were defined in the original studies. For example, Gottman et al. (1975) assessed the behaviors in a role-play situation, whereas Ladd (1981) used direct observation in the classroom, while Oden and Asher (1977) did not assess them at all. Increased correspondence between the measurements used to assess specific behaviors in correlational and experimental studies may result in increased effects.

ISSUES IN THE USE OF SOCIOMETRIC PROCEDURES

The use of sociometrics as a diagnostic and outcome tool in the treatment of socially problematic children raises a number of important methodological, ethical, clinical, and interpretative issues. In this section, we will discuss a number of those we considered most critical for the effective use of sociometrics, and we will provide some suggestions for future consideration.

The Distinction Between Friendship and Popularity

In spite of the long and continued use of sociometric procedures as an assessment tool for examining social relationships among children, there continues to be confusion in defining friendship and distinguishing friends from wishful playmates. Many investigators refer to positive nominations as indices of friendship (i.e., a child's choices of those children he or she *wishes* to play with are considered to be that child's friends). However, the available data indicate that the relationship between a child's play choices and the children actually played with is quite low. Greenwood et al. (1979) compared the amount of social interaction accounted for by each child's three positive choices, the three children who actually shared most of the subject's interactions, and a randomly selected group of three peers. The sociometric choices accounted for only half of the social interactions that involved the child's most frequent playmates (50%–60%), which was nearly four times as much as that provided for by the random group (15%). Furthermore, sociometric choices accurately identified only one-third of the three peers who accounted for most of a child's interactions.

Similar evidence was provided by Chapman, Smith, Foot, and Pritchard (1979) who noted that only 27% of the children in one classroom played the most with their selected best friend. In a more recent study (Hops, Higgins, & Stevens, in preparation), we found that more than 25% of a class of 21 second graders identified as their "best friend" a peer other than one of their first six choices as preferred playmates! This suggests that for a significant number of children, the peers with whom they wish to play are not likely to be the children they interact with normally and who are their "current" best friends.

It is also surprising that the developmental literature has not considered in full the concept of reciprocated choices and, instead, has ignored the mutuality inherent in the concept of friendship as a dyadic relationship. Hartup (1975) noted that friendships are characterized as partnerships and are assumed to be "mutually regulated" (p. 14). Kandel (1978) studied "friendship pairs" of high school students and found that only 41% of the choices were reciprocated. These data suggest that friendships should be defined reciprocally rather than unilaterally, regardless of which sociometric procedure is used. We found that mutually selected friends accounted for twice as much of a specific child's positive social behavior than did unilateral or unreciprocated choices, whether that individual was the subject's choice of a peer or the peer's choice of the subject (Hops & Finch, 1982). Future studies should distinguish more carefully between reciprocated choices (friends) and unilateral selections.

Identifying Targets for Treatment

After reviewing the literature, it is difficult to find any consistency in defining specific children who are considered to be at risk for later problematic behavior. Using positive nominations alone, the percentage of low status children has included approximately 30% with a 3-choice format (Hops et al., in preparation; Hymel & Asher, 1977), 18% with a 5-choice format (Gronlund, 1959), and 8% when six choices were allowed (Hops et al., in preparation). Hops (1982) and Hops and Greenwood (1981) have shown this same problem to exist whether the selection criterion is based on sociometrics or direct observation.

Peer ratings provide no better solution to this problem. In a recent study of social skills training, LaGreca and Santagrossi (1980) intervened with subjects whose mean rating on a 5-point scale was 2.57. Their failure to achieve changes in sociometric status may have been due in part to the number of children with mean ratings above 3.00. The diagnostic groups suggested by Peery (1979) and Coie et al. (1982) also require more specific identification strategies. In two studies by the same authors, slightly different computations were used (Coie et al., 1982; Dodge et al., 1982).

The percentage of children selected in each class must be considered in evaluating the impact of specific treatment procedures. Interventions found to be effective with large proportions of the class (e.g., Ladd, 1981) may be less powerful with more severely handicapped children (Hops, 1982).

It is becoming increasingly clear that negative nominations are critical for identifying various subgroups of high-risk children (i.e., the rejected, neglected, and controversial) (Coie et al., 1982). Several recent studies have also identified specific behavioral correlates of these diagnostic groups (Coie et al., 1982; Dodge et al., 1982). For many, however, use of negative choices raises important ethical issues. There is a growing concern that allowing children to make negative nominations: (a) sanctions the behavior, and/or (b) induces them to view others and interact with them more negatively in the future (Asher & Hymel, 1981). Yet, no study has been conducted which supports or refutes these hypotheses! The only available data are the anecdotal reports by every investigator who has used negative nominations indicating no apparent deleterious effects of this procedure (Asher & Hymel, 1981).

Unfortunately, these concerns have added additional confounds to the existing assessment procedures. For example, Roff et al. (1972) used four positive and two negative choices in their study and phrased the negative choices "choose the ones you like least" rather than "those you don't like" (the phrase used in other studies). Some have changed the criterion phrase to "Who you don't play with" which may confound the distinction between neglected and rejected. Others use only positive nominations. Although Asher suggests that positive nominations and peer ratings can be used to identify such children, our review of the literature suggests that it would not be as precise. Certainly, future studies will have to consider this problem, and clinicians who intend to use sociometrics to diagnose children for treatment should attempt to use both positive and negative nominations carefully and cautiously as suggested by Asher and Hymel (1981).

CASE STUDY

This case study illustrates the use of a positive and negative nomination procedure as an assessment instrument and to evaluate treatment effects. The child was a 7-year-old second grader who was not receiving any special educational or psychological services at the time of the intervention. He was selected using a two-stage screening process involving schoolwide teacher referrals for social isolation and playground interaction rates that were one standard deviation below his grade-level mean.

The selection procedure and treatment components are contained in the PEERS social skills training program (Hops, Fleischman, Guild, Paine, Street, Walker, & Greenwood, 1978), originally designed for the treatment of socially withdrawn or isolate children. Intervention consisted of: (a) social-skills tutoring, (b) a recess point system in which the target child earned points for social interaction that were traded in for rewards shared by the entire class, and (c) a peer pairing arrangement involving cooperative tasks between the target child and a selection of different peers. On the playground, program consultants prompted and reinforced the target child's and peers' social behavior. After the child had reached a preset criterion of social interaction rates one standard deviation above the grade-level mean, the program components were gradually and systematically withdrawn.

Process evaluation consisted of daily playground observations of social interaction with peers and repeated administration of a restricted positive plus negative 3-choice nomination procedure. Figure 7.1 shows the daily interaction rates during *Baseline* (B), *Intervention* (I), *Fading* (F), *Short-term follow-up* (FU), and *1-year follow-up* (FU1). Dotted lines represent the mean and ±1 standard deviation for grade-level norms.

The child's average baseline data (35.04) was just below −1 S.D. (38%) of the appropriate norms. During intervention, his mean rate (68.3%) increased to twice that of baseline and approximately equal to +1 S.D. of the norms (70%). The mean rate increased again during fadeout to 81.9%. Short- and long-term follow-up data continue to show maintenance above +1 S.D. of the normative data for second (70%) and third (88%) grade, respectively.

Figure 7.2 shows the sociometric results using Peery's (1979) two-dimensional framework. Social preference (positive nominations minus negative nominations) is represented on the horizontal axis. Social impact (positive plus negative nominations) is represented on the vertical axis. Social impact and preference scores for each phase are expressed as percentile ranks allowing comparisons across different classrooms over the 2 years. The number of times the sociometric procedure was administered is shown at the bottom of figure 7.1.

Figure 7.2 clearly shows that the impact of the Peers program changed the

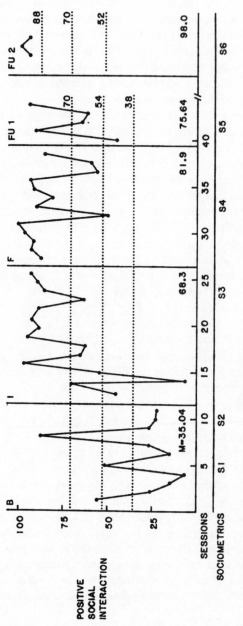

Fig. 7.1. Percentage of daily positive social behavior observed.

142

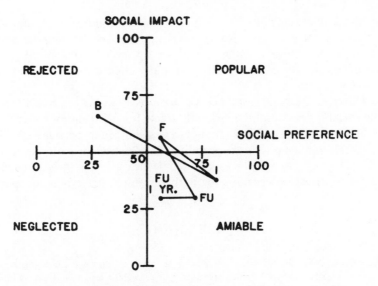

Fig. 7.2. The child's social status across phases.

child's status from *Rejected* to *Amiable* during intervention and at 1-month and 1-year follow-up assessments. Overall the program served to decrease his social impact score by about 35 percentile points while increasing his preference score by 25 points. An examination of the positive and negative nominations received during each phase indicates that the changes were primarily due to decreases in the number of negative nominations received. Positive nominations remained relatively stable throughout.

These data again show the relative independence of the positive and negative nominations and provide further support for their continued use. These data also show the relationship between increased positive social behavior and improvements in social status. While the initial change in status may have been due to the introduction of the group back-up procedure, maintenance of these gains into the following year suggests that the results of the intervention on the subject were more durable.

SUMMARY

The sociometric method has become more popular in recent years for the assessment of children's social relationships. In this chapter, we have compared the major types of sociometric procedures and have tried to evaluate the usefulness of each as a diagnostic tool and as an outcome measure of treatment effectiveness. The positive and negative nomination procedures appear to be the most useful for specifying children at risk. Ratings and paired-comparison procedures may be more useful for younger children or for studying dyadic relationships. Cost-effectiveness is another issue that must be given consideration in clinical practice. For this purpose, the nomination procedure seems to have the edge, especially for older children who remain relatively stable over time.

However, research is still needed to precisely and experimentally identify the specific behavioral deficits and targets for intervention for each group of high-risk children. Recent studies have attempted to provide such a knowledge base and the results are promising. At present, the sociometric method can be best used as one of a set of multiple measures that includes teacher ratings and direct observation for both screening and evaluation purposes.

REFERENCES

Achenbach, T. M., & Edelbrock, C. S. Behavioral problems and competencies reported by parents of normal and disturbed children aged four through sixteen. *Monographs of the Society for Research in Child Development,* 1981, *46* (Serial No. 188).

Asher, S. R., & Hymel, S. Children's social competence in peer relations: Sociometric and behavioral assessment. In J. D. Wine & M. D. Smye (Eds.), *Social competence.* New York: Guilford Press, 1981.

Asher, S. R., & Renshaw, P. D. Children without friends: Social knowledge and social skill training. In S. R. Asher & J. M. Gottman (Eds.), *The development of children's friendships.* New York: Cambridge University Press, 1981.

Asher, S. R., Singleton, L. C., Tinsley, B. R., & Hymel, S. The reliability of a sociometric method with preschool children. *Developmental Psychology,* 1979, *15,* 443–444.

Baer, D. M., & Wolf, M. M. The entry into natural communities of reinforcement. In R. Ulrich, T. Stachnik, & J. Mabry (Eds.), *Control of human behavior.* Glenview, IL: Scott Foresman, 1970.

Ballard, M., Corman, L., Gottlieb, J., & Kaufman, M. J. Improving the social status of mainstreamed retarded children. *Journal of Educational Psychology,* 1977, *69,* 605–611.

Bellack, A. S., & Hersen, M. (Eds.). *Research and practice in social skills training.* New York: Plenum Press, 1979.

Bonney, M. E. Assessment of effort to aid socially isolated elementary school pupils. *Journal of Educational Research,* 1971, *64,* 359–364.

Bower, E. M. *Early identification of emotionally handicapped children.* Springfield, IL: Charles C Thomas, 1960.

Busk, P. L., Ford, R. C., & Schulman, J. L. Stability of sociometric responses in classrooms. *Journal of Genetic Psychology,* 1973, *123,* 69–84.

Cartledge, G., & Milburn, J. F. *Teaching social skills to children: Innovative approaches.* New York: Pergamon Press, 1980.

Chapman, A. J., Smith, J. R., Foot, H. C., & Pritchard, E. Behavioral and sociometric indices of friendship in children. In M. Cook & G. D. Wilson (Eds.), *Love and attraction.* Oxford: Pergamon Press, 1979.

Cohen, A. S., & Melson, G. F. The influence of friendship on children's communication. Paper presented at the annual meeting of the Midwestern Psychological Association, Chicago, May, 1979.

Cohen, A. S., & Van Tassel, E. A. Comparison: Partial and complete paired comparisons in sociometric measurement of preschool groups. *Applied Psychological Measurement,* 1978, *2,* 31–40.

Coie, J. D., Dodge, K. A., & Coppotelli, H. Dimensions and types of social status: A cross-age perspective. *Developmental Psychology,* 1982, *18*(4), 557–570.

Condry, J., & Siman, M. L. Characteristics of peer- and adult-oriented children. *Journal of Marriage and the Family,* 1974, *35,* 543–554.

Cone, J. D. Psychometric considerations. In M. Hersen & A. S. Bellack (Eds.), *Behavioral assessment: A practical handbook.* (2nd ed.). New York: Pergamon Press, 1981.

Connolly, J., & Doyle, A. Assessment of social competence in preschoolers: Teachers versus peers. *Developmental Psychology,* 1981, *17,* 454–462.

Cowen, E. L., Pederson, A., Babigian, H., Izzo, L. D., & Trost, M. A. Long-term followup of early detected vulnerable children. *Journal of Consulting and Clinical Psychology,* 1973, *41,* 438–446.

Deutsch, F. Observational and sociometric measures of peer popularity and their relationship to egocentric communication in female preschoolers. *Developmental Psychology,* 1974, *10,* 745–747.

Dodge, K. A., Coie, J. D., & Brakke, N. P. Behavior patterns of socially rejected and neglected preadolescents: The roles of social approach and aggression. *Journal of Abnormal Child Psychology,* 1982, *10,* 389–410.

Dunnington, M. H. Behavioral differences in sociometric status groups in a nursery school. *Child Development,* 1957, *28,* 103–111.

Dygdon, J. A., Conger, A. M., & Ward, D. G. *The role of clique formation and individual choice patterns in sociometric status.* Paper presented at the annual meeting of the Association for Advancement of Behavior Therapy, Toronto, 1981.

Field, T. Early peer relations. In P. S. Strain (Ed.), *The utilization of classroom peers as behavior change agents.* New York: Plenum Press, 1981.

Flanders, T. Z., & Havumaki, S. The effect of teacher-pupil contacts involving praise on the sociometric choices of students. In J. M. Seidman (Ed.), *Education for mental health.* New York: Thomas Y. Crowell, 1963.

Glidewell, J., Kantor, M. B., Smith, L. M., & Stringer, L. A. Socialization and social structure in the classroom. In M. L. Hoffmann & L. W. Hoffmann (Eds.), *Review of child development research* (Vol. 2). New York: Russell Sage Foundation, 1966.

Gottlieb, J., & Leyser, Y. Friendship between mentally retarded and nontreated children. In S. R. Asher & J. M. Gottman (Eds.), *The development of children's friendships.* New York: Cambridge University Press, 1981.

Gottman, J. M., Gonso, J., & Rasmussen, B. Social interaction, social competence, and friendship in children. *Child Development,* 1975, *46,* 709–718.

Gottman, J. M., Gonso, J., & Schuler, P. Teaching social skills to isolated children. *Journal of Abnormal Psychology,* 1976, *4,* 179–197.

Green, K. D., Forehand, R., Beck, S. J., & Vosk, B. An assessment of the relationship among measures of children's social competence and children's academic achievement. *Child Development,* 1980, *51,* 1149–1156.

Greenwood, C. R., Walker, H. M., Todd, N. M., & Hops, H. Selecting a cost-effective screening device for the assessment of preschool social withdrawal. *Journal of Applied Behavior Analysis,* 1979, *12,* 639–652.

Gresham, F. M. Validity of social skills measures for assessing social competence in low-status children: A multivariate investigation. *Developmental Psychology,* 1981, *17,* 390–398.

Gresham, F. M., & Nagle, R. J. Social skills training with children: Responsiveness to modeling and coaching as a function of peer orientation. *Journal of Consulting and Clinical Psychology,* 1980, *48,* 718–729.

Gronlund, N. E. *Sociometry in the classroom.* New York: Harper, 1959.

Hallinan, M. T. Recent advances in sociometry. In S. R. Asher & J. M. Gottman (Eds.), *The development of children's friendships.* New York: Cambridge University Press, 1981.

Hartup, W. W. Peer interaction and social organization. In P. H. Mussen (Ed.), *Carmichael's manual of child psychology* (Vol. 2, 3rd ed.). New York: Wiley, 1970.

Hartup, W. W.The origins of friendships. In M. Lewis & L. A. Rosenblum (Eds.), *Friendships and peer relations.* New York: Wiley, 1975.

Hartup, W. W. The peer system. In P. H. Mussen (Ed.-in-chief) and E. M. Hetherington (Ed.), *Carmichael's manual of child psychology* (Vol. 4, 4th ed.). New York: Wiley, in press.

Hartup, W. W., Glazer, J. A., & Charlesworth, R. Peer reinforcement and sociometric status. *Child Development,* 1967, *38,* 1017–1024.

Hops, H. Social skills training for socially withdrawn/isolated children. In P. Karoly & J. Steffen (Eds.), *Enhancing children's competencies.* Lexington, MA: Lexington Publishing Co., 1982.

Hops, H., & Finch, M. *The relationship between observed social behavior and reciprocated sociometric choices: A dyadic view of friendship.* Paper presented at the biennial meeting of the Society for Research in Child Development, Detroit, April 1983.

Hops, H., Finch, M., & Stevens, T. Stability and validity of the paired-comparison sociometric procedure for preschoolers. In preparation.

Hops, H., Fleischman, D. H., Guild, J. J., Paine, S., Street, A., Walker, H. M., & Greenwood, C. R. *Procedures for establishing effective relationship skills (PEERS): Consultant manual.* Eugene: University of Oregon, Center at Oregon for Research in the Behavioral Education of the Handicapped, 1978.

Hops, H., & Greenwood, C. R. Social skills deficits. In E. J. Mash & L. G. Terdal (Eds.), *Behavioral assessment of childhood disorders.* New York: Guilford Press, 1981.

Hops, H., Higgins, B., & Stevens, T. A brief note on the meaning of friendship, sociometric and popularity. In preparation.

Hymel, S., & Asher, S. R. *Assessment and training of isolated children's social skills.* Paper presented at the biennial meeting of the Society for Research in Child Development, New Orleans, March 1977.

Kandel, D. B. Adolescent marihuana use: Role of parents and peers. *Science,* 1973, *181,* 1067–1070.

Kandel, D. B. Similarity in real-life adolescent friendship pairs. *Journal of Personality and Social Psychology,* 1978, *36,* 306–312.

Kane, J. S., & Lawler, E. E., III. Methods of peer assessment. *Psychological Bulletin,* 1978, *85*(3), 555–586.

Kazdin, A. E. Sociopsychological factors in psychopathology. In A. S. Bellack & M. Hersen (Eds.), *Research and practice in social skills training.* New York: Plenum Press, 1979.

Koch, H. L. Popularity in preschool children: Some related factors and a technique for its measurement. *Child Development,* 1933, *4,* 164–175.

Ladd, G. W. Social skills and peer acceptance: Effects of a social learning method for training social skills. *Child Development,* 1981, *52,* 171–178.

LaGreca, A. M. Peer acceptance: The correspondence between children's sociometric scores and teachers' ratings of peer interactions, *Journal of Abnormal Child Psychology,* 1981.

LaGreca, A., & Santagrossi, D. Social skills training with elementary school students: A behavioral group approach. *Journal of Consulting and Clinical Psychology,* 1980, *48,* 220–228.

Lilly, M. S. Improving social acceptance of low sociometric status low achieving students. *Exceptional Children,* 1971, *37,* 341–348.

Lippitt, R., & Gold, M. Classroom social structure as a mental health problem. *Journal of Social Issues,* 1959, *15,* 40–58.

Marshall, H. R., & McCandless, B. R. A study in prediction of social behavior of preschool children. *Child Development,* 1957, *28,* 149–159.

McCandless, B. R., & Marshall, H. R. A picture sociometric technique for preschool children and its relation to teacher judgments of friendship. *Child Development,* 1957, *28,* 139–148.

Mischel, W. *Personality and assessment.* New York: Wiley, 1968.

Moore, S., & Updegraff, R. Sociometric status of preschool children related to age, sex, nurturance-giving and dependency. *Child Development,* 1964, *35,* 519–524.

Moreno, J. L. *Who shall survive?: A new approach to the problem of human interrelations.* Washington, DC: Nervous and Mental Disease Publishing Co., 1934.

Mueller, E. The maintenance of verbal exchanges between young children. *Child Development,* 1972, *43,* 930–938.

Northway, M. L. Social relationships among preschool children: Abstracts and interpretations of three studies. *Sociometry,* 1943, *6,* 429–433.

Oden, S., & Asher, S. R. Coaching children in social skills for friendship making. *Child Development,* 1977, *48,* 495–506.

Peery, J. C. Popular, amiable, isolated, rejected: A reconceptualization of sociometric status in preschool children. *Child Development,* 1979, *50,* 1231–1234.

Pekarik, E. G., Prinz, R. J., Liebert, D. E., Weintraub, S., & Neale, J. M. The Pupil Evaluation Inventory: Sociometric technique for assessing children's social behavior. *Journal of Abnormal and Child Psychology,* 1976, *4,* 83–97.

Putallaz, M., & Gottman, J. M. An interactional model of children's entry into peer groups. *Child Development,* 1981, *52,* 986–994.

Renshaw, P. D. The roots of current peer interaction research: A historical analysis of the 1930s. In S. R. Asher & J. M. Gottman (Eds.), *The development of children's friendships.* New York: Cambridge University Press, 1981.

Rinn, F. C., & Markle, A. Modification of social skill deficits in children. In A. S. Bellack & M. Hersen (Eds.), *Research and practice in social skills training.* New York: Plenum Press, 1979.

Robin, K. H. Relationship between egocentric communication and popularity among peers. *Developmental Psychology,* 1972, *7,* 364.

Roff, M., Sells, S. B., & Golden, M. M. *Social adjustment and personality development in children.* Minneapolis: The University of Minnesota, 1972.

Schmidt, B. A. *The relationship between social status and classroom behavior.* Unpublished study. St. Louis, MO.: Washington University, 1958.

Singleton, L. C., & Asher, S. R. Peer preferences and social interaction among third-grade children in an integrated school district. *Journal of Educational Psychology,* 1977, *69,* 330–336.

Singleton, L. C., & Asher, S. R. Racial integration and children's peer preferences: An investigation of developmental and cohort differences. *Child Development,* 1979, *50,* 936–941.

Steigelman, G., & Hops, H. The effect of age and motor performance on the social status of preschoolers. In preparation.

Van Hasselt, V. B., Hersen, M., & Bellack, A. S. The validity of role play tests for assessing social skills in children. *Behavior Therapy,* 1981, *12,* 202–216.

Vaughn, B. E., & Waters, E. Attention structure, sociometric status and dominance: Interrelations, behavioral correlates and relationships to social competence. *Developmental Psychology,* 1980, *17,* 275–288.

Wytrol, S. L., & Thompson, G. G. A critical review of the stability of social acceptability scores obtained with the partial-rank-order and the paired-comparison scales. *Genetic Psychology Monographs,* 1953, *48,* 221–260.

8

Self-Monitoring Procedures

Edward S. Shapiro

The procedure known as self-monitoring requires an individual to first self-observe and then systematically self-record the occurrences of behavior (Haynes, 1978). As an assessment procedure, self-monitoring can serve as an effective method for gathering baseline data on the frequency of the target behavior as well as its antecedents and consequences. For example, a child having difficulty participating in class discussions may be asked to record the number of instances when he or she speaks out, and to note the type of question answered, the response of peers, and the response of the teacher. Such data would be useful in planning remediation strategies.

In addition to self-monitoring for purposes of assessment, self-monitoring alone has been found to sometimes result in behavior change. Numerous studies have been published where such reactive effects of self-monitoring were found (e.g., Glynn, 1970; Maletzky, 1974; Nelson, Lipinski, & Black, 1976). However, all investigators have not found that reactivity consistently occurs (e.g., Fixsen, Phillips, & Wolf, 1972; Hall, 1972; Shapiro & Ackerman, in press). When self-monitoring is being used as an assessment device, it sometimes produces reactive effects on behavior. Thus, it is difficult to separate use of self-monitoring as an assessment tool and an intervention strategy.

The present chapter will present a concise overview of the technique and will detail methodological concerns in using self-monitoring with children. Rather than an exhaustive literature review, studies illustrative of the specific points being made will be discussed. Two case studies, one from a school setting and the other from a clinical setting, will be presented at the end of the chapter.

METHODOLOGY OF SELF-MONITORING

Instruments typically used to collect data via self-monitoring are rather simple. Watson and Tharp (1972) suggested that primary consideration be given to devices that are portable, easy to use, of low cost, and obtrusive enough to serve as a reminder to self-monitor. The method most frequently used involves recording behavioral occurrences. Individuals may be instructed to place a tally mark on a data sheet describing specific and well-defined behaviors. At other times, more narrative descriptions of behavior might be indicated, in which case a behavioral diary might be recorded.

Another common method of self-monitoring involves the use of counting devices such as golf counters, grocery store counters, or wrist counters. These devices provide a very efficient, practical means for keeping track of behavior and allow the individual to self-monitor unobtrusively.

While such methods of self-monitoring have been used with both children and adults, certain considerations must be realized when self-monitoring is being done by children. Younger children may have some difficulty remembering how behaviors are defined. Likewise, they may need additional prompts to be vigilant in the use of the procedures. Kunzelman (1970) recommended the use of *countoons,* simple stick figure drawings that demonstrate the specific behavior to be self-monitored. Children are instructed to place a tally mark next to each picture when the behavior occurs. For example, a child self-monitoring out-of-seat behavior may be given an index card with a picture of a boy out of his seat and instructed to mark each time or or she does what the boy in the picture is doing. This device may actually serve as a visual prompt for self-monitoring.

Another consideration when self-monitoring is done with children relates to the amount of data recorded. It is unlikely that children will be able or willing to record a narrative description of their behavior. Data obtained from narratives are usually helpful when trying to ascertain if specific antecedents or consequences are relevant to the occurrences of behavior. With children, the recording of events surrounding the behavior must be objectively defined and easy to record. For example, in having a child self-monitor his or her amount of study time, it would be helpful to ask him or her to record for each instance the setting in which he studied, what he or she did after he or she finished studying, and what subjects he/she actually examined. To obtain this information, a checklist should be provided on which the child can quickly mark the information of interest.

In general, the methods of self-monitoring are simple. Any procedure in which the child records the presence of behavior can be used. This includes the use of paper and pencil, counters, and other such procedures. For example, Shapiro, McGonigle, and Ollendick (1980) had children self-monitor by placing gummed stars on their data sheets contingent upon on-task behavior.

The key in any self-monitoring procedure with children is that the behaviors are well defined and clearly understood and the recording procedures are un-complicated.

METHODOLOGICAL ISSUES IN SELF-MONITORING

Actual techniques of self-monitoring are rather straightforward and can be taught to a wide range of child and adolescent populations, including the mod-erately mentally retarded (Litrownik, Freitas, & Franzini, 1978; Shapiro et al., 1980), emotionally disturbed/mentally retarded children (Shapiro & Klein, 1980), psychiatrically hospitalized adolescents (Santogrossi, O'Leary, Roman-czyk, & Kaufman, 1973), and children in regular elementary classrooms (Glynn, 1970). These techniques also can be applied to a wide variety of child behavioral problems such as nervous tics (Ollendick, 1981), academic and work behaviors (Hundert & Batstone, 1978; Hundert & Bucher, 1978; Pier-sall, Brody, & Kratochwill, 1977), and other school related difficulties such as out-of-seat behavior (Bornstein, Hamilton, & Quevillon, 1977), study skills (Broden, Hall, & Mitts, 1971), and disruptiveness (Kunzelman, 1970; Santo-grossi et al., 1973). Methodological issues germane to using self-monitoring with adults are applicable to children. Specifically, the two primary concerns raised when self-monitoring is used as an assessment procedure relate to the reactivity and accuracy of self-monitoring.

REACTIVITY

Like other observation methods, self-monitoring may result in behavioral change without the aid of additional intervention strategies. This effect, known as reactivity, has been the subject of extensive discussion concerning both theoretical and practical considerations (Nelson, 1977, 1981). Ciminero, Nelson, and Lipinski (1977); Haynes (1978); Haynes and Wilson (1979); and Nelson (1977) have identified numerous factors that have been found poten-tially to influence the occurrence of reactivity. In this section, each of these variables will be discussed in regard to studies that have examined them when used with children. As noted previously, studies presented are meant to be illustrative and not representative of an exhaustive literature review.

Valence of the Target Behavior

Kanfer (1970) first discussed the notion that the degree of reactivity present during self-monitoring may be related to whether the behaviors monitored are considered to be positive (desirable) or negative (undesirable). He predicted that those behaviors positive in valence would have a tendency to increase when self-monitored; those with negative valences would decrease. Studies involving children have investigated this hypothesis. Broden et al. (1971), in one of the first investigations of self-monitoring, had two eighth-grade students self-monitor specific behavior. In the initial study, a girl who was instructed to self-monitor study behavior periodically during the school day displayed significant increases in that behavior (positively valenced). Likewise, a boy instructed to self-monitor talking out in class (negatively valenced) displayed decreased episodes in his behavior once self-monitoring was implemented.

In contrast, Litrownik and Freitas (1980), in a study investigating reactivity of self-monitoring as a function of valence among moderately mentally retarded adolescents, found that when positively valenced behaviors were monitored, students outperformed those who recorded negatively valenced behaviors on a bead-stringing task. However, the ability of subjects to learn the task and the accuracy of self-monitoring did not differ between those recording positive or negative behaviors. Litrownik and Freitas interpreted their results as evidence that, while behavioral valence plays a part in controlling reactivity of the response, it is unclear whether for a mentally retarded population the valence of the target behavior can account for all reactive effects. This conclusion has been supported by other studies (Gottman & McFall, 1972; Kunzelman, 1970; Nelson et al., 1976).

Motivation

Another variable which can potentially affect the reactivity of self-monitoring is the degree to which the individual wishes to change that behavior. Studies examining adult behavior such as smoking (McFall, 1970; McFall & Hammen, 1971) have found that those subjects who expressed willingness to change their behavior showed the greatest gains. Unfortunately, no studies can be found which have specifically examined this variable with children. It would be particularly interesting to investigate whether children who express the desire to reduce classroom disruptiveness or increase social interaction show greater reactivity when such behavior is self-monitored, compared to children who were selected for treatment for identical behavior without regard to an expressed desire to change.

Experimenter Instructions

The type of instructions given to the individual by the experimenter may also affect the degree of reactivity. Nelson, Lipinski, and Black (1975) informed college students that, by self-monitoring, the frequency of face-touching would either increase, decrease, or not change. Observation of the students found decreases in face-touching regardless of the instructional set. Glynn and Thomas (1974), in a class of third-grade pupils, found that consistent reactivity only occurred when the behavior to be self-monitored was specifically cued. Obviously, while the instructions given to the individual may be important, it is unclear whether instructions alone always result in reactivity.

Nature of the Target Behavior

The type of behavior self-monitored has frequently been found to have a strong effect on reactivity with adults (Hayes & Cavior, 1977, 1980; Romanczyk, 1974). Few studies involving child populations have been reported which have investigated this variable. Gottman and McFall (1972) found that self-monitoring of actual classroom participation resulted in increases in talking, whereas self-monitoring of unfulfilled urges to participate reduced the degree of participation. Humphrey, Karoly, and Kirschenbaum (1978) had children self-monitor by taking tokens from a designated container contingent upon accurate performance on a reading task or self-monitor by self-imposing a response-cost procedure (removing tokens from their containers) when they made errors. Results indicated that both procedures improved daily reading rates over baseline levels. However, self-monitoring of accurate performance consistently resulted in better performance. Clearly, the specific behavior chosen may have direct effects on the degree of reactivity present.

Goal Setting

The setting of specific goals for performance can result in significantly more reactivity than when standards are not prearranged. Spates and Kanfer (1977), in an evaluation of Kanfer's (1970) multistage model for self-regulation, found that among first-grade students performing an arithmetic task, training in criteria setting was the critical variable resulting in improved performance. However, Sagotsky, Patterson, and Lepper (1978) specifically compared the effects of goal setting, self-monitoring, and the combination of both procedures for fifth- and sixth-grade elementary school students performing an arithmetic task. Results indicated that for both the amount of time spent engaged in the task and the rate of correct problem solving, self-monitoring alone improved behavior significantly more than goal setting alone. Further, the addition of goal setting to the self-monitoring procedure did not significantly increase changes in the behaviors. While other studies have not supported Sagotsky et al.'s findings (Lyman, Rickard, & Elder, 1975), relatively few studies investigating this issue with children have been reported. Additional research specifically evaluating the effects of goal setting upon self-monitoring are obviously needed.

Timing of Self-recording

Reactivity frequently has been found to be related to when the self-observed behavior is actually observed and recorded. In general, studies with adults have found that the highest degree of reactivity is likely to occur if self-monitoring occurs before the behavior actually occurs (Bellack, Rozensky, & Schwartz, 1974; Rozensky, 1974). Few studies, however, have investigated this variable with children. Nelson, Hay, Devany, and Koslow-Green (1980) reported that, with elementary school-age children, self-monitoring of classroom verbalizations was unaffected if the behavior was monitored prior to or following the verbalization.

Related to this is the contiguity between when self-observation and self-recording occur. No research specifically examining this issue can be found. However, it would be expected that the longer the delays between self-observation and self-recording, the less reactivity is likely. This is clearly an empirical question in need of validation.

Nature of Self-recording Device

Although the types of devices typically used to self-monitor are rather simple (a counter, paper and pencil), reactivity may be related to the specific method of self-recording. Broden et al. (1971) reported that a child instructed to self-monitor study behavior displayed increases in the behavior compared to when he forgot to self-record. The authors attributed the finding to the presence of slips of paper on which self-recording was to have occurred. Similarly, Nelson, Lipinski, and Boykin (1978), in a study designed to increase the appropriate verbalizations of mentally retarded adolescents, found that while the use of hand-held counters and belt-worn counters both resulted in reactivity, the hand-held counters resulted in more accurate self-recording and more appropriate verbalizations. Viewing the hand-held counters as more obstrusive, Nelson et al. (1978) suggested that this may be responsible for the differences in levels of appropriate verbalizations.

Other Variables

Additional variables that have been found potentially to be related to reactivity are the number of behaviors monitored (Hayes & Cavior, 1977), the schedule of self-monitoring (Mahoney, Moore, Wade, & Moura, 1973), awareness of whether accuracy of self-monitoring is being assessed (Drabman, Spitalnik, & O'Leary, 1973; Santogrossi et al., 1973), and when training for accuracy in self-monitoring was given (Nelson et al., 1978; Shapiro et al., 1980). Only the latter two have been investigated with child or adolescent populations.

Santogrossi et al. (1973) found that when psychiatrically hospitalized adolescent boys discovered that reinforcement for their behavior was not contingent upon accurate self-monitoring, dramatic increases in disruptiveness were evident. However, in a follow-up study with younger children, Drabman et al. (1973) were able to demonstrate effective self-monitoring when students were initially informed that their accuracy was being monitored.

Finally, Shapiro et al. (1980) found that, among a group of mentally retarded children, reactivity appeared only after training in accurate self-monitoring. However, Nelson et al. (1978) found training to increase the accuracy of self-monitoring but to have no effect on reactivity.

Conclusions

It is important to recognize that behavioral change which may occur as a result of self-monitoring may not always be desirable. When one is attempting to obtain a preintervention baseline by using self-monitoring, reactivity of the behavior would provide a distorted picture of the initial levels of behavior. Because reactivity cannot always be predicted, individuals recommending self-monitoring as an assessment procedure must be prepared to recognize the potential effect of the assessment device. This may be a particularly important concern of the researcher interested in using self-monitoring as a means of evaluation.

In a similar way, one can capitalize on the therapeutic potential of self-monitoring. Clinicians interested in achieving behavioral change in their clients should consider suggesting self-monitoring as an initial intervention strategy. The relative simplicity and ease with which this measure results in behavioral change should make it quite appealing. However, it should be recognized that reactivity does not always result in change and may have to be supplemented by more complex intervention strategies.

Clearly, reactivity of self-monitoring is a double-edged sword. As an assessment strategy, it is a simple and efficient mechanism for data collection. As an intervention, it can result in significant and lasting change. However, the assessor evaluating a particular behavioral technique while using self-monitoring as an assessment strategy might be disappointed should reactivity emerge. Likewise, one expecting self-monitoring to result in behavioral change might be equally disappointed when reactivity is absent. Evaluators electing to use self-monitoring should be acutely aware of the variables likely to result in such effects.

ACCURACY OF SELF-MONITORING

Accuracy of self-monitoring refers to the degree to which the individual is accurately recording occurrences of his or her behavior. Typically, this is assessed by having data collected by independent observers while self-monitoring is also being performed. Inter-observer agreement between the two sets of data reflects the degree to which the subject is actually self-recording incidents of the behavior. It may be false, however, to treat such a measure as a degree of accuracy. Even though the individual self-monitoring and the external observer agree that the behavior occurred the same number of times, it is possible that neither is truly accurate. To determine accuracy, self-recorded behavior should be compared with a specific criterion that can be directly verified. For example, Shapiro and Ackerman (in press) used a permanent product measure (the number of units produced) as a dependent variable in a study examining the use of self-monitoring to improve production rates of mentally retarded clients. Accuracy of self-monitoring was assessed by comparing the self-recorded data with the actual count of completed products. While the obtained measure is similar to inter-observer agreement, agreement on the criterion variable can be easily assessed by using permanent product data. In general, most studies examining accuracy of self-monitoring are actually evaluating inter-observer agreement rather than accuracy. Regardless, a number of issues concerning the accuracy with which data can be recorded have been raised by numerous investigators (Ciminero et al., 1977; Haynes, 1978; Haynes & Wilson, 1979; Nelson, 1977). As in the previous section, these points will be discussed in relation to the assessment of child and adolescent populations. Studies reported here will again be illustrative and not representative of an exhaustive literature review.

Awareness of Accuracy Assessment

Reid (1970); Romanczyk, Kent, Diament, and O'Leary (1973); Taplin and Reid (1973); and many others have demonstrated that agreement levels between observers may be directly affected by knowledge that inter-observer agreement is being checked. Likewise, a few studies have investigated whether similar effects would be present if an individual is aware that his or her self-monitored behavior is being assessed for accuracy (Lipinski & Nelson, 1974; Nelson et al., 1975). In one of the studies specifically tackling this issue with children, Santogrossi (1974) reported improved agreement between children's self-recording and that of independent observers when children were informed that a teacher or peer also was monitoring their behavior.

Reinforcement for Accurate Self-monitoring

When self-monitoring accuracy is determined to be low, studies have found that contingent reinforcement for accurate self-monitoring could improve accuracy (Fixsen et al., 1972; Risley & Hart, 1968). Additionally, Drabman et al. (1973), Robertson, Simon, Pachman, and Drabman (1979), and Turkewitz, O'Leary, and Ironsmith (1975) evaluated whether it was possible to maintain high levels of accuracy by thinning the schedule of checking for accuracy. In the Drabman et al. (1973) and Turkewitz et al. (1975) studies, decreases in accuracy were reported as the number of children checked and reinforced decreased.

Valence of the Behavior

Kanfer (1977) proposed that self-recording of undesirable or negative behavior might result in lower accuracy than if desirable behavior were being self-recorded. Nelson, Hay, Hay, and Carstens (1977) had classroom teachers self-monitor positive and negative classroom verbalizations assessing both accuracy and reactivity. They found that positive verbalizations were recorded more accurately than negative verbalizations. Similarly, Nelson et al. (1980) found children to more accurately self-monitor positive verbalizations compared to negative verbalizations. In contrast, Litrownik and Freitas (1980), using moderately mentally retarded adolescents, found no differences in self-monitoring accuracy related to the valence of behavior, and accuracy in all groups ranged from 94 to 100% across all phases of the study.

Training in Self-monitoring

Another variable related to accurate self-monitoring is the degree to which subjects are trained in self-recording. Nelson et al. (1978), after training subjects in self-monitoring procedures, found higher correspondence between self-recorded and observer-recorded data for trained subjects than for those who were untrained. Shapiro et al. (1980), using five moderately to mildly mentally retarded children, investigated the need to train in self-observation and self-recording independently. They found substantial improvements across all subjects when trained in self-observation and self-recording procedures compared to pretraining phases. It also was reported that one subject demonstrated substantially improved accuracy in self-recording after training in self-observation alone.

Other Variables Affecting Accuracy

The nature of the behavior being self-recorded (Bailey & Peterson, 1975; Lipinski & Nelson, 1974), the requirements to perform other behavior simultaneously with self-recording (Epstein, Miller, & Webster, 1975; Epstein, Webster, & Miller, 1976), the schedule of self-monitoring (Frederiksen, Epstein, & Kosevsky, 1975), and the nature of the recording device (Nelson et al., 1978) all have been found to be related to accuracy of self-recording. All of the studies, with the exception of Nelson et al., (1978), used adults rather than children or adolescents. No other investigations of these variables in child behavioral assessment have been reported.

Conclusions

In general, the accuracy of self-monitoring is influenced by variables in a way similar to reactivity. It is important that those applying self-monitoring should attempt to maximize accuracy. Nelson (1977) has suggested carrying out frequent inter-observer checks, making checks on a random basis, and using mechanical recording devices as methods to improve accuracy of self-recording. In addition, consideration should be given to the valence of the target behavior and to providing training in accurate self-monitoring.

RELATIONSHIP BETWEEN ACCURACY AND REACTIVITY

A very important issue related to self-monitoring concerns the exact nature of the relationship between reactivity and accuracy. Nelson and McReynolds (1971) suggest that even though self-recording is inaccurate, reactivity may still be evident. Broden et al. (1971), Fixsen et al. (1972), Herbert and Baer (1972), Lipinski and Nelson (1974), Nelson et al., (1980), and Shapiro et al. (1980) demonstrated this effect in studies involving child populations. For this to occur, some cause for reactivity must be found. Peterson, House, and Alford (1975) argue that minimal accuracy must be present to achieve accurate self-monitoring. Simkins (1971) has noted that it is possible that individuals self-observe but neglect to self-record, resulting in behavioral change and low levels of accuracy. Such a finding was also speculated from the results of Shapiro et al. (1980) who found one subject displaying reactivity who could accurately self-observe but consistently omitted self-recording. At present, the data seem clear that while accurate self-monitoring is desirable, reactive behavioral change may still occur without it.

CASE STUDIES

Two case studies will be presented to illustrate the use of self-monitoring in child behavioral assessment. As previously noted, because self-monitoring can serve as a device creating reactive behavioral change as well as a methodology for preintervention assessment, the distinction between self-monitoring for assessment and treatment is quite blurred. In the cases presented, self-monitoring was carried out simultaneously with assessment and intervention strategies (the conditions under which they most often are used by clinicians). The initial case describes a school-based problem while the second a problem more likely to be treated in clinical settings.

Case Number 1 (from Piersall & Kratochwill, 1979) – KEN

Ken was described as a 15-year-old, ninth-grade student who had been labeled hyperactive and had been treated with Ritalin from the second through sixth grades. In the semester when he was referred, he had not completed any work and was failing all subjects due to failure in turning in assignments. He frequently was truant and spent a good deal of time while at school in the principal's office for behavioral problems.

Contingency management programs through weekly meetings with the psychologist were implemented to reduce classroom disruptiveness and truancy. Other forms of intervention, such as parent conferences, contingency management, counseling, and psychological testing, had been previously tried.

It was decided that the appropriate target behavior should be completion of academic assignments. The SRA reading series was chosen along with current teacher-designed math assignments. SRA divides the curriculum sequence into small, discrete units developed to teach specific skills. In language arts class, the teacher required one SRA unit to be completed per week. During math class, students were expected to complete one assignment each day. At the time the study began, Ken had finished two reading assignments and no math assignments during the initial 6 weeks of class.

A multiple baseline design across subjects (reading and math) was chosen to evaluate the strategy. Baseline data were collected on both subjects, using the number of completed SRA units and math assignments each day as dependent measures. After 5 days, self-monitoring for reading assignments was implemented. Baseline continued to be taken for math assignments for 10 additional days.

Self-monitoring procedures involved a pencil-and-paper technique. Ken was given a piece of notebook paper and told to simply record the number of SRA units he completed each day. Two weeks later, self-monitoring for math assignments was initiated by having Ken record the number of daily problems worked out and whether math assignments were accurately completed (using 75% as a criterion).

Figure 8.1 illustrates the results of the intervention. Immediately after self-monitoring was implemented for reading, increases in completed SRA units were observed. During this period, math assignments remained at zero. Once self-monitoring was also implemented for math, increases in completed assign-

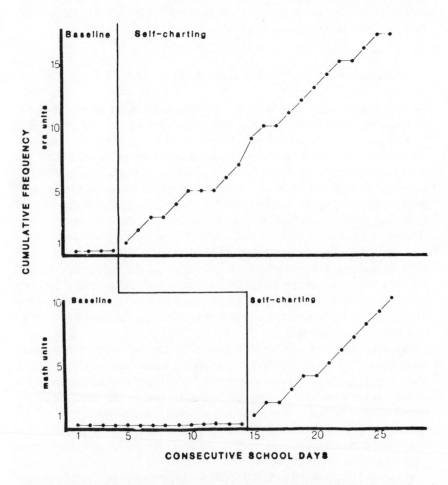

Fig. 8.1. KEN—Performance in reading and math during baseline and after implementation of self-monitoring. (*From:* Piersall, W. C., & Kratochwill, T. R., Self-observation and behavior change: Applications to academic and adjustment problems through behavioral consultation. *Journal of School Psychology,* 1979, *17,* 151–161; reprinted by permission).

ments were immediately evident. Accuracy of self-monitoring was checked throughout the study by having the teacher unobtrusively monitor Ken's behavior. Inter-observer agreement was found to be 100% for reading and math. In addition, the psychologist checked Ken's accuracy at correcting the math problems during weekly meetings and found it to be 100%, also.

Quite clearly, the use of a simple assessment procedure (self-monitoring) had quite dramatic effects. Behavior found to be unresponsive to other approaches was significantly changed by using this technique. Also, the reactive effects of self-monitoring were quite evident in this case study. No additional intervention other than self-monitoring was needed to achieve the degree of change observed. Whether such change would have been maintained and/or generalized to other subjects or behaviors is not known. Regardless, the power of this procedure was clear.

Case Number 2 (from Ollendick, 1981) — MARTY

Marty was described as a 9-year-old boy who exhibited excessive eye-blinking behavior. It was reported by his mother that the behavior first began when his maternal grandfather suffered a stroke which left him with numerous tremors and loss of sight in the right eye. Marty, who was 6 years old at the time, was reported to be "close" to his grandfather. At the time of referral, Marty's eye-blinking had become more pronounced following the death of his grandfather. This involved eye-blinking and simultaneous "bunching up" of the cheek. He also refused to sleep in his own bed. School records found Marty to be a superior student but not well liked by other children.

Using a multiple baseline design across settings, a self-monitoring procedure was developed to be implemented first at school and then at home. Baseline measures were taken by having Marty's mother or teacher record the number of occurrences of the tic behavior during specified study periods at school and after the evening meal at home. Observations were continued for 20 consecutive minutes each day.

Following 5 days of baseline, self-monitoring was implemented in the classroom throughout the day. Marty was given a wrist counter with which to count each instance of the behavior. He was instructed to write down the frequency on an index card at specified intervals. During this time, data continued to be collected at home without any self-monitoring.

After 5 days, the same self-monitoring procedures were implemented at home. Marty counted the behaviors throughout the evening and recorded the frequency at specified intervals.

Figure 8.2 illustrates the results of the study. Immediately after self-monitoring had begun, the rate of Marty's tics in school dramatically decreased. No changes were observed at home, however, until self-monitoring was begun

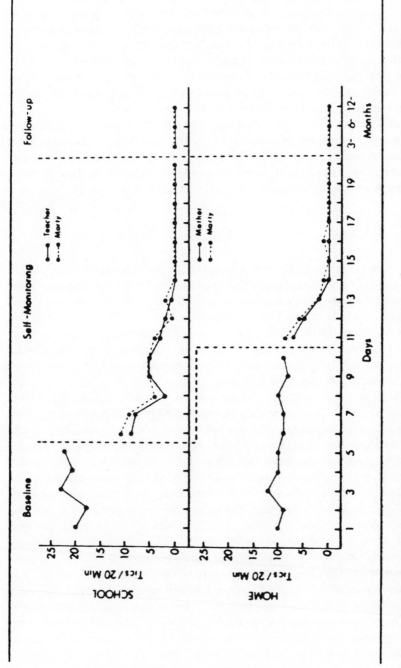

Fig. 8.2. MARTY — Rate of tic behavior in school and at home during baseline and after implementation of self-monitoring. (*From*: Ollendick, T. H., Self-monitoring and self-administered overcorrection: The modification of nervous tics in children. *Behavior Modification*, 1981, 5, 75–84; reprinted by permission).

in that setting. When implemented at home, immediate decreases in tic behavior were again observed. Accuracy of self-monitoring was evaluated throughout the study by having the teacher and parent continue to unobtrusively record Marty's behavior for one 20-minute period each day. Pearson product-moment correlations computed between rates obtained by the observer and the self-recorded rate resulted in a high correspondence ($r = .88–.89$) throughout the study. Follow-up data obtained at 3, 6, and 12 months after treatment found the behavior to have been eliminated.

This case provides a good illustration of the utility of self-monitoring in a clinical setting. Marty was only seen for four treatment sessions and three follow-up sessions; a minimal investment to reduce a behavior which had lasted over 3 years. In addition, the rather simple assessment procedure of counting instances of the behavior led to very strong reactive effects.

SUMMARY

Self-monitoring clearly has the potential to become a standard technique for use with children. It has been found to be applicable to a wide range of child behavioral problems across school, home, clinical, and institutional settings. As both an assessment and intervention procedure, self-monitoring offers the clinician a practical and efficient means to collect data and evaluate the progress of intervention procedures. The simplicity of the technique also provides an opportunity to design interventions requiring minimal effort or investment on the part of the therapist or client.

Despite the wide-ranging effectiveness of self-monitoring, the literature is replete with contradictory evidence regarding why it works or does not work as an intervention strategy. While a large number of variables related to the issues of reactivity and accuracy have been investigated with adult populations, there has been limited research on these variables with children. For example, very few studies involving child or adolescent populations have examined the effects of the valence of behavior upon reactivity and accuracy. This is an important issue since reactivity may be predicted from this variable, at least with adults (Kanfer, 1970). Results of these studies with children, however, have been far from consistent. Clearly, additional research is needed to clarify the effects of behavioral valence with children. Another issue that has been neglected with regard to children is that of motivation. While this variable is more difficult to operationalize, it would be important to determine the child's motivation for change prior to self-monitoring.

The importance of investigating the parameters of self-monitoring, specifically with child or adolescent populations, should be underscored. Results of studies in which adult populations were used may not be generalizable to children. As previously noted, numerous parameters, not typically accounted for when adults self-monitor, must be considered when children are the target subjects. Until such parameters are evaluated, it will be difficult to enumerate those components of self-monitoring that are critical to achieving accurate assessment or desired reactivity.

REFERENCES

Bailey, M. I., & Peterson, G. I. *Reactivity and accuracy on self-monitored verbal responses.* Unpublished manuscript, Ohio University, 1975.

Bellack, A. S., Rozensky, R., & Schwartz, J. A. A comparison of two forms of self-monitoring in a behavioral weight reduction program. *Behavior Therapy,* 1974, *5,* 523–530.

Bornstein, P. H., Hamilton, S. B., & Quevillon, R. P. Behavior modification by long distance. Demonstration of functional control over disruptive behavior in a rural classroom setting. *Behavior Modification,* 1977, *1,* 369–380.

Broden, M., Hall, R. V., & Mitts, B. The effect of self-recording on the classroom behavior of two 8th grade students. *Journal of Applied Behavior Analysis,* 1971, *4,* 191–199.

Ciminero, A. R., Nelson, R. O., & Lipinski, D. P. Self-monitoring procedures. In A. R. Ciminero, K. S. Calhoun, & H. E. Adams (Eds.), *Handbook of behavioral assessment.* New York: Wiley, 1977.

Drabman, R. S., Spitalnik, R., & O'Leary, K. D. Teaching self-control to disruptive children. *Journal of Abnormal Psychology,* 1973, *82,* 10–16.

Epstein, L. H., Miller, P. M., & Webster, J. S. The effects of reinforcing concurrent behavior on self-monitoring. *Behavior Therapy,* 1975, *7,* 89–95.

Epstein, L. H., Webster, J. S., & Miller, P. M. Accuracy and controlling effects of self-monitoring. *Behavior Therapy,* 1976, *6,* 654–666.

Fixsen, D. L., Phillips, E. L., & Wolf, M. M. Achievement place: The reliability of self-reporting and peer-reporting and their effects on behavior. *Journal of Applied Behavior Analysis,* 1972, *5,* 19–30.

Frederiksen, L. W., Epstein, L. H., & Kosevsky, B. P. Reliability and controlling effects of the procedures for self-monitoring smoking. *Psychological Record,* 1975, *25,* 255–264.

Glynn, E. L. Classroom applications of self-determined reinforcement. *Journal of Applied Behavior Analysis,* 1970, *3,* 123–132.

Glynn, E. L., & Thomas, J. D. Effects of cueing on self-control of classroom behavior. *Journal of Applied Behavior Analysis,* 1974, *7,* 299–306.

Gottman, J. M., & McFall, R. M. Self-monitoring effects in a program for potential high school dropouts: A time-series analysis. *Journal of Consulting and Clinical Psychology,* 1972, *39,* 275–281.

Hall, S. M. Self-control and therapist control in the behavioral treatment of overweight women. *Behaviour Research and Therapy,* 1972, *10,* 59–68.

Hayes, S. C., & Cavior, N. Multiple tracking and the reactivity of self-monitoring: I. Negative behaviors. *Behavior Therapy,* 1977, *8,* 819–831.

Hayes, S. C., & Cavior, N. Multiple tracking and the reactivity of self-monitoring: II. Positive behaviors. *Behavioral Therapy,* 1980, *2,* 283–296.

Haynes, S. N. *Principles of behavioral assessment.* New York: Gardner Press, 1978.

Haynes, S. N., & Wilson, C. C. *Behavioral assessment: Recent advances in methods, concepts, and applications.* San Francisco: Jossey-Bass, 1979.

Herbert, E. W., & Baer, D. M. Training parents as behavior modifiers. Self-recording of contingent attention. *Journal of Applied Behavior Analysis,* 1972, *5,* 139–149.

Humphrey, L. L., Karoly, P., Kirschenbaum, D. S. Self-management in the classroom: Self-imposed response cost versus self-reward. *Behavior Therapy,* 1978, *9,* 592-601.

Hundert, J., & Batstone, D. A practical procedure to maintain pupils' accurate self-rating in a classroom token program. *Behavior Modification,* 1978, *2,* 93-111.

Hundert, J., & Bucher, B. Pupils' self-scored arithmetic performance: A practical procedure for maintaining accuracy. *Journal of Applied Behavior Analysis,* 1978, *11,* 304.

Kanfer, F. H. Self-monitoring: Methodological limitations and clinical applications. *Journal of Consulting and Clinical Psychology,* 1970, *35,* 143-152.

Kanfer, F. H. The many faces of self-control. In R. B. Stuart (Ed.), *Behavioral self-management: Strategies, techniques, and outcomes.* New York: Brunner/Mazel, 1977.

Kunzelman, H. D. (Ed.). *Precision teaching.* Seattle: Special Child Publications, 1970.

Lipinski, D. P., & Nelson, R. O. The reactivity and unreliability of self-recording. *Journal of Consulting and Clinical Psychology,* 1974, *42,* 110-123.

Litrownik, A. J., & Freitas, J. L. Self-monitoring in moderately retarded adolescents: Reactivity and accuracy as a function of valence. *Behavior Therapy,* 1980, *11,* 245-258.

Litrownik, A. J., Freitas, J. C., & Franzini, L. R. Self-regulation in retarded persons: Assessment and training of self-monitoring skills. *American Journal of Mental Deficiency,* 1978, *82,* 499-506.

Lyman, R. D., Rickard, H. C., & Elder, I. R. Contingency management of self-reported cleaning behavior. *Journal of Abnormal Child Psychology,* 1975, *3,* 155-162.

Mahoney, M. J., Moore, B. J., Wade, T. C., & Moura, N. G. M. The effects of continuous and intermittent self-monitoring on academic behavior. *Journal of Consulting and Clinical Psychology,* 1973, *41,* 65-69.

Maletzky, B. M. Assisted covert sensitization in the treatment of exhibitionism. *Journal of Consulting and Clinical Psychology,* 1974, *42,* 34-40.

McFall, R. M. Effects of self-monitoring on normal smoking behavior. *Journal of Consulting and Clinical Psychology,* 1970, *35,* 135-142.

McFall, R. M., & Hamman, C. L. Motivation structure and self-monitoring: The role of nonspecific factors in smoking reduction. *Journal of Consulting and Clinical Psychology,* 1971, *37,* 80-86.

Nelson, R. O. Methodological issues in assessment via self-monitoring. In J. D. Cone & R. P. Hawkins (Eds.), *Behavioral assessment: New directions in clinical psychology.* New York: Brunner/Mazel, 1977.

Nelson, R. O. Theoretical explanations for self-monitoring. *Behavior Modification,* 1981, *5,* 3-14.

Nelson, R. O., Hay, L. R., Devany, J., & Koslow-Green, L. The reactivity and accuracy of children's self-monitoring: Three experiments. *Child Behavior Therapy,* 1980, *2,* 1-24.

Nelson, R. O., Hay, L. R., Hay, W. M., & Carstens, C. B. The reactivity and accuracy of teachers' self-monitoring of positive and negative classroom verbalizations. *Behavior Therapy,* 1977, *8,* 972-985.

Nelson, R. O., Lipinski, D. P., & Black, J. L. The effect of expectancy on the reactivity of selfrecording. *Behavior Therapy,* 1975, *6,* 233-249.

Nelson, R. O., Lipinski, D. P., & Black, J. L. The reactivity of adult retardates' self-monitoring: A comparison among behaviors of different valences, and a comparison with token reinforcement. *Psychological Record,* 1976, *26,* 189-201.

Nelson, R. O., Lipinski, D. P., & Boykin, R. A. The effects of self-recorders' training and the obtrusiveness of the self-monitoring device on the accuracy and reactivity of self-monitoring. *Behavior Therapy,* 1978, *9,* 200-208.

Nelson, R. O., & McReynolds, W. Self-recording and control of behavior. Reply to Simkins. *Behavior Therapy,* 1971, *3,* 594-597.

Ollendick, T. H. Self-monitoring and self-administered overcorrection: The modification of nervous tics in children. *Behavior Modification,* 1981, *5,* 75-84.

Peterson, G. L., House, A. E., & Alford, H. F. Self-monitoring: Accuracy and reactivity in a patient's recording of their clinically targeted behavior. Paper presented at the meeting of the Southeastern Psychological Association, Atlanta, March, 1975.

Piersall, W. C., Brody, G. H., Kratochwill, T. R. A further examination of motivational influences on disadvantaged minority group children's intelligence test performance. *Child Development*, 1977, *48*, 1142–1145.

Piersall, W. C., & Kratochwill, T. R. Self-observation and behavior change: Applications to academic and adjustment problems through behavioral consultation. *Journal of School Psychology*, 1979, *17*, 151–161.

Reid, J. B. Reliability assessment of observation data: A possible methodological problem. *Child Development*, 1970, *41*, 1143–1150.

Risley, T. R., & Hart, B. Developing correspondence between the non-verbal and verbal behavior of school children. *Journal of Applied Behavior Analysis*, 1968, *1*, 267–281.

Robertson, S. J., Simon, S. J., Pachman, J. S., & Drabman, R. S. Self-control and generalization procedures in a classroom of disruptive retarded children. *Child Behavior Therapy*, 1979, *1*, 347–362.

Romanczyk, R. G. Self-monitoring in the treatment of obesity: Parameters of reactivity. *Behavior Therapy*, 1974, *5*, 531–540.

Romanczyk, R. G., Kent, R. N., Diament, C., & O'Leary, K. D. The reliability of observational data: A reactive process. *Journal of Applied Behavior Analysis*, 1973, *6*, 175–186.

Rozensky, R. H. The effect of timing of self-monitoring behavior on reducing cigarette consumption. *Journal of Behavior Therapy and Experimental Psychiatry*, 1974, *5*, 301–303.

Sagotsky, G., Patterson, G. J., & Lepper, M. R. Training children's self-control: A field experiment in self-monitoring and goal setting in the classroom. *Journal of Experimental Child Psychology*, 1978, *25*, 242–253.

Santogrossi, D. A. *Self-reinforcement and external monitoring of performance on an academic task*. Paper presented at the 5th Annual Conference on Applied Behavior Analysis in Education, Kansas City, KS, October 1974.

Santogrossi, D. A., O'Leary, K. D., Romanczyk, R. G., & Kaufman, K. Self-evaluation by adolescents in a psychiatric hospital school token program. *Journal of Applied Behavior Analysis*, 1973, *6*, 277–297.

Shapiro, E. S., & Ackerman, A. Increasing productivity rates in adult mentally retarded clients: The failure of self-monitoring. *Applied Research in Mental Retardation*, 1983, *3*, in press.

Shapiro, E. S., & Klein, R. D. Self-management of classroom behavior with retarded/disturbed children. *Behavior Modification*, 1980, *4*, 83–97.

Shapiro, E. S., McGonigle, J. J., & Ollendick, T. H. An analysis of self-assessment and self-reinforcement in a self-managed token economy with mentally retarded children. *Applied Research in Mental Retardation*, 1980, *1*, 223–240.

Simkins, L. The reliability of self-recorded behavior. *Behavior Therapy*, 1971, *2*, 83–87.

Spates, C. R., & Kanfer, F. H. Self-monitoring, self-evaluation, and self-reinforcement in children's learning: A test of a multistage self-regulation model. *Behavior Therapy*, 1977, *8*, 9–16.

Taplin, R. S., & Reid, J. B. Effects of instructional set and experimenter's influence on observer reliability. *Child Development*, 1973, *44*, 547–554.

Turkewitz, H., O'Leary, K. D., & Ironsmith, M. Generalization and maintenance of appropriate behavior through self-control. *Journal of Consulting and Clinical Psychology*, 1975, *43*, 577–583.

Watson, D. L., & Tharp, R. G. *Self-directed behavior: Self-modification for personal adjustment*. Monterey, CA: Brooks/Cole, 1972.

9

*Direct Observation**

Edward J. Barton
and
Frank R. Ascione

. . . precise specification of the target problems . . . a search for the current determinants of the problems . . . and documentation of changes in the target problems. . . .

—Achenbach, 1982

These contributions to psychology are often made, in part, through use of the direct observation of behavior. In fact, recent surveys of major journals in behavioral analysis indicate that over the past decade more than 70% of the research studies incorporated direct behavioral observations (Bornstein, Bridgwater, Hickey, & Sweeney, 1980; Serna & Ascione, 1981). The purposes of this chapter are: (a) to define and provide a rationale for the use of direct observations in child behavioral assessment, (b) to describe the techniques currently available for conducting direct observation (including their advantages and shortcomings), and (c) to discuss pragmatic and ethical aspects of the use of direct observation of child behavior.

*We express our appreciation to Cathryn Peterson, Debbie Ascione, Gayle Mender, and Kelly Gahn for their assistance in preparation of this chapter. Completion of this chapter was facilitated by a Utah State University Faculty Research Grant to the second author.

DIRECT OBSERVATION

Definition of Direct Observation

Direct observation of behavior is at the core of child behavioral assessment. It is the process by which human observers, using operational definitions as their guide, record the overt motor and/or verbal behavior of other humans. These characteristics differentiate direct observation from other clinical assessment strategies that use electrically or mechanically activated devices (e.g., in measuring physiological responding), use evaluative judgments (as with some rating forms and sociometric techniques), or use clients' records of their own behavior (as in self-monitoring). Use of direct observation of child behavior is not restricted to any particular context. Recording may be conducted in naturalistic environments (e.g., a classroom), analogue settings (e.g., a room furnished to resemble a family's living room), or clinical laboratories (e.g., a room used for recording individualized therapist-child interactions). Furthermore, recording through direct observation need not necessarily be contemporaneous with the original occurrence of behavior nor be conducted in the place where the behavior occurred (e.g., viewing an audio-video tape).

Rationale for the Use of Direct Observation

As noted by Nelson and Hayes (1979), "the goals of behavioral assessment are to identify meaningful response units and their controlling variables . . . for the purposes of understanding and altering behavior" (p. 1). Direct observation of behavior is well suited to assisting in the achievement of these goals for child behavioral assessment. First, the age of the child, especially limitations of a child's verbal repertoire, may preclude the use of assessment strategies that require verbal responses (e.g., interviews and self-reports). Second, the use of objective definitions as a guide to recording a child's behavior implies that the response units to be recorded will require less inference and be less influenced by subjective criteria than other recording methods. For example, it has been shown that global ratings of behavior are more likely to be affected by biasing contextual factors and expectancies than objective behavioral observations (Cunningham & Tharp, 1981). Third, direct observation of problem behavior may yield measures having greater face validity for assessing treatment outcome than more indirect methods of assessment. For example, actual records of physical fighting and verbal abuse may be a better reflection of deviant social behavior than reports of sociometric status. Fourth, data generated through direct observation have been shown to be sensitive dependent measures of therapeutic effectiveness, thus contributing to the internal validity of clinical research with children (Foster & Ritchey, 1979). Fifth, because direct observation includes recording of the contextual antecedents and consequences of a child's problem behavior as well as collateral behaviors, it establishes a data base from which hypotheses about the variables controlling behavior can be generated. It also guides the selection of potentially effective treatment approaches. Sixth, direct observation of peer behavior in the target setting provides an objective basis upon which to decide (a) if a behavioral problem warrants treatment, and (b) if treatment produces subsequent behavioral changes that are clinically significant (Barton, 1983).

Deciding What, When, Where, and How to Record

It would be imprudent and presumptuous, at best, to expect parents, teachers, and children to arrive at a clinic or therapist's office with a carefully developed set of objectively defined problem behaviors. Even before a therapist[1] can begin to generate an objective definition of a problem behavior, he or she must consider numerous pieces of information. The therapist needs to ascertain answers to the following questions. What are the overt behaviors considered to be the problem? In whose presence does the child display the problem? Does the behavior occur in a single context or in multiple settings? What events set the occasion for problem behavior? What are the consequences that follow the behavior? What setting events may be implicated in the appearance of problem behavior? Tentative answers to some of these questions, in part, may be derived from complementary assessment strategies. For example, the behavioral interview (see chap. 4) can be used to solicit information on: the topographies of the deviant behavior, the social agents and environmental contexts in which the behavior is displayed, and potential sources of antecedent and consequent control. The use of behavioral checklists (see chap. 5) may suggest other behaviors with which deviant responses covary. Achievement test results (see chap. 10) may indicate potential setting events (e.g., deficient reading skills) that are contributing to problem behavior (e.g., classroom disruption). Thus, other assessment strategies may be used for initial screening of the types of behaviors and contexts to be analyzed through direct observation.

We also recommend that prior to the design and implementation of a direct observation procedure, one should perform a narrative recording. This consists of a written or dictated running account of ongoing overt behavior as well as changes in the environmental setting in which the behavior occurs (e.g., behavior of others or changes in group composition). The primary purpose of a narrative recording is to provide a basis for developing a more specific and quantifiable recording method. Using a narrative record, the therapist can begin to identify the classes of behavior and environmental events worthy of further analysis. He or she can identify the variability in the forms in which particular deviant/deficit behavior is displayed, suggesting elements that will need to be included in objective definitions of behavior. Finally, narrative recording may suggest hypotheses about factors controlling the target behavior that were not evident from other indirect assessment strategies. This process should sample as many settings and time periods in which the problem behavior is displayed as are feasible because the topography and functions of behavior and the variables that control it may not have setting or temporal generality. The use of narrative recording in the development of direct observation systems will be elaborated in the next section.

THE DEVELOPMENT OF A DIRECT OBSERVATIONAL SYSTEM

A direct observational system can best be developed by reference to the three-term relation of antecedent-behavior-consequence (A-B-C). Antecedents may be single events or sequences of events. Behavior may correspond to a single response or a constellation of responses. Consequences may, likewise, be simple or complex environmental changes. In addition, the entire three-term relation may be examined in a single setting (e.g., a particular classroom), multiple settings (e.g., the school cafeteria, home kitchen, and a local park), or in the presence of different setting events (e.g., changes in diet or peer group). Given this framework, the first task to be accomplished is selection of the categories of antecedents, behaviors, and consequences to be recorded.

Selecting Stimuli and Responses

Determining which antecedents-behaviors-consequences to select is of the utmost importance. Because most behavioral interventions focus on the effects of consequence stimuli (e.g., rewards contingent on academic performance; noxious stimuli contingent on self-injurious behavior), antecedent stimuli are often neglected in developing a direct observational system. However, it has been well documented that manipulation of antecedent stimuli can facilitate behavioral change (Barton, Olszewski, & Madsen, 1979; Center, Deitz, & Kaufman, 1982) and that antecedent behaviors are often good predictors of how effective a particular intervention will be (e.g., Karpowitz & Johnson, 1981). With regard to the behavior links in the A-B-C relation, the wrong behavior is often inadvertently selected. Lahey, Vosk, and Habif (1981) have noted that some target behaviors (e.g., on-task behavior) may not be related to more critical indices of successful treatment (e.g., academic performance measures). Likewise, in selecting consequences (e.g., adult-delivered praise), salient consequences (e.g., peer approval) are often overlooked. Therefore, selection of antecedents, behaviors, and consequences should be made only after careful examination of both the child's unique situation and the literature pertinent to the particular deviant/deficit response. It is imperative to remember that the child's circumstances may be idiosyncratic.

Narrative recording provides an excellent avenue for beginning to identify potentially salient antecedents, behaviors, and consequences. An example of a hypothetical narrative recording is given in the top half of table 9.1 for a young boy who was referred for fighting. After obtaining the running narrative (i.e., the preliminary recording), it can be restructured into the A-B-C format. As can be seen from the lower half of table 9.1., this additional step results in a number of revelations. First, it appears that Billy's critical problem is not fighting but rather a sharing deficit. More specifically, it appears that Billy does not know how or fails to: share physically, offer to share, and accept "offers to share." In addition, the restructured narrative recording reveals Billy responds inappropriately to key antecedent stimuli and is reinforced for refusing to share by access to the desired toys. Thus, A-B-C analysis of narrative recordings provides a very powerful method for selecting the critical antecedents, behaviors, and consequences.

There have been numerous other suggestions proffered in the literature for selecting the behaviors to be observed (Nelson & Hayes, 1979). One of the most common suggestions is to strive for face validity. Thus, the behavior

Table 9.1. Narrative Recording.

I. Preliminary Recording

Billy the Bully is constructing a tower with the Legos by himself. He stops to watch Tom play with the wooden block set. He runs over to Tom and tries to grab all the blocks. Tom resists and yanks some of the blocks back. Both boys start to yell and punch each other. Billy wins and takes all the blocks over to his former play area and proceeds to construct a building with the blocks. Joan comes over to Billy and asks if she can play with some of the blocks. Billy yells no and pushes Joan away from the blocks and continues to construct his building.

II. Restructured Recording

Antecedents	Behaviors[a]	Consequences
Legos present	Plays with Legos	Constructs tower
Tom plays with blocks	Watches; runs to; takes blocks	Gets some blocks
Tom resists	Yells; punches Tom	Gets all the blocks
Blocks present	Plays with blocks	Constructs building
Joan asks for blocks	Yells no; pushes Joan	Retains all blocks

---

[a]Billy was the target child.

observed should bear an obvious relation to the referral problem (e.g., physical fights for aggression; number of bites of food for anorexia). Behaviors may also be selected by noting differences in the behaviors between the client who displays the problem behavior and a group that does not (e.g., recording negative social interactions for a sociometrically unpopular child and for popular children). The clinician may also use subjective ratings by others (see chaps. 5 and 7). This latter approach is also a form of social validation which asks, "Will subjective ratings by social agents who have referred the child and by significant others in the child's life be more positive if changes in this particular behavior are effected?" Responses can also be selected by using, as criteria, local norms (e.g., mean classroom social interaction rates) or more general developmental norms (e.g., the Gesell Scales). By following these guidelines, one should be able to identify the salient antecedents, behaviors, and consequences that should be directly observed.

Objective Definition

Once specific environment-behavior relations have been identified, the next task is to develop objective definitions of the target behaviors. Defining behavior in objective terms means that the definition refers to observable aspects of behavior (characteristics that a human observer can see or hear).[2] The assumption is that any trained human observer would be able to assess accurately the presence or absence of a behavior using the objective definition as a guide. In essence, an objective definition should provide the observer with as comprehensive a set of decision rules as is feasible for detecting the behaviors being recorded and distinguishing these from other responses. The greater the vagueness of a definition, the fewer decision rules the observer has at his or her disposal and the greater the likelihood of subjective judgments affecting recording.

Let us examine examples of an objective definition and characteristics that make them appropriate for direct observation. In a study of 9- to 10-year-old children diagnosed as hyperactive, Jacob, O'Leary, and Rosenblad (1978) recorded a number of behaviors including solicitation and weird sounds. Solicitation was defined as:

> attempts to initiate interaction with teacher . . . [including] raising hand, calling teacher, walking up to teacher, or unsolicited physical contact with teacher . . . [and excluding] raising hand in response to teacher's question (p. 51).

Weird sounds were defined as:

> audible vocal sound that is not language communication . . . vocalization loud enough to be heard through a wall . . . [including] singing, whistling, crying

or screaming . . . imitating animals . . . demonstrative coughing, sneezing or
clearing of throat . . . monotonous repetition of a sentence or word . . . [and
excluding] intelligible verbalizations unless repetitious, screamed or sung . . .
coughing, sneezing, clearing of throat when the child has a cold (p. 51).

First, it should be noted that the general categories of solicitation and weird
sounds are ambiguous and, by themselves, would not specify the behaviors
in question. They do serve as descriptive shorthand labels that simplify communication such that, once defined, the labels may be used instead of the detailed descriptions. Second, the authors go on to provide not only general definitions of the behaviors but also extensive examples of instances that would
be included and excluded. These provide observers with concrete referents
(e.g., approximate sound level of vocalizations) to assist them in their decision making during observations.

Objective definitions have obvious advantages over less clearly defined categories. They avoid the ambiguity and idiosyncratic meanings often inherent
in colloquial or general terms (e.g., aggressive, "hard to manage"). Objective definitions can also improve communication between the therapist and
client because both will use the same referents in discussing problem behavior.

Although one of the hallmarks of applied behavioral analysis is that it is
technological in the sense that all procedures are described in detail from the
point of replication (Baer, Wolf, Risley, 1968), the steps that one should
follow to develop an operational definition, surprisingly, are blatantly absent from the literature. Thus, one learns how to develop an adequate operational definition through trial and error and, hopefully, feedback from a
mentor.

In the technological spirit, we analyzed the steps that we go through in developing an operational definition, and we offer them here as a rough guide
(see table 9.2). The first step we call "Quick Shot" because that is exactly what
we do. We write down as a definition the first thing that we think of (sometimes this includes informal observation). The second step we call "Examples
Add" because we think of all sorts of examples of the behavior. If the quick-
shot definition handles all the examples, we proceed to the next step; if not,
we add more verbiage to our definition such that all these examples are in-

Table 9.2. Steps for Developing Operational Definitions

1. Quick Shot
2. Examples Add
3. Nonexamples Add
4. List Examples
5. List Nonexamples
6. Reliability Test
7. Validity Test

cluded in our definition. Step 3 represents the reverse of Step 2 and is called "Nonexamples Add" because we think of similar but nonexamples of the behavior. If our definition precludes these nonexamples, we proceed to Step 4; if not, we add verbiage to our definition such that all the nonexamples are precluded by our revised definition. Anyone who has ever struggled with developing an operational definition knows that it may seem to be an impossible task to get past Steps 2 and 3. That is, for certain behaviors, some examples and nonexamples cannot be covered in, or excluded from, a definition by adding verbiage, without destroying the value of the definition. Therefore, Steps 4 and 5 are called "List Examples" and "List Nonexamples," respectively. In these steps, examples and nonexamples that do not lend themselves to added verbiage are simply listed in the definition. We call Step 6 the "Reliability Test." Here, naive, *untrained* observers are given the definition and a written explanation of how to observe. If they are able to reliably record the occurrence of the behavior without any oral explanation and clarification, the definition passes the reliability test. Step 7, which is critical but sometimes neglected, is an attempt at social validation and is called the "Validity Test." Although there are many approaches to social validation (Van Houton, 1979), one method is to have a number of *trained observers armed with the definition* and a number of *significant others in the child's life without training or access to the definition* score videotapes of children. If their scorings correlate, the definition passes this validation test. Twardosz, Schwartz, Fox, and Cunningham (1979), in an exemplary study, used this approach to validate their definition of children's affection.

To get started in developing an operational definition, there are two additional avenues. First, many excellent definitions of common target behaviors (e.g., fighting) exist in the literature (e.g., the *Journal of Applied Behavior Analysis*). Second, *significant others* in the child's life can describe the target behavior. These two strategies can save a tremendous amount of time and frustration.

Before closing this section, we wish to underscore that developing a good operational definition takes perseverance. Before reading further, take a moment to define "sharing an object" using the quick-shot approach. Here is what we came up with using the above 7-step approach.

Physical sharing was defined as: (a) handing a material to another child, (b) allowing another child to take his/her material, (c) using a particular material that another had used during the same observation interval, or (d) simultaneously using a material with another to work on a common project. Two or more children were considered to be using a particular material simultaneously when they were facing each other or the material and each was using a part of it to work on a common project (e.g., each child using separate logs to build one cabin). Physical sharing did not include instances where children indicated either verbally or nonverbally that they did not want to share physically with other group members (e.g., crying, screaming, or complaining to the experimenter). (Barton & Ascione, 1979, p. 420)

Note that this definition of physical sharing is quite detailed and includes examples and nonexamples. Nevertheless, after many attempts at social validation, we had to make minor changes in the definition (Barton, 1981). The salient point here is that a good operational definition requires not only a lot of work but an awareness that these definitions need to be modified to meet the needs of unique children and situations.

Molecular and Molar Response Categories

Once the behaviors have been selected and objectively defined, there remains one additional task to be addressed. It involves deciding how general behavioral categories should be. Should different responses be placed into separate molecular categories or grouped into molar categories? This issue is illustrated in a very basic manner by our research on children's sharing behavior. This behavior is made up not only of physical sharing, but also verbal sharing, which can be subdivided into "offers to share" and acceptance of "share offers." Although some therapists use the more molar term "sharing," we have found the molecular categories to be essential. For example, when the facilitation of "sharing" is the goal, it is more advantageous to train verbal rather than physical sharing (Barton & Ascione, 1979). Furthermore, whereas training both forms of verbal sharing is desirable (Barton, 1982), training only "offers to share" produces an undesirable increase in refusals to share (Warren, Rogers-Warren, & Baer, 1976). Thus, use of molecular categories has allowed for discoveries in the children's prosocial literature that would not have been realized with more molar classification.

The decision to lump or not lump behaviors can be critical when side effects of treatment procedures are examined (Kazdin, 1982). A study conducted by Singh, Manning, and Angell (1982) serves to underscore this point. The ruminating behavior of a set of profoundly retarded adolescent twins was the focus of treatment. One other molar category of interest was that of stereotyped behavior, which was separated into three molecular parts: self-stimulation, object manipulation, and self-injurious behavior. In examining the results of their study, as rumination decreased stereotyped behavior increased. However, this increase predominantly reflected increases in self-stimulation and *not* self-injury (a fact staff considered to be a tolerable side effect). Without the molecular subdivisions of behavior, conclusions regarding the severity of negative side effects might not have been possible or would at least have been based on nonobjective criteria.

Decisions on whether to lump or split response categories can at times be made based on generalizable relations between responses, as reported in the research literature. In general, molecular categories maximize opportunities for microanalyses and discovery. However, it should be noted that some response relations may be idiosyncratic, and, thus, appropriate categorizations may be difficult to arrive at a priori. The reader is referred to an excellent conceptual analysis of behavioral interrelations in a paper by Voeltz and Evans (1982).

DIRECT OBSERVATION RECORDING PROCEDURES

Dimensions of Behavior

Figure 9.1 displays a portion of a hypothetical record made for an interaction sequence between a father and his daughter; the latter was referred to a clinic for her noncompliance. The records appear as they would if made by using an event recorder. Five molar categories were observed in this ex-

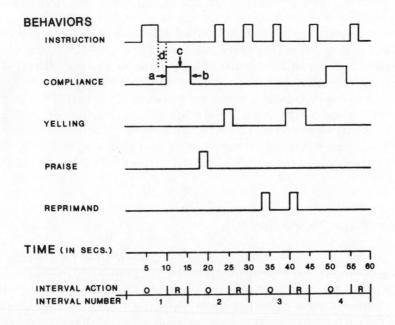

Fig. 9.1. A hypothetical event record for a one-minute behavioral interaction between a father and his daughter. Instruction, praise, and reprimand are parental behaviors and compliance and yelling are child behaviors. The behavioral dimensions *a, b, c,* and *d* are described in the text. *O* refers to the observation segment of an interval and *R* refers to the record segment.

ample: father gives an instruction, daughter complies with father's instruction, daughter yells, father delivers a praise statement, and father delivers a reprimand. In such a record, the temporal characteristics of each behavior and the temporal relations between behaviors are preserved. The potential dimensions of behavior that could be recorded are illustrated by examining the first instance of compliance in the event record. Let us assume that the father has asked his daughter to pick up and store some play materials that are on the living room floor. The point marked a in the record indicates the onset of the child's compliant behavior (e.g., picking up one of four play items), and b indicates the offset of compliance (e.g., the last play item is retrieved and stored). The time during which the child complied is represented by the temporal interval marked c. The latency between the parent's instruction and the onset of child compliance is shown as the segment marked d. Using this information, we can now describe some of the behavioral dimensions of importance in child behavioral assessment.

The frequency dimension of behavior is represented when observers attend to and record the *onsets* of a behavior, regardless of how long the behavior takes to be executed. Thus, in the 60-sec. sample shown in figure 1, the following frequencies would have been recorded: six instructions, two compliances, two yelling episodes, one instance of praise, and two reprimands. For duration measures, observers record the temporal period between the onset and completion of each response. In this example, the total duration was 11 secs. for compliance and 7 secs. for yelling. A variation of this type of duration measure is that of latency: the time between the offset of one response and the onset of another. For the first instruction in this example, the latency was 2 secs. One further dimension of behavior can be gleaned from this type of record: sequential relations between responses. For example, we may wish to record how often the offset of an instruction is followed within 3 secs. by yelling. In this record, this sequence occurs twice. We now turn to a discussion of the recording methods used for each of these dimensions.

Recording Techniques

Frequency Recording. The recording of the number of times a behavior occurs within a temporal interval is referred to as frequency (tally or event) recording. This recording approach is best suited for use with behaviors that fulfill three criteria. First, the behavior should be discrete (the beginning and end of the behavior should be clear and easily specified). For example, physical affection begins with some form of contact between the bodies of two people and ends when that contact is broken. With other behaviors, however, onset and termination are more difficult to specify (e.g., "excessive noise").

Second, each time the behaviors occur, it should take approximately the same amount of time to complete each response. For example, frequency recording would be appropriate for recording temper tantrums if each occurrence lasted approximately the same amount of time. Obviously if some tantrums last one minute and others last for an hour, the frequency method would not be appropriate as it would not be sensitive to this difference. Third, frequency recording cannot be used for behaviors that occur so frequently that separating each occurrence becomes difficult. If a child presented a problem of very rapid rubbing of her lower lip, each rub might be difficult to count.

Because frequency recording requires counting *every* instance of a behavior in a certain period of time, the observer must be free to record each response whenever it occurs. The alertness that is required may be difficult for observers who have other tasks to complete (e.g., a classroom teacher). This continuous monitoring of every occurrence of the behavior also restricts the number of behaviors and clients that can be observed simultaneously.

There are three basic ways of reporting data using the frequency recording method. First, if each observation period lasts the same amount of time, the "actual" frequency with which the behavior occurred can be reported. Second, if observation periods are not constant in length, the data should be reported in terms of rates (i.e., the number of responses divided by the time period observed). Third, if recording a behavior that is supposed to follow a certain type of cue (e.g., eye contact following the instruction "Look at me"), the data should be reported in terms of the percentage of opportunities that a behavior occurred. This method of reporting allows one to control for differences in the number of opportunities available for a behavior to be displayed. Referring back to the compliance data in figure 9.1, the actual frequency of compliance was 2, the rate was 2 compliances per minute, and the percentage compliance per opportunity was 33% (2 compliances per 6 instructions).

There are numerous examples of the use of frequency recording in the literature. For example, in one study, Barton and Madsen (1980) taught a severely retarded child to control the negative side effects of his excessive drooling by wiping his face. Thus, they recorded the number of times that he wiped his face dry per session, but more meaningfully presented their data as the percentage of opportunities that wiping occurred per session.

In discussing selection of the target behavior, we stressed the importance of validity. It is also imperative that the recording method be reliable. The type of reliability we are referring to is the degree to which the observational records of two or more independent observers correspond with one another. Assessment and intervention are based on the premise that the data recorded are accurate. If accurate data are not available, the quality of assessment is compromised and intervention effects cannot be gauged. The reliability of the recordings is typically determined by calculating the observers' agreement.

The formula for computing percentage observer agreement[3] for frequency recording is as follows:

$$\frac{\text{smaller tally number}}{\text{larger tally number}} \times 100$$

For example, if one observer recorded 50 instances of a behavior and the other recorded 43 instances, observer agreement would equal 86% (i.e., $43/50 \times 100$).

Duration Recording. How much time a child engages in a behavior can often be viewed as the reason the behavior is a problem. Duration recording is a direct measure of the amount of time an individual engages in a behavior or, less often, the amount of time that elapses between a reference point and the behavior (i.e., latency). An example of the latter would be the amount of time that elapses between sitting at a desk and beginning to study.

Behaviors recorded with the duration method should meet two criteria. First, as with frequency recording, the behavior should be discrete (one must be able to specify clearly when the behavior begins and ends). Second, each time the behavior occurs, it should last for more than a few seconds. For example, if a child presents a problem of sneezing more often than desirable, recording the duration of each sneeze would be cumbersome.

Duration data are reported in two ways. First, if observation periods are of the same length, the total duration of each period is reported. Second, if observation periods differ in length, data must be reported as the percentage of the total time that the observations occurred. Referring back to the yelling data in figure 9.1, total duration equaled 7 secs., and the percentage of time equaled 12%.

The use of duration recording is illustrated in a study on prolonged eating behavior in a 5-year-old girl conducted by Sanok and Ascione (1978). The objective of the study was to reduce (to a level more acceptable to the parents) mealtime duration, defined objectively as "the amount of time between the placement of food in front of the child to the time when no food was left on her plate" (p. 177). Using this duration measure, the authors demonstrated a reduction in duration of mealtime as a function of praise, time limits, and tokens. Data in this study were reported as the total time in minutes it took the child to complete each of three daily meals.

Computing observer agreement for duration recording is similar to the procedure used with frequency recording, except amounts of time are used instead of number of times. The formula is as follows:

$$\frac{\text{smaller observed duration}}{\text{larger observed duration}} \times 100$$

For example, if one observer recorded a behavior as having a total duration of 120 minutes and the other recorded a total duration of 145 minutes, observer agreement would equal 83% (i.e., $120/145 \times 100$).

Frequency/Duration Recording. When use of both frequency and duration recording is appropriate and time and situational costs are not excessive, the simultaneous use of both is often advantageous. By doing so, one has access not only to all the frequency and duration measures mentioned previously, but also to the mean length of each response. For example, referring back to figure 9.1, we find the mean length of each yell was 3.5 seconds. For some behavioral problems whose onset have an organic basis, the most appropriate treatment goal is to reduce the mean length of the response; as such, this combination of recording techniques is necessitated.

Interval Recording. Recording occurrence or nonoccurrence of a behavior in a series of equal time intervals is referred to as interval recording. Although it is usually desirable to determine how often or for how long a behavior occurs, practical considerations often make these types of exact recordings unfeasible. For example, if one needs to keep track of four behaviors simultaneously, duration recording by one observer would be difficult. Likewise, some behaviors occur at such a high rate that event recording is precluded. Still other behaviors do not have a clear-cut beginning and end and, thus, eliminate use of the duration method. These factors, however, do not influence whether or not interval recording can be used because all that is recorded is presence or absence of a behavior in short intervals of time.

In most instances, interval recording involves observation periods lasting 60 minutes or less. Therefore, if a behavior is very infrequent (e.g., occurring twice a day), the interval method would be an insensitive method of recording. Except for this restriction, interval recording can be applied to any behavior. It is best suited for situations where more than one response is being recorded, more than one individual is being observed (e.g., a class of 20 students), and/or for behaviors that cannot be recorded using the frequency or duration methods.

Interval recording requires an observer's undivided attention. Because of this, it is not practical for use by observers if the intervals are of relatively short length and if they have to attend to other tasks (e.g., cooking a meal). Another drawback is that some sort of signaling device (e.g., an audio or video timer, a precorded cassette, etc.) is needed to indicate onset of the observe-and-record intervals. In addition, training individuals to use the interval recording method requires more time and practice than either frequency or duration recording. Finally, interval recording gives only an estimate of the frequency or duration of a behavior and not an exact measure of these response dimensions.

In order to use the interval method, the total observation period is divided into identical time intervals. Part of the time, the observer observes the client to see if a behavior occurred, and, part of the time, he or she records whether or not the behavior occurred. Therefore, separate time intervals for both observing and recording are needed.[4] This is illustrated at the bottom of figure 9.1, where observe (O) and record (R) intervals are indicated below the time line. The size of observation intervals depends on how frequently the behavior occurs.[5] A rule to follow is that the more frequent the behavior, the shorter the observation interval should be. In general, intervals should never be less than 5 secs.

For illustrative purposes, assuming 10-secs. observation and 5-secs. record intervals, the observer would at the start of a 10-secs. observation interval look at the client(s) for 10 secs., deciding whether or not any of the behaviors are present. It does not matter how often the behavior occurs in an interval. The only question the observer asks himself or herself is "Was the behavior present at all during any part of the 10 secs.?" At the end of 10 seconds, the observer looks away from the client(s) and, during the next 5-secs. record interval, notes which behaviors were present in the previous 10-secs. observation interval on an observation sheet. An example is presented in figure 9.2. This cycle of observe-record is repeated throughout the entire observation period: 10 secs. observe, 5 secs. record, 10 secs. observe, 5 secs. record, and so forth.[6]

As noted earlier, the interval method provides an estimate of frequency or duration and does not yield exact measurement of these response dimensions. This can be seen by referring back to figure 9.1. For example, for the category of yelling, an observer would have scored the presence of this behavior for two observation intervals (2 & 3). However, in one of the intervals (2), yelling comprised 2 secs. of the interval while in the remaining interval (3) it involved 5 secs. Although duration of yelling varied across intervals, this dimension is not represented in the interval data. A similar problem occurs with the frequency of father reprimands. The actual frequency in figure 9.1 is 2 intervals across 60 seconds, yet only 1 interval would be scored. The second reprimand occurred in a record interval (R_3), a time when the observer was looking away from the clients and entering scores.

The type of interval recording system described thus far is referred to as partial interval. In another variation (whole-interval recording), a behavior is scored as occurring only if it recorded throughout the entire observation interval. For example, in the previous illustration, it would have required the behavior to occur throughout the entire 10-secs. interval. In still yet another variation, momentary time sampling, a behavior is scored as occurring only if it occurs at the signal. For example, upon hearing the signal "Observe," an observer would make an immediate determination as to whether the behavior occurred. The duration of the session until the next signal functions as a record interval.

REFERRAL CODE:
CLIENT CODE:
DATE OF OBSERVATION:
TIME OF OBSERVATION: START END
SETTING:
OTHERS PRESENT:

SESSION NUMBER:
OBSERVER:
RELIABILITY OBSERVER:

PS SO AC	PS SO AC	PS SO AC	PS SO AC	PS SO AC	PS SO AC
1	2	3	4	5	6
RF FI TA	RF FI TA	RF FI TA	RF FI TA	RF FI TA	RF FI TA
PS SO AC	PS SO AC	PS SO AC	PS SO AC	PS SO AC	PS SO AC
7	8	9	10	11	12
RF FI TA	RF FI TA	RF FI TA	RF FI TA	RF FI TA	RF FI TA
PS SO AC	PS SO AC	PS SO AC	PS SO AC	PS SO AC	PS SO AC
13	14	15	16	17	18
RF FI TA	RF FI TA	RF FI TA	RF FI TA	RF FI TA	RF FI TA
PS SO AC	PS SO AC	PS SO AC	PS SO AC	PS SO AC	PS SO AC
19	20	21	22	23	24
RF FI TA	RF FI TA	RF FI TA	RF FI TA	RF FI TA	RF FI TA
PS SO AC	PS SO AC	PS SO AC	PS SO AC	PS SO AC	PS SO AC
25	26	27	28	29	30
RF FI TA	RF FI TA	RF FI TA	RF FI TA	RF FI TA	RF FI TA
PS SO AC	PS SO AC	PS SO AC	PS SO AC	PS SO AC	PS SO AC
31	32	33	34	35	36
RF FI TA	RF FI TA	RF FI TA	RF FI TA	RF FI TA	RF FI TA
PS SO AC	PS SO AC	PS SO AC	PS SO AC	PS SO AC	PS SO AC
37	38	39	40	41	42
RF FI TA	RF FI TA	RF FI TA	RF FI TA	RF FI TA	RF FI TA
PS SO AC	PS SO AC	PS SO AC	PS SO AC	PS SO AC	PS SO AC
43	44	45	46	47	48
RF FI TA	RF FI TA	RF FI TA	RF FI TA	RF FI TA	RF FI TA
PS SO AC	PS SO AC	PS SO AC	PS SO AC	PS SO AC	PS SO AC
49	50	51	52	53	54
RF FI TA	RF FI TA	RF FI TA	RF FI TA	RF FI TA	RF FI TA
PS SO AC	PS SO AC	PS SO AC	PS SO AC	PS SO AC	PS SO AC
55	56	57	58	59	60
RF FI TA	RF FI TA	RF FI TA	RF FI TA	RF FI TA	RF FI TA

BEHAVIOR CODES   COMMENTS
PS - PHYSICAL SHARING
SO - SHARE OFFERS
AC - ACCEPTED OFFERS
RF - REFUSALS
FI - FIGHTING
TA - TEACHER ATTENTION

Fig. 9.2. A sample interval recording observation sheet.

At the end of the observation session, regardless of the type of interval recording, the number of intervals in which each behavior was scored is counted. If all of the observation sessions will be the same length (e.g., 30 minutes), one may report these totals. If, however, on different days, session lengths differ (e.g., Day 1 – 30 minutes, Day 2 – 20 minutes, Day 3 – 25 minutes), one must convert totals into percentages. The formula for doing this is as follows:

$$\frac{\text{number of intervals the behavior was scored}}{\text{total number of observation intervals}} \times 100$$

The use of interval recording is illustrated by one of our investigations of prosocial behavior (Barton & Ascione, 1979). We had our observers monitor five behaviors of preschool children for 10 seconds and record for 5 seconds, using partial-interval recording. Although the sessions were scheduled to be equal in length, because of illness, the number of children ($n = 32$), and natural interfering events, this goal was not met. As a consequence, we presented the data for each behavior as the percentage of interval occurrence.

To assess observer reliability for interval recording we must determine if the observers agreed, interval by interval. Before presenting the formula, two terms need to be defined. Agreements on occurrences refer to all intervals where *both* observers recorded that the behavior occurred. Intervals where neither observer recorded the behavior are *not* counted as agreements. Disagreements refer to intervals where one observer recorded the behavior and the other observer did not. The formula for computing observer agreement is:

$$\frac{\text{number of agreements on occurrences}}{\text{number of agreements on occurrences} + \text{number of disagreements}} \times 100$$

This method of computing agreement is referred to as the *Exact Agreement-Response Intervals Only Procedure* (Repp, Deitz, Boles, Deitz, & Repp, 1976) or, more simply, the scored-interval method. A similar procedure, computing observer agreement on nonoccurrences, has been proposed by Hawkins and Dotson (1975) and is referred to as the unscored-interval method. These authors note that both methods can yield an inflated agreement percentage depending on the base rates of behaviors. Use of the former with high rate, and the latter with low rate, behavior will result in spuriously inflated agreement percentages. Therefore, they recommend that the mean of these two methods be presented. Although debate continues on the most appropriate method for computing interval observer agreement (e.g., Hartmann, 1977), the mean scored-interval/unscored-interval method can be considered adequate in most instances (Lech & Ascione, 1981).

Sequential Data Recording. Sequential data recording refers to the class of methods that preserves in the observation record the temporal relation between behaviors and/or interactions. At the simplest level, the therapist may be interested in the sequential relation between only two events. For example, in figure 9.1 we can examine the sequence between the father giving an instruction and the child complying or the child complying and the father praising the child. To do this, we need to define the temporal limits of a sequence (e.g., by stating that offset of the first behavior has to precede the onset of the second behavior by no more than 3 seconds). In figure 9.1, there are two instances of the instruction-compliance sequence and four instances of the instruction–no compliance sequence. Likewise, the compliance-praise sequence occurred once and the compliance–no praise sequence occurred once. We can express these data as probabilities for this small sample of an instructional record. The probability of compliance given an instruction was .33, and the probability of praise given compliance was .50.

At a more complex level, we may wish to assess sequential relations between a number of different behaviors. This is illustrated in a study of peer social interactions conducted by Tremblay, Strain, Hendrickson, and Shores (1981). The authors were interested in the types of social behavior initiated by preschoolers that resulted in positive, negative, or no response from peers. Six-minute observation periods were divided into 10-secs. intervals. A maximum of three initiated behaviors could be recorded in each interval. A response to initiation was scored only if it followed an initiation within 3 seconds. Using this system, the authors not only were able to collect data on frequency of different types of initiations, but also the probability of positive, negative, and no response following each type of initiation behavior. In fact, the authors found that "target subjects' most frequent social initiations were not the behaviors that were most effective in gaining positive, reciprocal behavior from peers" (p. 247).

Sometimes in sequential analysis, rather than analyzing relations between behavior, we are concerned with how client(s) engage in a certain behavior sequentially with other individuals. This is illustrated in a study of sharing within, and across, groups of preschoolers by Barton and Bevirt (1981). The authors used a 5-secs. observe and 5-secs. record partial-interval recording system. However, during the record interval, the observers recorded who was sharing with whom. Thus, Barton and Bevirt (1981) were able to track sequentially with whom, for example, Erica shared. In addition, they were able to assess the effect of trained (to share) versus untrained peers on Erica's behavior.

Computing observer agreement for interval sequential analysis is similar to the procedure for interval data. However, the unit of agreement is the sequence instead of individual responses. Barton and Bevirt (1981) have provided a detailed discussion of how to define agreements for sequential analysis.

> As a stringent test of the accuracy of their observations, agreement was defined as both observers recording the same children sharing with another. For any given observation, their recordings had to be exactly the same. For example, if the primary observer marked Subjects 1, 2, and 3 as sharing, and the second observer marked Subjects 1 and 2 as sharing, then their recording was scored as a nonagreement, even though both observers agreed that Subjects 1 and 2 shared. Interobserver agreement for a session was computed by dividing the total number of agreements by the total number of observations and multiplying by 100. (p. 509)

Unlike the other recording approaches previously described, sequential recording has been used less frequently. We feel sequential recording has tremendous potential — especially for recording social behavior. Sequential data recording has been proposed as a desirable assessment approach by others in areas such as assessment of maladaptive parent-child interactions (Roberts & Forehand, 1978). It is clearly a method appropriate for the analysis of antecedent-behavior-consequence relations. A more extensive treatment of the conceptual and methodological issues related to sequential analysis can be found in the excellent volumes by Cairns (1979), Hops (1982), Lamb, Suomi, and Stephenson (1979), and Sackett (1978).

Qualitative Recording

One of the hallmarks of child behavior therapy has been objective functional analyses of quantitative changes in behavior. . . . However, treatment also may produce qualitative changes in behavior. . . . Qualitative analyses of the response components . . . are crucial for an accurate assessment of the operant level, as well as the effect of treatment. For example, if little Jonathon is taught to allow others to use his crayons, but does so sarcastically and with a frown on his face, quantitative analyses would probably indicate that treatment was successful. Nonetheless, his teacher would probably evaluate the treatment as being a failure. (Barton, 1982, p. 42)

Qualitative recordings can be made from direct observations; however, like sequential recording, they are blatantly absent from the literature. Two or three qualitative aspects of a behavior can be operationally defined and then monitored using the more common direct observation techniques of frequency, duration, or interval recording.

In the above example, qualitative analyses could be accomplished by counting the number of sharing responses that are emitted with a smile on Jonathon's face and in the absence of sarcastic remarks and frowns. By monitoring these latter three behaviors, for which excellent operational definitions currently exist, qualitative changes in addition to quantitative changes in Jonathon's sharing could be evaluated. (Barton, 1982, p. 43)

Qualitative recording is especially well suited for extremely low-frequency behavior emitted at a very high intensity, for which the more common quantitative recording methods are less sensitive. The tantrum behavior of young children is a classic example. It usually occurs very infrequently, but, when it does, the social environment is totally disrupted. A case study by DeWulf, Hamm, and Barton (1982) exemplifies the advantages of qualitative recording in just such a situation. An 8-year-old student in a special education classroom was referred for therapy by his teacher because of intermittent disruptive tantrum behaviors in response to teacher instructions. Tantrum behavior was defined in terms of a hierarchy of five different types of tantrum responses. Starting with the least intense, a point value of 1 was assigned, and, moving to the most intense, a point value of 5 was assigned. Thus, tantrums were defined as: (1) discontinuing activity, (2) emitting negative verbal gestures,

(3) producing negative verbal comments, (4) nondirective destructive behavior, and (5) destructive behavior. Each of these five response categories was operationally defined. The recording system used by the authors can best be described as a frequency-qualitative system. Each response was tallied and a corresponding qualitative score was assigned. The authors presented their results in terms of total responses and mean intensity per session. The desirability of using qualitative analyses is reflected in their results that the intervention did not affect total number of responses, but it did positively influence the mean intensity of the tantrums!

DeWulf et al. (1982) developed the following formula to test for observer agreement on the qualitative intensity of the behavior:

$$[1 - .2 \,(|x-y|)] \times 100$$

In this formula, x refers to Observer 1's rating and y refers to Observer 2's rating. For example, if Observer 1 and 2's ratings were 3 and 4, respectively, the discrepancy of 1 would yield an agreement percentage of 80% (i.e., $100[1 - .2(|3-4|)]$). Likewise, if Observer 1's rating had been 2, the discrepancy of 2 would have yielded an agreement percentage of 60% (i.e., $100[1 - .2(|2-4|)]$). Use of this formula is restricted to rating scales having five values. This stringent formula has face validity and obvious appeal, but it has yet to receive scientific scrutiny.

In the past, most proponents of child behavioral assessment have not used qualitative recording for fear of incorporating subjectivity. However, the DeWulf et al. (1982) study clearly demonstrates that qualitative recording can be objective. Qualitative direct observation can be used with many other types of child behavioral assessment such as checklists (see chap. 5).

ISSUES IN USE OF DIRECT OBSERVATION

Pragmatic Issues

Throughout this chapter we already have made a number of pragmatic suggestions. In this section we will address additional issues and concerns that eventually confront users of direct observation technology. It is hoped that the information contained in this section will be of value to novice practitioners as well as veteran researchers. The suggestions that we will be proffering are based on both scientific findings reported in the literature and our own experiences in research, training, and clinical settings.

Observer Training and Monitoring. It has been well documented that a number of variables (including an observer's bias, drift, location, and presence) can potentially confound the data that are obtained through direct observation (Johnson & Bolstad, 1973). Two methods for reducing the likelihood of these confounds are through observer training and monitoring.

Optimal observer training, as we view it, can be thought of as a three-part process. The first step involves the trainee becoming thoroughly familiar with the operational definitions as well as the recording system.[7] To facilitate learning, we recommend not only providing the trainee with typed copies of the definitions and recording system but, also, study objectives to help them focus on key aspects of both. Once the trainee feels as if he or she has mastered these materials, he or she takes a quiz. It is recommended that a 100% mastery criterion be used before the trainee is allowed to proceed to Step 2.

The second step involves the trainee demonstrating mastery on an actual observation sheet while viewing a prerecorded audio-video tape of child-child and child-adult interactions. The first few sequences on the tape should be rather short in duration so as to provide an opportunity for coaching a trainee who might be having problems transferring the knowledge gained in Step 1 to actual audio-video taped situations. This coaching typically involves a number of behavioral intervention strategies, including shaping, feedback, instructions, modeling, behavior rehearsal, and/or praise. Once the trainee is competent on the short sequences, the length of subsequent sequences should become progressively longer, until eventually they equal the expected length of the actual observation sessions. This latter strategy helps the trainee gradually to condition himself or herself against the negative potential for observer fatigue. Again, the trainee should not be allowed to move to the next step until he or she has demonstrated mastery (at least 85%).

The third and final step involves *in vivo* observations either in the target, a similar, or an analogue, setting. This step should continue until he or she again demonstrates mastery. An illustration of Step 3 is the study by Greenwood, Walker, Todd, and Hops (1979). They had their observers practice in actual preschool classrooms during 15-minute sessions, using a sequential recording system. Their mastery criterion consisted of at least 85% agreement on all the child behaviors for three consecutive sessions.

The three-step training process is obviously quite time consuming, and, as such, most trainers do not do so thorough a job! However, without adequate training, the probability of obtaining reliable data is minimal. We have found that there is a direct relation between the quality of observer training and reliability. The 3-step process described here has its theoretical basis in errorless learning and the personalized system of instruction (Keller, 1968). We strongly recommend its use.

Although observers, after training, may record in a highly reliable fashion in the initial stages of a case study, reliability may deteriorate over time. The best strategy for preventing this is frequent monitoring and feedback. We have found the more frequent the monitoring, the more likely reliability will be maintained at an acceptable level. When possible, it is advantageous to monitor for reliability during every session (e.g., Barton & Ascione, 1979). Feedback on percentage observer agreement, however, need not be given daily. Instead, it is recommended that feedback be given on an irregular basis but on the average of approximately once every five sessions. If such monitoring discloses reliability deterioration, then the trainer should (a) check to make sure the observers are recording independently and not discussing their observations with one another; (b) interview the observer so as to determine what is causing the problem; and/or (c) provide coaching (like the type used in training).

Observation Sheet. A well-designed observation sheet can greatly facilitate accurate direct observation. An example of an observation sheet was presented earlier in this chapter (see fig. 9.2). Every observation sheet should include spaces for critical basic information at the top. This information typically includes: date, session number, location, observers' names, number and identity of children and adults present, starting and ending time of the observation, and a space for noting unusual incidents. If acronyms are used to connote the behaviors, codes and their definitions should be listed at the bottom of the sheet.

The observation sheet should be designed so as to miminize complexity and maximize usability. It should also be designed so that it can be used by any trained observer in any setting where observations occur. In addition, the observation sheet (as well as the observations system) should be designed so that it can be used through all phases of a study. For example, if the observer is also the therapist, will he or she be able to record his or her observations during treatment? In supervising practicum students, we have found overestimation of therapist ability to use an observation system to be a common error. Finally, the observation sheet should be designed so as to allow for recording of the therapist's behavior. This is especially important with respect to manipulation of the independent variables. Many researchers fail to do this!

Observation sheets may soon have a competitor: computer boards. Much more information can be gathered, and more quickly, using a computer board than with a system using handwritten entries. In addition, data analysis is facilitated because the raw data do not have to be transposed by humans. Data can be fed directly into a computer program at any point during a study.

The work of Burgess (1982) in assessing the proximity and social contact of 209 children in university and community sites is illustrative of the potential efficiency of computer-board recording. She had her observers gather two types of information. Upon entering the setting, the observers would enter on the board data concerning structural parameters of the group (e.g., number of teachers, sexual makeup of the group, developmental composition).

In addition, the observers recorded the functional characteristics. More specifically, they entered direct observations of children using a detailed sequential recording approach. The raw data were then submitted to a myriad of statistical tests. Her analyses revealed many subtle effects of mainstreaming on young children's social integration into natural settings. Thus, high technology may soon eliminate the need for observation sheets and undoubtedly greatly enhance the state of the art in direct observation.

How Much Data? In setting up a direct observation system, one has to ask a number of questions. How much data should be gathered? How many responses and how many settings should be monitored? How long should each observation session and the entire study last? Who and how many individuals should be observed?

In general, the more data that can be gathered, the better. For example, we have found treatment effects that have generalized across responses and settings (Barton & Ascione, 1979). Gathering too few data per session or across the study can seriously threaten the validity and reliability of the observations (Hersen & Barlow, 1976). Any individual common to the child's environment (e.g., parent, sibling, teacher, peer), who could be trained to observe, could potentially gather meaningful data. Thus, it would appear that one should gather as much data as possible. However, this conclusion is not warranted. In setting up an observation system, one should consider if (a) all the data will, and can, be analyzed and utilized; (b) the number of responses, settings, and/or observers will make the observation system unmanageable and/or unreliable; and (c) the observers' other responsibilities (e.g., to other children and/or a spouse) will cause task overload. Thus, there is no general answer to the question of how much data to gather. Like most practitioners and researchers, we sometimes have gathered too little, too much, or the wrong data. Experience, intuition, and behavioral analysis help to answer this question—but so does luck!

Ethical Concerns

Recent litigation (e.g., *Youngberg* vs. *Romeo,* 1982), U.S. Congressional actions such as the Buckley amendment (The Family Education Rights and Privacy Act, 1976), and policy statements on ethical behavior by the American Psychological Association (1977; 1981 a, b, c, & d) dictate the importance of considering the child's rights before implementing a direct observational procedure.

Prior to observing children, especially if an intervention is planned, the purpose of the study, the observational procedures, and methods to assure the confidentiality of the data should be explained to the child's parents or guardian. In addition, permission must be granted by the parents or guardians before starting to observe! Otherwise, the observer is violating the child's right to privacy.

The data generated by observing a child must be kept confidential. Thus, for example, on the observation sheet, a code or pseudonym should be used instead of the child's real name. In addition, all tangential cues to the child's identity must be avoided. For example, a reference to stuttering, if the child is the only one in the classroom who has a stuttering problem, would violate the child's rights because of its obvious association with him or her.

No one can be given access to information regarding a child that has been obtained through direct observation without the child's (or guardian's) permission. For example, observations of a child in his or her home cannot be discussed with his or her classroom teacher without the client's permission. The code of ethics of the American Psychological Association (1977; 1981 a, d) also dictates that a child has the right to request that an observation of him or her be stopped immediately. This policy is consistent with the child's right to privacy.

A child and/or his or her guardian also has the right to inspect any information that you have on file about him or her. This right is provided to the child by the Buckley amendment to assure that all statements about a child have a sound basis. Direct observation procedures, as distinct from subjective assessment, are consistent with this right. Direct observation should involve the use of objective, valid, and reliable procedures. Thus, a child should not be harmed by "unfounded" statements. Nonetheless, users of direct observation should be careful not to extend their comments about a child beyond the limits of the objective data.

These are but a few of the many ethical considerations that an individual must consider in setting up a direct observational procedure. Attention to ethical considerations must take precedence over all the suggestions we have given in the previous sections—even at the expense of developing a less than optimal observational system! The child's rights have to be of the utmost concern.

CASE STUDY

In closing, we offer the following hypothetical case as an example of how a direct observational system could be developed and implemented in child behavioral assessment.

Client: Billy (Age: 4 years, 5 months)
Referral Agency: Harmonious Day-Care Center
Reason for Referral: Fighting with other children at the day-care center.

An interview was conducted with Billy's parents who indicated they had sought the advise of a behavioral consultant (BC) on the recommendation of the day-care center director. The parents said that center staff had noted a substantial increase in the number of fights with other children Billy appeared to be involved with at the center. The parents were concerned that Billy would be disliked by his peers but were baffled because he did not present this problem at home. They noted that Billy is an only child and was at the center most of the day. They suggested that he did not have much opportunity to play with peers at home. The parents granted permission for BC to interview the center staff and observe Billy at the center.

In talking with center staff, BC learned that fighting was their principal concern about Billy. He seemed to be progressing well on the pre-academic work at the center and interacted well with center staff. The director noted that most of the fights occurred during free-play periods, both during morning and afternoon sessions. Reasoning with Billy and reprimanding him had not proven to be effective, and the staff said they would be appreciative of any suggestions that could be provided.

Given this information, BC was given permission to observe Billy during the two free-play periods. BC observed Billy and his peers for four half-hour periods of free play, over two separate days using a narrative recording procedure. Restructured recording of the narrative (part of which is shown in table 9.1) suggested to BC that fighting centered around possession and use of toys in the free-play area. Billy most often played by himself; positive interactions with peers seemed more like parallel play and occurred only when duplicates of toys (e.g., two trucks) were available. Other children attempted to play with Billy on occasion but were always rebuffed by him. Informal observation suggested to BC that Billy's fighting was excessive in comparison to the other children and went beyond the occasional altercations that occur in a day-care center.

BC speculated that fighting would be less frequent if Billy were taught appropriate skills in sharing toys with others and if center staff attended to him during appropriate play. Peer sociometric ratings completed on two separate occasions verified that Billy's status among his peers was low.

A checklist completed by center staff verified not only that fighting was a serious concern in Billy's case, but also that appropriate play would be a desired goal of any intervention that was designed.

Using this information from the narrative, especially topographical descriptions of behavior, BC developed definitions of six behavior categories: physical sharing, share offers, acceptance of share offers, refusal to share, physical fighting, and teacher attention. BC also consulted a paper by Barton and Ascione (1979) to assist in developing some of the definitions. The definitions were shown to two of the center teachers who worked most closely with Billy, and, with some minor revisions, the definitions were viewed as capturing both problem behaviors (e.g., refusals to share) and desirable alternatives (e.g., acceptance of share offers). The parents also reviewed and approved of the behavior categories indicating they would rely on teacher judgment in this area.

Given the number of behaviors to be recorded, BC selected a partial-interval recording system, using a format shown in figure 9.2. Three local college students working in a psychology practicum agreed to serve as observers. After studying the definitions, passing a criterion test, and reaching high reliability on a practice videotape, the observers were ready to record at the day-care center.

Each day, for one half hour of the morning and one half hour of the afternoon free-play period, two of the three observers recorded the categories using the data sheets and a cassette recorder signaling device. During this time, except for one day, reliability for each of the categories equaled or exceeded 80% (using the mean scored-interval/unscored-interval method).

Since all observation sessions did not last exactly 30 minutes, BC examined the percentage of intervals for each behavior and for selected sequences. The means for these data over one week were as follows:

Physical Sharing:	3%	Refusals to Share:	98%
Share Offers:	1%	Physical Fighting:	28%
Acceptance of Share Offers:	2%	Teacher Attention:	8%

Teacher attention given physical sharing: 0%
Teacher attention given physical fighting: 74%
Teacher attention given share offer or acceptance of share offer: .5%

Treatment could now begin.

SUMMARY

Direct observation in child behavioral assessment is a hallmark of applied behavioral analysis approaches to behavioral intervention with children. Assessment of the observable dimensions of behavior remains the criterion upon which therapists most often reach decisions regarding the current etiology, choice of intervention strategies, and treatment effectiveness for behavioral disorders in children. The evolution of direct observational methods has resulted in a level of sophistication that allows for reliable, valid, and ethical assessment technique. Continued development in this area promises an increase in our understanding of the processes that maintain deviant behavior in children and in our ability to design effective procedures for ameliorating child behavioral problems.

NOTES

1. "Therapist" is used in this chapter in its generic sense of referring to any change agent who uses intervention techniques to rectify a child's behavior problem. Thus, a therapist could be a clinician, researcher, parent, teacher, sibling, etc.
2. This restriction is a requirement of direct observation and does not imply the unimportance of more subjective data.
3. For more sensitive methods of computing observer agreement for each of the recording methods, refer to Gelfand and Hartmann (1975).

4. If recording is conducted by viewing videotapes, the pause function may be used to stop the tape during record intervals, avoiding loss of data during record periods.

5. Data suggest that observe intervals under 30 seconds do not seriously distort the actual frequency or duration dimensions of behavior (Powell, Martindale, & Kulp, 1975).

6. As a suggestion for observer training we recommend when an audio signal is being used, that as soon as the observer hears the "O" of observe that s/he start observing and as soon as s/he hears "R" of record, s/he stop observing. We have found that this strategy greatly facilitates reliability.

7. The observer, however, should be kept naive as to the purpose of the study until after its completion.

REFERENCES

Achenbach, T. M. *Developmental psychopathology* (2nd Ed.). New York: Wiley, 1982.

American Psychological Association. *Standards for providers of psychological services* (Rev. ed.). Washington, DC: Author, 1977.

American Psychological Association. Ethical principles of psychologists. *American Psychologist,* 1981, *36, 633*-638. (a)

American Psychological Association. Specialty guidelines for the delivery of services by clinical psychologists. *American Psychologist,* 1981, *36,* 640-651. (b)

American Psychological Association. Specialty guidelines for the delivery of services by counseling psychologists. *American Psychologist,* 1981, *36,* 652-663. (c)

American Psychological Association. Specialty guidelines for the delivery of services by school psychologists. *American Psychologist,* 1981, *36,* 670-681. (d)

Baer, D. M., Wolf, M. M., & Risley, T. R. Some current dimensions of applied behavior analysis. *Journal of Applied Behavior Analysis,* 1968, *1,* 91-97.

Barton, E. J. Developing sharing: An analysis of modeling and other behavioral techniques. *Behavior Modification,* 1981, *5,* 386-398.

Barton, E. J. Classroom sharing: A critical analysis of assessment, facilitation, and generalization procedures. In M. Hersen, R. M. Eisler, & P. M. Miller (Eds.), *Progress in behavior modification Vol. 13.* New York: Academic Press, 1982.

Barton, E. J. Modification of children's prosocial behavior. In P. S. Strain, M. Guralnick, & H. M. Walker (Eds.), *Children's social behavior: Development, assessment, and modification.* New York: Academic Press, 1983.

Barton, E. J., & Ascione, F. R. Sharing in preschool children: Facilitation, stimulus generalization, response generalization, and maintenance. *Journal of Applied Behavior Analysis,* 1979, *12,* 417-430.

Barton, E. J., & Bevirt, J. Generalization of sharing across groups: Assessment of group composition with preschool children. *Behavior Modification,* 1981, *5,* 503-522.

Barton, E. J., & Madsen, J. J. The use of awareness and omission training to control excessive drooling in a severely retarded youth. *Child Behavior Therapy,* 1980, *2,* 55-63.

Barton, E. J., Olszewski, M. J., & Madsen, J. J. The effect of adult presence on prosocial behavior among preschool children. *Child Behavior Therapy,* 1979, *1,* 271-286.

Bornstein, P. H., Bridgwater, C. A., Hickey, J. S., & Sweeney, T. M. Characteristics and trends in behavioral assessment: An archival analysis. *Behavioral Assessment,* 1980, *2,* 125-133.

Burgess, J. M. *Social interaction in developmentally integrated preschool classrooms.* Paper presented at the 6th Annual Meeting of the Association of Behavioral Analysis, Dearborn, Michigan, May 1982.

Cairns, R. B. *The analysis of social interactions: Methods, issues, and illustrations.* Hillsdale, NJ: Lawrence Erlbaum Associates, 1979.

Center, D. B., Deitz, S. M., & Kaufman, M. E. Student ability, task difficulty, and inappropriate classroom behavior: A study of children with behavior disorders. *Behavior Modification,* 1982, *6,* 355-374.

Cunningham, T. R., & Tharp, R. G. The influence of settings on accuracy and reliability of behavioral observation. *Behavioral Assessment,* 1981, *3,* 67-78.

DeWulf, M. J., Hamm, H., & Barton, E. J. Qualitative analysis of a behavioral program designed to modify intense tantrum behavior. In E. J. Barton (Ed.), *Psychology Practicum Summary Vol. 5.* Marquette: Northern Michigan University Press, 1982.

The Family Educational Rights and Privacy Act. *Federal Register,* June 17, 1976, *41* (No. 118).

Foster, S. L., & Ritchey, W. L. Issues in the assessment of social competence in children. *Journal of Applied Behavior Analysis,* 1979, *12,* 625-638.

Gelfand, D. M., & Hartmann, D. P. *Child behavior analysis and therapy.* New York: Pergamon Press, 1975.

Greenwood, C. R., Walker, H. M., Todd, N. M., & Hops, H. Selecting a cost-effective screening measure for the assessment of preschool social withdrawal. *Journal of Applied Behavior Analysis,* 1979, *12,* 639-652.

Hartmann, D. P. Considerations in the choice of interobserver reliability estimates. *Journal of Applied Behavior Analysis,* 1977, *10,* 103-116.

Hawkins, R. P., & Dotson, V. A. Reliability scores that delude: An Alice in Wonderland trip through the misleading characteristics of interobserver agreement scores in interval recording. In E. Ramp & G. Semb (Eds.), *Behavior analysis: Areas of research and application.* Englewood Cliffs, NJ: Prentice-Hall, 1975.

Hersen, M., & Barlow, D. H. *Single-case experimental designs: Strategies for studying behavior change.* Oxford: Pergamon Press, 1976.

Hops, H. Social skills training for socially withdrawn/isolated children. In P. Karoly & J. Steffen (Eds.), *Enhancing children's competencies.* Lexington, MA: Lexington Publishing Co., 1982.

Jacob, R. G., O'Leary, K. D., & Rosenblad, C. Formal and informal classroom settings: Effects on hyperactivity. *Journal of Abnormal Child Psychology,* 1978, *6,* 47-59.

Johnson, S., & Bolstad, O. Methodological issues in naturalistic observation: Some problems and solutions for field research. In L. A. Hamerlynck, L. C. Handy, & E. J. Mash (Eds.), *Behavior change: Methodology, concepts, and practice.* Champaign, IL: Research Press, 1973.

Karpowitz, D. H., & Johnson, S. M. Stimulus control in child-family interaction. *Behavioral Assessment,* 1981, *3,* 161-171.

Kazdin, A. E. Symptom substitution, generalization, and response covariation: Implications for psychotherapy outcome. *Psychological Bulletin,* 1982, *91,* 349-365.

Keller, F. S. "Good-bye teacher . . . " *Journal of Applied Behavior Analysis,* 1968, *1,* 79-89.

Lahey, B. B., Vosk, B. N., & Habif, V. L. Behavioral assessment of learning disabled children: A rationale and a strategy. *Behavioral Assessment,* 1981, *3,* 3-14.

Lamb, M. E., Suomi, S. J., & Stephenson, G. R. (Eds.). *Social interaction analysis: Methodological issues.* Madison: University of Wisconsin Press, 1979.

Lech, B., & Ascione, F. R. Different formulas for computing observer agreement: Does it *really* make any difference? Paper presented at the meeting of the Rocky Mountain Psychological Association, Denver, April 1981.

Nelson, R. O., & Hayes, S. C. Some current dimensions of behavioral assessment. *Behavioral Assessment,* 1979, *1,* 1-16.

Powell, J., Martindale, A., & Kulp, S. An evaluation of time-sample measures of behavior. *Journal of Applied Behavior Analysis,* 1975, *8,* 463-469.

Repp, A. C., Deitz, E. D., Boles, S. M., Deitz, S. M., & Repp, C. F. Differences among common methods for calculating interobserver agreement. *Journal of Applied Behavior Analysis,* 1976, *9,* 109-113.

Roberts, M. W., & Forehand, R. The assessment of maladaptive parent-child interaction by direct observation: An analysis of methods. *Journal of Abnormal Child Psychology*, 1978, *6*, 257–270.

Sackett, G. P. (Ed.). *Observing behavior Volume II: Data collection and analysis methods.* Baltimore: University Park Press, 1978.

Sanok, R. L., & Ascione, F. R. The effects of reduced time limits on prolonged eating behavior. *Journal of Behavior Therapy and Experimental Psychiatry*, 1978, *9*, 177–179.

Serna, R. W., & Ascione, F. R. Computing observer agreement: Recent trends in the *Journal of Applied Behavior Analysis*. Paper presented at the meeting of the Rocky Mountain Psychological Association, Denver, April 1981.

Singh, N. N., Manning, P. J., & Angell, M. J. Effects of an oral hygiene punishment procedure on chronic rumination and collateral behaviors in monozygous twins. *Journal of Applied Behavior Analysis*, 1982, *15*, 309–314.

Tremblay, A., Strain, P. S., Hendrickson, J. M., & Shores, R. E. Social interactions of normal preschool children. *Behavior Modification*, 1981, *5*, 237–253.

Twardosz, S., Schwartz, S., Fox, J., & Cunningham, J. L. Development and evaluation of a system to measure affectionate behavior. *Behavioral Assessment*, 1979, *1*, 177–190.

Van Houten, R. Social validation: The evolution of standards of competency for target behaviors. *Journal of Applied Behavior Analysis*, 1979, *12*, 581–591.

Voeltz, L. M., & Evans, I. M. The assessment of behavioral interrelationships in child behavior therapy. *Behavioral Assessment*, 1982, *4*, 131–165.

Warren, S. F., Rogers-Warren, A., & Baer, D. M. The role of offer rates in controlling sharing by young children. *Journal of Applied Behavior Analysis*, 1976, *9*, 491–497.

Youngberg vs. Romeo, No. 80-1429 (U.S. Supreme Court, June 18, 1982).

10

Intellectual and Academic Achievement Tests

Alan S. Kaufman
and
Cecil R. Reynolds

This chapter is intended to provide a brief overview and introduction to the assessment of intellectual functioning and academic attainment through the use of standardized tests. Many intelligence and achievement tests are available for use with children. Indeed, the relative publication rate of new intelligence tests has increased over the last decade (Reynolds & Elliott, in press). However, this chapter will not be a test recital detailing these tests for you to run out and learn. But, rather, it will provide a paradigm for intelligent testing to guide your assessments. The approach has been applied most often and most eloquently to intelligence tests (e.g., Kaufman, 1979), though application to other types of measures has frequently been suggested (e.g., Reynolds, 1982a). To learn the proper administration and scoring procedures for individually administered tests and to develop a healthy respect for following standardized procedures are no mean feats; they require intense practice. The principles and concepts developed in this chapter should aid you in the proper choice of test materials and their proper use and interpretation once you have mastered the technical skills of administration and scoring. Standardized tests of intelligence and achievement must be administered and scored correctly. If not, the scores are useless no matter how sophisticated your scheme of test interpretation. There is no adequate method for partialling out this type of error even if you are aware of it, though typically you will not be. With this admonition, it is appropriate to turn to the principal tasks of the chapter.

WHEN TO TEST INTELLIGENCE
AND ACHIEVEMENT

From the ages of 5 years to about 18 years, the vast majority of their non-adult lives, children attend school. Socialization and individuation are doubtless major developmental tasks of this period; many others could be named, but schooling and the acquisition of an education that allows one to become an independent, contributing member of the larger society take precedence over most other tasks of these years. Academic success, the acquisition of the knowledge base for life in a complex society, and the lack of it are major foci of school administrators, teachers, and parents (the individuals who fill most of the child's waking hours), and are a cause of great consternation and potential distress for the children themselves. It follows then that any evaluation that ignores intellectual and academic development is going to be inadequate for developing a good understanding of children and their reciprocal interactions with the environment. Our response to the question of when to assess intelligence and achievement in the context of a psychological evaluation, of which a behavioral assessment is one subset of possible approaches to evaluation, is virtually always. Additional reasons exist.

The intellectual level of a child will impact on the interpretation given to other assessment outcomes and observations of behavior. Many behaviors could be cited that are developmentally sequenced such that they are considered normal, progressive acts at one age but pathological if persisting beyond a particular age level. Such behaviors and acts are, in most instances, better evaluated relative to the child's mental age and not chronological age. Pathognomic indicators on certain projective tests, such as the Kinetic Family Drawing (KFD) and the Human Figure Drawing (HFD), are age related with regard to their personality interpretation. The failure to integrate intellectual level into such interpretations can cause considerable distortion in the final evaluation. Particularly for children, intellectual level can impact choice of therapeutic programs. A 12-year-old with an IQ of 60 is a poor prospect for cognitive behavioral therapy, particularly along the lines of Rational Emotive Therapy (RET); whereas the 12-year-old with an IQ of 120 may be very responsive to such an approach.[1]

An in-depth, comprehensive evaluation of intelligence and achievement, although always required when the primary referral questions are problems such as mental retardation or learning disabilities, is not always necessary. The reality of practice and the circumstances of the referral may indicate that only brief or screening measures of IQ and achievement are necessary. Such decisions to defer to a screening measure should not be made lightly, however.

A FEW WORDS ON SCREENING
OF INTELLIGENCE LEVEL

Comprehensive evaluation of intellectual functioning, though highly desirable, is time consuming, expensive, and not always necessary. Hence, a variety of brief measures of intelligence have been developed over the years. When deciding to use a brief measure of intelligence, one must recognize and accept the fact that there may be a considerable loss of clinical information. Thus, it is useful to review the purpose of screening and to evaluate the use of screening techniques. More detailed discussions of the issues to follow can be found in several sources (Kaufman, 1979; Kaufman & Kaufman, 1977; Kaufman & Reynolds, 1983; Reynolds, 1979b).

Although nearly all children with intellectual disorders will ultimately be identified during their public school careers, it is during the early years that corrective, habilitative efforts have the greatest probability of success. Additionally, parents, teachers, and pediatricians, though good sources of referral, cannot be relied upon entirely to identify these children or to report reliably on their intellectual skills. In the course of comprehensive psychological assessments of children, a brief screening measure of intelligence will sometimes be sufficient to meet the clinician's need for information. With young children, brief screening measures are more likely to be used to evaluate large numbers of children in a short time period. In this instance, screening has as its direct goal identifying children who are most likely to develop learning, behavior, or other problems.

In these circumstances screening is conducted on a probability basis and reduces the cost of identifying mentally handicapped children by selecting out (or screening out) those children *most likely* to have problems. However, a screening test is not a criterion measure. No matter how badly a child performs on a screening test, it does not necessarily mean he or she is mentally or cognitively handicapped. In fact, a good screening test has a built-in pathological bias. Because it is usually less tolerable to miss locating a handicapped child than to recommend comprehensive evaluation of a nonhandicapped child, whenever a screening test is "in doubt" about a child, it should identify him or her as potentially handicapped.

Children identified as potentially mentally handicapped through a screening test can then be referred for a thorough individual evaluation to assess accurately and in detail their true levels of intellectual functioning. The latter appraisal is multifaceted. It involves determination of an appropriate classification and delineation of an individual educational program or plan of therapy that capitalizes on children's assets, limits the effects of their liabilities, and makes treatment as palatable and successful as possible.

Screening tests, as a rule, provide very limited, restrictive samples of behavior and are all but useless with respect to diagnostic decision making and the development of instructional plans. Screening tests are usually designed to detect a child's areas of deficit or handicap, but they do not typically allow for the identification of his or her strengths. From a legal standpoint, the vast majority of screening tests do not meet the requirements of P.L. 94–142 for use in educational placement. The results of a screening test cannot substitute for comprehensive individual assessment information, and screening test information certainly cannot be allowed to override the results of the individual assessment of the referred pupil. However, when used appropriately, screening tests can enhance, economically, a clinician's or school district's ability to identify and to serve the handicapped. Used in an attempt to circumvent, stunt, or substitute for a comprehensive evaluation of intellectual functioning, screening tests can lead to major errors in the identification-programming process and provide a great disservice to the teachers, parents, and other individuals involved. All intellectual screening tests are not group administered. Some of the best screening tests are individually administered, although individual administration does not elevate the status of a screening measure within the total evaluation process.

A number of well-designed group tests are available for use in intellectual screening with youngsters who are at least at the beginning kindergarten stage. One need only review Buros's *Tests in Print* and the most recent of his yearbook series, *The Eighth Mental Measurements Yearbook,* to locate nearly all tests available for the group testing of cognitive skills. In addition to descriptive information on each test, comprehensive reviews of the technical adequacy and general quality of the measures are provided in the *Yearbooks.* There are far too many of these tests to be reviewed here. Thus, the reader is referred to the aforementioned sources for information on group tests for intellectual screening, and to Ebel (1982) for a more general discussion of the evaluation and selection of group tests.

Group tests are typically not available for use with children below age 5; these youngsters are far less accustomed to formal environments and do not have the necessary attentional, visual-motor, perceptual, and social skills to allow them to sit and concentrate on the test materials for the necessary amount of time without close supervision. Individual assessment of children should be the rule below age 5 and is recommended for older children as well. The use of group tests further removes the clinician from the process and takes away the possibility of obtaining good observational data.

The use of individually administered screening tests need not be an expensive or time-consuming enterprise. Individual screening instruments are available that are reliable, valid, informative, and require only 20–30 minutes for administration. Of these, the most reasonable methods seem to be the use of carefully developed short forms of the major individually administered intelligence tests. These short forms are typically at least as reliable as other brief tests, have more validity information available, are more familiar to educational and psychological personnel, and are traditionally better normed than nearly all other brief tests of intelligence. Short forms of the major scales have an added advantage in that, if an individual is noted to be at risk on the screening measure, the remainder of the scale can be administered without a duplication of effort.

The development of short forms of the Wechsler scales has been a popular topic in the psychometric literature for some time, and a variety of short forms have been proposed. Of these, some of the more useful ones appear to be the short forms proposed by Kaufman (1976) for the Wechsler Intelligence Scale for Children-Revised (WISC-R) and Wechsler Preschool and Primary Scale of Intelligence (WPPSI) (Kaufman, 1972), and by Reynolds, Wilson, and Clark (in press) for the Wechsler Adult Intelligence Scale-Revised (WAIS-R). Also of value is Kaufman's (1977) six-subtest short form of the McCarthy Scales of Children's Abilities (MSCA).

Frequently, short forms have been developed on purely empirical grounds without regard to rational and psychological bases for the inclusion of specific subtests from the parent scale. While empirical development is necessary, it seems insufficient as the sole method of choosing subtests for a short form. Kaufman's (1972) four-test short form of the WPPSI was developed on the basis of empirical and rational psychological characteristics of the various subtests. It uses data gleaned from the large national standardization sample of the test with careful delineation of the short form's psychometric properties. Subsequent short forms of the WISC-R, WAIS-R, and MSCA noted above were developed from a similar blend of clinical and empirical criteria. When choosing or developing short forms of existing or new intelligence tests, psychologists would be wise to adhere to the combination of psychological, clinical, and psychometric considerations proposed by Kaufman (1972, 1976, 1977).

A PHILOSOPHY OF INTELLIGENT TESTING

Conventional intelligence tests and even the entire concept of intelligence testing currently are the focus of considerable controversy. Always the subject of scrutiny, intelligence tests in the past decade have been placed on trial in the federal courts (*Larry P.,* 1979; *PASE,* 1980), state legislatures (e.g., New York's "truth-in-testing" legislation and similar Federal level proposals), the lay press, and open scholarly forums (Reynolds & Brown, in press; Sattler, Hilliard, Lambert, Albee, & Jensen, 1981). At one extreme of the issues are those such as Albee, Hilliard, and Williams who contend that IQ tests are inherently unacceptable measurement devices with no real utility. While at the other extreme are such well-known figures as Hernstein and Jensen who believe the immense value of intelligence tests is by now clearly self-evident. While critics of testing demand a moratorium on their use with children, psychologists are often forced to adhere to rigid administrative rules that require the use of *precisely* obtained IQs when making placement or diagnostic decisions. But there may be no consideration for: measurement error, the influence of behavioral variables on performance, or appropriate sensitivity to the child's cultural or linguistic heritage.

A middle ground is sorely needed. Tests need to be preserved along with their rich clinical heritage and their prominent place in the neurological, psychological, and educational literature. Yet the proponents of tests need to be less defensive and more open to rational criticisms of current popular instruments. Knowledge of the weaknesses as well as the strengths of individually administered intelligence tests can serve the dual functions of 1) improving examiners' ability to interpret profiles of any given instrument; and 2) enabling them to select pertinent supplementary tests and subtests so as to secure a thorough assessment of the intellectual abilities of any child, adolescent, or adult referred for evaluation. The quality of individual mental assessment is no longer simply a question answered in terms of an instrument's empirical or psychometric characteristics. High reliability and validity coefficients, a meaningful factor structure, and normative data obtained by stratified random sampling techniques do not ensure that an intelligence test is valuable for all, or even most, assessment purposes. The skills and training of the psychologist engaged in using intelligence tests will certainly interact with the utility of intelligence testing beyond the level of simple actuarial prediction of academic performance.

Indeed, with low-IQ children, the primary role of the intelligent tester is to use test results to develop a means of intervention that will enhance the prediction made by global IQs. A plethora of research during this century has amply demonstrated that very low IQ children show concomitantly low levels of academic attainment. The purpose of administering an intelligence test to a low-IQ child then is at least twofold: 1) to determine that the child is indeed at high-risk for academic failure, and 2) to help articulate a set of learning circumstances that defeat the prediction. For individuals with average or high IQs, the specific tasks of the intelligent tester may change, but the philosophy remains the same. When evaluating a learning-disabled (LD) child, for example, the task is primarily one of fulfilling the prediction made by the global IQs. Most LD children exhibit average or better general intelligence yet have a history of academic performance significantly below what would be predicted from their intelligence test performance. The intelligent tester then assumes the responsibility of preventing the child from becoming an outlier in the prediction (i.e., designing a set of environmental conditions that cause him or her to achieve and learn at least at the level predicted by the intelligence test).

When engaged in intelligence testing, the child becomes the primary focus of the evaluation and the tests fade into the background as only vehicles to understanding. The test setting becomes completely examinee oriented. Interpretation and communication of test results in the context of the child's particular background, referral behaviors, and approach to performance on diverse tasks constitute the crux of competent evaluation. Global test scores are deemphasized. Flexibility, a broad base of knowledge in psychology, and insight on the part of the psychologist are demanded. Thus, the intelligence test becomes a dynamic helping agent, not an instrument for labeling, placement in dead-end programs, or disillusionment of eager, caring teachers and parents. Intelligent testing through individualization becomes the key to accomplishment and is antithetical to the development of computerized or depersonalized form reporting for individually administered cognitive tests, such as espoused by some (e.g., see reviews by Reynolds, 1980a, 1980b). For the intelligent tester, it is imperative to be sensitive, socially aware, and to heed Halpern's (1974) plea to "recognize that intelligence and cognition do not comprise the total human being!" However, neither can intellectual skill be ignored.

Intelligent testing urges the use of contemporary measures of intelligence as necessary to achieve a true understanding of the individual's intellectual functioning. The approach to test interpretation adopted under this philosophy has been likened to that of a psychological "detective" (Kaufman, 1979). It requires a melding of clinical skill, mastery of psychometrics and measurement, and extensive knowledge of differential psychology, especially those aspects related to theories of cognitive development and intelligence. A far more extensive treatment of this approach to test interpretation appears in Kaufman's *Intelligent Testing With the WISC-R* and in Kaufman and Reynolds (1983). Discussion of applications of this philosophy to preschool children may be found in Kaufman and Kaufman (1977) and Reynolds and Clark (1983).

Observing Test Behavior

Clinical skills with children are obviously important to the intelligent tester in building rapport and maintaining the proper ambience during the actual testing setting. While adherence to standardized procedure and obtaining valid scores are quite important, the child must remain the lodestar of the evaluation. Critical to the dynamic understanding of the child's performance is close, insightful observation and recording of behavior during the testing period.

Fully half or more of the important information to be gathered during the administration of an intelligence test comes from observing behavior under a set of standard conditions. Behavior at various points in the course of the assessment will often dictate the proper interpretation of test scores but can not offer information on a child's characteristic approach to problem solving, reactions to frustrations or successes, or cognitive style. Many individuals earn IQs of 100 but each in a different manner, with infinite nuances of behavior interacting directly with a person's test performance.

Table 10.1 provides a sampling of behaviors that will frequently be of interest in the context of an individual assessment in general but particularly when assessing intelligence and achievement. It will be important, particularly to the generalizability of any inferences made on the basis of the child's behavior during testing, to observe his or her behavior in other settings, such as the waiting room, playground, day-care center, or a formal classroom setting. It is best to make such observations prior to formal testing so as to lessen the impact of the observation process on the behaviors of interest. Intelligence and achievement tests themselves can be evaluated from an applied behavioral analysis perspective (e.g., see Sattler, 1982, chap. 18, for a brief review), though such is not the featured approach here.

Concomitantly, intelligent testing requires the communication of results in a meaningful manner that is child oriented and not simply a test-by-test recital of results. Though results are often communicated verbally to some staff, the most universal means is through the psychological report. Table 10.2 gives a brief summary of the characteristics of effective reports. The key to the intelligent tester's report is that it is written about a child, not about a test or series of tests.

Psychometric Theory and Individual Differences

Knowledge and skill in psychometrics and measurement are requisite to intelligent testing. The clinical evaluation of test performance must be directed by careful analyses of the statistical properties of the test scores, the internal psychometric characteristics of the test, and data regarding the test's relationship to external factors. As one example, difference scores have long had inherent interest for psychologists, especially between subparts of an intelligence scale. Difference scores are unreliable, and small discrepancies between levels of performance may best be attributed to measurement error. If large enough, however, difference scores can provide valuable information regarding the choice of an appropriate remedial or therapeutic program. The psychometric characteristics of the tests in question dictate the size of the differences needed for statistical confidence in their reflecting real rather than chance fluctuations. Interpretation of subscale differences often requires integrating clinical

**Table 10.1. Examples of Observations and Behaviors
Useful in Intellectual and Academic Assessment.[a]**

1. Appearance – size, height and weight; facial and other physical characteristics; grooming and general cleanliness; clothing style, appropriateness for age.
2. Language development – articulation, syntax, language patterns, use of standard English, dialects, or slang.
3. Responses to test materials and setting:
   a. General activity level – evidence of tension, anxiety, or restlessness, e.g., nail biting, foot wiggling, fidgeting, excessive talking, blocks in talking, intermittent stutters, voice tremors.
   b. Attention span – resistance to extraneous stimuli, general distractibility, ability to focus behavior, remaining on task, and sustaining purposive acts.
   c. Cooperation or resistance – rapport, personal relationship with psychologist, attempts to cooperate, refusal of specific tasks, interest in the various tasks, attempts to perform at a high level of proficiency, motivation.
   d. Cognitive and problem-solving styles – impulsive, quick to respond, contemplates solutions, employs trial and error, develops systematic plan, checks answers, disregards obviously incorrect responses.
   e. Reactions to failure, challenges and success – continues to work as long as time limits allow, gives up at first hint of difficulty, frequently asks for assistance or special directions, failure on one task reduces interest in following tasks, difficulty heightens interest, seeks challenges, becomes aggressive when meeting failure, withdraws, becomes dependent.
   f. Attitudes toward self – displays confidence, a superior attitude, frequently says "I can't," seems defeatist, seeks examiner's approval, responds positively to praise and encouragement, sulks, makes disparaging remarks about self or about test materials.

[a]This list is suggestive, not exhaustive, and refers to both behaviors and inferences drawn from those behaviors. Typically, both levels of information are important and should be provided.

Table 10.2. Characteristics of Effective Psychological Reports.[a]

1. Reports answer the referral question.
2. Limitations of the report are clearly stated.
3. Reports describe behavior as a basis for interpretations and inferences.
4. Reports describe the uniqueness of the individual.
5. Reports are written in a clear, precise, and straightforward manner.
6. Standard English is employed, avoiding slang, jargon, and technical terms.
7. Reports synthesize and integrate information, avoiding a test-by-test recital of results, emphasizing the child.
8. Reports provide recommendations that are explicit, specific, and adaptable to the specific setting.
9. Reports are completed and returned in a timely fashion.

[a]After research reviewed and summarized by Shellenberger (1982).

observations of the child's behaviors with data on the relationship of the test scores to other factors and with theories of intelligence *but only after first establishing that they are real and not based on error.*

One of the major limitations of most contemporary intelligence tests is their lack of foundation in theories of intelligence, whether these theories are based on research in neuropsychology, cognitive information processing, factor analysis, learning theory, or other domains. Nevertheless, many profiles obtained by children and adults on intelligence tests are interpretable from diverse theoretical perspectives and can frequently be shown to display a close fit to one or another theoretical approach to intelligence. Theories then become useful in developing a full understanding of the individual. Competing theories of intelligence literally abound (e.g., see Reynolds, 1981; Vernon, 1979; White, 1979). Well-grounded, empirically evaluated models of intellectual functioning enable one to reach a broader understanding of the child and to make specific predictions regarding behavior outside of the testing situation. One will not always be correct. However, the intelligent tester has an excellent chance of making sense out of the predictable individual variations in behavior, cognitive skills, and academic performance by invoking the nomothetic framework provided by theory. The alternative often is to be stymied or forced to rely on trial-and-error or anecdotal, illusionary relationships when each new set of profile fluctuations is encountered. Theories, even speculative ones, are more efficient guides to developing hypotheses for understanding and treating problems than are purely clinical impressions and armchair speculations.

Through the elements of clinical skill, psychometric sophistication, and a broad base of knowledge of theories of individual differences emerges intelligent testing. None is sufficient; yet, when properly implemented, these elements engage in a synergistic interaction to produce the greatest possible understanding. Obviously, all of these factors cannot be presented here and occur only as the product of extensive training. The remaining portions of this chapter will focus on an introduction to some of the primary tools of intelligence testing, the general psychometric characteristics of intelligence tests, and examples of a general and a specific individual measure of achievement.

RELIABILITY AND VALIDITY OF INDIVIDUAL INTELLIGENCE MEASURES

Since their first presentation around the turn of the twentieth century, the psychometric characteristics of intelligence tests have been improving constantly. Nevertheless, in the early days of testing, and even as late as the 1949 WISC, it was not unusual for standardization samples of individually administered tests to be all white. Also, reliability and validity data were reported only for white children. Though the changes have been gradual, such is no longer the case for the premier intelligence scales now available for use with children: Kaufman Assessment Battery for Children (K-ABC: Kaufman & Kaufman, 1983), MSCA (McCarthy, 1972), WPPSI (Wechsler, 1967), WISC-R (Wechsler, 1974).[2] Other intelligence tests are continuing to be developed and published that do not meet the high standards of the above scales. Therefore, their use is not encouraged.

Today, the major intelligence scales are developed from large nationally stratified random samples of children. Samples are typically stratified on the basis of age, sex, race, socioeconomic status (usually determined by parental occupation), geographic region of residence (e.g., North, South, Central, West), and whether the child resides in an urban or rural setting. Such careful sampling is required to ensure the stability and the generalizability of scores in the battery. Less careful standardization and norming should not be considered acceptable for tests that will impact strongly on decisions about children's lives.

The reliability of the major intelligence scales has also reached an impressive level, though it has always been good. Reliability is the benchmark of the accuracy of test scores and is a prerequisite to validity. From the ages of 2½ to nearly 17 years, the scales mentioned above report general IQs or summary scores with reliability estimates routinely above .90 and frequently as high as .95 and .96. These, of course, are most impressive statistics, given that the limit of reliability is 1.00, and in itself unattainable. The high level of reliability available from the major scales argues strongly for their use as opposed to other more limited scales. The reliability of these measures also has been shown to be consistent across a host of demographic variables such as race, sex, and socioeconomic status (e.g., see Reynolds, 1982b, for a review).

The literature regarding validity of the major intelligence scales as well as the construct of intelligence itself is quite massive in its accumulation over the years. Sattler (1982) has provided a most thorough review of this plethora of evidence. Though one can debate the nature of the construct intelligence and defend many different points of view, the data regarding intelligence tests do demonstrate their utility in a number of areas. Intelligence tests are, outside of achievement tests, the best available predictors of academic achievement. Measures of general intelligence also turn out to be very good predictors of success in most job training and vocational training programs, though prediction of actual job performance is more difficult. Intelligence test scores predict a variety of other criteria as well. General intellectual level consistently has been shown to be one of the best predictors of success in psychotherapy, while premorbid IQ is the best available predictor of rehabilitative success of patients with acute brain trauma and a number of neurological diseases

(Golden, 1981; Reynolds, 1981). The diagnostic utility of IQ tests is also quite formidable in such categories as mental retardation and intellectual giftedness (though we do not recommend making any diagnostic statements about any individual on the basis of any single psychological test). Validity has, for the most part, been demonstrated across a host of demographic variables as well (e.g., see Jensen, 1980; Reynolds, 1982b).

Though intelligence is omnipresent in our daily activities and influences much of what we do and are able to accomplish, it is not omnipotent. Forgetting this rather simple distinction (omnipresent, not omnipotent) has resulted in many abuses of intelligence tests; abuses that can be avoided if we have an adequate understanding of validity and of the limitations of intelligence as a construct.

MAJOR CONTEMPORARY MEASURES OF INTELLIGENCE

The Wechsler Scales

The "Wechsler scales" refer to the WPPSI, the WISC-R, the WAIS-R, and their predecessors, the WISC, WAIS, and the Wechsler-Bellevue scales. The Wechsler-Bellevue, Form I, was the first serious challenge to the Binet monopoly, even though it was not published until 1939. The WPPSI is normed for ages 4–6½ years; the WISC-R is normed for ages 6 years–16 years, 11 months; and the WAIS-R is normed for ages 16–74 years.

All Wechsler scales include 10–12 subtests, with about half on a verbal scale and half on a performance scale. Three IQs are derived from the Wechsler scales: a verbal IQ, a performance IQ, and a summary or global full scale IQ. Each is scaled to a mean of 100 and a standard deviation of 15. The subtests of the Wechsler scales are scaled to a mean of 10 and a standard deviation of 3. Wechsler basically accepted the Terman/Binet definition of intelligence as a global construct, but he chose a different methodology for its measurement. Nevertheless, most Wechsler tasks are taken from the Binet or are direct analogues of Binet tasks. Wechsler's major contributions were to 1) group the tasks in such a way that each person was administered each subtest, 2) group the tests into what has been a clinically very useful division of verbal and nonverbal or performance scales, and 3) promote the use of deviation IQs and other scale scores to have a constant mean and standard deviation across age. Today, the WISC-R is the most frequently employed individual test of intelligence for school-age children.

The WISC-R has become a favorite among those who study and work with learning-disabled children. Its popularity in this regard stems primarily from the profile of scores it yields as well as the fruitful division of the test into verbal and nonverbal scales. Though useful in this regard, the scale has been abused through a clinical mythology that developed over the years. For example, most clinicians believed that verbal-performance IQ differences on the WISC-R of 10, 11, or 12 points were relatively unusual and pathognomonic. Wechsler, himself, even noted that 15-point differences were clinically significant and needed follow up evaluation. We now know that verbal-performance IQ differences of 12 points occur in one-third of the normal population of children and 15 points in one-fourth of a random sample of children nationwide (Kaufman, 1979). This distribution of differences also occurs for the WPPSI age range (Reynolds & Gutkin, 1981). However, though these data have been known for some time, the authors frequently encounter practitioners who are surprised at these frequencies. The intelligent tester then must also keep fully abreast of the literature on intelligence testing. The Wechsler Scales are quite useful in evaluation of learning problems and other disorders of the intellect. Recent reviews of research and use of the Wechsler scales can be found in Kaufman (1979, 1981, 1982a) and Kaufman and Reynolds (1983).

The McCarthy Scales of Children's Abilities

The MSCA was published in 1972 by Dorothea McCarthy and the Psychological Corporation (the latter also being the publisher for the Wechsler scales) and is designed and normed for use with children from 2½ to 8½ years of age. McCarthy was a developmental psycholinguist who had worked clinically with children for some 30 years. She developed a series of largely informal tasks that she used in her own assessment functions during this time. It is from this array of tasks that the child-oriented MSCA was formed.

The MSCA comprises 18 short tests of mental and motor ability, requiring about one hour to administer. The 18 subtests are grouped several ways to form six scales. The overall, global summary score of the MSCA is called the General Cognitive Index (GCI) and is scaled to a mean of 100 and standard deviation of 16 and is essentially cognate to a Wechsler full scale IQ or Stanford-Binet IQ (Kaufman & Kaufman, 1977). There are three nonoverlapping scales that constitute the GCI: Verbal, Perceptual-Performance, and Quantitative Scales. These scales are identified primarily on the basis of the content of their items. In addition, the Verbal Scale requires only vocal responses, while the Perceptual-Performance Scale requires only nonverbal responses. By contrast, the two remaining scales (Memory and Motor) are identified through their process orientation; the former assesses short-term memory and the latter motor coordination. The Memory Scale subtests all appear on at least one other scale as do two of the Motor Scale tasks: Draw-A-Design and Draw-A-Child. Each scale, other than the General Cognitive Index, yields a scale index that has a mean of 50 and a standard deviation of 10. The 18 MSCA subtests do not yield any type of scaled or standardized score and must be evaluated through a complicated process of transformation and comparison as age equivalents. This process is explained in detail in Kaufman and Kaufman (1977) and is also discussed by Reynolds and Clark (1983).

The last 10 years have produced a significant body of empirical evaluation of the fledgling MSCA that has recently been reviewed by Kaufman (1982b). This body of research has generally supported the reliability and validity of the scale for use in evaluating the intellectual skills of the young child, though, for reasons not yet adequately understood, the MSCA tends to yield lower global estimates of intelligence than the Wechsler scales and the Binet. This is especially so for groups of exceptional children (see Kaufman, 1982b, for a detailed review of these discrepancies). Factor analyses of the MSCA subtests show the multiscore profile to be meaningful for both normal and atypical children. The MSCA-GCI correlates with school achievement about as well as the Wechsler scales at the ages of overlap. Good evidence is also available to support the power of the MSCA to discriminate between learning disabled and normal children. Thus, it is a valuable tool for the assessment of such children. Research evidence on the efficacy of the MSCA for other atypical groups is meager (Kaufman, 1982b). Add to this attractive, child-oriented test materials; excellent norms; and readily understood directions for administration and scoring, and it is easy to see why it has become so popular in what, in clinical assessment, is a relatively brief period of time. Yet, the MSCA remains a complex instrument, and a good understanding of the research and methods presented in Kaufman and Kaufman (1977) and Kaufman (1982b) is necessary for its intelligent use.

The Kaufman Assessment Battery for Children (K-ABC)

The K-ABC (Kaufman & Kaufman, 1983) is the newest entry into the realm of major cognitive assessment scales. The K-ABC is designed to assess the intelligence and achievement of 2½- to 12½-year-old children. The battery consists of 16 subtests, but all are not administered at every age; 7 are administered at age 2½, 9 at age 3, 11 at ages 4 and 5, 12 at age 6, and 13 at ages 7–12½. For prekindergarten children, the battery requires about 35–50 minutes for administration, about 50–70 minutes for 5 to 6-year-old children, and about 75–85 minutes beginning at age 7.

The K-ABC results are divided into four major scores: three in the intelligence domain and one for achievement, all scaled to a mean of 100 and standard deviation of 15. All intelligence subtests yield scaled scores with a mean of 10 and standard deviation of 3, like the Wechsler scales, while the six achievement subtests are scaled to a mean of 100 and standard deviation of 15. The intelligence scales of the K-ABC are derived from theories of mental processing developed and researched by cognitive and neuropsychological researchers. The primary theoretical work influencing development of the mental processing scales of the K-ABC includes cerebral specialization research on differential hemispheric functioning and the neuropsychological information processing theories of Luria and his followers (cf. Reynolds, 1981).

The global intelligence or summary score of the K-ABC is the Mental Processing Composite (MPC) standard score. The MPC is a combination of the Sequential Processing and Simultaneous Processing scales. The Sequential Processing Scale primarily involves the solving of problems where the emphasis is on the serial or temporal order of the stimuli. The Simultaneous Processing Scale principally calls upon problem solving that invokes the use of a Gestalt-like or holistic approach to integrate many stimuli to solve the problems.

The Achievement Scale requires the child to demonstrate knowledge of facts, language concepts, and school-related skills and includes subtests entitled: *Faces & Places* (an informational/general knowledge test), *Arithmetic, Riddles* (a test of language concepts), *Reading/Decoding, Reading/Understanding,* and *Expressive Vocabulary.* Many of these subtests are quite innovative and place the problems presented into meaningful context. For example, the Arithmetic subtest presents items in the format of a family's trip to the zoo with calculations related to admission, numbers of animals, and so forth.

Though only recently published, the K-ABC is noteworthy because it has a strong theoretical base (a factor conspicuously lacking in most tests of intelligence) and was published with significantly more advanced validity research studies (over 40) than is typically the case, even for major assessment scales. The preliminary research on the battery offers much evidence of construct, predictive, and concurrent validity and shows particular promise for designing remedial programs that work for children with reading problems. Much research remains to be carried out and clinical experience needs to be accumulated. However, the K-ABC has the potential to be a major advance in the technology of intelligent testing.

ASSESSING ACHIEVEMENT

Thus far, we have focused principally on the assessment of the child's intellectual functioning. Academic attainment is another facet of the overall cognitive picture that is crucial in the evaluation of children, particularly since children devote so much of their time to its acquisition. (That is why the K-ABC covers both the intelligence and achievement domains.) Schools are constantly evaluating the achievement of children through observation and teacher-made classroom tests. Group comprehensive achievement tests are administered less frequently but on a regular basis that may be yearly or on another schedule such as at the end of grades 1, 4, 6, 9, and 12. Evaluation of learning problems is the most frequent of all referrals to psychologists in the schools. Even when this is not the referral question, an individual assessment of achievement level remains important to understanding the child's world, though a less vigorous assessment may be in order.

A variety of individual achievement tests is available for screening a child's general educational development. Several that have achieved widespread use are the Peabody Individual Achievement Test (PIAT: Dunn & Markwardt, 1970) and the Wide Range Achievement Test (WRAT: Jastak & Jastak, 1978). The WRAT is popular primarily due to its brevity. It is most useful when only a brief screening measure of academic level is needed. The WRAT has three subtests: Reading, Spelling, and Arithmetic. The Reading subtest is only a word recognition task, while the other subtests require paper and pencil responses. Though frequently used for diagnosis of educational disorders, the PIAT is ill equipped for this level of task but does provide a good general measure of academic attainment (Reynolds, 1979a). As given by its authors, the PIAT is intended as a broad screening measure and has more depth and breadth than the WRAT. The PIAT has five subtests: *Mathematics* (measuring fundamental computational skills), *Reading Recognition* (measuring skills in translating alphabetic symbols), *Reading Comprehension* (measuring the facility to take meaning from the printed page), *Spelling* (measuring accuracy of word construction in written language), and *General Information* (measuring "general encyclopedic knowledge"). Factor analyses of the PIAT do not support such specificity of content in the subtests, revealing that most reliable variance is accounted for by an Acquired Factual Knowledge and a Verbal Comprehension factor (Reynolds, 1979a).

General tests of achievement such as the PIAT are useful to gain a quick overview. Whenever learning or specific academic problems are present or suspected, a more in-depth assessment of the focal area is in order. One such test now in widespread use is the Woodcock Reading Mastery Test (WRMT: Woodcock, 1973). The WRMT has five subtests measuring different aspects of the reading process, including: Letter Identification, Word Identification, Word Attack, Word Comprehension, and Passage Comprehension, in addition to an overall summary score. Most major, well-designed individual measures of achievement have normative samples comparable to those of a major intelligence scale. These instruments do, however, tend to be somewhat less reliable and have a lesser research base regarding psychometric factors. Specific tests of achievement are available in most areas of functioning. Some that we have found most useful are the Keymath Diagnostic Arithmetic Test (Connolly, Nachtman, & Pritchett, 1971, the Gates-McKillop Reading Diagnostic Tests (Gates & McKillop, 1962), and the Stanford Diagnostic Reading Test (Karlsen, Madden, & Gardner, 1976).

CASE STUDY

The following case report provides an illustration of the intelligent testing approach. Though the report has been condensed, it is still longer than required in most reports. It is lengthy because it involves a complex case with a long history and includes personality test data, many behavioral observations, and further recommendations for the child's therapist. We have chosen this particular report because of the number of different aspects of the intelligent testing paradigm that it helps to illustrate. Also, our client, Richard, is an interesting child, and one who is gradually but consistently showing improvement. Names, locations, and several other details in the report have been modified to ensure Richard's anonymity.

Psychological Evaluation
Confidential
For Professional Use Only

Subject: Richard Richardson   School: Johnson Public
CA: 7–5   Grade: One
Date of Testing: 4-15-80   Examiner: Cecil R. Reynolds, Ph.D.

Tests Administered:
Wechsler Intelligence Scale for Children-Revised
McCarthy Scales of Children's Abilities — Number Questions, Draw-A-Design, and Draw-A-Child subtests
Ammons & Ammons Quick Test (Forms 1, 2, and 3)
Wide Range Achievement Test
Bender Visual-Motor Gestalt Test
Motor-Free Visual Perception Test

Background Information and Reason for Referral:
Richard is currently enrolled in therapeutic classes at Pleasant Center for Severely Disturbed Children. He previously attended the center's Early Childhood Project, where he began in 1976 and continued until its termination in 9/78 when he began classes. Beginning in 9/78 he divided his time between the center and his first-grade class at Johnson School. Richard was originally referred to the center by his teachers at a local day-care center. He was described at that time as demanding excessive attention, distractible, restless, overactive, resistant to discipline, manipulative, and aggressive toward chil-

dren and property. The parents' descriptions of his behavior at home closely paralleled the teacher's descriptions.

A psychiatric evaluation of 10/7/78 indicated difficulties with both verbal comprehension and expression and other motoric signs of left hemisphere dysfunction. The psychiatric impression was given as borderline intelligence, socioeconomic deprivation, hyperkinetic behavioral syndrome, and visual-perceptual difficulty.

Psychological evaluation at the center on 9/21/78, indicated functioning within the borderline range of intelligence (McCarthy GCI = 76). Richard displayed a significant strength in nonverbal-spatial reasoning and weakness in fine motor control. He performed exceptionally well on several short-term memory tasks (auditory and visual) but quite poorly on others. The previous examiner indicated that Richard's poor performance on one memory task was due to a conceptual deficit in understanding the directions and not due to poor memory. The 9/78 evaluation further indicated that while his physical size and build approximated that of about an 8-year-old, his motor coordination showed development consistent with his age of 6 years. Emotional indicators of impulsivity and aggression were also present. Behavioral observations included the full range of symptoms associated with hyperactivity, some attempts at manipulation, and a generally disorganized approach to assignments.

Richard lives with his parents, Mr. and Mrs. Richardson, a half-brother, and an older sister. The sister has a child of about 2 years living in the home. Richard's mother is concerned about him but is largely ineffective in setting limits and leaves discipline to the father. According to his teachers, Richard would come to school quite upset on particular days last spring. It was later determined that Mr. Richardson had been threatening Richard with a whipping, which he would receive upon coming home in the afternoon. Despite discussions with Mr. Richardson, this situation remains essentially unchanged. Richard's half-brother, Gabriel, is mentally retarded and has been at the center in the past.

Recently, Richard was placed on Ritalin to help control hyperactivity. Mrs. Richardson had resisted this, indicating that Richard needed "a strong hand" and not medication, until the school finally refused to allow him to attend without medication. The school reports improvements in Richard's behavior since medication began. In his center class, Richard has begun to show improvement and calms down whenever tight structural limits are imposed. Richard's teacher indicates that he has grown a lot in the past year and occasionally hurts other children without being aware of it. Currently, work with the parents is focusing on establishing consistent limits for Richard in the home to which both parents will adhere. Much difficulty has been encountered with Mr. Richardson, who resists any suggestions concerning management of Richard's behavior and avoids contact with the parent worker when possible.

The present evaluation was undertaken to determine proper placement for Richard next year and to provide recommendations for his therapist.

Observations of Test Behavior:

Richard was brought to the afternoon testing session from his center class by his therapist. He entered the testing session with ease and no apparent apprehension. Richard is a black male, large for 7½, his height and stocky build giving the appearance of a 10-year-old child. He was neatly dressed for the testing session and smiled occasionally at the examiner. Richard cooperated well except when asked to perform tasks which he felt were too difficult. On these occasions, he became hostile almost immediately when encouraged to continue. Second attempts to persuade him to try such tasks characteristically met with increased hostility, a loud no, and an aggressive banging of his fist on the table top. These behaviors are quite indicative of Richard's low tolerance for frustration and propensity for aggressive acting out in response to frustrating situations. Following his hostile outbursts, the task demands changed, and his hostility and aggression disappeared as quickly as they had arisen, indicating his severe behavioral lability.

Richard's attention span also demonstrated lability. During verbal tasks primarily, Richard had difficulty listening and was easily distracted by visual stimuli within the room. He also frequently tended to look toward the window. On nonverbal tasks (utilizing concrete, visual materials), Richard was able to concentrate much better. This seems to reflect an increase in Richard's usable attention span since his last evaluation and is possibly attributable to his medication. Other behavioral differences were observed during the verbal and nonverbal tasks. Richard appeared nervous and occasionally bit his fingernails during the verbal items. The verbal tasks seemed almost aversive to him, which is consistent with his psychiatric evaluation. In contrast, he appeared to enjoy the various nonverbal tasks, his favorite being one requiring him to arrange a series of pictures to tell a story. Thus, Richard demonstrated a behavioral preference for working with concrete, visual materials as opposed to utilizing abstractions such as language.

Richard did display difficulties on some nonverbal tasks. When copying abstract designs and drawing human figures, he typically used intense pressure and erased almost continually. He also attempted to rotate his drawing paper many times. When not allowed to rotate the paper as he drew each side of the figure, his drawing became more difficult. Richard dropped his pencil several times as well.

Richard was generally cooperative with the examiner and put forth sustained effort on most tasks. While sometimes slow to catch on to various tasks, he usually understood what was asked of him. On the basis of his behaviors during the evaluation, Richard's performance has provided a valid index of his typical level of cognitive functioning.

Test Results and Interpretation:

On testing with the WISC-R, Richard earned a verbal IQ of 74, performance IQ of 93, and a full scale IQ of 82 ± 5. This level of performance on the WISC-R indicates functioning within the low average range of intellectual skills and exceeds 12% of children his age. The chances that the range of scores from 77 to 87 contains Richard's true full scale IQ are 85 out of 100. However, a large discrepancy was observed between Richard's verbal and performance IQs, rendering the full scale IQ an inadequate summary statistic of Richard's abilities.

Richard demonstrated substantially greater nonverbal than verbal skills. The magnitude of the discrepancy observed here is also relatively unusual in that only about 7 out of 100 children show a difference this large. A significant amount of scatter was observed in Richard's scaled-score range on the WISC-R as well. Approximately 88% of children Richard's age show less variability in their performance (his scores ranged over 3 full standard deviations). His performance was best on nonverbal tasks throughout the test battery.

During a series of verbal tasks, an apparent dichotomy developed in Richard's performance. On what are basically language and verbal reasoning tasks (telling how two things are alike, defining various concrete and abstract words), Richard performed at a level commensurate with his nonverbal performance and near the average range of intellectual skills for his age. His performance on these tasks was further substantiated by his earning a Mental Age of 6-6 on the Ammons & Ammons Quick Test, a measure of receptive language and verbal reasoning. While this score is nearly a year below Richard's actual age, it falls within the average range of functioning. When his performance in these areas was contrasted, Richard demonstrated several weaknesses. On a task requiring him to answer factual questions and another task requiring explanations of socially acceptable responses to specified situations, Richard showed relative weaknesses in his ability spectrum. Each of these tasks presupposes exposure to certain basic types of information to which a socioeconomically deprived child such as Richard may not have had access. However, his relatively low performance on these two tasks is indicative of a poor fund of knowledge upon which to base decisions about proper behavior and is almost certainly related to his deficient social and cultural skills.

Richard also performed poorly on two verbal tasks involving numbers, the first requiring him to solve oral arithmetic problems and the second requiring him to repeat digits forward and backward. His low performance on these two tasks appears to stem from attentional and conceptual deficits as well as his preference for nonverbal, visual stimuli rather than memory or numerical reasoning problems. Richard was easily distracted during verbal tasks, as evidenced in his behavior and performance on untimed tasks requiring essentially equivalent abilities. On an untimed test of oral arithmetic, on the McCarthy Scales of Children's Abilities, Richard performed at about the level of the average 7-year-old, substantially better than his WISC-R performance and average for his own age. Richard's low score on a task requiring him to repeat digits stems primarily from his lack of knowledge of the basic concept "backward" rather than a memory deficit. Richard's overall performance on the WISC-R Verbal scale falls within the borderline range of skills, exceeding only 3% of children his age.

Richard demonstrated greater consistency of performance on a series of more concrete, nonverbal tasks. On a diverse group of tasks, such as telling what important part is missing in a picture, arranging pictures to tell a story, maze tracing, copying abstract designs with paper and pencil, Richard performed synonymously with only a single relative strength. On the motor-free visual-perception test, Richard performed at about the level of the average 8¾-year-old, earning him a perceptual quotient of 111 (76th percentile). Richard completed the Bender-Gestalt drawings within the critical time limits for his age and, using the Koppitz scoring criteria, earned a Perceptual Age equivalent of 7-0. The Bender is primarily a measure of visual-motor integration (a complex, high-level skill requiring the coordination of visual-perceptual input and motor output), and Richard's performance indicated that, while developmentally consistent with his chronological age, his developmental level of visual-motor integration lagged behind his perceptual development. This is a surprising finding in view of previous evaluations and indicates substantial development over the past nine months as well as possible beneficial effects from medication. These findings bear further support from Richard's performance on the McCarthy Drawing Tests (Draw-A-Design and Draw-A-Child), in which he earned age equivalents of 7-6 and 7-0, respectively. Richard's various nonverbal skills (e.g., nonverbal reasoning, psycho-motor speed, spatial reasoning, perceptual organization) appear to fall within the average range of cognitive abilities exceeding about 32% of children his age. These results are consistent with previous evaluations showing strengths in nonverbal, spatial reasoning.

Richard's current achievement levels appear to be commensurate with his nonverbal skill level. When administered the Wide Range Achievement Test, he earned the following scores and rankings:

Subtest	Grade Equivalent	Standard Score*	Percentile
Reading	1.4	88	21
Spelling	1.4	88	21
Arithmetic	2.4	103	55

*Similar to IQ scaling

While achievement in each area is consistent with measured aptitude levels, an obvious dichotomy exists. In the language related areas of reading and spelling, Richard's achievement falls below his attainment in arithmetic. This finding is consistent with previously discussed deficiencies in receptive and expressive language and other implications of left hemisphere dysfunction.

Recommendations:

1. Richard's achievement levels are quite satisfactory to recommend promotion to second grade. However, he meets the majority of criteria for an LD placement and should receive such placement next year at Johnson School.
2. Richard's LD resource teacher may wish to concentrate on the development of listening and verbal comprehension skills. Speech therapists sometimes teach such skills, and the therapist at Richard's school should be consulted, with actual placement made with the individual having the most available time for Richard. Instruction in listening and comprehension skills should begin with such short topics that the probability of failure is at or near zero. While always a good remedial practice, this will be especially important due to Richard's very low frustration tolerance.
3. Richard currently experiences difficulties with many basic concepts such as forward, backward, over, under, in, before, and so forth. A more specific delineation of Richard's knowledge of basic concepts may be obtained through administration of the Boehm Test of Basic Concepts. Boehm also suggests remedial activities for specific conceptual deficits. When attempting to teach Richard basic concepts, use concrete examples that demonstrate visually the meaning of such linguistic concepts as in, on, and so forth. Richard's teachers should always remember to structure his learning activities to take advantage of his relatively good nonverbal skills through the use of visual materials and demonstration.
4. Richard's medication appears to be helping in his behavioral control. Discontinuation over the summer, nevertheless, is recommended with a trial period at the beginning of second grade to determine if Richard can function at an acceptable level without being medicated.
5. Continued placement at the center is recommended for summer and fall quarters. Stated goals for continued center placement should include but are not limited to
   a. spontaneously participating in routines without physical intervention;
   b. verbally recalling and expressing understanding of group rules and procedures;
   c. contributing to the making of group expectations of conduct and procedures;
   d. verbalizing, understanding, and accepting the *consequences* of not reaching the group's behavioral expectations;

e. using *appropriate* words or gestures to show pride in own work or other activities performed independently;

f. using *appropriate* words or actions to show feeling responses to the environment.

6. An increase in parent work is necessary to assist the family in providing a consistent but not restrictive environment for Richard. Visits to the home should be made, if possible.

7. Along with the customary ongoing evaluation of Richard's behavioral progress, an academic reevaluation should be scheduled in nine months, preferably during March or April of the next school year. Such evaluation should include measurement of auditory comprehension skills and an extensive diagnostic reading evaluation such as the Gates-McKillop or the Woodcock Reading Mastery Test. This further evaluation should provide evidence to determine the need for continued LD resource placement as well as its past effectiveness.

SUMMARY

Throughout this chapter we have attempted to provide a model for the intelligent use and intelligent interpretation of tests of aptitude and academic attainment. This model stresses a meld of psychometric and statistical skill with a strong foundation of knowledge in differential psychology (the psychology of individual differences) and the right amount of clinical acumen. The model is itself a general one, although we have stressed its application to more cognitive domains.

This approach and many of its various aspects are illustrated in the case report of Richard, particularly the hypothesis testing or "detective" nature of the model. The use of the model is most appropriate in the development of remedial and therapeutic hypotheses for beginning and later refinement of work with children experiencing a variety of cognitive or affective disorders. However, it must be stressed that the model is flexible and centers around finding the best fit of the data to the child, not forcing the child to fit a preconceived rigid system of classification or inflexible remedial approaches that tend to treat every child the same.

Once therapeutic or remedial programs have been implemented, follow-up assessment and evaluation is demanded as well for fine-tuning or perhaps even major overhauls as the model also recognizes the error inherent in dealing with psychological constructs and the complexities of individual human behavior. Intelligent testing is a challenging, difficult enterprise but one that we believe offers the best model for using test scores *for* children and not merely as vehicles to classification.

NOTES

1. We would be the first to admit that there is little empirical basis for this particular argument, yet it is sound from the standpoint of the theoretical requirements of the particular therapeutic approaches mentioned.
2. The Revised Stanford-Binet Intelligence Scale, Form L-M (1972 Norms edition) is not discussed here or later in the chapter due to the lack of precise information regarding the 1972 normative sample, lack of recent reliability and validity data on this new form, the antequated nature of many of the test items, and the tendency toward racial and sexual stereotyping of behavior in the Binet test items. Although a revision of the Binet is underway, it does not appear likely that it will be available in the near future. Thus, for now, it is perhaps best to relegate the Binet to the history of psychological testing, but it will not be forgotten as it has influenced all its successors right up to the most recently published scales. However, we must concur with Friedes (1972), offering for the present: *Requiescat in pace.*

REFERENCES

Buros, O. K. (Ed.). *Tests in print.* Highland Park, NJ: Gryphon Press, 1974.

Buros, O. K. (Ed.). *Eighth mental measurements yearbook.* Highland Park, NJ: Gryphon Press, 1978.

Connolly, A., Nachtman, W., & Pritchett, E. *Key Math Diagnostic Arithmetic Test.* Circle Pines, MN: American Guidance Service, 1971.

Dunn, L. M., & Markwardt, F. *Peabody Individual Achievement Test.* Circle Pines, MN: American Guidance Service, 1970.

Ebel, R. Evaluation and selection of group measures. In C. R. Reynolds & T. B. Gutkin (Eds.), *The handbook of school psychology.* New York: Wiley, 1982.

Friedes, D. Review of the Stanford-Binet Intelligence Scale. In O. K. Buros (Ed.), *The seventh mental measurements yearbook.* Highland Park, NJ: Gryphon Press, 1972.

Gates, A., & McKillop, A. S. *Gates-McKillop reading diagnostic tests.* New York: Teachers College Press, 1962.

Golden, C. J. *Diagnosis and rehabilitation in clinical neuropsychology.* Springfield, IL: Charles Thomas, 1981.

Halpern, F. C. Clinicians must listen. In G. Williams & S. Gordon (Eds.), *Clinical child psychology.* New York: Behavioral Publications, 1974.

Jastak, J., & Jastak, S. *Wide Range Achievement Test.* Wilmington, DE: Jastak Associates, 1978.

Jensen, A. R. *Bias in mental testing.* New York: The Free Press, 1980.

Karlsen, B., Madden, R., & Gardner, E. *Stanford Diagnostic Reading Test.* New York: Harcourt Brace Jovanovich, 1976.

Kaufman, A. S. A short form of the Wechsler Preschool and Primary Scale of Intelligence. *Journal of Consulting and Clinical Psychology,* 1972, *39,* 361–369.

Kaufman, A. S. A four-test short form of the WISC-R. *Contemporary Educational Psychology,* 1976, *1,* 180–196.

Kaufman, A. S. A McCarthy short form for rapid screening of preschool, kindergarten, and first-grade children. *Contemporary Educational Psychology,* 1977, *2,* 149–157.

Kaufman, A. S. *Intelligence testing with the WISC-R.* New York: Wiley-Interscience, 1979.

Kaufman, A. S. The WISC-R and LD assessment: State of the art. *Journal of Learning Disabilities,* 1981, *14,* 520–526. 96–107.

Kaufman, A. S. Implications of WISC-R research for school psychologists. In C. R. Reynolds

& T. B. Gutkin (Eds.), *The handbook of school psychology*. New York: Wiley, 1982. (a)

Kaufman, A. S. A review of almost a decade of research on the McCarthy Scales. In T. Kratochwill (Ed.), *Advances in school psychology* (Vol. 2). Hillsdale, NJ: Erlbaum Associates 1982. (b)

Kaufman, A. S., & Kaufman, N. L. *Clinical evaluation of young children with the McCarthy Scales*. New York: Grune & Stratton, 1977.

Kaufman, A. S., & Kaufman, N. L. *Kaufman assessment battery for children*. Circle Pines, MN: American Guidance Services, 1983.

Kaufman, A. S., & Reynolds, C. R. Clinical evaluation of intellectual function. In I. Weiner (Ed.), *Clinical methods in psychology*. New York: Wiley-Interscience, 1983.

Larry P. et al. vs. Riles et al. U.S. District Court for the Northern District of California, C-71-227ORFP, October 1979, slip opinion.

McCarthy, D. *McCarthy Scales of Children's Abilities*. New York: Psychological Corporation, 1972.

PASE: Parents in Action on Special Education et al. vs. Hannon et al. U.S. District Court for the Northern District of Illinois, Eastern Division, C-74-3586RFP, July 1980, slip opinion.

Reynolds, C. R. Factor structure of the Peabody Individual Achievement Test at five grade levels between grades one and twelve. *Journal of School Psychology,* 1979, *17,* 270–274. (a)

Reynolds, C. R. Should we screen preschoolers? *Contemporary Educational Psychology,* 1979, *4,* 175–181. (b)

Reynolds, C. R. Review of the TARDOR Interpretive Scoring System for the WISC-R. *School Psychology Review,* 1980, *9,* 385–386. (a)

Reynolds, C. R. Two commercial interpretive systems for the WISC-R. *School Psychology Review,* 1980, *9,* 385–386. (b)

Reynolds, C. R. The neuropsychological basis of intelligence. In G. Hynd & J. Obrzut (Eds.), *Neuropsychological assessment and the school-aged child: Issues and procedures.* New York: Grune & Stratton, 1981.

Reynolds, C. R. Determining statistically reliable strengths and weaknesses in the performance of single individuals on the Luria-Nebraska Neuropsychological Battery. *Journal of Consulting and Clinical Psychology,* 1982, *50,* 525–529. (a)

Reynolds, C. R. The problem of bias in psychological assessment. In C. R. Reynolds & T. B. Gutkin (Eds.), *The handbook of school psychology*. New York: Wiley, 1982. (b)

Reynolds, C. R., & Brown, R. T. (Eds.). *Perspectives on bias in mental testing*. New York: Plenum Press, in press.

Reynolds, C. R., & Clark, J. H. Cognitive assessment of the preschool child. In K. Paget & B. Bracken (Eds.), *Psychoeducational assessment of preschool and primary aged children.* New York: Grune & Stratton, 1983.

Reynolds, C. R., & Elliott, S. N. Recent trends in test development and test publishing. *Professional Psychology,* in press.

Reynolds, C. R., & Gutkin, T. B. Test scatter on the WPPSI: Normative analyses of the standardization sample. *Journal of Learning Disabilities,* 1981, *14,* 460–464.

Reynolds, C. R., Wilson, V. L., & Clark, P. L. A WAIS-R short form for clinical screening. *Clinical Neuropsychology,* in press.

Sattler, J. M. *Assessment of children's intelligence and special abilities* (2nd ed.). Boston: Allyn & Bacon, 1982.

Sattler, J. M., Hilliard, A., Lambert, N., Albee, G., & Jensen, A. *Intelligence tests on trial: Larry P. and PASE.* Symposium presented at the annual meeting of the American Psychological Association, Los Angeles, August 1981.

Shellenberger, S. Presentation and interpretation of psychological data in educational settings. In C. R. Reynolds & T. B. Gutkin (Eds.), *The handbook of school psychology*. New York: Wiley, 1982.

Vernon, P. A. *Intelligence: Heredity and environment*. San Francisco: W. H. Freeman, 1979.

Wechsler, D. *Manual for the Wechsler Preschool and Primary Scale of Intelligence (WPPSI)*. New York: Psychological Corporation, 1967.

Wechsler, D. *Manual for the Wechsler Intelligence Scale for Children-Revised (WISC-R)*. New York: Psychological Corporation, 1974.

Wechsler, D. *Manual for the Wechsler Adult Intelligence Scale-Revised (WAIS-R)*. New York: Psychological Corporation, 1981.

White, W. (Ed.). Intelligence. Special issue of *Journal of Research and Development in Education*, 1979, *12* (1).

Woodcock, R. W. *Woodcock reading mastery tests*. Circle Pines, MN: American Guidance Service, 1973.

PART III
Comprehensive Assessment

11

Integrated Assessment and Treatment

Philip H. Bornstein
Marcy Tepper Bornstein
and
Brenda Dawson

Behavioral assessment is that field of inquiry focused upon the identification of target behaviors and their controlling conditions (Nelson & Hayes, 1979). While the purpose of this assessment format is to "understand" behavior, ultimately, all behavioral assessment leads to treatment. Thus, it is quite surprising that a paucity of the child behavioral assessment literature has attempted to discuss the integration of assessment and treatment functions (e.g., Ciminero & Drabman, 1977; Evans & Nelson, 1977; Ollendick & Cerny, 1981). Consequently, that shall serve as the purpose of this present chapter. To accomplish this, we will first discuss the assumptions and goals of behavioral assessment. Traditional and behavioral assessment theories will then be compared. A brief section on methods of behavioral assessment will be followed by a discussion of major behavioral assessment models. The pragmatics of integrated assessment and treatment will then be elaborated. Concluding our presentation will be a case study and a few, brief summary remarks.

ASSUMPTIONS AND GOALS OF BEHAVIORAL ASSESSMENT

A number of conceptual assumptions underlie the practice of contemporary behavioral assessment (see chap. 1). These are important to note, as such assumptions influence and direct the methods and goals of such assessment. First, and perhaps the most important assumption held by behavioral assessors, is the interdependence of assessment and treatment. Treatment strategies depend upon the accurate identification of target behaviors. Precise specification of behaviors and their controlling conditions is the *sine qua non* of both behavioral assessment and treatment. Second, behavioral assessment places emphasis upon quantitative data collection methods. Quite simply, quantification increases accuracy and thereby influences both reliability and validity of the assessment practice. Third, behavioral assessment is interested in the antecedent and consequent conditions which serve to maintain problem behavior. Thus, "history" may tend to take a subordinate role (Cone & Hawkins, 1977). However, when the conditions which gave rise to the problem behavior are facilitating its maintenance, "history" becomes of critical importance. Last, behavioral assessment assumes the uniqueness of individual behavior patterns; that is, assessment and treatment are highly idiographic in nature.

The primary goals of behavioral assessment are to (a) accurately identify and describe target behaviors, (b) isolate proximate controlling variables, and (c) determine the most appropriate therapeutic intervention which can be implemented and evaluated (Hartmann, Roper, & Bradford, 1979). Certainly, these goals are not entirely unique to behavioral assessment. The more important question, however, is whether behavioral assessment can more effectively achieve these purposes.

ALLEGED BENEFITS OF BEHAVIORAL ASSESSMENT VERSUS TRADITIONAL ASSESSMENT

The broad categories of behavioral and traditional assessment encompass a wide variety of differing methods. For this reason, it is recognized that a global comparison between the two necessarily entails some oversimplification. Nevertheless, such a comparison is useful. It serves to elucidate the defining characteristics of both approaches and focuses attention upon the questions and procedures of primary importance in the assessment of human behavior.

Hartmann et al. (1977) synthesized the major differential characteristics of behavioral and traditional assessment procedures (see table 11.1). As indicated, the two approaches view the nature of personality and causes of behavior quite differently. Traditional approaches infer a personality construct which causes and directs behavior from within the individual. This construct (i.e., personality) is what is consistent in an individual's behavior over time and across various environmental contexts. In behavioral analysis, the notion of personality refers to patterns rather than causes of behavior. Thus, emphasis is placed on what a person *does* rather than what a person *is*. As a result, it is the influence of environmental antecedents and consequences that are said to be the causes of behavior.

Table 11.1 Differences Between Behavioral and Traditional Approaches to Assessment

	BEHAVIORAL	TRADITIONAL
I. Assumptions		
1. Conception of personality	Personality constructs mainly employed to summarize specific behavior patterns, if at all	Personality as a reflection of enduring underlying states or traits
2. Causes of behavior	Maintaining conditions sought in current environment	Intrapsychic or within the individual
II. Implications		
1. Role of behavior	Important as a sample of person's repertoire in specific situation	Behavior assumes importance only insofar as it indexes underlying causes
2. Role of history	Relatively unimportant, except, for example, to provide a retrospective baseline	Crucial in that present conditions are seen as a product of the past
3. Consistency of behavior	Behavior thought to be specific to the situation	Behavior expected to be consistent across time and settings
III. Uses of data	To describe target behaviors and maintaining conditions To select the appropriate treatment To evaluate and revise treatment	To describe personality functioning and etiology To diagnose or classify To make prognosis; to predict
IV. Other characteristics		
1. Level of inferences	Low	Medium-high
2. Comparisons	More emphasis on intraindividual or idiographic	More emphasis on interindividual or nomothetic
3. Methods of assessment	More emphasis on direct methods (e.g., observations of behavior in natural environment)	More emphasis on indirect methods (e.g., interviews and self-report)
4. Timing of assessment	More ongoing; prior, during and after treatment	Pre- and perhaps posttreatment, or strictly to diagnose
5. Scope of assessment	Specific measure of more variables (e.g., of target behaviors in various situations, of side effects, contexts, strengths as well as deficiencies)	More global measures (e.g., of cure, of improvement) but only of the individual

The differing assumptions underlying behavioral and traditional assessment result in divergent views as to the purposes of assessment, as well. Traditional psychological tests are interpreted as a sign of the existence of particular personality constructs. Behavioral assessment, on the other hand, interprets test behavior as a representative sample of situationally specific behavior.

Selection of test item content also differs for the two assessment approaches. Traditional assessors believe that test behavior is a function of inner dynamics rather than item content. As a result, they are not particularly concerned with representative item selection. Alternatively, behavioral assessors emphasize the adequate sampling of behaviors in specific environmental contexts. "Thus, the *content validity* of the test becomes particularly crucial, as one must obtain a representative sample of those situations in which a particular behavior of interest is likely to manifest itself" (Goldfried, 1977, p. 6).

Perhaps the greatest discrepancy between traditional and behavioral assessment, however, is with regard to the assessment-treatment relationship. The goal of traditional assessment has been the description of personality functioning, diagnostic labeling, and prognosis. Only secondarily does traditional assessment lead to a specific treatment recommendation. Mischel (1968) and Stuart (1970) argue that traditional assessment procedures provide little useful information in the selection of appropriate treatment strategies. Behavioral assessment, however, purports to focus on information that is directly relevant to treatment and treatment evaluation. In fact, behavioral assessment attempts to provide a descriptive analysis of the target behavior and its controlling conditions. In so doing, behavioral assessment operationally defines and functionally analyzes target behaviors of interest. This is conducted across assessment and treatment phases. Thus, behavioral assessment provides ongoing evaluation of client progress and the effects of treatment prior to, during, and following therapeutic intervention.

Hartmann et al. (1979) indicate that the above characterization of behavioral assessment may be somewhat idealized. In actuality, many of the behavioral assessment procedures utilized tend to be of a more "qualitative" than "quantitative" nature (Kazdin & Wilson, 1978). Wade, Baker, and Hartmann (1979) report that nearly one-half of the behavior therapists, responding to a national survey, employed traditional interviews and/or assessment procedures in their clinical practice. Obviously, the costs of behavioral assessment in professional time and resources present some practical problems. Complex observational coding schemes and sophisticated psychophysiological data collection methods are not within the financial and pragmatic capabilities of most clinicians. Thus, development of a practical framework for integrated assessment and treatment becomes of even greater importance. Toward that goal, let us now examine the methods of behavioral assessment.

METHODS OF BEHAVIORAL ASSESSMENT

The purpose of this section is to briefly review methods of behavioral assessment as background for the development of a comprehensive, integrated assessment-treatment model. To accomplish this, both indirect and direct methods of assessment will be briefly noted (Cone, 1978).

Indirect Methods of Assessment

Among those indirect methods to be discussed are the behavioral interview, self-report questionnaire, behavioral checklist, peer ratings, and traditional psychological tests. The first method of assessment to be considered is the behavioral interview. The purpose of the interview is to diagnose, assess, and begin the formulation of treatment plans. Behavioral interviews differ from traditional interviews in that the focus is on specific problem behaviors of the child and the environmental variables that maintain those behaviors. To accomplish this, child, parent, teacher, and *significant others* may be called upon as informants. Further, these interviews may be of a structured or unstructured nature. Interrater reliability may increase as a result of structured interviews (Herjanic, Herjanic, Brown & Wheatt, 1975). Alternatively, information relevant to the development of a functional analysis may be more readily acquired via unstructured methods. In any case, there are a number of advantages which are attested to by the popularity of the interview as an assessment tool. First, behavioral interviews are flexible enough to allow response to clients' immediate concerns and thereby aid in the establishment of a therapeutic relationship. Second, interviews potentially provide the therapist with a sample of individual and interactive behavior. Third, interviewing the child allows for the assessment of how behavioral events are cognitively and emotionally processed. This, in turn, may give direction to the evolving individualized treatment plan.

While self-report questionnaires may be of limited utility with very young children, parent behavioral checklists have been widely employed in clinical settings. Advantages include: (a) comprehensive sampling of potential problem behaviors, (b) improved reliability and validity, and (c) ease of administration. Unfortunately, most checklists do not provide information relevant to the maintenance of problem behaviors nor are the items always specific and quantifiable enough to aid in formulating behavioral change programs. Peer ratings of sociometric status have similar limitations. However, such ratings appear to be excellent predictors of later, serious psychopathology (Evans & Nelson, 1977).

Traditional personality tests may also be of some use to behavioral clinicians. First, they are apt to provide a more thorough analysis of children's strengths and deficits. Second, such tests broaden the evaluation base and provide a rich sample of potentially relevant information. Third, traditional psychological tests may indicate further areas in need of assessment. Finally, these nonbehavioral instruments often aid in defining the parameters of treatment efficacy. Thus, the authors of this chapter have no argument with traditional psychological tests per se. Rather, our concern is with the manner in which test information has been inappropriately used in the past (i.e., diagnosis, classification, etc.).

Direct Methods of Assessment

Our discussion here will focus upon self-monitoring, direct observation, and permanent product measures.

There is ample evidence attesting to the value of self-monitoring in children (Bornstein, Hamilton, & Bornstein, in press). In fact, a number of therapeutic benefits may be derived. First, of course, are the potentially reactive effects of self-monitoring. Second, as an assessment device, self-monitoring is an economical and frequently informative data collection method. Third, increased feelings of self-control and responsibility may result from the use of self-monitoring procedures. Unreliability, however, may limit the clinical usefulness of self-monitored data collection methods.

Direct naturalistic observation still remains the hallmark of behavioral assessment. Unfortunately, inadquate psychometric evaluation, lack of normative data, and cost of the procedures often limit application in nonresearch settings. One obvious alternative is the use of direct observation in contrived, nonnaturalistic situations. In fact, analogue observation of both free behavior (e.g., a clinic playroom) and behavior created in response to a role-play situation has greater practicality for use in clinical settings: One must remain cautious, however, in extrapolating from the laboratory to the natural environment (e.g., see Van Hasselt, Hersen, & Bellack, 1981).

Finally, permanent product measures also may serve as behavioral assessment methods. For example, behaviors of interest can be inferred by physical trace erosion or accretion (Webb, Campbell, Schwartz, & Sechrest, 1966). Nocturnal enuresis serves as the exemplar case. Other permanent product measures might include school assignments completed, soiled clothing, weight gain/loss, and so forth. Archival records may also serve as permanent products. These could include school grades, medical reports, or records of juvenile offenses. Obviously the number and type of unobtrusive measure utilized are limited only by the ingenuity of the behavioral assessor.

In summary, behavioral assessment methods require a careful knowledge of currently available instruments, their psychometric properties, and the cost/practicality of administration. In all instances, however, instruments become the tools of operative conceptual models. Consequently, those models will now be discussed.

BEHAVIORAL ASSESSMENT MODELS

Behavioral assessors have generally rejected traditional methods of assessment and diagnostic classification. Unfortunately, however, no single alternative model has emerged as the "champion" of contemporary behavioral assessment. Instead, a host of conceptual schemes exists. Some of the more popular models will be presented below. All share in an attempt to describe the problem behavior, select an appropriate treatment, and evaluate the efficacy of the therapeutic intervention. Moreover, as with all models, each provides a conceptual "superstructure" within which specific behavioral assessment methods may be employed.

Functional Analysis of Behavior

Initially proposed by Peterson (1968), the "functional analysis of behavior" model is an empirically-based assessment approach. The cardinal features of the method are:

> (1) systematic observation of the problem behavior to obtain a response frequency baseline, (2) systematic observation of the stimulus conditions following and/or preceding the behavior, with special concern for antecedent discriminative cues and consequent reinforcers, (3) experimental manipulation of a condition which seems functionally, hence causally, related to the problem behavior, and (4) further observation to record any changes in behavior which may occur. (Peterson, 1968, p. 114)

Thus, as noted by Ciminero (1977), the "functional analysis of behavior" approach is basically an A-B experimental design, where A represents baseline and B represents some therapeutic intervention. By manipulating those variables that control the behavior, the efficacy of a particular treatment can be evaluated. While giving direction to early behavioral assessment efforts, the functional analysis model may be unnecessarily narrow and limited in applicability (Evans & Nelson, 1977).

Kanfer and Saslow's S-O-R-K-C

The Kanfer and Saslow (1969) S-O-R-K-C model has had great appeal to behavior modifiers. The various elements are as follows: *S* (stimulus) refers to antecedent events, *O* (organism) refers to biological conditions, *R* (response) refers to observed behaviors, K (contingency) refers to schedules or contingency-related conditions, C (consequence) refers to events which follow R. Accompanying the S-O-R-K-C framework are seven specific component areas which theoretically yield information relevant to the target, treatment, and goals of intervention. These include:

1. *an initial analysis of the problem situation* in which behavioral excesses, deficits, and assets are specified;
2. *clarification of the problem situation* in which affected individuals are identified and conditions of occurrence are elaborated;
3. *a motivational analysis* in which incentive and aversive conditions are determined;
4. *a developmental analysis* in which biological, sociological, and behavioral changes relevant to the problem behavior are specified;
5. *an analysis of self-control* in which situations, limitations, and methods of self-regulation are defined;
6. *an analysis of social relationships* in which *significant others* are identified and social resources noted;
7. *an analysis of the socio-cultural-physical environment* in which norms, settings, and environmental constraints are examined.

While the model is extremely thorough and allows for a wide diversity of assessment methods, there do appear to be a number of limitations. First, it may be so thorough that it becomes clinically impractical. Second, the information obtained is still interpreted in a subjective manner (Dickson, 1975). Third, the model does not really aid in the selection of the most appropriate treatment strategy. Last, S-O-R-K-C does not specify the "how, what, when, where" of continuous monitoring and evaluation. Still, the model has proven quite useful, especially with its emphasis on multichannel assessment and behavioral asset information (see chap. 1 for a further discussion of this model).

The BASIC ID

Arnold Lazarus (1973, 1976) has posited that faulty specification of target behaviors is probably the greatest impediment to successful treatment. Moreover, misidentification of problem behaviors is apt to result from a failure to assess the BASIC ID. The BASIC ID is an acronym specifying the major domains that should be a part of all preintervention assessment; behavior, affect, sensation, imagery, cognition, interpersonal, and drugs (includes organic and physiological processes). In the *behavioral* domain, Lazarus suggests that target characteristics (i.e., frequency, intensity, duration) shall be directly observed with an emphasis on antecedents and consequences of the problem response. *Affectively*, the clinician should explore those client experiences which give rise to strong emotional response. In the domain of *sensation*, physical complaints (e.g., nausea), sensory experience (appetite, odor, etc.), and sensory channel information (e.g., touch, sight, sound, etc.) should be explored. In the *imagery* domain, Lazarus calls upon his client to create a series of "mental pictures." *Cognitively*, the therapist must identify misconceptions, mistaken beliefs, attributions of self-efficacy, and faulty illogical thinking. Regarding *interpersonal relationships*, Lazarus recommends that clients be both heard and observed vis-à-vis their significant relationships with others. Lastly, the domain of *drugs* refers generally to the clients' state of physical being, including appearance, dress, exercise, and diet.

As should be apparent from the above, BASIC ID is a conceptual guideline for the conduct of initial interviews and problem description. Domains are clearly interdependent, and problems can occur both within and across categories. While one need not accept the technical eclecticism of multimodal therapy to do multimodal assessments, there does seem to be significant overlap between this and the Kanfer and Saslow (1969) S-O-R-K-C model. If differences do exist, they no doubt result from a lack of explicit criteria used in the selection of differing treatment techniques. Thus, this continues to be a problem for most major behavioral assessment and treatment models.

The Behavioral Assessment Grid (BAG)

Cone (1978) has recently presented a detailed conceptual scheme that may be used as a model for the conduct of behavioral assessments (see fig. 11.1) This model is actually a three-dimensional system for classifying and evaluating behavioral measures. The three aspects of assessment to be simultaneously considered include contents, methods, and types of generalizability. In the content category, Cone is generally referring to cognitive, motor, and physiological domains of behavior. While tripartite assessment is clearly being advocated, a distinction is drawn between the measurement mode and the content area itself; that is, the three domains may be measured by a variety of behavioral techniques or devices. For example, an individual may self-report behavioral avoidance, such as motor domain. Similarly, motor responses may be assessed via direct observation in laboratory situations. The second dimension, methods, is ordered along a continuum of directness regarding the extent to which these procedures (a) measure the clinically relevant target response, and (b) do so at the time and place of its natural occurrence. At the indirect end of the continuum fall interview, self-report, and "rating-by-other" methods. Five types of direct observation methods are noted. These include self-observation, analogue role-play, analogue free behavior, naturalistic role-

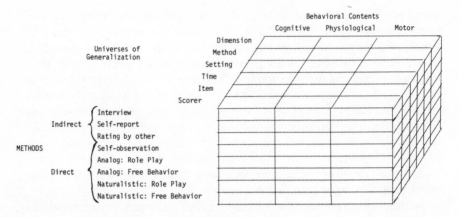

Figure 11.1 The behavioral assessment grid (BAG); a taxonomy for behavioral assessment.

play, and naturalistic free behavior. If content and method categories were juxtaposed, a 24-category behavioral taxonomic system would result. This is only theoretically possible, however, since a limited number of method categories are available for the measurement of cognitive contents. We will not discuss the third dimension of generalizability at this time as that aspect of the model is more restricted to an evaluation of particular assessment instruments. However, the combined content by method matrix clearly is of relevance in our present discussion. Specifically, Cone's BAG model allows for more comprehensive assessment in that behaviors can be measured both across method and content categories. In so doing, greater organization is provided both to the field of behavioral assessment and the evaluation of the individual client. Unfortunately, BAG does not, in and of itself, aid in clinical decision making or in the establishment of therapeutic goals. We should not be too critical in this respect, however, as its intended purpose was neither of the above. Rather, it was a system devised for the classification and evaluation of behavioral assessment instruments and measures.

Multimethod Clinical Assessment

Nay (1979) has proposed a behavioral assessment guide that is perhaps more comprehensive and systematic than any of the models formerly cited. This multimethod clinical assessment strategy provides suggestion regarding the planning, implementation, and utilization of behavioral assessment information. Specifically, the model focuses on five categories of information (referred to as "modalities") and four major methods of assessment. The five modalities and their "facets" (specific information) include:

1. *a description of potential targets* in which attributions and overt/covert referents are defined; further, frequency, duration, and intensity information is obtained;
2. *conditions of occurrence* in which the target behavior is examined with regard to location, activity, time antecedents, consequences, and modeling influences;
3. *historical information* in which case history data are collected with respect to the following: birth, developmental milestones, medical, family, interpersonal, educational, sexual, and occupational background;
4. *client resources* in which internal (i.e., personal abilities and skills) and external (i.e., environmental) strengths and weaknesses are evaluated; these may include such areas as intellect, physical abilities, social skills, support, physical surroundings, finances, and so forth;
5. *client motivation* in which information is obtained regarding client's desire to bring about changes in his or her behavior, environment, or both.

While the above modalities refer to *what* is being assessed, the four major methods of assessment refer to *how* it is assessed: interview, written, observation, and physiological. In addition, each of the methods categories can be further subdivided into the facets of operations, supplier, setting, and sampling components. In summary, a matrix (similar to Cone's [1978] BAG model) can be formed indicating the various method by modality interactions. Each cell within such a matrix represents another possible method-modality combination available for the clinical assessment. Clearly, the above model may potentiate a truly comprehensive assessment. However, if one were to sketch out the complete matrix prior to actually conducting the assessment, the task would simply be overwhelming (see Nay, 1979, table 12.5). This occurs because each modality and methods facet is afforded independent status within the assessment matrix. Of paradoxical interest, however, the reader may note that Nay's methods categories are, in fact, less detailed than Cone's BAG typology. The irony is that, with less methods specification, Nay's model appears to result in even greater complexity.

THE PRAGMATICS OF INTEGRATED ASSESSMENT AND TREATMENT

While the above behavioral assessment models provide clinicians with data-gathering strategies, they must be placed within the broader context of a thoroughly integrated assessment-treatment framework. Once this is accomplished, child behavioral therapists can obtain both a comprehensive view of the client and an assessment of a particular therapeutic program's likelihood of success. Thus, the purpose of this section is to translate the principles and strategies of behavioral assessment into a practical framework for clinical application. To accomplish this, we have artificially divided the process into five sequential phases: (a) the task of assessment, (b) problem identification and target behavior selection, (c) choosing and designing a treatment program, (d) measurement during intervention, and (e) therapeutic evaluation.

The Task of Assessment

A number of years ago, one of the authors of this chapter, P. H. Bornstein, received an intake card from a referring physician which read as follows:

Name:	John S.
Age:	10 yrs.
Address:	1000 Main St., Middleamerica, Iowa
Phone:	727-0001
Presenting Complaint:	Psychological problems
Purpose of Assessment:	Please do a psychological

Although name, address, and phone number have been changed to protect the client's identity, all other information is exactly how it was received at the time of referral. Thus, the point should be clear. We often begin the process of assessment with extremely vague, essentially undefined questions to be answered. Yet, at its conclusion we are expected to draw rather specific recommendations which logically weave together the assessment-treatment package. Certainly, the job is difficult enough without the added burden of ignorance; that is, ignorance with regard to the nature of the assessment task itself.

What, then are the most frequent reasons for conducting a behavioral assessment? Kanfer and Nay (1982) cite six common purposes of assessment: (a) assignment to a diagnostic category; (b) evaluation of specific aptitudes, behaviors, abilities, or skills; (c) transformation of vague complaints into specific assessment questions; (d) as preintervention assessment; (e) to predict future behavior under given conditions; and (f) to assess the availability of personal and environmental resources. The present authors consider the above list to be quite extensive. Of paramount importance, however, is the relationship between the assessment task and the assessment process. Specifically, there is no doubt that the content and methods utilized in the process of assessment will vary widely depending upon the original purpose of assessment. Moreover, since purpose and process are inexorably linked, the two will reactively affect one another. Thus, as the task first defines the process, the process may later redefine the task. In essence, establishing an integrated assessment-treatment framework is clearly a dynamic rather than static process.

Problem Identification and Target Behavior Selection

Broadly stated, the major goal in this phase of the integrated assessment-treatment framework is that of defining the problem. Certainly, in the case of most child referrals, the leading target behavior "contender" is often pre-established by parents, teachers, or some other agents of society. But, as Hawkins (1975) has so aptly stated, "Who decided *that* was the problem?" That is, just because the behavior has been nominated as problematic by others does not, ipso facto, define it as the target behavior of choice.

If one does not simply accept the presenting complaint as the behavior to be modified, how then is the problem to be identified? Birnbrauer (1978) suggests that a task and situation analysis be performed. More specifically, we must come to understand the behaviors required for success in that particular situation. Then, we select as targets only those behaviors that will facilitate more effective adjustment. For example, let us assume parent-child observations reveal that 6-year-old Herbie does not comply with parental requests. Having become convinced that both Herbie and his family will develop a more effective living situation if compliance were to occur, compliance becomes justifiable as a target behavior of choice. Furman and Drabman (1981), on the other hand, provide three alternatives to traditional target behavioral selection methods. First, using a *normative* approach, data may be collected on the targeted child and some other normative group (typically, this would include similarly aged peers or classmates). Undesirable behaviors occurring above rate or desirable behaviors occurring below rate then become prospects for target behavior selection. Second, social validation procedures may be used to identify problems and behaviors of some significance. The identification of relevant behaviors is accomplished by correlating behavioral rates of occurrence with subjective ratings of performance across some larger identified class. Thus, initiating a conversation may be highly correlated with judges' ratings of social skill effectiveness. Consequently, initiation of conversations is a viable target behavior choice. Third, Furman and Drabman (1981) recommend that target behaviors be empirically related to *current and future adjustment*. This approach is very similar to that noted by Birnbrauer (1978) except that emphasis is placed on an empirically derived decision-making model. In any case, any one of the above procedures probably should not serve as the sole basis for selecting target behaviors. However, when criteria are combined in the decision-making process, target behavioral selection appears more firmly rooted in objective rather than subjective bases.

Unfortunately, all assessors are typically provided with only limited information at the time of referral. Yet, a myriad of procedural methods exists, and an overwhelming number of "facts" about the client could theoretically be assessed. How then does one decide upon an appropriate assessment method? The answer, regrettably, is not all that simple. In fact, the question only raises further questions; namely, as should be apparent from earlier sections of this chapter, (a) What is the task of assessment (b) What is the behavioral assessment model adopted by the clinician? and (c) What methods of assessment are available, economical, and potentially of greatest utility? Independent of the answers to these questions, however, all behavioral assessors strive toward a number of similar goals at this point: (a) developing a functional analysis of behavior, (b) pinpointing the problem behavior, and (c) generating a measurement system. Functional analytic concepts have already been discussed. Suffice it to note that behavioral assessors are most interested in uncovering those variables that control the problem behavior (Nelson & Hayes, 1979). This most frequently takes the form of examining and/or manipulating antecedent, consequent, or organismic conditions. In a related manner, pinpointing the behavior allows the assessor to operationalize his or her analysis of the problem. Thus, the difficulty may be a social skills deficit. Pinpointing may yield an emphasis on the client's inability to maintain eye contact and provide positive conversational feedback. Finally, once all of the above has been accomplished, the identified target behavior must be measured in some manner. This usually involves a determination of response characteristics (i.e., frequency, intensity, duration measures) and the establishment of a baseline level of performance. Once this information is obtained, the behavioral assessor is ready to consider design and treatment alternatives.

Choosing and Designing a Treatment Program

As indicated by Ciminero and Drabman (1977), there is no general model that has been developed to aid in the selection of treatment strategies. However, it is generally agreed that treatment program selection is a function of numerous factors. First, as indicated earlier in this chapter, behavioral assessment procedures (by their very nature) are constructed so as to guide in the selection of therapeutic alternatives. Thus, when assessment information reveals that parents do not consequate "hitting" behavior among siblings, a number of treatment options should immediately become apparent (e.g., time out, response cost, DRO, etc.). Second, all treatment procedures are not created equal! Moreover, there is growing evidence that some techniques are more appropriate with some clients when administered under certain kinds of conditions (Ollendick & Cerny, 1981). For example, Bornstein, Sturm, Retzlaff, Kirby, and Chong (1981) found that paradoxical instruction dramatically reduced encopretic behavior in a 9-year-old male when soiling was partially the result of exacerbation-based phenomena. Third, not all therapists are equally trained or experienced in the use of a wide band of therapeutic procedures. One of the authors (P. H. Bornstein) can recall an instance where the treatment of choice within a family appeared to be negotiation training.

The colleague responsible for the case, however, had never actually implemented such a technique. As a consequence, a more standard parent-training program was implemented in its place. Finally, a variety of practical matters will influence the actual selection of a treatment program. For example, the law of parsimony is not restricted in usage solely to the philosophy of science. Rather, simpler (i.e., less restrictive, less costly, less disruptive) therapeutic procedures are to be preferred over those of a more complex nature. Similarly, client preference and treatment acceptability are matters that should also be of some concern to the practicing clinician (Bornstein, Fox, Sturm, Balleweg, Kirby, Wilson, Weisser, Andre, & McLellarn, in press).

A number of recommendations are also in order regarding treatment program design; namely, (a) targets of intervention initially should be relatively few in number, (b) behaviors with a high probability of success should be focused upon first, (c) therapeutic programs should remain narrow and concentrated (e.g., contingencies put into effect at bedtime) until a treatment effect is obtained, (d) only require of clients that which can be realistically accomplished (do not program failure!), and (e) continue to collect data even as the program is being implemented. Appropriately, then, we now turn to the measurement of behavior during intervention.

Measurement During Intervention

One of the unique aspects of behavioral modification is the manner in which assessment extends into the treatment phase. In fact, Keefe, Kopel, and Gordon (1978) have indicated that there are three major ongoing assessment tasks: (a) checking upon the client's use of therapeutic procedures; (b) monitoring the effectiveness of treatment; and (c) modifying the treatment program if necessary. Measuring the client's use of therapeutic procedures is actually a compliance-related issue; namely, Is the treatment being implemented as prescribed by the clinician? This becomes particularly important in the child behavioral therapy area since a great many treatments are, in fact, implemented by parents or other agents of society. Thus, whenever possible, data should be collected on the validity of treatment implementation.

Perhaps the most important measurement function during intervention, however, relates to the monitoring of treatment effectiveness. The importance here lies in a number of factors. First, even during treatment, target behaviors continue to be operationally defined and, therefore, objectively monitored. Second, ongoing measurement precludes arbitrary and capricious decisions regarding continuation/noncontinuation of current therapeutic procedures. Third, in most instances, the methods of assessment employed during baseline can also be used during the intervention phase. Thus, the evaluative continuity afforded allows clinicians to modify treatment when inadequate progress occurs. In so doing, minor adjustment or complete modification of therapeutic programs may occur. In either case, however, the process increases the probability of success since failing procedures are replaced by potentially more active treatment techniques.

Therapeutic Evaluation

As should be obvious from the above, evaluation of therapy outcome is a natural by-product of the integrated assessment-treatment framework. This evaluation is usually accomplished by means of a between-group or within-subject design. These designs have certainly been discussed at length in the behavior modification literature (see Hersen & Barlow, 1976; Kazdin, 1982; Kratochwill, 1978). Consequently, they will not be elaborated upon here. Instead, we will briefly mention that at posttreatment clinicians may want to consider two other forms of outcome evaluation: measures of social validity and consumer satisfaction. Social validity has already been discussed earlier in this chapter. Such measures refer to whether the effects of intervention produce changes of clinical or applied significance. These assessments are typically accomplished via social comparison or subjective evaluation methods (Kazdin, 1977). Consumer satisfaction, on the other hand, provides an evaluation of therapeutic outcome as perceived by recipients of the service (Bornstein & Rychtarik, in press). Both of the above appear to be of increasing importance in the evaluation of behavioral therapy/behavioral modification programs.

INTEGRATED ASSESSMENT AND TREATMENT: THE CASE OF BILLY

As one increases the number of methods and informational categories within his or her assessment plan, he or she decreases the likelihood of failing to find relevant clinical material. Thus, behavioral modifiers have eschewed the use of multimethod assessment in the conduct and practice of clinical behavioral therapy (Bornstein, Bridgwater, Hickey, & Sweeney, 1980). Unfortunately, given the time, cost, personnel, and equipment requirements, alternative assessment strategies must sometimes be developed. Nelson (1981) has eloquently described one such alternative model. Rather than recommending the employment of as many method by modality strategies as possible, she outlines the concept of "realistic dependent measures." As a consequence, Nelson's empirical clinician chooses among a minimal, intermediate, and maximal battery. The case study which follows is representative of an intermediate battery.

CASE STUDY

Billy J. was a 10-year-old male Caucasian referred to the senior author (P. H. Bornstein) for treatment of "dental phobia." The case had been referred for psychological intervention because local pedodontists had been unable to carry out the restorative work necessary to effect adequate oral hygiene. Billy's mouth had so deteriorated that at the time of referral gums were swollen, teeth were decaying, and root canal work was a pressing priority. Unfortunately, Billy had been unable to undergo any form of dental treatment as a result of his intense and persistent fear.

Assessment consisted of a variety of behavioral methods applied across numerous informational categories. First, separate *behavioral interviews* were conducted with the referring pedodontists, parents, and child. While the parent interview was based upon the Holland (1970) guide, both the pedodontist and child interviews were more unstructured in nature. These interviews revealed a number of significant findings:

1. Billy had never successfully completed a dental visit;
2. at age 6, his first dental experience occurred; it was traumatic; ending in the dentist's use of a loud voice, hand-over-mouth management, and physical restraint; Billy's response was to vomit on the dentist!
3. aside from this particular problem area, the remainder of Billy's adjustment appeared rather unremarkable; academically, he was an average student; socially, peer relationships were of great importance to him; athletically, he was regarded as one of the outstanding football players for his grade level.
4. by both Billy's and the pedodontist's reports, there appeared to be particular aspects of the dental situation that gave rise to increased tension, fear, and anxiety; these included: (1) the whirling, buzzing sound of the drill, (2) receiving an injection, (3) exploratory exam using dental instruments, and (4) use of technical language or equipment (e.g., X-ray machine); and
5. if the problem was not corrected soon, irreparable health damage would soon occur.

Following the clinical interviews, Billy was placed in an analogue role-play situation and asked to "think out loud" as a variety of common dental scenes were imaginally presented (e.g., arrival at the office, prophylaxis, etc.). This provided highly significant information. It was revealed that Billy was exacerbating his own anxiety by telling himself (a) he was scared, (b) the pain would be great, or (c) that he simply could not go on any longer. In addition, Billy completed the self-report Fear Survey Schedule for Children (FSS-FC: Scherer & Nakamura, 1968; Ollendick, in press). Results on this instrument indicated specific fears related to "going to the dentist" and the general "medical" factor.

Billy was then taken on a visit to the dentist's office. Three additional methods of assessment were employed during this baseline period: (a) the Behavior Profile Rating Scale (BPRS: Melamed, Hawes, Heiby, & Glick, 1975) was used for purposes of *naturalistic observation*; (b) Billy completed three short *self-rating inventories* (see Chertock & Bornstein, 1979) assessing attitude, anxiety, and level of physiological activity; and (c) the pedodontists provided separate *global behavioral ratings* on fear and cooperativeness. Collectively, these results indicated a variety of inappropriate behaviors: crying, choking, verbal complaints, inappropriate mouth closing, and so forth. Further, Billy's attitude was very poor. He self-reported high degrees of anxiety/physiological activity (e.g., heart racing), and both pedodontists in the office considered him extremely fearful and uncooperative.

Thus, assessment methods employed included behavioral interviews, analogue role play, self-report, naturalistic observation, self-rating inventories, and global behavioral ratings by others. Moreover, the use of these methods provided highly detailed cognitive, motor, and physiologic information. Based upon the above, an integrated assessment-treatment program was developed. This treatment was composed of the following components:

1. relaxation was first taught as means of controlling increased tension and anxiety in the dental situation;
2. covert modeling (an empirically demonstrated effective procedure) was then employed as the prime therapeutic technique;
3. since peer relationships were of great import to Billy, a multiple modeling procedure was used (see Chertock & Bornstein, 1979); further, because the dental situation normally elicits some degree of anxiety, coping rather than mastery models were chosen for imaginal presentation;
4. during covert modeling scene rehearsal, Billy was provided with more effective cognitive self-instructions (e.g., "I know this may hurt a little, but if I just take a deep breath and relax, it will probably be okay") than those used in the past;
5. a hierarchy of dental-related situations was constructed with a focus on Billy's idiosyncratic fears (i.e., drilling sound, X-ray machine, etc.).

Research indicates that having children experience the phobic object subsequent to observing a model enhances treatment effects. Consequently, after each covert modeling session, those scenes successfully completed were, in fact, enacted in the pedodontists' office. In addition, naturalistic observation, self-rating inventories, and pedodontists' global behavioral ratings were collected on a weekly basis throughout the course of treatment. Further, at the conclusion of the therapeutic program, the FSS-FC was re-administered, pedodontists' provided a social validity rating of improvement, and parents completed a consumer satisfaction measure.

Quite simply, results were overwhelmingly successful. Over the course of treatment, the BPRS demonstrated significant declines in the measurement of disruptive dental behavior (pretreatment = 13; posttreatment = 1). All self-rating inventories corroborated these reductions. Moreover, pedodontists' global ratings evinced improvement in cooperativeness and decreased fear-related behavior (pretreatment $\overline{X} = 9.0$; posttreatment $\overline{X} = 2.5$, using a Likert scale 1-10). Similarly, prepost and posttest-only measures were also indicative of therapeutic improvement. At posttest, the FSS-FC no longer revealed any dental or medical fears. The pedodontists considered Billy greatly improved and parents rated themselves as "completely satisfied" with the treatment. In summary, the behavioral assessment information obtained clearly aided in the development of a specific treatment program. More importantly, this program was highly effective in remediating a personally and clinically significant problem.

SUMMARY

In this chapter we have presented an integrated model of behavioral assessment and treatment. To accomplish this, the assumptions and goals of behavioral assessment were discussed first. Behavioral assessment was then compared to traditional assessment. Methods and models of behavioral assessment were elaborated. A 5-step, practical model of integrated assessment and treatment was presented and illustrated by means of an actual clinical case study.

REFERENCES

Birnbrauer, J. S. Some guides to designing behavioral programs. In D. Marholin (Ed.), *Child behavior therapy*. New York: Gardner Press, 1978.

Bornstein, P. H., Bridgwater, C. A., Hickey, J. S., & Sweeney, T. M. Characteristics and trends in behavioral assessment: An archival analysis. *Behavioral Assessment*, 1980 *2*, 125-133.

Bornstein, P. H., Fox, S. G., Sturm, C. A., Balleweg, B. J., Kirby, K. L., Wilson, G. L., Weisser,, C. E., Andre, J. C., & McLellarn, R. W. Treatment acceptability of alternative marital therapies: A comparative analysis. *Journal of Marital and Family Therapy*, in press.

Bornstein, P. H., Hamilton, S. B., & Bornstein, M. T. Self-monitoring procedures. In A. R. Ciminero, H. S. Calhoun, & H. E. Adams (Eds.), *Handbook of behavioral assessment* (2nd ed.). New York: Wiley, in press.

Bornstein, P. H., & Rychtarik, R. G. Consumer satisfaction in adult behavior therapy: Procedure, problems, and future perspectives. *Behavior Therapy*, in press.

Bornstein, P. H., Sturm, C. A., Retzlaff, P. D., Kirby, K. L., & Chong, H. Paradoxical instruction in the treatment of encopresis and chronic constipation: An experimental analysis. *Journal of Behavior Therapy and Experimental Psychiatry*, 1981, *12*, 167-170.

Chertock, S. L., & Bornstein, P. H. Covert modeling treatment of children's dental fears. *Child Behavior Therapy*, 1979, *1*, 249-255.

Ciminero, A. R. Behavioral assessment: An overview. In A. R. Ciminero, K. S. Calhoun, & H. E. Adams (Eds.), *Handbook of behavioral assessment*. New York: Wiley, 1977.

Ciminero, A. R., & Drabman, R. S. Current developments in the behavioral assessment of children. In B. B. Lahey & A. E. Kazdin (Eds.), *Advances in clinical child psychology* (Vol. 1). New York: Plenum Press, 1977.

Cone, J. D. The behavioral assessment grid (BAG): A conceptual framework and taxonomy. *Behavior Therapy*, 1978, *9*, 882–888.

Cone, J. D., & Hawkins, R. P. Introduction. In J. D. Cone & R. P. Hawkins (Eds.), *Behavioral assessment: New directions in clinical psychology*. New York: Brunner/Mazel, 1977.

Dickson, C. R. Role of assessment in behavior therapy. In P. McReynolds (Ed.), *Advances in psychological assessment* (Vol. 3). San Francisco: Jossey-Bass, 1975.

Evans, I. M., & Nelson, R. O. Assessment of child behavior problems. In A. R. Ciminero, K. S. Calhoun, & H. E. Adams (Eds.), *Handbook of behavioral assessment*. New York: Wiley, 1977.

Furman, W., & Drabman, R. S. Methodological issues in child behavior therapy. In M. Hersen, R. M. Eisler, & P. M. Miller (Eds.), *Progress in behavior modification* (Vol. 11). New York: Academic Press, 1981.

Goldfried, M. R. Behavioral assessment in perspective. In J. D. Cone & R. P. Hawkins (Eds.), *Behavioral assessment: New directions in clinical psychology*. New York: Brunner/Mazel, 1977.

Hartmann, D. P., Roper, B. L., & Bradford, D. C. Some relationships between behavioral and traditional assessment. *Journal of Behavioral Assessment*, 1979, *1*, 3–21.

Hawkins, R. P. Who decided *that* was the problem? Two stages of responsibility for applied behavior analysis. In W. S. Wood (Ed.), *Issues in evaluating behavior modification*. Champaign, IL: Research Press, 1975.

Herjanic, G., Herjanic, M., Brown, F., & Wheatt, T. Are children reliable reporters? *Journal of Abnormal Child Psychology*, 1975, *3*, 41–48.

Hersen, M., & Barlow, D. H. *Single-case experimental designs: Strategies for studying behavior change*. New York: Pergamon Press, 1976.

Holland, C. J. An interview guide for behavioral counseling with parents. *Behavior Therapy*, 1970, *1*, 70–79.

Kanfer, F. H., & Nay, W. R. Behavioral assessment. In G. T. Wilson & C. M. Franks (Eds.), *Contemporary behavior therapy: Conceptual and empirical foundations*. New York: Guilford Press, 1982.

Kanfer, F. H., & Saslow, G. Behavioral diagnosis. In C. M. Franks (Ed.), *Behavior therapy: Appraisal and status*. New York: McGraw-Hill, 1969.

Kazdin, A. E. Assessing the clinical or applied significance of behavior change through social validation. *Behavior Modification*, 1977, *1*, 427–452.

Kazdin, A. E. *Single-case research designs: Methods for clinical and applied settings*. New York: Oxford, 1982.

Kazdin, A. E., & Wilson, G. T. *Evaluation of behavior therapy*. Cambridge, MA: Ballinger, 1978.

Keefe, F. J., Kopel, S. A., & Gordon, S. B. *A practical guide to behavioral assessment*. New York: Springer, 1978.

Kratochwill, T. R. (Ed.). *Single-subject research: Strategies for evaluating change*. New York: Academic Press, 1978.

Lazarus, A. A. Multimodal behavior therapy: Treating the "BASIC ID." *Journal of Nervous and Mental Disease*, 1973, *156*, 404–411.

Lazarus, A. A. *Multimodal behavior therapy*. New York: Springer, 1976.

Melamed, B. G., Hawes, R., Heiby, E., & Glick, J. The use of film modeling to reduce uncooperative behavior of children during dental treatment. *Journal of Dental Research*, 1975, *54*, 797–801.

Mischel, W. *Personality and assessment*. New York: Wiley, 1968.

Nay, W. R. *Multimethod clinical assessment*. New York: Gardner Press, 1979.

Nelson, R. O., & Hayes, S. C. The nature of behavioral assessment: A commentary. *Journal of Applied Behavior Analysis*, 1979, *12*, 491–500.

Ollendick, T. H. Reliability and validity of the Revised Fear Survey Schedule for Children (FSSC-R). *Behaviour Research and Therapy*, in press.

Ollendick, T. H., & Cerny, J. A. *Clinical behavior therapy with children*. New York: Plenum Press, 1981.

Peterson, D. R. *The clinical study of social behavior*. New York: Appleton-Century-Crofts, 1968.

Scherer, M. W., & Nakamura, C. Y. A fear survey schedule for children (FSS-FC): A factor analytic comparison with manifest anxiety (CMAS). *Behaviour Research and Therapy*, 1968, *6*, 173–182.

Stuart, R. B. *Trick or treatment: How and when psychotherapy fails*. Champaign, IL: Research Press, 1970.

Van Hasselt, V. B., Hersen, M., & Bellack, A. S. The validity of role play tests for assessing social skills in children. *Behavior Therapy*, 1981, *12*, 202–216.

Wade, T. C., Baker, T. B., & Hartmann, D. P. Behavior therapists' self-reported views and practices. *The Behavior Therapist*, 1979, *2*, 3–6.

Webb, E. J., Campbell, D. T., Schwartz, R. D., & Sechrest, L. *Unobtrusive measures: Non-reactive research in the social sciences*. Chicago: Rand McNally, 1966.

12
Ethical Issues in Child Behavioral Assessment
George A. Rekers

A number of ethical issues regarding rights, consent, professional judgment, and social values are raised in the clinical practice of child behavioral assessment. The professional conducting child behavioral assessment may be a psychologist, psychiatrist, educator, social worker, pediatrician, or marriage and family therapist. The accepted ethical practices of these professions prescribe, for example, that the professional should value objectivity, integrity, professional competence, and concern for the welfare of the children served. The practicing professional accepts responsibility for the consequences of his or her behavioral assessment procedures and should make appropriate attempts to have assessment services used properly. Professionals should avoid any procedure which may be expected to cause harm to the child, whether passively or actively.

Beyond these commonly shared general ethical obligations of the professional, there are a number of specific, identifiable ethical issues which need to be carefully considered by any practitioner conducting child behavioral assessment.

ISSUES REGARDING CHILDREN'S RIGHTS

Professional ethical standards typically require the clinician or educator to identify clearly who the client is, what the client's rights are, and whose interests are being served by conducting behavioral assessment with a child (see for example, the Ethical Standards of Psychologists of the American Psychological Association, 1977). If a behavioral assessment procedure is to be

244

carried out, the professional needs to make clear who is being served: the designated child client, the parents, an agency, and/or the broader community.

MacKay (1979) has presented an extensive ethical argument that accountability is essential to avoid objectionable forms of manipulation in behavioral interventions:

> What kind of manipulation is it, then, that is objectionable? The key question, I suggest, is how far in principle the manipulator is or wants to be answerable to the person he is manipulating. Any contrived way of handling our fellow men that destroys or evades the answerability of the manipulator to the manipulated person is unacceptable. (p. 72)

It is a commonly held assumption that the professional should protect the welfare of the consumer, in part by providing full and appropriate information regarding the planned intervention, by providing for confidentiality, and by providing the consumer with freedom of choice with regard to participation in the procedure. When a minor child is the recipient of a behavioral assessment service, implications of these ethical responsibilities are more complex than if the consumer were a full legal adult. This makes it all the more necessary to clarify the consent issue involved and to determine who is being served when we provide behavioral assessment services.

We must be sensitive to protect the inalienable rights of the individual child against any possible violation of his or her deserved freedom and dignity as a human being. But as professionals, we need to be simultaneously diligent in our efforts to ensure that the child retains the rights and opportunities to obtain the potential positive benefits of receiving behavioral assessment procedures (see Shore, 1979). Occasionally, it may appear that attempts to guarantee the child's rights against possible intrusion into his or her freedom are in conflict with our efforts to provide a potentially beneficial clinical or educational intervention involving behavioral assessment. Professionals must make every reasonable attempt to guarantee that behavioral assessment procedures are not used to merely manipulate the child or to be applied contrary to his or her own best interests.

ISSUES REGARDING PROPER AND LEGAL CONSENT

Normally, the right of an adult consumer of behavioral assessment procedures would be substantially safeguarded by the ethical principles regarding full and proper consent for the intervention, along with fully appropriate disclosure as to the purpose and nature of the behavioral assessment procedures proposed. But in the case of a child, we must raise the question: Should we require him or her to give direct consent for behavioral assessment procedures?

A legal specialist on issues raised by behavioral modification, Reed Martin (1975), has stated:

> Even though capacity is presumably lacking in children, there is a current trend to secure their "consent" when they are to be involved. This does not really alter anything from a legal standpoint nor does it preclude the necessity for parental consent, but it seems to have a valuable therapeutic basis and seems admirable from a human viewpoint. (p. 28)

But realistically and legally, can the child actually grant full and proper consent to a behavioral assessment procedure? To answer this question, we must make a conceptual distinction between the three equal and yet necessary conditions for consent to be both ethically and legally proper: competence or capacity to consent, voluntariness, and information.

Competent Consent

The first requirement of competence or "capacity" implies that the individual has a "sound mind" and is of suffecient age to be capable of acting on one's own behalf. Legally, children, some "disturbed" prisoners, retarded individuals, or incompetent or psychotically disturbed patients are typically presumed to lack the capacity to consent.

In recent years, some professionals and governmental agencies have raised questions about the possibility of establishing an "age of discretion" for children at some point (e.g., at 7 years). The suggestion is made that we should require consent from a child older than this "age of discretion" before prescribing an intervention. However, these proposals for a chronological cut-off age prior to adolescence tend to ignore the wide variation in mental age of children at any given chronological age. They also overlook critical limitations in the child's intellectual decision-making capacity. In practice, therefore, it is common hospital policy, for example, to regard a minor's consent to be unnecessary for medical assessment or treatment if he or she is under 18 years of age, unmarried, and having no special circumstances (e.g., California Hospital Association, 1975). Instead, when the child is judged to be unable to consent, the consent of a legal surrogate such as the parent or guardian may be secured instead.

Similarly, most state laws grant to the parent or guardian the "privilege" for confidential communication between child and the professional. Therefore, when professional ethical standards mandate confidential professional communication, it is the parent or guardian who can authorize or provide consent for releasing confidential information to another party regarding the child.

Ferguson (1978) has outlined four distinct developmental periods which might be taken into consideration for developing separate criteria for obtaining proper consent directly from the child, depending upon his or her developmental capacities. Her discussion is related to the participation of children in research studies, and, as Martin (1975) has suggested, it can be therapeutically valuable to attempt to obtain commitments of cooperation from the child depending upon his or her developmental level. Nevertheless, it is generally concluded that the limited mental capabilities and restrictions in the child's legal status result in a relative lack of social decision-making power of children in most situations. Professionals and the law alike generally conclude that the child is not capable of providing competent consent for all kinds of social interventions; therefore, consent decisions must be made by a responsible legal surrogate.

Voluntary Consent

The second criterion for proper consent is the assurance that such consent is voluntary. Legally, voluntariness is usually defined in terms of the absence of coercion or duress. Of the three criteria for proper consent, perhaps the voluntariness criterion might be most easily met by the child himself or herself. But if the capacity to consent has not been established, it is not considered legally possible for the voluntariness criterion to have been met (Martin, 1975). Therefore, the voluntariness criterion must be met by the legal surrogate (the parent or guardian of the child).

Serious questions about satisfying the "voluntariness" criterion arise when there is a direct or indirect suggestion for a reward or punishment contingent upon the client's offer to "voluntarily" permit one's child to enter into a behavioral assessment and treatment program. For example, a school official might imply a direct threat ("either you allow your child to enter this special behavioral assessment and treatment program or we will have to suspend him immediately from school"). But here we must make a careful logical distinction between "coercion" and fair description of normal consequences.

For example, I might tell you that last month I bought a brand new sportscar and today I just won a sportscar of the identical model. If I told you that I would give you a sportscar for a sum of $2, there would certainly be a tremendous amount of pressure on you to give me $2. However, although there would be tremendous psychological pressure put upon you to buy the brand new car from me for $2, it would not fulfill the legal definition of "coercion" because there would be no unfair consequences imposed upon you if you declined my offer.

On the other hand, if a criminal held a gun to the head of your child and asked you to give him $2 or he would shoot your child, you could not legally grant "voluntary" consent because of the *coercion* involved. That is, if you "freely chose" not to give the $2 to the criminal, an unfair consequence would occur to you—namely, your child would be shot in the head.

Therefore, the definition of "coercion" is not dependent upon how strong the psychological pressure is on the client to conform, but rather is dependent upon a determination of whether or not an unfair consequence will occur if the client chooses not to consent.

Therefore, the ethical issue that the professional must face is this: Am I making a fair proposal to the parent or guardian of the child for conducting behavioral assessment? As long as the professional does not threaten unfair consequences for the child or his or her parents in the event that the parents fail to grant consent, then coercion is not likely to be present.

However, on the other hand, the professional needs to be sensitive to the fact that professional authority can create substantial psychological pressure on the parent to grant consent to an intervention such as behavioral assessment. If the doctor in psychology or psychiatry, for example, recommends behavioral assessment to the parent who is unschooled in behavioral psychology, there would be a strong psychological pressure to conform to the expert's implied recommendation for behavioral assessment. This places a heavy responsibility on the professional to be making a proper and appropriate recommendation for behavioral assessment and not to be overutilizing the procedure nor to be misapplying the procedure to an inappropriate situation.

Philosophically, legal systems in western civilization imply the concept of true freedom to choose among alternative courses of action. But many professionals who conduct behavioral assessment may have a basic theoretical disagreement with the entire legal concept of "voluntariness," which is one of the accepted criteria for judging whether or not consent is proper and legal. Skinner (1971) has highlighted the issue at the level of philosophic presuppositions. Much of current law is based on historical and traditional views of human freedom and responsibility. In Skinner's words:

> In the traditional view, a person is free. He is autonomous in the sense that his behavior is uncaused. He can therefore be held responsible for what he does and justly punished if he offends. That view, together with its associated practices, must be re-examined when a scientific analysis reveals unsuspected controlling relations between behavior and environment.
>
> . . . Many anthropologists, sociologists, and psychologists have used their expert knowledge to prove that man is free, purposeful and responsible. Freud was a determinist—on faith, if not on the evidence—but many Freudians have no hesitation in assuring their patients that they are free to choose among different courses of action and are in the long run the architects of their own destinies.
>
> This escape route is slowly closed as new evidences of the predictability of

human behavior are discovered. Personal exemption from a complete determinism is revoked as a scientific analysis progresses, particularly in accounting for the behavior of an individual (pp. 17–18).

Adopting a consistent Skinnerian behaviorism, based as it is on the presupposition that *all* the individual's actions are either predetermined by heredity or immediately determined by environment, a behavioral assessment specialist may sincerely disagree with the possibility of "voluntary consent." Martin (1975), an attorney, has pointed out the ethical and legal danger here for the practicing professional:

> Behavior therapists, who work through changing features in the environment in order to change behavior, often argue that "freedom" and "voluntariness" are illusory concepts and that in fact all behavior is coerced to some degree. Some practitioners say that for this reason they do not take the issue of voluntary consent seriously. But they certainly must learn to, if they want to avoid legal challenges in the future. (p. 29)

According to an orthodox Skinnerian position, the entire democratic framework in which the legal concept of proper consent rests should be challenged. One commentator put it this way:

> Skinner himself recognizes very well the implications of his behaviorism. For example, he recognizes that within behavioral terms democracy is essentially impossible. Since all behavior is controlled by the environment, it is possible to manipulate the environment so as to produce the kind of behavior one wants. For Skinner a democracy is controlled by the concept of autonomous man, a false concept. Far more effective control can be wielded by those who recognize and utilize the tenets of behavioral psychology. (Schaeffer, 1972, pp. 37–38)

It appears that if a professional logically carries Skinner's thesis in *Beyond Freedom and Dignity* to its logical conclusion, then the democratic form of government and law upon which we emphasize the necessity of proper consent for intervention should be discarded. This, indeed, could be a concern of parents who may have read about Skinnerian behaviorism in popular periodicals. For example, Harris (1971) summarized Skinner's approach to a public audience in this way:

> But man in his conceit refuses to accept himself as an organism shaped by his environment. The trouble starts, Skinner says, with the proud belief that underlies democracy: the notion that in each of us there is a mentalistic being— an ego, personality, anima, spirit, character, soul or mind—that is somehow free.

He denies the existence of this Autonomous Man and of any other cognitive entity able to claim, as Americans did in the Declaration of Independence, to hold "unalienable rights." In cold passion, Skinner seeks to destroy our pretentions to the freedom and dignity whose literature is written in brave blood.

To take their place, Skinner offers the passionless hypothesis of his experimental laboratory: each man and woman is a unique bundle of behaviors determined by environment; only that, and nothing more. Through evolution the environment selected the behaviors that survive in our genes, and environmental conditioning shapes each of us in this life. If you would control, or change, human behavior, you need only control environment. (p. 33)

MacKay (1979), a professor at Keele University in England, has made a distinction between what he calls *positive* and *negative* behaviorism:

By "positive" behaviourism I mean simply a particular scientific method or habit of approach to the understanding of human behaviour which looks for causal connections only between observable acts and events in the environment. By contrast, I shall use "negative" behaviourism to mean a particular metaphysical doctrine, which is characterized by what it *denies* and is parasitic on the scientific theory and data, though in fact having no logical support from them. (pp. 45–46)

Negative behaviourism, however — behaviouristic *philosophy* as distinct from science — is anything but neutral. It is characterized by what it *denies*. In the writings of Skinner, for example, it goes with the idea that concepts like "freedom" or "dignity" are "pre-scientific" relics which are designed to be outdated by a scientific understanding of human behaviour purely in terms of conditioning, contingencies of reinforcement and the like. . . . Freedom of choice is held to be an illusion based on ignorance of the psychological mechanisms involved in the shaping of behaviour; and so on. (p. 47, *emphasis* added)

Similarly, MacKay (1979) points out that the word "determinism" can be used in more than one way. On the one hand, he defines *positive* determinism as a neutral scientific hypothesis: "the speculation (essentially untestable) that for every event in the physical world there exist (even if you cannot find them) prior events which constitute sufficient causes of those events. . . . It expresses only a positive confidence in the reliability of scientific precedent as a guide to our future expectations. 'Determinism' is often used, however, in a *negative* sense to stand for a particular metaphysical doctrine, which denies human freedom and responsibility. Like negative behaviourism, negative determinism is often presented as if it had logical support from deterministic science; but as we shall see, this too is a bogus claim" (pp. 48–49).

The professional using behavioral assessment techniques can take a logically defensible position (and be able to explain it as such to parents granting consent) that behavioral assessment techniques can be used for the benefit of the child without making all the *negative* deterministic assumptions of Skinner. Schaeffer (1972) provides an example of a "positive behaviorism" as the theoretical underpinnings for behavioral assessment, which would make the legal requirement of obtaining voluntary consent meaningful: "though man may undergo a good deal of conditioning, he is not only the product of conditioning. Man has a mind; he exists as an ego, an entity standing over against the machine-like part of his being" (p. 36).

Informed Consent

The client or the client's legal surrogate (in the case of a child) must meet the competence and voluntariness criteria for proper consent. But once these criteria have been met, the third criterion of being *informed* must be satisfied. In the case of a child, there are many situations in which obtaining direct *informed* consent from him or her would be either impossible, impractical, or countertherapeutic.

Often, implied expectations of adults or self-expectations of the child may contribute to an adverse developmental outcome in the child. For example, if we were to proceed with obtaining informed consent from a child, we might be put in the difficult position of having to inform the child that we wish to embark upon a behavioral assessment procedure because he or she is potentially at high risk for criminal behavior, sexual deviance, academic failure, or some other equally unfortunate outcome. In such a case, the very process of obtaining informed consent from the child might adversely affect the child's current and future psychological adjustment.

The perceived authority of a professional giving such information to a child can constitute a potentially strong and harmful labeling effect. Of course, there is a range of possible reactions of a child to an implied label which may result in attempting to satisfy the information criterion of proper consent. A variety of complex variables can be involved, including: (a) the salience of the label to the child, (b) the severity of the current conditions of the child leading to the labeling, (c) the visibility of the child's condition to others, (d) any possible distressing features of the behavioral assessment procedure to be conducted, and (e) any potential protection provided by such a label or implied intervention related to that label (Guskin, Bartel, & MacMillan, 1975).

Not only is the child usually seen as lacking in the ability to satisfy the competence and voluntariness criteria, but also, if we were to have the child satisfy the information criterion as well, we would encounter difficulties of informing him or her of the potential adverse outcome which would result in the absence of our behavioral assessment procedure. This raises the possibility of a "self-fulfilling prophecy." According to Rosenthal and Jacobson (1968), this could involve the risk that the professional's perspective concerning the child's acceptability or competence might be learned and accepted by him or her. He or she then may behave in accordance with that learned perspective inherent in the labeling process.

Because the professional's goals are usually to improve the condition or status of the child, such a possibility of adversely labeling a child should be considered. The variables related to the consequences of labeling are quite complex (for a review, see Guskin et al., 1975), and the ethical issue raised here pertains to the professional's responsibility to consider this possibility prior to deciding whether or not to obtain "informed consent" from the child or from the parent.

These issues also exist at another level. The parent or guardian of the child may receive information from the professional and then may label the child in ways that result in adverse consequences. The professional should also be aware of this possibility. But it might be argued that the adult has potentially greater maturity and competence to understand and act upon appropriate warnings given by the professional against adversely labeling the child.

In the professional's relationship to the child in a behavioral assessment procedure, deception (misinformation given) should be avoided, but concealment (information withheld) might be judged to be the most therapeutic approach with such a child with regard to the issue of informed consent. If the process of obtaining informed consent from the child directly would pose a risk of psychological harm or social injury to him or her, the information criterion of proper consent should be satisfied with the parent or guardian instead.

The Parent or Guardian as Legal Surrogate

Although we have concluded that it is typically unreasonable to expect a child to be able to give competent, voluntary, and informed consent for behavioral assessment intervention, we should nevertheless simultaneously emphasize the desirability of informing the child (as much as possible under the prevailing circumstances) regarding the purposes and nature of the proposed evaluation. This matter becomes a very delicate issue, and all due regard must be given to guaranteeing the child's rights. Because the child is not competent to make a fully informed or voluntary decision regarding participation in a behavioral assessment intervention, there must be a proper balance among merging (a) the responsibilities of the parent or guardian with (b) the expert consultation with the professional in (c) a society which has legal boundaries within which both parents and professionals can collaborate with the child's best interests.

Some critics would question the initiation of any behavioral assessment or behavioral therapy techniques in response to a request of the parent only, without an effort to elicit the child's proper consent. But, certainly, it is widely held in our society to be proper and, in fact, mandatory for parents to subject their child to an educational process whether the child consents or not. If the elementary school-age child decides not to attend school, both parents and society have the right to enforce both educational assessment and educational interventions upon the child. Both the parents and society intervene in the child's life to guarantee his or her right to the potential benefits of education. Similarly, over the protests of a child, parents and physicians may collaborate to inoculate him or her against polio, diphtheria, or other dreaded childhood diseases. In a parallel fashion, a behavioral assessment procedure may be entirely appropriate for the parent to request of a professional over the objections of a noncompliant child. The nature of behavioral assessment intervention thereby can be conceptualized to be essentially equivalent to medical, dental, or educational assessment procedures, insofar as the proper consent issues are involved.

Society clearly does not expect a child to grant full proper consent for educational assessment in school, psychological evaluation or medical diagnosis, or dental evaluation because it is widely recognized that a child is unable to grant competent and informed consent, even though the voluntariness criterion might occasionally be met. This issue can be illustrated by considering the case of a parent who completely accepts a child's decision not to obtain a medical assessment where there is a severe physical symptom of illness. Assuming, for the moment, that no religious constitutional issue is involved, and, assuming that the parent completely comprehends the desirability of obtaining medical diagnosis to prevent a life-endangering illness, we would conclude that the parent's complete acceptance of the child's decision to forego medical assessment would be condemned by society's moral and legal codes. It would be ethically more appropriate for the parent and the professional to collaborate in using educational or other persuasive approaches to inform the child regarding the actual dire consequences of failing to obtain medical intervention. However, the critical issue is this: The failure of the parent or professional to succeed in obtaining the child's consent in the situation would not be sufficient to remove the parent and professional from the moral or legal responsibilities to intervene on behalf of the child.

To guarantee the child's right to obtain potentially beneficial forms of educational, medical, dental, or behavioral assessment, it is simply the case that there are times when the parent and professional must collaborate to override his or her lack of consent to a procedure. From a humanitarian and clinical perspective, it is certainly desirable to obtain the child's active cooperation and consent to a behavioral assessment procedure. Nevertheless, there are ethically justifiable circumstances in which the child's consent is not essential, and attempts to satisfy the information criterion of proper consent would be inappropriate for the child's best welfare. These considerations, of course, do not remove the necessity of obtaining proper consent from a suitable legal surrogate (a parent or guardian) because a representative of the child's welfare must grant proper consent for him or her to protect the rights, freedoms, and human dignity of the individual child.

Therefore, the parent or guardian of the child should be informed in advance of the intended behavioral assessment procedures. The information should be accurate and presented both in an oral and written format that can be comprehended by the legal surrogate who may not be conversant with technical or behavioral terminology. The parent or guardian should be informed that he or she has a right to refuse to grant consent on behalf of the child. It must be clearly communicated to the parent that there is no condition or penalty which will be contingent upon refusal to grant consent, otherwise the voluntariness criterion of proper consent will be destroyed. The parent or guardian should be informed that consent may be withdrawn at any time in the future. Therefore, even if behavioral assessment has begun, consent could be withdrawn to terminate the procedure before it is completed.

The legal surrogate for the child should also be informed of any potential risks involved in the behavioral assessment procedure. The potential benefits of the behavioral assessment procedure should be described in realistic terms. And, together with a description of the risks and benefits of the proposed behavioral assessment procedure, information should be provided about the risks and benefits of alternative assessment techniques.

In summary, a primary professional ethical issue raised by behavioral assessment is that of obtaining proper consent which satisfies the three separate criteria of competence, voluntariness, and information. Because the child is not capable of granting full proper consent, a legal surrogate (such as the parent, guardian, or other legal representative of the child) must provide full proper consent on behalf of the child.

ISSUES REGARDING PROFESSIONAL JUDGMENT

Once proper consent has been obtained to conduct behavioral assessment, the professional has a number of decisions to make which have ethical ramifications. The professional conducting the behavioral assessment faces at least four ethical issues in this regard: (1) decisions regarding which assessment procedures should be used, (2) a determination of what behavior pattern should be conceptualized as deviant, (3) a professional judgment regarding the child's prognosis with and without assessment intervention, and (4) the formulation of specific intervention strategies based on behavioral assessment data collected.

Which Assessment Procedures Should Be Used?

Specific behavioral assessment procedures must be selected in order to document whether a given pattern constitutes an intolerable excess or a functional deficit for the child. In many cases, behavioral histories are obtained by interviewing the parent, the child, and (where the legal surrogate has consented) other individuals such as school teachers, physicians, or other relatives and family members. Because the parent or guardian of the child holds the right to consent and the privilege of confidentiality, the professional conducting initial stages of behavioral assessment needs to make available the results of such an inquiry, the professional anticipations and judgments made, and, where appropriate, the original data on which the final professional judgments were based. Based upon these sources of information, additional behavioral assessment procedures may be formulated and proposed to the parent or guardian.

The institutional setting in which the professional is working has implications for the presumed authority of that clinician to conduct a behavioral assessment. If a behavioral assessment is to be proposed in the classroom and is a standard procedure for a number of the students there, it might be conceptualized as part of the general educational process not needing specific additional consent of a parent or guardian. However, any procedure which is individually prescribed for a student raises the potential need for obtaining proper consent from the parent or guardian. Furthermore, once the parent or guardian has given consent for behavioral assessment procedures, there is a responsibility that the professional conduct an assessment only in areas of relevance to the problem situation. The authority to assess might be challenged if the professional probes areas of questionable relevance (Martin, 1975, p. 117)

In selecting appropriate assessment procedures, language bias and cultural bias should be avoided. The language used in administering the assessment procedure to the child should not (a) be culturally biased, (b) include language beyond the child's educational level, or (c) be in a different area than the language fluency of the child. Otherwise, inaccurate results may be produced, thereby subjecting the professional to legal liability or constituting inappropriate professional judgment. For example, in some schools, Spanish-speaking children have been incorrectly classified as retarded on the basis of assessment procedures administered in the English language, resulting in court action (Martin, 1975, pp. 17–18).

It is the responsibility of the professional to use assessment procedures with reasonable reliability and validity. Measures of observer reliability for *in vivo* behavioral assessment procedures are not only scientifically necessary but are ethically compelled. The professional holds responsibility for developing a proper rationale for the procedure and for conducting the behavioral assessment procedures up to the standards of the profession (see for example, the ethical principle in the 1977 *Ethical Standards of Psychologists* concerning "utilization of assessment techniques").

What Is Deviant?

The professional has the responsibility to make decisions involving the child based upon the behavioral assessment results. To make such decisions, the professional needs to have a competent understanding of psychological and educational measurement, validation issues, and other assessment research findings.

After conducting a behavioral assessment procedure, the professional is often asked to confirm or disconfirm for the parent or teacher or other referral agent: "Is this behavior pattern deviant or not?" Deviant can be conceptualized as a clinical, statistical, or theoretical concept. The behavioral assessment clinician must be familiar with the available body of empirical data on the question, must assess the child with appropriate assessment procedures, and then form a professional judgment regarding the presence and magnitude of potential deviant behavior in the child. The professional must be familiar with available data regarding the base rates of the target behaviors in normal children of the same sex, developmental level, intelligence status, and so forth. By using identical measures for an individual clinical case as have been used by comparison groups, the professional can make a judgment regarding deviance. Even if a behavior pattern is not labeled deviant, there may be a sufficient and appropriate rationale for making a professional recommendation that a behavior pattern be altered for the more optimal functioning of the individual child. In our discussion of social values below, we shall see that such professional judgments need to recognize the larger views of the society and community in which the child lives and must take into account the prevailing moral and legal standards of the environment in which the child lives (see Rosen, Rekers, & Bentler, 1978).

What Is the Prognosis?

One of the tasks of behavioral assessment is to compare the data obtained for the individual child with comparable data reported in the literature for the purpose of formulating a prognostic forecast regarding the anticipated outcome for the child without further intervention. The professional's interpretation of the behavioral assessment data should interact with the parents' judgment to form an intervention plan.

Ethically speaking, the professional is obliged to recognize the boundaries of one's competence and the limitations of the behavioral assessment techniques and thereby prescribe intervention that meets recognized standards in current clinical practice. The professional, therefore, has an ethical obligation to be aware of published data in the area of the behavior in question. He or she should be able to interpret responsibly the behavioral assessment data for the individual child in the context of published normative data on normal and disturbed children.

One of the professional judgment issues facing the clinician is the possibility that an intervention may have no useful benefit, in which instance it would be ethically appropriate to recommend no intervention at all. Or, if the child's behavior is within normal limits, the ethically appropriate recommendation would be that no intervention be introduced.

On the other hand, if a professional judgment is made that the individual child has a behavioral pattern which is sufficiently deviant to have a poor prognosis without treatment, then a decision to intervene is appropriate if it is likely that treatment would produce a better prognostic outcome. Of course, there are many areas of "uncharted territory" in the area of behavioral intervention, and in these cases it is possible to use intrasubject designs to evaluate intervention effectiveness for the individual child. In this sense, then, conducting a pretreatment baseline and then collecting behavioral assessment data (throughout the period of time in which various behavioral interventions are introduced) becomes a method of carrying out the professional's obligation to evaluate one's work and be accountable for interventions which are introduced.

What Is the Treatment Goal?

One of the uses of behavioral assessment data is to provide baseline information which is needed to formulate an intervention goal. One model of adaptive behavior in individual children holds that the child should be provided an increase of diversity and choice in his or her behavioral repertoire (Mahoney & Thoresen, 1974). That is, a treatment goal is to expand the child's repertoire of appropriate behaviors, thereby increasing his or her choices among a larger number of alternative behaviors.

The availability of behavioral assessment procedures makes it possible to increase our accountability in clinical service and educational programming, in that it is now possible to record the effect of a behavioral change intervention. Martin (1975) has observed: "The basic behavioral model offers a workable system for increasing compliance with legal changes and effectiveness of treatment: concrete goals, sequences tasks, feedback on progress, and rewarding desired performance" (p. 97).

ISSUES REGARDING SOCIAL VALUES

It is common for formal ethical standards of professionals to require that they show a sensible regard for the moral and legal standards of the community in which they work. Delicate issues arise when the professional would like to provide new leadership for changing the social codes and moral expectations of his or her community. On the one hand, it is not entirely appropriate or necessary to establish our professional standards after the "average behavior" in our social environment. For example, if 99% of all children lie during their childhood, it is not necessarily appropriate to lower our moral expectation to allow dishonesty to be included among our treatment goals. It may be desirable to have an intervention goal to increase certain behaviors above such an "average" level.

But, if we concede that the child cannot grant full proper consent for intervention goals, we then face the questions: Who in society should determine intervention goals? Who should define the appropriate range of child behavior? Should teachers decide? Should parents alone decide? Should legislators decide? Should the courts define the appropriate goals? Should concerned professionals alone define intervention standards? Does a select group of social advocates really represent the child's rights in the matter?

These and related questions pose ethical issues concerning the social values that the professional follows in conducting behavioral assessment procedures with children. Some critics vociferously argue that it is inappropriate for professionals or parents to impose their standards for values on children. But, it is clear that there are competing values and that some subset of social values will ultimately be applied to the children's lives. The question is not whether or not values should be imposed upon children because some values are inevitably imposed upon them. The real question turns out to be: Which values should be imposed upon the children and by whom?

Clearly, it is possible that the parents may possess one set of social values, while clinical professionals may hold a different set of values. At the same time, certain social advocates may possess a vastly different set of values altogether, while the children themselves may have a different and limited subset of social values they hold dear. If behavioral assessment is requested or recommended, whose values should be followed?

MacKay (1979) has convincingly argued that there is an appropriate role for parents to intervene in their children's lives:

> The danger then is that we may slide in one of two opposite directions. On the one hand there are many people today who react with horror. "Who am I," they say, "to impose my views on my children? I must do my best to avoid conditioning them, and to let them make up their own minds on everything." As a result, their offspring grow up deprived of much of the early "programming"

necessary for healthy normal development. The opposite reaction, perhaps less common, is to rush for all the latest textbooks on behavioural manipulation, adopt a depersonalized calculating attitude, and design home life inhumanly around mechanical "schedules of reinforcement." Both of these extremes, I suggest, violate human dignity by denying the rights and needs of the young people to whom we are potentially answerable. (p. 75)

Statements of ethical standards for professionals often make reference to the obligation of the professional to be aware of the prevailing moral, ethical, and legal standards in the community in which professional services are rendered. Therefore, in providing a professional service, no action should be taken that would violate or interfere with the legal and civil rights of children or of their families. It should be recognized that the community norms are not established by an elitist or "informed" minority group. Instead, there is a delicate ethical balance in making judgments which include the legitimate rights and responsibilities of children, parents, the community, and the greater society. Therefore, we may conclude that issues of social values should not be resolved by simply following the opinions of a professional alone or the opinions of a minority extremist group alone. Instead, the most responsible and ethical decisions regarding professional intervention will take into account information from a variety of sources and will take into account the rights and responsibilities of a variety of interrelated individuals in society.

This means that the professional should seriously consider complaints made by parents or teachers regarding a child's behavior. The parent or guardian is the legal agent holding responsibility for the child's welfare, and the teacher has mandated duties to educate him or her. Ethically speaking, the professional must make a judgment as to whether the parent or teacher truly has the best welfare of the child in mind. Then, the professional may conduct a behavioral assessment (with proper consent having been granted) to focus upon the presenting problem as it relates to normative data published in the literature. At the same time, the professional must consider the broader social values of the community and society in which the child lives. Therefore, such behaviors as school truancy, stealing, physical aggression, destruction of property, academic failure, gender deviance, sexual deviance, noncompliance, and social skill development all suggest potential target behaviors for behavioral assessment (which are of concern to parents, teachers, the community, or the larger society).

Often, a child is referred for evaluation and behavioral assessment by a variety of different community individuals who have perceived a problem to be serious enough to merit intervention. Teachers, counselors, physicians, parents, and others may request assessment of a child. Although these referring individuals may not have the expertise to provide specific behavioral assessment recommendations, nonetheless their request for information and evalua-

tion typically is very valuable and, thereby, contributes to professional decisions regarding the ethics of intervening in the case of an individual child.
This has been illustrated at greater length for the case in which a child is
judged to be at high-risk for adulthood sexual deviances such as transsexual-
ism, transvestism, or homosexuality (see Rekers, 1977; 1981; 1982a, 1982b;
Rekers, Bentler, Rosen, & Lovaas, 1977; Rekers & Mead, 1980; Rekers,
Rosen, Lovaas and Bentler, 1978). In these articles, Rekers and his colleagues
have articulated the ethical case for providing behavioral assessment and treatment for a gender disturbed child, even in the presence of objections by a
small minority such as certain "gay liberation" activists. These general ethical principles are highlighted by considering the example of that one particular childhood disorder in which parents and teachers and physicians request
behavioral assessment and treatment on behalf of the child's welfare.

In recent years, the popular press has publicized the opinions of some elements of society who call for a "right" to help children despite their parents.
In some cases, some professionals (especially school personnel) advocate elim-
inating the step of attempting to gain the consent of a parent or guardian when
a child's problem is one that would likely result in a different intervention
strategy by a parent (e.g., in the areas of drugs, sex, or abortion) (Martin,
1975, pp. 8–9). Martin (1975) cites court cases and state agency actions that
have sought to remove a child from the legal custody of parents if the parent
is unwilling to authorize life-supporting surgery, on the one hand, or if a state
employee made a judgment that the parents were not providing "sufficient
intellectual stimulation" to the child. From a legal perspective, Martin makes
the following recommendation:

> Some behavior change practitioners feel that they know what is best for chil-
> dren, and they might welcome the opportunity to relocate children in new en-
> vironments. Child counselors in general, frustrated by unresponsive parents,
> might wish they could just take the child away. But the "right" of state agents
> to decide that they can do a better job of child raising, that they have rights,
> on behalf of the child, superior to the parent, is a dangerous trend. It is one
> being challenged by civil liberties lawyers in several states. Behavior change prac-
> titioners would be well-served to direct their efforts toward improving services
> to parents at home so that families can be kept together and children's inter-
> ests can be served — and so that another area of legal conflict can be avoided.
> (1975, pp. 9–10)

SUMMARY

In the context of the complexity of children's rights to receive help and be
treated with dignity as individual human beings, it is consistent with accepted
professional ethics and with present community standards to provide appro-

priate behavioral assessment for children who exhibit maladaptive behavior. Because it is not possible to obtain full and proper consent from the individual child which truly satisfies the three legal criteria of being *competent, voluntary,* and *informed,* it is necessary to obtain consent from his or her parent or legal guardian. Some vocal social critics claim that it is inappropriate for certain behavioral assessment procedures to be carried out for children because of the implied imposition of external values or standards made upon them by parents, guardians, or professionals. However, in the realm of competing social value judgments, there appear to be no more appropriate ethical agents to make such decisions regarding children other than the parents in consultation with professionals (who are, as well, responsive to the broader moral, legal, and social codes of the community). Decisions to intervene with behavioral assessment should not be conceptualized as following a different set of ethical standards than other forms of assessment for children, such as educational assessment, dental evaluation, or medical diagnosis. Instead, all the helping professions have the same ethical obligations to work for the welfare, rights, and opportunities of children to have assistance for their basic needs.

REFERENCES

California Hospital Association. *Consent manual* (9th ed.). 1975.

Ethical standards of psychologists. *APA Monitor,* March 1977, pp. 22–23.

Ferguson, L. R. The competence and freedom of children to make choices regarding participation in research: A statement. *Journal of Social Issues,* 1978, *34,* 114–121.

Guskin, S. L., Bartel, N. R., & MacMillan, D. L. Perspective of the labeled child. In N. Hobbs (Ed.), *Issues in the classification of children* (Vol. 2). San Francisco: Jossey-Bass, 1975.

Harris, T. G. Editorial. *Psychology Today,* August 1971, p. 33.

MacKay, D. M. *Human science and human dignity.* Downers Grove, IL: InterVarsity Press, 1979.

Mahoney, M. J., & Thoresen, C. F. *Self-control: Power to the person.* Monterey, CA: Brooks/Cole, 1974.

Martin, R. *Legal challenges to behavior modification.* Champaign, IL: Research Press, 1975.

Rekers, G. A. Atypical gender development and psychosocial adjustment. *Journal of Applied Behavior Analysis,* 1977, *10,* 75–87.

Rekers, G. A. Psychosexual and gender problems. In E. J. Mash & L. G. Terdal (Eds.), *Behavioral assessment of childhood disorders.* New York: Guilford Press, 1981.

Rekers, G. A. *Growing up straight: What every family should know about homosexuality.* Chicago: Moody, 1982. (a)

Rekers, G. A. *Shaping your child's sexual identity.* Grand Rapids: Baker Book House, 1982. (b)

Rekers, G. A., Bentler, P. M., Rosen, A. C., & Lovaas, O. I. Child gender disturbances: A clinical rationale for intervention. *Psychotherapy: Theory Research and Practice,* 1977, *14,* 2–11.

Rekers, G. A., & Mead, S. Female sex-role deviance: Early identification and developmental intervention. *Journal of Clinical Child Psychology,* 1980, *9,* 199–203.

Rekers, G. A., Rosen, A. C., Lovaas, O. I., & Bentler, P. M. Sex-role stereotypy and professional intervention for childhood gender disturbances. *Professional Psychology,* 1978, *9,* 127–136.

Rosen, A. C., Rekers, G. A., & Bentler, P. M. Ethical issues in the treatment of children. *Journal of Social Issues,* 1978, *34,* 122–136.

Rosenthal, R., & Jacobson, L. *Pygmalion in the classroom: Teacher expectation and pupils' intellectual development.* New York: Holt, 1968.

Schaeffer, F. A. *Back to Freedom and Dignity.* Downers Grove, IL: InterVarsity Press, 1972.

Shore, M. F. Legislation, advocacy, and the rights of children and youth. *American Psychologist,* 1979, *34,* 1017–1019.

Skinner, B. F. *Beyond freedom and dignity.* New York: Bantham/Vintage Books, 1971.

Author Index

Achenbach, T. M. 21, 23, 25, 31, 43, 82, 83, 84, 85, 86, 89, 90, 92, 93, 94, 125
Adelman, H. S. 15
Ackerman, A. 148, 155
Albee, G. 199
Alford, H. F. 157
Allen, L. 10, 34
Anderson, L. L. 92, 96
Andre, J. L. 237
Angell, M. J. 174
Aries, P. 3
Ascione, F. R. 166, 174, 178, 181, 182, 187, 188, 190
Asher, S. R. 127, 128, 129, 130, 131, 132, 135, 137, 138, 140
Atkeson, B. M. 88, 107

Bachrach, R. 114
Bacon, A. 84
Baer, D. M. 157, 172, 174
Baert, A. E. 34
Bahn, A. K. 38
Bailey, M. I. 157
Baker, T. B. 226
Baldwin, A. L. 21
Ballard, M. 127, 137
Balleweg, B. J. 237
Bandura, A. 6, 16
Barbigian, H. 11, 125
Barkley, R. A. 49, 85, 87
Barlow, D. H. 52, 188, 238
Barnard, C. 114
Barrett, C. L. 13, 83
Barrett, R. P. 12
Bartel, N. R. 251

Barton, E. J. 168, 169, 174, 177, 181, 183, 184, 187, 188, 190
Bastein, R. 15
Batstone, D. 150
Battle, E. S. 114
Bauer, D. 13
Bauske, B. W. 82
Beamesderfer, A. 112
Beck, A. 112
Beck, S. 84, 134
Behar, L. B. 83
Bellack, A. S. 6, 125, 134, 153, 228
Bem, D. J. 10
Bennett, B. 112
Bentler, P. M. 256, 260
Berg, I. 13
Bevirt, J. 183
Bialer, I. 114
Bijou, S. W. 4
Birch, H. G. 72
Birleson, P. 113
Birnbrauer, J. S. 235
Black, J. L. 148, 151
Blanchard, J. P. 112
Blouin, A. 94, 95
Boles, S. M. 182
Bolstad, O. 186
Bonney, M. E. 137
Bornstein, P. H. 80, 150, 166, 228, 236, 237, 238, 240
Boykin, R. A. 153
Bradford, D. C. 28, 224
Bradley, M. 109
Brakke, N. P. 133
Bridgewater, C. A. 80, 166, 238
Broden, M. 150, 151, 153, 157

Broderick, J. E. 93
Brody, G. H. 50
Brown, F. J. 3, 73
Brown, R. T. 95, 227
Brummett, B. 82
Bucher, B. 150
Bugental, B. D. 16
Burgess, J. M. 187
Burton, N. 44
Burton, R. V. 72
Busk, P. L. 130
Butler, L. F. 112, 113

Cairns, R. B. 80, 81, 100, 184
Calkins, R. P. 12
Campbell, D. R. 228
Campbell, J. D. 72
Campbell, S. B. 86
Cantor, S. 45
Cantwell, D. P. 41, 47, 48, 51, 112,
    113
Caputo, J. 90, 95
Carlson, G. 112, 113
Carr, E. G. 44, 54
Carstens, C. B. 156
Cartledge, G. 125
Casteneda, A. 107, 110
Cavior, N. 152, 153
Center, D. B. 169
Cerny, J. A. 4, 6, 7, 8, 11, 12, 20, 65,
    107, 223, 236
Cerreto, M. C. 39
Chalesworth, R. 1, 127
Chapman, A. J. 139
Charlesworth, R. 11, 127
Chertock, S. L. 240
Chess, S. 35, 72
Chong, H. 236
Ciminero, A. R. 4, 11, 65, 68, 81, 90,
    91, 92, 150, 155, 223, 229, 236
Clark, J. H. 199, 201
Clement, P. W. 84
Cohen, A. S. 130, 131, 132, 136
Cohen, M. N. 94
Coie, J. D. 15, 128, 134, 135, 136, 140
Compas, B. E. 15
Condry, J. 108
Cone, J. D. 9, 10, 52, 80, 81, 86, 87,
    89, 90, 134, 224, 227, 231, 232,
    233
Conger, A. M. 132

Conger, R. E. 69
Conners, C. K. 80, 81, 82, 83, 84, 88,
    92, 94, 95
Connolly, A. 210
Connolly, J. 134
Cook, R. 44
Coppotelli, H. 128, 134
Corman, L. 127
Cormier, W. H. 62
Costello, A. J. 87
Cowen, E. L., 11, 125
Cunningham, J. L. 173
Cunningham, T. R. 167

Dannenburg, M. A. 111
Davidson, K. S. 110
Davies, G. R. 89
Deardorff, P. A. 91, 110
Deitz, D. E. 169
Deitz, S. M. 169, 182
Deluty, R. H. 107
Devany, J. 153
DeWulf, M. J. 184, 185
Diament, C. 155
DiClemente, C. C. 46
Dodge, K. A. 128, 133, 134, 135, 140
Doll, E. A. 83
Dollinger, S. J. 15
Doster, J. A. 71
Dotson, J. A. 182
Doyle, A. 134
Drabman, R. S. 4, 11, 65, 68, 89, 90,
    154, 156, 223, 235, 236
Dragovich, S. L. 84
Dreger, R. M. 39
Dugas, F. 94
Duke, M. P. 115, 116
Dunnington, M. H. 126
Dygdon, J. A. 132

Earls, F. 41
Ebel, R. 198
Edelbrock, C. 21, 23, 25, 30, 31, 82,
    83, 84, 85, 86, 87, 89, 90, 92, 93,
    94
Eisenberg, J. B. 35
Elder, I. R. 152
Elliott, S. N. 195
Elliott, W. R. 16
Emmelkamp. P. M. G. 91
Epstein, L. H. 157

Evans, I. M. 4, 6, 11, 23, 34, 82, 87, 175, 223, 227, 229
Evans, J. 45
Eyberg, S. M. 83, 85, 92, 95, 96

Ferguson, H. B. 94
Ferguson, L. R. 25, 247
Field, T. 124, 125
Finch, A. J., Jr. 91, 107, 110, 111, 112, 115, 116, 119, 120
Finch, M. 132, 136, 139
Fixen, D. L. 148, 156, 157
Flanigan, P. J. 108
Fleishman, D. H. 141
Fleming, C. F. 119, 120
Fleming, E. L. 39
Foot, H. C. 139
Forehand, R. 88, 107, 134, 138
Ford, R. C. 130
Foreman, J. B. W. 41
Foster, R. 83
Foster, S. L. 168
Fox, J. 173
Fox, S. G. 237
Franzini, L. R. 150
Frederiksen, L. W. 137
Freitas, J. C. 150, 151, 156
Freund, R. D. 89
Friedland-Bandes, R. 15
Friedman, R. J. 112, 113
Furey, W. M. 89
Furman, W. 14, 28, 235

Garber, J. 95
Gardner, E. 211
Gates, A. 211
Gelder, M. G. 13
Gelfand, D. 5
Gersten, J. C. 35
Gittleman-Klein, R. 49
Glazer, J. A. 11, 127
Glick, J. 240
Glidewell, J. 125
Glow, P. W. 90
Glow, R. A. 90
Glynn, E. L. 148, 150, 152
Goetz, L. 54
Gold, R. S. 46
Golden, C. J. 206
Golden, M. M. 125, 134
Goldfried, M. R. 4, 5, 52, 63, 226

Gonso, J. 134, 137
Gordon, S. B. 68, 237
Gorsuch, R. L. 114
Gottlieb, J. 127
Gottman, J. M. 134, 137, 138, 151, 152
Goyette, C. H. 94, 95
Graham, P. 34, 35, 73, 85
Graziano, A. M. 13
Green, J. A. 80, 81, 100
Green, K. D. 134, 135
Greenwood, C. R. 125, 130, 133, 134, 139, 140, 141, 186
Gresham, F. M. 10, 11, 131, 135, 137
Griest, D. L. 88
Gronlund, S. E. 140
Gross, A. M. 61
Grounds, L. 90
Guild, J. J. 141
Guskin, S. L. 251, 252
Gutkin, T. B. 207
Guy, W. 84

Habif, V. L. 169
Haley, R. 90
Hall, R. V. 148
Hall, S. M. 150
Hallinan, M. T. 125
Halpern, F. C. 201
Hamilton, S. B. 150, 228
Hamm, H. 184
Hamman, C. L. 151
Hampe, E. 13, 83
Harris, S. L. 41
Harris, T. G. 249
Hart, B. 156
Hartmann, D. P. 5, 28, 224
Hartup, W. W. 11, 125, 127, 130, 133, 136, 139
Hawes, R. 240
Hawkins, R. P. 9, 52, 53, 80, 81, 86, 87, 224, 235
Hay, L. R. 153, 156
Hay, W. M. 156
Hayes, S. C. 52, 61, 152, 153, 167, 170, 223, 236
Haynes, S. N. 61, 65, 67, 69, 70, 71, 73, 92, 148, 150, 155
Heiby, E. 240
Hendrickson, J. M. 183
Henigan, R. P. 114

Henker, B. 16, 51
Herbert, E. W. 157
Herjanic, G. 72, 73, 227
Hersen, M. 3, 6, 125, 134, 188, 228,
    238
Herzbergen, S. D. 116
Hickey, J. S. 166, 238
Higa, W. R. 12
Higgins, B. 139
Hilliard, A. 199
Hirshoren, A. 92
Holland, C. J. 69, 239
Holleran, P. A. 89
Hollon, S. D. 5
Holmes, F. B. 3
Honzik, M. P. 34
Hooke, J. F. 116
Hops, H. 29, 83, 125, 130, 132, 136,
    137, 138, 139, 140, 141, 186, 184
House, A. E. 157
Humphrey, L. L. 81, 83, 91, 92, 132
Hundert, J. 150
Hymel, S. 127, 128, 129, 131, 132,
    135, 137, 140

Irwin, M. 44
Ironsmith, M. 156
Izzo, L. D. 11, 125

Jacob, T. 90, 93, 171
Jacobson, L. 251
Jensen, A. R. 199, 200, 206
Johnson, S. 169, 186
Johnson, S. B. 86, 89, 91
Johnstone, E. E. 46
Jones, M. C. 3
Jones, R. R. 69

Kagan, J. 35
Kane, J. S. 124
Kandel, D. B. 139
Kanfer, F. H. 4, 7, 52, 63, 64, 150,
    152, 156, 162, 229, 231
Kantor, M. B. 125
Karlsen, B. 211
Karoly, P. 152
Karpowitz, D. H. 169
Kaufman, A. S. 195, 197, 199, 201,
    205, 207, 208
Kaufman, K. 150
Kaufman, M. E. 169

Kaufman, M. J. 127
Kazdin, A. E. 13, 29, 49, 88, 125, 174,
    226, 238
Keefe, F. J. 68, 237
Kelley, C. 92
Kelly, M. M. 119
Kendall, P. C. 5, 83, 95, 111
Kent, R. N. 4, 5, 52, 155
Kessler, M. D. 87
King, C. 95
Kirby, K. L. 236, 237
Kirschenbaum, D. S. 152
Klein, D. F. 49
Klein, R. D. 150
Knopf, J. 34
Koch, H. L. 125, 128
Kopel, S. A. 68, 237
Kosevsky, B. P. 157
Koslow-Green, I. 153
Kovacs, M. 112, 113
Kramer, M. 38
Kratochwill, T. R. 150, 159, 238
Kunzelman, H. D. 149, 150, 151

Lacey, H. M. 83
Ladd, G. W. 131, 137, 138, 140
LaGreca, A. M. 135, 137, 140
Lahey, B. B. 169
Lamb, M. E. 184
Lambert, N. 49, 199
Lang, P. J. 7
Lange, M. 113
Langner, T. S. 35
Lapouse, R. 25
Laprade, K. 94
Lawler, E. E., III 124
Lazarus, A. A. 52, 64, 230, 231
Lech, B. 182
Lefkowitz, M. M. 44
Leland, H. 83
Leon, G. R. 95
Lepper, M. R. 152
Lester, B. M. 25
Lewis, P. M. 39
Leyser, Y. 127
Liebert, D. E. 124
Lightfall, F. F. 110
Lilly, M. S. 137
Lindholm, B. W. 86, 93
Linehan, M. M. 61, 62, 72, 90
Linney, J. A. 116

Lipinski, D. P. 148, 150, 151, 153, 155, 157
Lipsedge, M. 13
Litrownik, A. J. 150, 151, 156
Littman, D. C. 89
Loney, J. 90, 95
Lovaas, O. I. 260
Lyman, R. D. 152
Lynch, G. 94

MacDonald, A. P. 114
MacDonald, M. 61
MacFarlane, J. W. 34
Mackay, D. M. 245, 250, 258
Macmillan, D. L. 251
Madden, R. 211
Madsen, J. J. 169, 177
Mahoney, M. J. 153, 257
Maletzky, B. M. 148
Maloney, M. P. 69, 70, 71
Manning, P. J. 174
Marholin, D. 84
Markle, A. 125
Marks, I. 13
Marshall, H. R. 12, 126, 133
Martin, R. 246, 247, 249, 255, 257, 260
Mash, E. J. 4, 5, 6, 7, 8, 9, 11, 13, 20, 23, 28, 52, 81, 84, 88, 90
Matarazzo, J. D. 70
Matson, J. L. 16, 84
Mattison, R. 41, 47, 48
Mayer, G. R. 5
Mayer, J. 13
McAdoo, G. 111
McCandless, B. R. 12, 107, 126, 133
McCarthy, D. 205
McCarthy, E. D. 35
McFall, R. M. 9, 151, 152
McGonigle, J. J. 149
McGuire, R. 13
McKillop, A. S. 211
McLellarn, R. W. 237
McMahon, R. J. 89
McReynolds, P. 4
McReynolds, W. 157
McNamara, J. R. 84
Mead, S. 260
Mednick, S. A. 34
Meichenbaum, D. H. 5, 6
Melamed, B. G. 240

Melson, G. F. 129
Meyers, C. E. 84
Miezitis, S. 112
Milburn, J. F. 123
Milich, R. 90, 95
Miller, K. S. 39
Miller, L. C. 13, 83, 84, 157
Mischel, W. 6, 10, 62, 63, 64, 132, 226
Mitchell, S. 25
Mitts, B. 150
Monk, M. A. 25
Montgomery, L. E. 91, 110, 111, 116, 117
Moore, S. 130, 133, 153
Moreno, J. L. 125
Morgan, J. R. 111
Morganstern, K. P. 63, 71
Morris, T. 111
Moss, H. A. 35
Moss, J. H. 107, 119
Moura, N. G. M. 153
Mueller, E. 125

Nachtman, W. 210
Nagle, R. J. 37
Nakamura, C. Y. 12, 107, 239
Nathan, P. E. 41
Nay, W. R. 89, 232, 233, 234
Neale, J. M. 124
Nee, J. 40
Nelson, R. O. 4, 11, 52, 61, 82, 87, 89, 91, 148, 151, 153, 154, 155, 156, 157, 167, 170, 223, 227, 229, 236, 238
Nelson, W. M., III 107, 115, 116, 119, 120
Newmark, C. S. 110
Newmark, L. 110
Newsom, C. D. 44
Nihira, K. 83, 84
Noble, H. 83
Nowicki, S., Jr. 114, 115, 116

O'Brien, P. A. 113
Oden, S. 128, 131, 137, 138
O'Donnell, J. P. 92
O'Leary, K. D. 85, 89, 91, 93, 95, 150, 154, 155, 156, 171
O'Leary, S. G. 95
Ollendick, T. H. 3, 4, 6, 7, 8, 9, 10, 11, 12, 13, 16, 20, 65, 68, 107, 149, 150, 160, 223, 236, 239

Olszewski, M. J. 169
Oltmanns, T. F. 93
Olweus, D. 11, 14
Overlake, D. C. 39

Pachman, J. S. 156
Packard, D. 44
Paget, K. D. 108, 109
Paine, S. 141
Palermo, D. S. 107
Parsons, J. E. 12
Parton, D. A. 83
Partyka, L. B. 25
Patterson, G. R. 4, 49, 69, 114, 132
Pearce, J. 45
Pederson, A. 11, 125
Peery, J. C. 127, 135, 140
PeKarik, E. G. 124
Pela, O. A. 108
Pelham, W. E. 95
Pennington, B. F. 15
Peoples, A. 44
Peters, C. J. 108
Peterson, D. R. 62, 64, 83, 92, 229
Peterson, G. I. 157
Peterson, R. F. 4
Pezzot-Pearce, T. 45
Pezzuti, K. A. 115
Phillips, E. L. 148
Piersall, W. C. 150, 159
Pomeranz, D. 63
Prentice-Dunn, S. 81, 83, 86, 87, 89
Prinz, R. 124
Pritchard, E. 139
Pritchett, E. 210
Putallaz, M. 134

Quay, H. C. 83, 86, 92

Rappaport, J. 116
Raskin, A. 34
Rasmussen, B. 134
Rayner, R. 3
Reed, M. L. 93, 94
Reid, J. B. 69, 82, 155
Reid, M. P. 39
Reimherr, F. W. 43
Rekers, G. A. 14, 256, 260
Renshaw, P. W. 128
Repp, A. C. 182
Repp, C. F. 182

Retzlaff, P. D. 236
Reynolds, C. R. 108, 109, 195, 197, 199, 201, 204, 205, 206, 207, 209, 210
Rich, T. A. 39
Richard, R. C. 84
Richmond, B. O. 108, 109
Rickard, H. C. 152
Rie, H. E. 3
Rincover, A. 44
Rinn, F. C. 125
Risley, T. R. 156, 172
Ritchey, W. L. 168
Roberts, M. A. 90, 95, 100
Roberts, M. W. 183, 184
Robertson, S. J. 156
Robins, L. N. 34, 35
Robinson, E. A. 85, 92, 95, 96
Roff, M. 125, 134, 140
Rogers-Warren, A. 174
Romanczyk, R. G. 150, 152, 155
Roper, B. L. 28, 224
Rosen, A. C. 256, 260
Rosen, B. M. 38
Rosenblad, C. 171
Rosenthal, R. 251
Ross, A. O. 83
Ross, A. W. 85, 95, 96
Ross, J. 12
Rotter, J. B. 114
Roundtree, J. 115
Rozensky, R. 153
Ruebush, B. K. 100
Rulon, P. J. 118
Rump, E. E. 90
Ruple, D. N. 12
Russell, A. T. 41, 47, 48
Rutter, M. 21, 25, 34, 35, 41, 42, 45, 48, 50, 73
Rychtarik, R. G. 238

Sackett, G. P. 184
Sagotsky, G. 152
Sandoval, J. 49, 83, 85
Sanok, R. L. 178
Santogrossi, D. 137, 140, 150, 154, 155
Sarason, S. B. 110
Saslow, G. 4, 7, 52, 63, 64, 229, 231
Sassone, D. 49
Sattler, J. 202, 205
Saylor, C. F. 112, 113

Schacht, T. 41
Schaeffer, F. A. 251
Scheiderer, E. G. 70
Scherer, M. W. 12, 107, 239
Schmaling, K. B. 89
Schnelle, J. F. 72
Schnittjer, C. J. 92
Schuler, A. L. 54
Schuler, P. 137
Schulman, J. L. 130
Schulsinger, F. 34
Schulterbrandt, J. G. 34
Schwartz, J. A. 153, 173, 228
Sechrest, L. 228
Seidman, E. 116
Sells, S. B. 125, 134
Serna, R. W. 166
Shaffer, D. 41, 42, 48, 50
Shapiro, E. S. 12, 148, 149, 150, 154,
    155, 156, 157
Shectman, A. 25
Shellhaas, M. 83
Shepherd, M. 25
Shores, R. E. 183, 245
Shuller, D. Y. 84
Siegel, L. J. 84, 85, 87
Siman, M. L. 108
Simcha-Fagan, O. 35
Simkins, L. 157
Simon, S. J. 156
Singh, N. N. 174
Singleton, L. C. 127, 128, 129, 135
Sitarz, A. M. 110
Skinner, B. F. 248, 249, 250
Skinner, H. A. 86
Skudol, A. E. 39, 42
Smith, J. R. 139
Smith, L. M. 125
Spates, C. R. 152
Spielberger, C. D. 109, 110, 111
Spirito, A. 112
Spitalnik, R. 154
Spitzer, R. L. 39, 41, 42, 51
Spivack, G. 82, 83, 92
Spotts, J. 82
Sprafkin, J. N. 52, 63
Sprague, R. L. 94
Stabler, B. 110
Steele, C. 109
Stein, A. B. 116
Steinert, Y. 86

Stephenson, G. R. 184
Stevens, T. 132, 139
Strain, P. S. 183
Street, A. 141
Strickland, B. R. 114
Stringer, L. A. 125
Stringfield, S. 83
Stuart, R. B. 63, 64, 226
Sturm, C. A. 236, 237
Sulzer-Azaroff, B. 5
Suomi, S. J. 184
Swan, G. E. 61
Sweeney, T. M. 80, 166, 238
Swift, M. 82, 83, 92

Taffer, C. 39
Taplin, R. S. 155
Taylor, J. A. 107
Terdal, L. G. 4, 5, 6, 7, 8, 9, 11, 13,
    20, 23, 28, 52, 84, 88, 90
Tevlin, H. E. 63, 71
Tharp, R. G. 12, 149, 167
Thelen, M. H. 15
Thomas, A. 35, 72
Thomas, J. D. 152
Thompson, G. G. 129, 131
Thoresen, C. F. 257
Tinsley, B. R. 127, 135
Tisher, M. 113
Tizard, J. 25, 34
Todd, N. M. 130, 186
Touliatos, J. 86, 93
Treece, C. 40
Tremblay, A. 183
Trites, R. L. 94
Trost, M. A. 11, 125
Tuma, J. M. 39
Turkewitz, H. 156
Twardosz, S. 173

Ulrich, R. F. 94
Updegraff, R. 130, 133

Van Hasselt, V. B. 134, 135, 228
Van Houton, R. 173
Van Tassell, E. A. 129, 130, 132,
    136
Van Tuinan, M. 92
Vaughn, B. E. 129
Voeltz, L. M. 23, 34
Vosk, B. 134, 169

Wade, T. C. 153, 226
Wahler, R. G. 62
Waite, R. R. 110
Walker, H. M. 29, 118, 130, 141, 186
Walls, R. T. 84, 92
Walsh, M. L. 15
Ward, D. G. 132
Ward, M. P. 69, 70, 71
Warren, S. F. 124
Waters, E. 129
Watson, D. L. 149
Watson, J. B. 3
Webb, E. J. 228
Webb, L. J. 46
Webster, J. S. 157
Webster-Stratton, C. 96
Weinrott, M. R. 82, 83, 84, 87
Weintraub, S. 124
Weisser, C. E. 237
Wells, K. C. 72, 88
Wender, P. 43
Werner, T. J. 84
Werry, J. S. 81, 88, 94, 95
Whalen, C. K. 16, 51
Wheatt, T. 73, 227
Wheeler, D. 110

Whitmore, K. 25, 34
Wiens, A. 70
Wiggins, J. S. 91
Wilcox, L. E. 83
Will, L. 41, 47, 48
Williams, J. B. W. 39, 42, 199
Wilson, C. C. 150, 155
Wilson, D. R. 61, 70, 81, 83, 86, 87, 89
Wilson, G. L. 226, 237
Wilson, V. L. 199
Wolf, M. M. 13, 148, 172
Wolff, S. 25
Wood, D. R. 43
Wynne, M. E. 95
Wytrol, S. L. 129, 132

Yarrow, M. R. 72
Young, R. D. 95
Yule, W. 34

Zane, T. 84
Zeiss, A. 114
Zeiss, R. 114
Zetlin, A. 84

Subject Index

Academic achievement, 209–211
Accuracy of self-monitoring, 155–157
Adaptive Behavior Scale, 54, 83
Aggressive behavior, 14, 32–33, 47
Anger, 116–119
Anxiety, 32–33, 43–44, 47, 107–111, 119–120, 239–241
Assertive behavior, 107
Attention deficit disorder, 42, 47, 73–77, 87, 158–160, 211–217

Basic ID, 220–231
Behavior Problem Checklist, 83, 92–93
Behavior Profile Rating Scale, 240–241
Behavioral assessment grid, 231–232
Behavioral checklists, 80–101, 240, 255
Behavioral interviewing, 61–79, 240, 255

Case study
  with behavioral interview, 73–77
  with behavioral checklists, 96–99
  with self-report instruments, 119–120
  with sociometric ratings, 141–143
  with self-monitoring, 158–162
  with direct observation, 189–191
  with intellectual tests, 211–217
  with integrated assessment, 239–241
Child Behavior Checklist, 25, 31–35, 83, 93–94, 96–99
Child Behavior Profile, 25, 31–35, 83
Child behavioral assessment
  definition, 4–6, 61–62, 166–168
  characteristics of, 7–15, 22–24
  history of, 3–4
  role of the child, 15–16

goals of, 223–224
assumptions of, 223–224
Childhood schizophrenia, 45, 47
Children's Depression Inventory, 112–114
Children's Inventory of Anger, 116–119
Children's Manifest Anxiety Scale, 107–111
Children's Nowicki-Strickland Locus of Control Scale, 114–116
Children's rights, 15–16, 244–245
Clinical significance, 29
Conduct disorder, 43, 47, 73–77
Conners Rating Scales, 83, 94–99
Consent
  competent, 246–247
  voluntary, 247–251
  informed, 251–252
Cross-gender behavior, 14

Depressive behavior, 27, 28, 32–33, 47, 112–114
Delinquent behavior, 15, 32–33, 47
Developmental issues
  in child assessment, 11–15
  in behavioral assessment, 20–36
  in diagnosis, 48–49
  in intellectual assessment, 196
Devereux Child Behavior Rating Scale, 82
Diagnostic and Statistical Manual, 38–54, 85–86
Diagnostic issues, 38–54
Direct observation, 166–191, 240, 255

Eating disorders, 44

Epidemiology, 85–86
Ethical issues, 188–189, 244–261
Eyberg Child Behavior Inventory, 83, 85, 95–99

Fear, 12, 14, 26, 32–36, 47, 119–120, 239–241
Fear Survey Schedule for Children, 12, 239–240
Functional analysis, 7–9, 166–169, 229

Hyperactive behavior, 15, 32–33, 47, 73–77, 158–160

Infantile autism, 45, 47
Intellectual disorders, 42, 127
Intellectual tests, 195–217, 240

Kaufman Assessment Battery for Children, 205, 208–209

Learning disability, 200–201, 211–217
Locus of control, 114–116
Louisville Child Behavior Checklist, 84
Louisville Fear Survey Schedule, 83

Multimethod assessment, 7–9, 129–130, 232–233
McCarthy Scales of Children's Abilities, 199, 205, 207–208, 211–217

Normative comparisons, 11–15, 21–22, 24–31, 235–236

Oppositional behavior, 26, 32–33, 47, 73–77, 175–176

Peabody Individual Achievement Test, 210
Pittsburgh Adjustment Survey Schedule, 83
Preschool Behavior Questionnaire, 83

Reactivity of self-monitoring, 150–154
Reliability
  of diagnosis, 47–51
  of behavioral interviewing, 72–73

  of behavioral checklists, 89–92
  of self-report measures, 107–111, 113, 116–119
  of sociometric ratings, 130–133
  of self-monitoring, 150–157
  of direct observation, 175–185
  of intelligence tests, 204–207
Ruminating behavior, 174

Self-monitoring, 148–162, 240, 255
Self-report instruments, 106–120, 240, 255
Social skills, 141, 170–174
Social validation, 8–9, 29–30
Social values, 258–260
Socioeconomic Issues
  in assessment, 7–8
  in rating forms, 28
  in diagnosis, 49–50
Sociometric ratings, 12, 124–144, 255
State-Trait Anxiety Inventory for Children, 108–111
Statistical significance, 29
Stereotyped movement disorder, 44, 47, 160–162

Validity
  of diagnosis, 47–51
  of behavioral interviewing, 72–73
  of behavioral checklists, 89–92
  of self-report measures, 107–111, 113, 116–119
  of sociometric ratings, 133–136
  of self-monitoring, 150–157
  of direct observation, 175–185
  of intelligence tests, 204–207

Wechsler Intelligence Scale for Children-Revised, 199, 205–207, 211–217
Wechsler Preschool and Primary Scale of Intelligence, 199, 206–207
Wide Range Achievement Test, 210–217
Withdrawn behavior, 14, 32–33, 47, 127

About the Contributors

Frank R. Ascione (Ph.D., University of North Carolina at Chapel Hill, 1973) is Associate Professor of Psychology at Utah State University (USU). He chairs the Analysis of Behavior doctoral program in the Department of Psychology and holds a joint appointment at USU's Exceptional Child Center, a University Affiliated Program. He has authored and co-authored numerous articles in behavior analysis and developmental psychology. He has been a guest reviewer for the *Journal of Applied Behavior Analysis* and *Behavioral Assessment* and his major research interests are in the development of pro-social behavior.

Edward J. Barton (Ph.D., Utah State University, 1978) is Vice-President of Drake Beam Morin, Inc. in Detroit, Michigan. He is the past Director of the Behavior Technology Curricula at Northern Michigan University, where he was an associate professor of psychology. Dr. Barton also has served as a Staff Psychologist for the North Central Michigan Mental Health Center. He has authored numerous research articles and chapters on child behavior assessment.

Marcy Tepper Bornstein (B.A., East Carolina University, 1968) is a graduate student in clinical psychology at the University of Montana. Her major areas of interest include children of divorce and naturalistic observation strategies with families. Ms. Bornstein's most recent research has appeared in *Behavior Therapy*; she is also co-author of a forthcoming chapter in the *Handbook of Behavioral Assessment*.

Philip H. Bornstein (Ph.D., University of South Dakota, 1972) is Professor of Clinical Psychology at the University of Montana. His major areas of interest include practice of behavior therapy, and interventions for marital/family dysfunction. Dr. Bornstein is co-editor of the forthcoming *Handbook of Clinical Behavior Therapy with Children* and author of the forthcoming *Loving: A Self-Help Guide to Relationship Satisfaction*. He has published and presented over 100 articles/papers and presently is on the editorial board of four major professional journals.

Brenda Dawson (M.A., University of the Pacific, 1980) is a doctoral student in clinical psychology at the University of Montana. She is presently completing her clinical internship at the University of Mississippi Medical Center, Jackson, Mississippi. Ms. Dawson's major areas of interest include child behavior analysis, the effects of television advertising on children's eating behavior, and issues in behavioral medicine. Her most recent research has appeared in *Behavioral Assessment, Developmental Psychology,* and *Behaviour Research and Therapy.*

Craig Edelbrock (Ph.D., Oregon State University, 1976) is Assistant Professor of Psychiatry at the University of Pittsburgh and Director of the Child Assessment Project at Western Psychiatric Institute and Clinic. After completing postdoctoral training at NIMH, he was a Research Scientist for two years at the Center for the Study of Youth Development near Omaha. Dr. Edelbrock serves on the editorial boards of the *Journal of Consulting and Clinical Psychology* and the *Journal of Abnormal Child Psychology* and recently received a Research Scientist Development Award from NIMH to further his research on the assessment of child psychopathology.

A. J. Finch, Jr. (Ph.D., University of Alabama, 1970) is a Professor of Psychiatry and Behavioral Sciences at the Medical University of South Carolina. He is an ABPP in Clinical Child Psychology and has authored numerous research articles and chapters. Former positions have been at the Devereux Foundation and the Virginia Treatment Center for Children, Division of Child Psychiatry, Medical College of Virginia.

Alan M. Gross (Ph.D., Washington State University, 1979) is an Assistant Professor of Psychology at Emory University. His research interests include Child Behavior Therapy and Behavioral Pediatrics. Dr. Gross is the recent recipient of two NIMH research grants in the area of behavioral aspects of the treatment of diabetes.

Sandra L. Harris (Ph.D., State University of New York at Buffalo, 1969) is Professor of Psychology at Rutgers, the State University of New Jersey (Faculty of Arts & Sciences and Graduate School of Applied and Professional Psychology). She is also Director of the Douglass Developmental Disabilities Center. She co-authored with Peter E. Nathan *Psychopathology and Society* and has written several other books and chapters including *Teaching Speech to a Nonverbal Child* and *Families of the Developmentally Disabled: A Guide to Behavioral Intervention.* The author of a number of articles focused primarily in the area of developmental disabilities and child psychopathology, she is currently an Associate Editor of *Behavior Therapy* and on the editorial boards of several other journals.

Michel Hersen (Ph.D., State University of New York at Buffalo, 1966) is Professor of Psychiatry and Psychology at the University of Pittsburgh. He is the Past President of the Association for Advancement of Behavior Therapy. He has co-authored and co-edited 18 books including: *Single-Case Experi-*

mental Designs: Strategies for Studying Behavior Change, Behavior Therapy in the Psychiatric Setting, Behavior Modification: An Introductory Textbook, and *Introduction to Clinical Psychology.* With Bellack, he is editor and founder of *Behavior Modification* and *Clinical Psychology Review.* He is Associate Editor of *Addictive Behaviors* and Editor of *Progress in Behavior Modification.* Dr. Hersen is the recipient of several NIMH research grants.

Hyman Hops (Ph.D., University of Oregon, 1971) is Research Scientist at the Oregon Research Institute. Previously, he was Program Director at the Center for Research in the Behavioral Education of the Handicapped (COR-BEH) at the University of Oregon. He is on the Oregon Psychological Association's Board of Directors as Chair of the Ethics Committee. The author of over 40 research articles and chapters, he is currently on the editorial boards of *Behavioral Assessment* and *Analysis and Intervention in Developmental Disabilities.* Dr. Hops is the recipient of several research grants from NIMH and NICHD.

Alan S. Kaufman (Ph.D., Columbia University, 1970) is Professor of Psychology at California School of Professional Psychology, San Diego. As Assistant Director of The Psychological Corporation (1968–74) he worked closely with David Wechsler and Dorothea McCarthy in the development and standardization of the WISC-R and McCarthy Scales. Before accepting his present position in 1982, he trained school and clinical psychologists at the University of Georgia, University of Illinois at Chicago, and National College of Education. Dr. Kaufman, who serves on seven editorial boards, authored *Intelligent Testing with the WISC-R* and co-authored (with Nadeen L. Kaufman) *Clinical Evaluation of Young Children with the McCarthy Scales* and the recent *Kaufman Assessment Battery for Children (K-ABC).*

Lewis M. Lewin (Ph.D., Ohio University, 1975) is Associate Professor of Psychology at California State College, Stanislaus. He is a licensed clinical psychologist and serves as consultant to various community agencies in the areas of childhood academic and social skills and marital and family therapy.

Robert J. McMahon (Ph.D., University of Georgia, 1979) is Assistant Professor of Psychology at the University of British Columbia. He has co-authored *Helping the Noncompliant Child: A Clinician's Guide to Parent Training* with Rex Forehand, and co-edited *Advances in Clinical Behavior Therapy* with Kenneth Craig. He is the author of more than 30 research articles and chapters pertaining to child behavioral assessment and therapy.

Thomas H. Ollendick (Ph.D., Purdue University, 1971) is currently Professor of Psychology and Associate Department Head at Virginia Polytechnic Institute and State University. He has held former positions at the Devereux Foundation, Indiana State University, and Western Psychiatric Institute and Clinic. He has co-authored *Clinical Behavior Therapy with Children* with Jerome Cerny and co-edited the *Handbook of Child Psychopathology* with Michel Hersen. The author of over 75 research articles and chapters, he is currently on the editorial board of six journals and on the Executive Committee of APA's Division 12 Section I on Clinical Child Psychology.

Michael D. Powers (M.A. Columbia University, 1980) is a doctoral candidate at the Graduate School of Applied and Professional Psychology, Rutgers, the State University of New Jersey. He has been a teacher, supervisor, and consultant with autistic and severely/profoundly retarded children and adults, and is co-author with Jan S. Handleman of a forthcoming book, *Behavioral Assessment of Severe Developmental Disabilities.* He has co-authored several book chapters and has published in the areas of behavioral assessment and intervention with developmentally disabled children, family therapy, and the assessment of families with developmentally disabled children. He is currently on internship at Child and Family Services, Inc., Hartford, CT.

George A. Rekers (Ph.D., University of California at Los Angeles, 1972) is Professor of Family and Child Development at Kansas State University and the current Chairman of the Family Research Council of America. He is a Diplomate in Clinical Psychology from the American Board of Professional Psychology. He has served previously as a Visiting Scholar at Harvard University and as Chief Psychologist and Associate Professor, Division of Child and Adolescent Psychiatry, University of Florida College of Medicine. The author of over 55 research articles and chapters, he has written several books including *Shaping Your Child's Sexual Identity* (Baker, 1982) and *Growing Up Straight* (Moody, 1982). Dr. Rekers has been the recipient of several NIMH and NIAAA research grants.

Cecil R. Reynolds (Ph.D., University of Georgia, 1978) is Associate Professor of Educational Psychology and Director of Doctoral Training in School Psychology at Texas A&M University. He is former Acting and Associate Director of the Buros Institute of Mental Measurement and has co-authored and co-edited four books including, *The Handbook of School Psychology,* and has more than 150 scholarly publications to his credit. In 1980 he received the APA Division 16 Lightner Witmer Award, in 1981, Division 5's Outstanding Contributor in First 10 Postdoctoral Years Award, and in 1983, Division 15's Early Career Award. He is editor of Plenum's Perspectives on Individual Differences Series and serves on the editorial boards of 9 journals, among them *Journal of School Psychology, Journal of Special Education,* and the *Journal of Psychoeducational Assessment.* For 2 years, he served as staff psychologist at the Rutland Center for Severely Emotionally Disturbed Children.

Tim R. Rogers (Ph.D., University of Georgia, 1983; internship at the Medical University of South Carolina, Charleston, SC, 1982–1983) is currently the Program Director of St. Vincent's Parenting Resource Center in New Orleans, LA. Clinical and research interests include child behavioral assessment and therapy, parent training, and pediatric psychology. He has published in the *Journal of Behavioral Assessment, Behaviour Research and Therapy,* and

Journal of Clinical Child Psychology, as well as others. He has served on the editorial board of the *Journal of Behavioral Assessment.*

Edward S. Shapiro Ph.D., University of Pittsburgh, 1978) is currently Assistant Professor and Director, School Psychology Program, School of Education, Lehigh University. He has authored or co-authored over 20 research articles and book chapters in the areas of self-control processes with the mentally retarded, behavioral assessment, strategies to reduce stereotypic behavior, and behavioral approaches to school psychology. A reviewer for many journals, Dr. Shapiro was recently appointed to the editorial board of *Behavior Modification.*

Other books by The Oatmeal

 How to Tell If Your Cat Is Plotting to Kill You

 My Dog: The Paradox

 If My Dogs Were a Pair of Middle-Aged Men

 The Terrible and Wonderful Reasons
Why I Run Long Distances

 Why Grizzly Bears Should Wear Underpants

 404 Not Found (A Coloring Book)

 How to Be Perfectly Unhappy

 5 Very Good Reasons to
Punch a Dolphin in the Mouth

TheOatmeal.com

🐦 @Oatmeal   f @TheOatmeal   📷 @TheOatmeal